Intersectionality in Social Work

This groundbreaking book is an innovative, passionate and provocative exploration of intersectionality. The sustained emphasis on activism and practice reasserts the potency of intersectionality borne out of Black feminism. The rare and pioneering international reach of this book crosses four continents. In this book context matters: there is no intersectionality without context!

Resting on the premise that we cannot work for the liberation of individuals, communities and societies without intersectionality, this book asks: How does intersectionality challenge the structures and discourses of social work education, management and organisation? What is the revolutionary potential of intersectionality? Intersectional in its method and content, the blend of practice, activism, research and theory troubles geopolitical and disciplinary boundaries. The range of topics include: Islamophobia, immigration, feminist movements, social work education, violence against women and girls, gender, sexuality, race, disability, age, religion, nationality, citizenship policy and legal frameworks.

This book will appeal to activists for social justice, social work practitioners, researchers, lecturers, students and those working in the field of Black feminist thinking. The focus on the activism of intersectionality provides a clear pathway into Black feminist thinking and its application to social work internationally and to emancipatory collective political activism worldwide.

Suryia Nayak is a Senior Lecturer in social work at the University of Salford, UK. Suryia has been working with intersectionality for over 30 years for social justice in ending violence against women and girls, primarily within the Rape Crisis Movement. Suryia has set up services dedicated to BAMER women and girls. Suryia applies models of education as liberation and the activism of Black feminism to raise consciousness about the psychological and political impact of oppressive social constructions.

Rachel Robbins is a Research Fellow at the University of Central Lancashire. She researches in the areas of domestic violence, adult social care and social justice. In particular she has an interest in feminist theory and intersectionality. Rachel is research active in the area of social work and social policy and is a member of the Connect Centre for International Research on New Approaches to Prevent Violence and Harm. Prior to entering the academy, Rachel worked in a range of social work and social policy settings.

Routledge Advances in Social Work

Everyday Social Justice and Citizenship
Perspectives for the 21st Century
Edited by Ann-Marie Mealey, Pam Jarvis, Janis Fook and Jonathan Doherty

Critical Ethics of Care in Social Work
Transforming the Politics and Practices of Caring
Edited by Bob Pease, Anthea Vreugdenhil and Sonya Stanford

Reconceptualising Transitions from Care to Independence
Supporting Care Leavers to Fulfil Their Potential
Jennifer Driscoll

Reciprocal Relationships and Wellbeing
Implications for Social Work and Social Policy
Edited by Maritta Törrönen, Carol Munn-Giddings and Laura Tarkiainen

Forthcoming

Neoliberalism, Nordic Welfare States and Social Work
Current and Future Challenges
Edited by Masoud Kamali and Jessica H. Jönsson

Participatory Pedagogic Impact Research
Co-production with Community Partners in Action
Mike Seal

Consciousness-Raising
Critical Pedagogy and Practice for Social Change
Nilan Yu

Intersectionality in Social Work
Activism and Practice in Context
Edited by Suryia Nayak and Rachel Robbins

Conversation Analysis for Social Work
Talking with Youth in Care
Gerald deMontigny

For a full list of titles please visit www.routledge.com/Routledge-Advances-in-Social-Work/book-series/RASW.

Intersectionality in Social Work

Activism and Practice in Context

Edited by
Suryia Nayak and Rachel Robbins

Routledge
Taylor & Francis Group
LONDON AND NEW YORK

First published 2019
by Routledge
2 Park Square, Milton Park, Abingdon, Oxon OX14 4RN

and by Routledge
711 Third Avenue, New York, NY 10017

Routledge is an imprint of the Taylor & Francis Group, an informa business

British Library Cataloguing-in-Publication Data
A catalogue record for this book is available from the British Library.

Library of Congress Cataloging-in-Publication Data
Names: Nayak, Suryia, editor. | Robbins, Rachel, editor.
Title: Intersectionality in social work : activism and practice in context / edited by Suryia Nayak and Rachel Robbins.
Description: 1st Edition. | New York : Routledge, 2018. |
Series: Routledge advances in social work | Includes bibliographical references and index.
Identifiers: LCCN 2018009961 | ISBN 9781138628168 (hardback) | ISBN 9781315210810 (ebook)
Subjects: LCSH: Intersectionality (Sociology) | Womanism. | Social service. | Women political activists.
Classification: LCC HM488.5 .I585 2018 | DDC 320.082—dc23
LC record available at https://lccn.loc.gov/2018009961

ISBN: 978-1-138-62816-8 (hbk)
ISBN: 978-1-315-21081-0 (ebk)

Typeset in Times New Roman
by Florence Production Ltd, Stoodleigh, Devon, UK

Contents

Figures

Tables

Contributors

Rashida Bibi is currently a PhD student at the University of Manchester. She completed a BA Hons Humanities at the University of Huddersfield and went on to complete an MRes entitled, 'Mussafirs of the 21st Century: British South Asian Muslim Women, higher education and changing notions of Britishness'. Her current PhD research involves multi-level analysis of the everyday lives and interactions of BSA Muslim women within and across spaces of home, work and wider public spaces. Research interests include intersectionality, higher education and employment for BSA Muslim women.

Elena Calvo-Gonzalez, social anthropologist, is a lecturer in the Department of Sociology and Postgraduate Programme in Social Sciences at the Federal University of Bahia.

Itzia Gandarias Goikoetxea is a teacher at the Faculty of Psychology and Education at the University of Deusto. Degree in Psychology by the University of Deusto and PhD in Social Psychology at the Autonomous University of Barcelona. Interested research areas are intersectionality and de-colonial feminisms, feminist epistemologies, migration and gender and activist methodologies. Some of the last publications include: 'From below: Alliances for a feminist cooperation' (2014), 'Other forms of (re)know: Reflections, tools and applications from feminist research' (2015) and recently a research about strategies of survival and resistance of Sub-Saharan African women (2017) with the NGO Cear-Euskadi.

Nina Held works as a Research and Teaching Fellow at the University of Sussex. She is one of the researchers of the ERC-funded project *SOGICA – Sexual Orientation and Gender Identity Claims of Asylum*, a comparative study that looks at the social and legal experience of LGBT people seeking asylum in Germany, Italy and the UK. Her current research interests in sexuality and asylum have developed through her previous role as Centre Co-ordinator at Freedom from Torture and through her voluntary role as the Chair of the Lesbian Immigration Support Group since 2009.

Andrew Hollingworth is undertaking a PhD at the University of Huddersfield into the care leaver birth father experiences of having a child involved in child protection. Andrew is also a HCPC registered social worker on a child protection team at Salford Local Authority.

Edward Hon-Sing Wong is a doctoral student at York University's Social Work PhD program. He is also a graduate of York University's Masters of Social Work program. With a background in mental health practice and community organising, his work weaves together critical perspectives on psychiatry with anti-colonial and anti-racist theory. His published writings and presentations include a historical examination of processes of disablisim within Canadian immigration policy, Canadian social work and colonialism, experiences of non-status students in accessing education and discourses of race in Canadian mental hygiene movement literature.

Dorett Jones has worked at Imkaan and in the ending Violence against Women and Girls (VAWG) sector for many years, from frontline advocacy, training and therapeutic provision to strategic development and management of services. She works internationally, including with Indigenous communities in Aotearoa, which has influenced her practice. Dorett is a filmmaker and published writer in the UK and Europe and holds an MA in Culture Diaspora Ethnicity. She developed and wrote Imkaan's national Accredited Quality Standards for specialist by and for Black and 'minority-ethnic' ending VAWG services in the UK. They are the only standards of their kind.

Camille Kumar has worked in the ending VAWG sector/ movement for 15 years in the UK, Australia and briefly in Bangladesh. Camille Kumar is currently Membership and Sustainability Coordinator at Imkaan, UK. Camille's work involves coordinating the network of 34 Black-led women's organisations working to end VAWG. Camille is also a member of Black Feminists UK, Freedom Without Fear Platform and LGBTQI community-based organising groups. Camille graduated in Social Work in 2004 (RMIT, Australia).

Kaltrina Kusari was born and grew up in Kosovo, but moved to North America six years after the war. Her Master's in Social Work thesis (from the University of Calgary) explored the experiences of rejected asylum seekers from Kosova. She interviewed Kosovar rejected asylum seekers and analysed Kosova's National Strategy for Reintegration of Repatriated Persons to highlight the voices of a largely hidden migrant population. She is now working to ensure that the voices of those interviewed will inform policy-makers. She is involved with research projects that focus on the settlement and integration experiences of refugees in Canada.

Marai Larasi is the Executive Director of Imkaan and Co-Chair of the End Violence Against Women Coalition. Her ending violence against women and girls work has spanned over two decades at both operational and strategic levels; and she has developed and led cutting-edge services which address violence against minoritised/marginalised women and girls. Her activism, advocacy and teaching have been framed by alliances with other Black and

Indigenous feminist activists and practitioners. She has produced papers for, and delivered presentations to, a range of audiences in the UK and internationally, and her work has appeared in a number of publications.

Karen McCarthy holds an MA in Sociology and Global Change. Karen is a volunteer of the Lesbian Immigration Support Group and one of its founder members, since 2007. She works as a lecturer in Youth and Community Work at MMU. Her previous professional experience is over 20 years' experience as a community development worker, working with a wide range of communities and on a variety of issues, including provision for Asian women and the establishment of youth work provision for Black young people.

Marisela Montenegro is a lecturer in Social Psychology Department of Autonomous University of Barcelona and foundational member of FIC: Fractalities in Critical Research group, a group devoted to the study of present and alternative forms of governmentality from a critical epistemological perspective. She is an activist in feminist, LGTB and antiglobalisation movements in Barcelona. Her research activity focuses on critical and postcolonial analysis of research and social work in areas such as social services for migrant women, social movements and the relationship between new technologies and the social construction of gender and sexuality.

Ilana Mountian is a post-doctoral researcher, lecturer at the Postgraduate Program of Psychology at the University of Sao Paulo (CAPES/PNPD), member of the Discourse Unit, Manchester, and psychoanalyst.

Kamaria Muntu is a Black American writer and experienced activist, whose work centres on domestic human rights concerns with an emphasis on food sovereignty and women's cooperatives. She is the founder of the online arts journal *Sinister Guru* (formerly *Femficatio*). She has been published in both academic and literary journals, including, *The Journal of Pan African Studies, Call and Response: The Riverside Anthology of the African American Literary Tradition, Stand Our Ground: Poems for Trayvon Martin and Marissa Alexander* and *A Lime Jewel: An Anthology of Poetry and Short Stories in Aid of Haiti*. She is also a proud working-class single mother and cancer survivor.

Suryia Nayak is a qualified social worker and psychoanalytic psychotherapist and currently training as a psychoanalytic group practitioner. She has over 30 years of practice and training experience within the Rape Crisis Movement working to confront all forms of violence against women and girls. She has set up two specific services for Black, Asian and Minoritised ethnic women and girls. She has extensive experience as a clinical supervisor (for example, eating disorders, intensive psychiatric in-patient therapeutic work with adolescents, prisons) as well as in community education, research and clinical practice with asylum seekers, refugees and issues of migration.

Joan Pujol is Lecturer in Social Psychology Department of Autonomous University of Barcelona and foundational member of Fractalities in Critical

Research group, a group devoted to the study of present and alternative forms of governmentality from a critical epistemological perspective. He is an activist in the feminist and LGBT movement in Barcelona. His research analyses governmental practices in current liberal democracies in the areas of sex/gender, gender and technology, queer subjectivities and postcolonial feminisms, using critical research methods.

Annette Rimmer is a freelance radio producer, experienced in community development, social work and teaching. She is currently involved in radio production with excluded groups, is a community radio volunteer and an honorary lecturer at the University of Manchester.

Rachel Robbins researches in the areas of domestic violence, adult social care and social justice. In particular, she has an interest in feminist theory and intersectionality. Rachel researches actively in the area of social work and social policy and is a member of the Connect Centre for International Research on New Approaches to Prevent Violence and Harm at UCLAN. Prior to entering the academy, Rachel worked in a range of social work and social policy settings. She is also a blogger on issues of social justice at: https://socialpolicyandthe dorisdayfan.wordpress.com/

Dr Rekha Sethi is a researcher, scholar, writer, translator, editor and an educationist. As Associate Professor at Indraprastha College for Women, University of Delhi, Rekha, has been teaching Hindi Language, Literature and Media Studies to graduate and postgraduate students of Delhi University for more than two decades. Rekha's main areas of work are post-independence Hindi poetry and fiction and translation, and translation studies. Rekha also works as a language expert.

Dr Hannana Siddiqui is a renowned multi-award-winning consultant on violence against Black and minority women and girls. She has worked for 30 years at a leading organisation, Southall Black Sisters, and led successful campaigns on domestic violence, immigration and battered women who kill, particularly the landmark case of Kiranjit Ahluwalia. She was on the first Home Office Working Group on Forced Marriage; helped to introduce the Forced Marriage (Civil Protection) Act 2007 and statutory guidance; and helped bring to justice high-profile 'honour killings'. She co-edited *Moving in the Shadows: Violence in the Lives of Minority Women and Children* (Ashgate, 2013).

Sonia Soans was awarded her PhD in 2016. Her training is in Psychology and she has worked in both clinical and academic settings. Her work explores the intersections between mental health, gender, media and nationalism. Using feminism to illustrate the discrepancies in how nationalism formulates narratives around women and issues such as addiction, she poses a challenge to clinical ideas of mental illness.

Dr Ravi Thiara is a Principal Research Fellow and Director of the Centre for the Study of Safety and Well-being, University of Warwick, a centre specialising in research on violence against women and children, and on marginalised communities. Her work spans national and international research, evaluation and practice development over more than 25 years. She has published widely and books include: *Violence against Women in South Asian Communities: Issues for Policy and Practice* (Jessica Kingsley, 2010); *Disabled Women and Domestic Violence: Responding to the Experiences of Survivors* (Jessica Kingsley, 2012); *Preventing Violence Against Women and Girls: Educational Work with Children and Young People* (Policy Press, 2014).

Introduction

Suryia Nayak and Rachel Robbins

This book rests on the premise that we cannot act socially to enable the liberation possibilities of individuals, communities and societies without intersectionality. Thus, this book opens up critical analysis of questions such as: How and why does intersectionality challenge the structures and discourses of social work education, management and organisation both within a multinational, multicultural, multi-faith UK and wider global context? How does intersectionality work to disrupt political, social and discursive constructions that act as defence mechanisms designed to disavow complicity with oppression? What is the internal revolutionary potential of practices founded on intersectionality?

Too much of the debate about intersectionality remains at a conceptual and methodological level – this book argues for the 'activism of intersectionality' to invoke the action of social work without borders. The book disrupts convenient demarcated zones of thinking and action that are contingent upon the fetish for categorisation. Thus, this book performs Minh-ha's (2011) 'the boundary event' and calls the reader into the happenings of the boundary. In other words, this book opens up the happenings in the 'boundary event' that function to delimit representations, articulations, movements and positions.

This book emphasises context as the agent of intersectionality. The constitutive imperative of context in relation to axes of differentiation is that, 'if you can't locate the other, how are you going to locate yourself?' (Minh-ha, 1991: 73). Of relevance is Brah's (1996) use of 'diaspora spaces' privileging 'routes' over 'roots'; invoking the idea of 'subjects in movement', where axes of differentiation are temporary and in constant transformation. Thus, picking up on the Black feminist concepts of 'situated knowledge' developed by Hill-Collins (2000: 270; Haraway, 1988), 'situated knowers' (2000: 19) and situated standpoints (2000: 25), we could speak of a 'situated intersectionality'. Taking this stance, what becomes clear is that 'intersectionality is not being offered here as some new, totalising theory of identity' (Crenshaw, 1991: 1244).

Situated intersectionality understands that particular differences in particular contexts produce particular relationships of discrimination and subalternisation. This book recognises the complexity of social work within contexts of increasingly diverse, cosmopolitan families, communities and societies; where the term 'cosmopolitan' certainly captures the element of diversity, but is, perhaps, lacking in the element (found in most dictionary definitions of the word 'cosmopolitan') of how we relate 'across our human differences as equals' (Lorde, 1980: 115). How can intersectionality enable social work to grapple with the complexity of being a second- or third-generation British-born Muslim woman carer for her Pakistani born, first-generation migrant mother with dementia and survivor of domestic violence? Or, how can intersectionality enable social work with a Nigerian-born asylum-seeking lesbian in the UK with no recourse to public funds? Or, how might insights into the impact of the intersectionality of caste and gender structures for Dalit and Adivasi women in India translate into learning for migrant women's struggles in the Basque Country or Brazil? Or, how might social workers resist collusion with racist Islamophobic discursive practices whilst seeking to liberate survivors of female genital mutilation, forced marriage and honour-based violence?

The international imperative of this book is its insistence on a re-framing of spatial and temporal notions of 'the international', which transcend geopolitical borders. This book includes examples from diverse geographical contexts that pick up the specificity and complexity of grappling with geographical, regional, religious, racial, colonial and cultural issues manifest in, for example, productions of migration, asylum and Islamophobia. The sustained emphasis on activism and practice reasserts the potency of intersectionality born out of Black feminism to provoke wider debates about the position of the activism of Black Feminist Theory in social work.

In this book, the applications of the activism of intersectionality in context occupy, rather than resolve, uncomfortable questions at the core of social justice movements such as: Can the subaltern speak? (Spivak, 1988); and '[a]t what point, and in what ways . . . does the specificity of a particular social experience become an expression of essentialism? (Brah, 1996: 95). Examination of activist methods such as community radio, Black women-only spaces and services, poetic literary practices and feminist street actions provide examples of the complexity of intersectionality in action.

Configured on the dialectic of being born out of injustice in order to confront injustice, intersectionality is a refusal of dividing practices (Foucault, 1975, 1982; Parker and Spears, 1996: 4) and, as such, this book insists on the explicit dialogical and dialectical relationship between context, experience, practice and scholarship (Hill-Collins, 2000: 30). In short, this book sustains an argument for resistance to the split between theory and practice, centre and margin, individual and collective, subject and context, and paternalistic service provider/professional and service recipient/user binary relations.

Structure

Structuring a book on intersectionality is an inherently anti-intersectional conundrum that mirrors the tension within activism of '[h]ow to be both free and situated' (Morrison, 1998: 5). Intersectionality is a refusal of single axes of differentiation and the chapters within this book assert that refusal, as they weave, whilst troubling particular discursive weaves of, theory, empirical research and activism. The book is structured across the intersection of two mutually constitutive axes: Understandings of Intersectionality, here the chapters contextualise the question of how and why '[t]he shadow obscuring this complex Black women's intellectual tradition is neither accidental nor benign' (Hill-Collins, 2000: 3); and Realizations of the Activism of Intersectionality, here, the chapters contextualise experience of the 'activism of intersectionality' as a tool with political potential to be reclaimed and yet to be discovered.

Understandings of intersectionality

Nayak and Rekha, focus on Dalit and Adivasi women's poetry about intersectional oppression in the Indian context as a basis to argue for text as a practice of intersectionality. Siddiqui and Thiara insist on a 'returning home' where intersectionality concerned with racialised structural inequalities experienced by BME women and girls in particular contexts and historical moments might accommodate 'mature multiculturalism' and 'mature multi-faithism'. Hon-Sing's analysis of three Ontario-based social service training texts reveals the absence of historicisation and interlocking oppression. Hon-Sing argues that individualised social services are diametrically opposed to social change through collective action integral to Black feminist thought. Hollingworth reflects on two journeys of international social work to deliberately dislocate the reader between the refugee camp in Calais, France, called 'the Jungle' and Fort Portal, Uganda, including the Kyaka II refugee camp. Bibi offers empirical research with British South Asian Muslim women in the context of Islamophobia in the UK. Bibi's analysis navigates intersectional micro-embodied discursive practices in the minutiae of everyday ordinary spaces. Mountian and Calvo-Gonzalez's feminist research on public health and immigration in Brazil argues for consideration of colonial heritage and its contemporary discursive repetition as a dynamic of intersectionality.

Realisations of the activism of intersectionality

Jones and Larasi's auto-ethnography [re]imagination of non-statutory social work practice as a critical site for transformation in work to end violence against Black women and girls asks: How can we build collective Black women spaces of recovery and accountability, while disrupting the impact of white, patriarchal, colonial social work practices? What would those spaces look like, and would we survive the psychic ruptures and practical challenges of removing the 'walls' of Social Work? Muntu's detailed analysis of the position of Black women in the Black Lives Matter Movement denounces patriarchal microstructural macro-aggressions, such as, misogynistic cultural narratives. Muntu insists that Black Lives Matter activists bring state crimes against Black women into focus: the action will determine the change. Held and McCarthy draw on research with the Lesbian Immigration Support Group (LISG) in Manchester, UK, to examine the complexities for Black, African and Asian lesbian asylum seekers within the

British asylum system. Here, Held and McCarthy illustrate that 'refugeeness' troubles the intersections gender, class, religion and 'race'. Soans demonstrates the ways in which Dalit feminists seeking a new approach to empower Dalit women in areas they have historically been excluded from such as political, economic and religious social arenas, attempt to create a new consciousness. Kumar's reflective activist scrutiny highlights historical and contemporary 'fault lines' within the violence against women's and girls' movements, where 'fault lines' are a site of survival and creation of new intersectional possibilities. This reflective chapter investigates some of the current fault lines using an intersectional analysis.

Robbins uses the example of the avoidable death by drowning of 18-year-old Connor Sparrowhawk in a UK NHS unit for people with learning disabilities as a searing indictment of complicit oppressive discursive practices within social care systems. Robbins argues that scholars of intersectionality and social movements need to consider the relevance of the digital space and the context of social media activism. Gandarias Goikoetxea's application of intersectionality in political activism focuses on feminist collectivity between autochthonous and migrant women in the Platform of the World March of Women of the Basque Country. Gandarias Goikoetxea examines three tensions: (i) the crystallisation of 'lacking' and 'emptied' intersectional subjects; (ii) the 'coat rack' subject or the danger of classification and univocality; and (iii) the utopia of the 'etcetera'. Rimmer draws an empirical research study entitled 'Breaking the Silence: community radio, women and empowerment' that considers community radio as a vehicle of women's empowerment.

Conclusion

The conversation on contextual intersectionality, between Nayak, Montenegro and Pujol, is a fitting conclusion to this edited collection of international perspectives on the activism of intersectionality. In the same way as the conversation took place, the chapter is structured by a series of questions that could be used as a social work framework for critical intersectional reflexivity.

The interminable tensions inhabited within 'Intersectionality in Social Work: Activism and Practice in Context' are captured by Anzaldúa, in the following words:

> it is not enough to stand on the opposite river bank, shouting questions, challenging patriarchal, white conventions. A counterstance locks one into a duel of oppressor and oppressed; locked in mortal combat, like the cop and the criminal, both are reduced to a common denominator of violence . . . All reaction is limited by, and dependent on, what it is reacting against . . . At some point, on our way to a new consciousness, we will have to leave the opposite bank, the split between the two mortal combatants somehow healed so that we are on both shores at once and, at once, see through serpent and eagle eyes. Or perhaps we will decide to disengage from the dominant culture, write it off altogether as a lost cause, and cross the border into a wholly new

> territory. Or we might go another route. The possibilities are numerous once we decide to act and not react.
>
> (Anzaldúa, 2007: 100–101)

Whether we speak in terms of 'opposite river bank[s]' or finding new shores and territories, the conclusion is that there is no intersectionality without context.

References

Anzaldúa, G. (2007) *Borderlands/La Frontera: The New Mestiza*. 3rd ed., San Francisco: Aunt Lute Books.

Brah, A. (1996) *Cartographies of Diaspora: Contesting Identities*. London: Routledge.

Crenshaw, K. (1991) 'Mapping the Margins: Intersectionality, Identity Politics, and Violence Against Women of Color'. *Stanford Law Review*, 43(6): 1241–1299.

Foucault, M. (1975) *The Birth of the Clinic: An Archaeology of Medical Perception* (trans. A. M. Sheridan Smith). New York: Vintage.

Foucault, M. (1982) 'The Subject and Power'. In Dreyfus, H. L. and Rabinow, P. (eds.) (1993) *Michel Foucault: Beyond Structuralism and Hermeneutics*. 2nd ed. Chicago, IL: University of Chicago Press.

Haraway, D. (1988) 'Situated Knowledges: The Science Question in Feminism and the Privilege of the Partial Perspective'. *Feminist Studies*, 14(3): 575–599.

Hill-Collins, P. (2000) *Black Feminist Thought: Knowledge, Consciousness, and the Politics of Empowerment*. 2nd ed. London: Routledge.

Lorde, A. (1980) 'Age, Race, Class, and Sex: Women Redefining Difference'. In Lorde, A. (ed.) (1984) *Sister Outsider: Essays and Speeches*. Trumansburg, NY: The Crossing Press.

Minh-ha, T. T. (1991) *When the Moon Waxes Red: Representation, Gender and Cultural Politics*. New York: Routledge.

Minh-ha, T. T. (2011) *Elsewhere, Within Here: Immigration, Refugeeism and the Boundary Event*. New York: Routledge.

Morrison, T. (1998) 'Home'. In Lubiano, W. (ed.) (1998) *The House that Race Built*. New York: Vintage Books.

Parker, I. and Spears, R. (1996) *Psychology and Society: Radical Theory and Practice*. Chipping Norton, UK: Pluto Press.

Seshadri-Crooks, K. (2000) 'Surviving Theory: A Conversation with Homi K. Bhabha'. In Afzal-Khan, F. and Seshadri-Crooks, K. (eds.) (2000) *The Pre-occupation of Postcolonial Studies*. Durham, UK: Duke University Press.

Spivak, G. C. (1988) 'Can the Subaltern Speak?' In Nelson, C. and Grossberg, L. (eds.) (1988) *Marxism and the Interpretation of Culture*. Basingstoke, UK: Macmillan.

Part 1

Understandings of intersectionality

1 Textual practice as intersectional practice

Situated caste and gender knowledge in India

Suryia Nayak and Rekha Sethi

Literary texts are marked with multi-layered, interdependent sensibilities that challenge binary positions of social conditioning. Literary texts, both in terms of composition and content, are intersectional. Thus, the practice of writing and reading literary text is a practice of intersectionality, opening up questions about the politics of knowledge production that correspond with unequal intersecting power relations. If, as 'social beings, women [and clients of social services] are constructed through effects of language and representation' (De Lauretis, 1984: 14), then the role of text in this construction is rudimentary to intersectionality. Using the lens of intersectionality to think about the production and analysis of literary texts in terms of social work has both an international reach and holds the specificity of diverse social work practice contexts. This analysis of intersectionality, reaching across India and the UK, intersects a diversity of disciplinary fields, including social work, Black feminism and literary textual analysis, and as such, both the content and the method are intersectional. In the spirit of the Black feminist theory of intersectionality, this transgression of geographical and disciplinary borders reflects intersectionality as a theory of the deconstruction of borders (Nayak, 2015: 101–103).

The questions being asked are: what can social work learn from the literary works of Indian women, and more specifically, Dalit and Adivasi women poets, writing about their experience of intersectional oppression in the Indian context? How might social workers and service users take up 'strategies of writing and reading [as] forms of cultural resistance' (De Lauretis, 1984: 7)? Can the example (examined in this chapter) of the Indian Adivasi activist Nirmala Putul, who uses poetry to record/transcribe her work with women and girls that have been trafficked, offer a different method of social work documentation? How can social work occupy an insider-outsider position within and through the very texts that frame the profession and practices? How might the creation of literature form social work interventions for recovery and empowerment? The subversive potential of Dalit and Adivasi women texts is that:

> [n]ot only can they work to turn dominant discourses inside out (and show that it can be done), to undercut their enunciation and address, to unearth the archaeological stratifications on which they are built; but in affirming

> the historical existence of irreducible contradictions for women in discourse, they also challenge theory in its own terms, the terms of a semiotic space constructed in language, its power based on social validation and well-established modes of enunciation and address. So well established that, paradoxically, the only way to position oneself outside of that discourse is to displace oneself within it.
>
> (De Lauretis, 1984: 7)

It is of significance to note that the meaning of the word 'text' is 'a tissue, a woven fabric' (Barthes, 1977: 159). This chapter performs an intersection or weave of apparently unconnected field of practice. It is not usual for literary textual analysis to form a core component of social work education. For example, how many social work books direct students to the work of Roland Barthes? Indeed, the situation of social work and the situation of social service users are not 'self-contained systems' but are constituted in terms of relational socio-political, historical and cultural structures/contexts that mirror intertextuality:

> There are always other words in a word, other texts in a text. The concept of intertextuality requires, therefore, that we understand texts not as self-contained systems but as differential and historical, as traces and tracings of otherness, since they are shaped by the repetition and transformation of other textual structures.
>
> (Martínez Alfaro, 1996: 268)

Social work is a prime example of a professional practice based on the relationality of texts, where no piece of documentation exists in isolation. Thus, '[m]eaning becomes something which exists between texts and all other texts to which it refers and relates, moving out from the independent text into a network of textual relations. The text becomes the intertext' (Allen, 2000: 1). In accord with Crenshaw's proposition that 'intersectional experience is greater than the sum of racism and sexism' (Crenshaw, 1989: 539), intertextuality as intersubjectivity 'operates in an equation whereby the sum of the parts [text(s)] is greater than the individual elements [for example, words, grammar and spaces], as in intersectionality' (Nayak, 2015: 57). Proposing the idea of intertextuality as intersubjectivity (1980), Kristeva, explains that:

> each word (text) is an intersection of word (texts) where at least one other word (text) can be read . . . [as] the absorption and transformation of another . . . The word as minimal textual unit thus turns out to occupy the status of mediator, linking structural models to cultural (historical) environment, as well as that of regulator.
>
> (Kristeva, 1969: 37; parentheses and emphasis in original)

The texts of social work, including the array of documentation about service users, are mechanisms whereby the 'absorption' and, as such, the 'transformation' of the problem of the service user is translated into words; these words link 'structural models' of socially constructed representations, positions and discourses about service users 'to cultural (historical) environment[s]'. In other words, the 'spatialized' materiality of words reflects the 'spatialized' materiality of subjects (as social workers, activists, service users and poets). Application of intertextuality as intersectionality enables scrutiny of social work's regulatory function, particularly, in regards to documentation as a 'mediator' that regulates recognition of the importance of the social contexts that produce service users. Conversely, in the tradition of Dalit and Adivasi women poets in India, perhaps the application of intertextuality as intersectionality is the revolutionary potential of social work, to enable 'new strategies, new semiotic contents and new signs . . . a habit change in readers, spectators, etc.' (De Lauretis, 1984: 186). The point is, that, the concept of 'textuality does not mean a reduction of the world to linguistic texts, books, or a tradition composed of books' (Spivak, 1998: 104).

The politics of knowledge production

The application of intertextuality as intersectionality exposes the power/knowledge relationship, whereby 'subjugated knowledges' are relegated. Foucault explains:

> By 'subjugated knowledges' I mean two things. On the one hand, I am referring to historical contents that have been buried and disguised in a functional coherence or formal systemization. . . . By 'subjugated knowledges' one should understand something else . . . namely a whole set of knowledges that have been disqualified as inadequate to the task or insufficiently elaborated; naïve knowledges, located low down on the hierarchy, beneath the required level of cognition or scientificity.
>
> (Foucault and Collin, 1980: 81–82)

This chapter demonstrates 'a politics of close reading practice' (Nayak, 2015: 24–50) of 'a set of knowledges' 'disqualified as inadequate' due to the intersection of caste, gender and poverty. The focus is on the work of contemporary female poets of India including Dalit and Adivasi women poets, as a feminist praxis of intersectionality 'resolutely, political, directly involved in effecting social change' (Locke Swarr and Nagar, 2010: 55). This chapter demonstrates that warranted critiques of 'the invocation of praxis as code word for an 'activist knowledge' (ibid.) are transcended by the situated knowledge of intersectional subjugation articulated in the work of contemporary Indian feminist poetry. Situated knowledge as 'activist knowledge' is feminist praxis in poetry; not a 'code word' (ibid.). It is clear that for Indian women poets including Dalit and Adivasi women poets, that:

> poetry is not a luxury. It is a vital necessity of our existence. It forms the quality of the light within which we predicate our hopes and dreams toward survival and change, first made into language, then into idea, then into more

> tangible action. Poetry is the way we help give name to the nameless so it can be thought. . . . And where that language does not yet exist, it is our poetry which helps to fashion it.
>
> (Lorde, 1984: 37–38)

The situated knowledge of Dalit and Adivasi women poet-activists give 'name to the nameless' so that the particularity of gender and caste 'can be thought' as a production of the particularity of situated meanings:

> the experience of a Dalit migrant woman accessing health services cannot be understood simply by her gender experience and her experience of being dalit. The experience of being a woman itself differs for dalits and non-dalits, i.e. gender (and prescribed norms and behaviours) can be constituted differently by cultural meanings, policies and institutional practices and aspects of historical violence and discrimination . . . In essence, the simultaneous operation of structures of oppression make the experience at the intersection of these structures qualitatively distinct.
>
> (Kapilashrami and Ravindran, 2016: 181)

The point is that all movements, sectors, and/or services that purport to empower, support, protect and advocate for those violated by oppression must do so on a foundation of situated knowledge of situated intersectionality.

The relevance to social work of reading literary text as a practice of intersectionality

Social work involves the construction, analysis and utilisation of a diverse range of texts, including: case notes, assessment forms, files about services users, court reports, minutes of meetings and referral documentation (Ames, 1999; Kagle, 1991, 1993, 1995; Monnickendam, et al., 1994; Cormican and Cormican, 1977). The enduring importance of text as 'a product and a process' within social work (Fox and Gutheil, 2000) is pivotal to concepts of evidence-based practice and co-production involving multi-disciplinary working and service user participation. The production of texts to document narrative processes of phronesis through critical reflection, clinical supervision, social work education and qualitative social work research are fundamental to non-defensive human rights-based social work and social policy practice principles (Robbins, 2013).

The social work practices of life story and reminiscence work are examples of the therapeutic potential and impact of (auto) biographical memory work. Social work research and scholarship is undisputed in identifying, either explicitly or implicitly, that the therapeutic benefits of narrative textual work with service users lies in the production of the text as a process of intersecting the past with the present, the social with the psychological, discursive practices with representation of self-identity (Barnardos, 2013; Baynes, 2008; Burnell and Vaughan, 2008; Cook-Cottone and Beck, 2007; Goddard, et al., 2010; Habermas and Bluck, 2000;

Horrocks and Goddard, 2006; Humphreys and Kertesz, 2012; Murray, et al., 2008; Nelson and Fivush, 2004; Rose and Philpot, 2006; Ryan and Walker, 2007; Shotton, 2010, 2013). The question is: how can the therapeutic textual practices within social work be a force for a mutual activism of resistance between those who use social services and those who provide social services, where the therapeutic potential rests in turning 'dominant discourses inside out' (De Lauretis, 1984: 7)?

Intersectionality in the matrix of gender, caste and class within the context of India

Hindi literature has a tradition that dates back to the eighth century but women poets who have registered a significant presence are numbered to the likes of Mirabai and Mahadevi Varma. Kumkum Sangari identifies a strong streak of protest in the poetry of *bhakti poet* Mirabai (Sangari, 1990). Mahadevi Varma's collection of essays written, between 1931 and 1937 (published in 1941) and entitled *Shrankhla ki Kadiyan*, translated as *Links in the Chain* (Varma, 2003), speak for the economic independence and citizen rights of women. Mahadevi Varma highlights the necessity of women understanding their judicial rights and examines the processes of subject formation within patriarchy in relation to women's identity, representation and position. Within postcolonial Indian feminist literature, the emphasis on the assertion of feminist voice as an assertion of self-existence is evident in the work of Kirti Chaudhary, Snehmayi Chaudhary and Indu Jain (Anamika, 2015). Since the nineties there has been resurgence in women's writing owing to the spread of education and assertion of identity discourses globally, including the socio-political locale of the country. Many Indian women writers face intersectional marginalisation because of their gender and caste or class and their poems carry images of the intersectionality of women as the subject of their poetry and emphatically denounce all kinds of oppression and violence. The situated poetic knowldege of Indian women in this chapter testifies that: 'socio-spatial embeddedness of village-level activists places them in a unique position to analyse the multiple webs of power in which their everyday lives, struggle, and aspirations are inserted' (Sangtin Writers and Nagar, 2006: 151).

The writings of contemporary female poets, from the field of Hindi literature, including: Gagan Gill (2017), Katyayni (1999, 2002), Anamika (2007, 2015), Savita Singh (2013, 2017), Sushila Takbhaure (2011, 2013, 2015), Nirmala Putul (2003, 2014, 2017) and Neelesh Raghuvanshi (1997), are challenging the horizon of their poetic expression and in doing so challenge the horizon and experience of simultaneous multiple structural oppression. The challenge is of 'recasting 'women's' issues from a plurality of vantage points and an acknowledgement that gender plays out differently depending on one's many intersecting identities' (Kapilashrami and Ravindran, 2016: 178). The contextual intersectionality of caste, class and gender translate into the convergence constructions of identity that function in the subjugation of women. Kumar's (2009) analysis of the counter-hegemonic activist practices of Indian poet-activist women to the multiple oppressions suffered by women and girls is captured in her reference to the power of Katyayni's poetry. The overtones of her poetry are immensely political. On one hand she condemns the social order that parades an activist bare bodied, to add insult to her being a woman (Katyayni, 2002). Similarly, she is upset at the communal riots in wake of the upsurge in Ayodhya (Katyayni, 1999).

> [w]riting in response to an incident in which a girl-activist is paraded naked in Andhra Pradesh by the state's police, the poet [Katyayni] underlines the urgency of writing direct poetry:
>
> Pushing great religious luminaries in the background
> Should we postpone poetry? (Kya Sthagit Kar Dein Kavita)
>
> (Kumar, 2009: 352)

It is important to note the deliberate decision to discuss these issues through the writings of contemporary female poets of India, writing in Hindi: the predominant language of an otherwise multilingual country. These are voices from the margins, speaking in a language that is located in a country positioned geo-politically on the margins; it is an intervention to contest the politics of the hierarchies of language. Thus, both the method (in terms of language and location) and the content (literature from women positioned as marginal) are co-productive as an action of feminist consciousness-raising to resist oppressive centre/margin positions.

Intersectionality: A case study of Dalit and Adivasi women poets

Though the plural texture of multicultural and multilingual Indian nation is a matter of pride for its citizens, it has also been plagued by identity conflicts resulting in divisive social structures. Caste-based hierarchies have pushed lower caste groups to peripheral positions. Dalits and Adivasis, being on the lowest rung of the ladder, are two groups who face multiple converging indignities, derision, abuse and forms of exploitation at the hands of influential upper caste groups. Thus, to say that all Indian 'women suffer the same oppression simply because [they] are women is to lose sight of the many and varied tools of patriarchy' (Lorde, 1979: 67) namely, the intersectional experience of caste.

Dalits refer to the group of people who were known as the depressed classes, prior to 1935, during British rule. After independence, they came to be known as scheduled castes. According to the 2011 census they comprise 16.6% of India's population. The Adivasis are small ethnic, tribal groups. The constitution refers to them as scheduled tribes. They are considered to be the original inhabitants of their native lands, so they assert their right on the natural resources of the area. Industrialisation and global onslaught on the economy has resulted in their massive displacement. Adivasis are spread in different parts of the country and form 7.5% of the total population in India. Even after six decades of independence, Adivasis have not been included in mainstream national development programmes. The marginalisation of both Dalits And Adivasis has, more or less, remained constant.

The writings of Dalit and Adivasi poets represent a desire to tell their own story for 'the transformation of silence into language and action' (Lorde, 1977: 40); it is a rewriting of the history of their social existence with the corresponding complexities of Spivak's question, *Can the Subaltern Speak?* (1988). Dalit and Adivasi poets demand an equal and just society, not only for themselves but for their entire class, insisting on equality as enshrined in the constitution, to be granted irrespective of caste, class, gender, religion, race or any such external social construction. The lens of intersectionality is extended to achieve inclusivity. More specifically, Dalit and Adivasi poets ask for an equal space for women in democratic processes; foregrounding the differential treatment meted out to women repeatedly at home and in the workplace. Although a human rights framework underlies the work of these poets, there is a clear articulation that in a patriarchy women's needs are not the same as that of men. The caution is not to fall into the trap of translating the notion of universal human rights into universal women's rights because of the diversities of women's experiences, representation and positionality at the grassroots lived level. This tension is alive in Sushila Takbhaure's poetry, fiction and autobiography (Takbhaure, 2011, 2013a, 2013b) located at the crossroads of marginalised identities; the intersection of being feminist and Dalit in the fight against mutltiple oppression. Takbhaure reiterates (Takbhaure, 2013b: 16) that the treatment meted out to Dalits reflect a particular cultural colonisation where upper caste parties, groups and individuals grab all the opportunities, take control over national resources and push the Dalits to the peripheries of urban centres.

Dalit literature in India seems to have discovered a new aesthetics and poetics for their writings. The main thrust of their literature is on struggle and awakening. Their entire writings are a mission to fight intersecting inequalities. In that sense Takbhaure's poetry can be termed as a cry for justice predicated on intersectionality. Thematically, most of her poems are based on the trauma of being both a Dalit and a woman, as well as the resolution to fight these oppressive systems and stand up for one's rights. Takbhaure's poetry articulates resistance as resilience to multiple oppressions through an intersectional lens. Dalit women have an arduous realisation of self; often their caste identities superseding their gender identity, placed in an impossible position of being split in their experience of the intersectionality of caste and gender. Tilak, a contemporary poet and Dalit ideologist writes:

> *Dalit* women inhabit two worlds; in one world they stand with their brothers, husband, father, companion, friend, fighting against caste system and in the other world they find themselves being pushed to the margin in their own houses, societies and social movements. Despite this since the *dalit* consciousness is inspired by the ideology of Savitri Bai Phule, Ambedkar and Buddha, the entire *dalit* community stands against capitalism, feudalism and fascism. *Dalit* women writers have also spoken against these social evils.

> In their own poetry and especially Hindi poetry at large they have touched upon the themes where they reject the distinctions of race, class, caste or gender and have worked towards realizing the vision of equitable society.
>
> (Tilak, 2011: 91–92, trans. Sethi)

Dalit women navigate the complexity of intersectional oppression; on the one hand they navigate standing in solidarity with the Dalit men of their community to fight caste oppression. On the other hand, the subversive voices of Dalit women poets seek to alter the agenda of feminist discourses in India. Dalit women refuse to join the ranks of upper caste women sloganeering against gender alone. In her 1992 essay *Dalit Movement and the Women's Movements*, Dietrich 'criticised the mainstream women's movement's blindness to the caste dimensions of violence against Dalit women and its tendency to frame it exclusively as a gender issue' (Kapilashrami and Ravindran, 2016: 176). Dalit women's poetry articulates the crossroads of being torn apart between feminist discourses and subaltern discourses. Dietrich, observes:

> The cause of *Dalit* woman can only be strengthened if we in the autonomous women's movement also make an effort to reach out to Dalit movements. This, in turn, also requires drastic rethinking in the Dalit movement on patriarchy and on the women's movement.
>
> (Rao, 2003: 79)

Takbhaure recognises the necessity and opportunities of this 'rethinking':

> I need an endless infinite skyline
> Not merely a part of open sky seen from the terrace
> Need sky as my roof
> I need an infinite sky.
>
> (Takbhaure, 2013a: 86; trans. Rekha Sethi)

In terms of intersectionality, 'an infinite skyline' means not being confined within the 'distorted analysis of racism and sexism because the operative conceptions of race and sex become grounded in experiences that actually represent only a subset of a much more complex phenomenon' (Crenshaw, 1989: 539). Or, translated into the Indian context, the Dalit women's movement seeks more than 'a part of open sky' represented by a women's movement, which 'treats upper caste Hinduism as the norm and treats women from minority communities as representatives of their respective groups' (Kapilashrami and Ravindran, 2016: 178). The point is that, Dalit women's experience cannot be 'subsumed within the traditional boundaries of race and gender discrimination as these boundaries are currently understood' (Crenshaw, 1991: 1244). Takbhaure pleads for untying a knot within (herself, within the Dalit community and within feminism itself); asserting the power of education as liberation; where every subjugated woman is a 'situated knower' (Hill-Collins, 2000: 19).

From Dalits we move to Nirmala Putul, an Adivasi activist, who raises her voice from the peripheral world of Adivasis against the plight of Adivasis. Putul primarily writes in local dialect Santhali but has been widely translated in Hindi and accepted in the plural tradition of Hindi language and literature. Of significance in Putul's poetry is the theme of 'location' and 'voice'; two significant issues in intersectionality. The intersection of, location and voice in the lives of Adivasis, including the intersections on the continuums of violence to exploitation, discrimination to oppression, unemployment to human trafficking. Adivasi pockets are generally located in the areas rich in natural resources. The development agenda of the nation is an infringement on their independence. The mesh of dams and roads, aimed to utilise the resources, is perceived as equivalent to exploitative colonial rule; resulting flood and famine situations. Putul writes, 'Globalisation is a new aggressive phase of neo-colonialism. It is the start of a new corporate politics. Their thirst for money is polluting the civilizations and cultures. Human values are fast disintegrating. In such circumstances the survival of many groups, civilizations and cultures seem unbelievable' (Putul, 2014a: 65, trans. Sethi).

Putul questions this power structure and reminds people of her clan not to fall prey to the ideas and designs of the new ruling class. Perhaps the poet warns all political activists not to fall prey, to the seductive machinations of the oppressor. The aggressive globalisation of markets is a threat to the culture and society of Adivasis who struggle for reclaiming their land, forest, water resources. The poetry of Putul explores all these areas of human suffering:

> They are traders . . . Understand this . . .
> Identify them dear daughter Murmu
> Know them!
>
> (Putul, 2005: 15, trans. Sethi)

Sethi's research based on the readings of Adivasis and Dalit poets, and interviews, evidences their sustained resolution to configure the impact of their gender and social realities on their poetry. In one such interview Putul accepted that at times she feels very lonely yet continues to march on with courage and confidence (Putul, 2017).

The feminism of this poet arises from the vulnerability of women in her own community, Jharkhand, who live in constant fear of the intersection of physical abuse, hunger and the vagaries of social superstitions. The superstitious belief of *dayan* constructs women as a curse of misfortune, for which they are paraded naked and abandoned. There are narratives of women being picked up by upper caste men and abused while husbands keep playing flute to cover their helplessness; of women subject to poverty, exploitation and hard labour. Endemic deprivation makes these regions prime hunting ground for human trafficking. Thousands of girls and women from these areas are trafficked to work as domestic help in Delhi and other metropolitan cities. Putul works with these girls reported missing from their homes and this field work is transcribed in her poetry:

Where are you, Maya?
Where are you?
Are you there safe and sound, or,
Has Delhi swallowed you?

Delhi is not meant for people like us.
Don't you feel it is a graveyard (?)
Where people were queued up to be buried alive;

Come back, Maya;
Wherever you are;
These jungles are calling you;
Come back!

(Putul, 2003: 31, trans. Sethi)

In her poetry collection '*Homeless Dreams*' Putul reiterates that only an intersectional assessment and assertion of self will liberate women. Putual points to the paradoxes and contradictions but relies greatly on the resilience of women themselves as the tool for empowerment. She feels the power within is the only recourse for a woman:

History has not given any space to women;
So we the women will write our own history;
We will write our own history with blood;
And not with tears . . .

(Putul, 2014b: 74; trans. Sethi)

Intersectionality exposes the complexities involved in multiple identities and helps to address them in the specificity of context. The poetic literature of Sushila Takbhaure and Nirmala Putul are located primarily in their immediate realities and background. Their feminist inheritance is complex and many-sided. They have been able to develop interlinkages between gender, caste and other inequalities. The rise of education and increased participation of women in socio-political life has given them the confidence to navigate the complex grid of ideology, reality and aesthetics. Women have probably had the longest history of oppression in all civilisations. Her choice to write is definitely seen as an expression of her freedom, an insightful analysis of a non-sectarian, non-hierarchical social structure. Anamika has examined how the Hindi writings of Indian women propose a feminist poetics as a tool of peace activism:

> a transformative politics with a potential to initiate change towards a more equitable society. If it may be called an ideology in the established sense of the term, it is an ideology of support for those who are deprived and exploited by the institutionalized structures of control and operate in different forms indifferent social formations.
>
> (Anamika, 2007: vi–vii)

Literary writings of Takbhaure and Putul do not hesitate to carve out new spaces, scoping a transformative picture of democratic rights ensuring equality; conjectures created in and through intersectionality that are realistic and assertive. Their images and narratives interweave in a lasting trace or imprint enabling the emotional component of intersectionality to breathe (Nayak, 2015: 85–117).

Conclusion

In repeated assertions these poets react against the hypocrisy of upper caste women who have hijacked the feminist movement, seated on the podium, engaged in changing power hierarchies in politics, whilst conveniently ignoring lower caste women's economic, social and political contexts. The logic of intersectionality is opposed to universalising experience: the logic of intersectionality is premised on situated experience, situation knowledge and situated standpoints. Intersectionality facilitates processes which begin with the realisation of subjugation and moves on to create negotiations between different registers of identity. In a democracy, representative institutions sometimes strengthen identity politics, while the success of intersectionality lies in helping dissolve barriers.

This chapter calls for social work engagement with textual practice as intersectional practice to achieve a:

> shift prevailing practices of knowledge production – that is, shifts in dominant expectations about (a) which actors can produce knowledge, (b) the methodology and content of knowledges produced, (c) the languages, genres and forms in which knowledges are produced, and (d) the manner in which new knowledges gain relevance as they reach different audiences and enable new kinds of socio-political interventions.
>
> (Sangtin Writers and Nagar, 2006: 150)

References

Allen, G. (2000) *Intertextuality*. Oxford, UK: Routledge.

Ames, N. (1999) 'Social work recording: A new look at an old issue'. *Journal of Social Work Education*, 35(2): 227–237.

Anamika. (2007) *Feminist Poetics: 'As Kingfishers Catch Fire'*. New Delhi: Research & Publishing House.

Anamika. (2015) *Beesvin Sadi ka Hindi Mahila Lekhan, Khand 2* [*Twentieth Century's Women Writing in Hindi*, Vol. 2] New Delhi: Sahitya Akademi.

Barnardos. (2013) *Still Our Children: Case for Reforming the Leaving Care System in England*. London: The Stationary Office Ltd.

Barthes, R. (1977) *Image, Music, Text*. ed. and trans. S. Heath, London: Fontana Press.

Baynes, J. (2008) 'Untold stories: A discussion of life story work'. *Adoption and Fostering*, 32(2): 43–49.

Burnell, A. and Vaughan, J. (2008) 'Remembering never to forget and forgetting never to remember: Re-thinking life story work'. In B. Luckock, and M. Lefevre (Eds.) *Direct Work: Social Work Children and Young People in Care*. London: BAAF.

Cook-Cottone, C. and Beck, M. (2007) 'A model for life-story work: Facilitating construction of a personal narrative for foster children'. *Child and Adolescent Mental Health*, 12(4): 193–195.

Cormican, E. J. and Cormican, J. D. (1977) 'The necessity of linguistic sophistication for social workers'. *Journal of Education for Social Work*, 13(2), 18–21.

Crenshaw, K. (1989) 'Demarginalizing the intersection of race and sex: A Black feminist critique of anti-discrimination doctrine, feminist theory and antiracist politics'. *University of Chicago Legal Forum*, 14: 538–554.

Crenshaw, K. (1991) 'Mapping the margins: Intersectionality, identity politics, and violence against women of color'. *Stanford Law Review*, 43(6): 1241–1299.

de Lauretis, T. (1984) *Alice Doesn't: Feminism, Semiotics, Cinema*. London: Macmillan.

Foucault, M. and Colin, G. (1980) *Power/Knowledge: Selected Interviews and Other Writings, 1972–1977*. New York: Pantheon Books.

Fox, R. and Gutheil, I. A. (2000) 'Process recording a means for conceptualizing and evaluating practice'. *Journal of Teaching in Social Work*, 20(1–2): 39–55.

Gill, G. (2017) *Katore Mein Sikka Girne Ke Intezaar Mein: Gagan Gill Se Baatcheet (Interview) Naya Gyanoday*. Ed. Mandloi, L. New Delhi: Bharatiya Jnanpith.

Goddard, J., Duncalf, Z. and Murray, S. (2010) 'Access to child care records: A comparative Analysis of UK and Australian policy and practice'. Paper for the Social Policy Association Annual Conference, Lincoln, UK, 5–7 July 2010.

Habermas, T. and Bluck, S. (2000) 'Getting a life: The emergence of the life story in adolescence'. *Psychological Bulletin*, 126(5): 748–769.

Hill-Collins, P. (2000) *Black Feminist Thought: Knowledge, Consciousness, and the Politics of Empowerment*, 2nd ed. London: Routledge.

Horrocks, C. and Goddard, J. (2006) 'Adults who grew up in care: Constructing the self and accessing care files'. *Child and Family Social Work*, 11(3): 264–272.

Humphreys, C. and Kertesz, M. (2012) '"Putting the heart back into the record". Personal records to support young people in care'. *Adoption & Fostering*, 36(1): 27–39.

Kagle, J. D. (1991) *Social Work Records*, 2nd ed. Belmont, CA: Wadsworth.

Kagle, J. D. (1993) 'Recordkeeping: Directions for the 1990s'. *Social Work*, 38: 190–196.

Kagle, J. D. (1995) 'Recording'. In R. L. Edwards (Ed.), *Encyclopaedia of Social Work*, 19th ed. Washington, DC: NASW Press.

Kapilashrami, A., Bisht, R., and Ravindran, S. (2016) 'Feminist movements and gender politics: Transnational perspectives on intersectionality'. *The Delhi University Journal of the Humanities and the Social Sciences*, 3: 171–184.

Katyayni. (1999) *Is Paurushpurn Samay Mein* [*In This Time of Virility*]. New Delhi: Vani Prakashan.

Katyayni. (2002) *Jaadu Nahi Kavita* [*Poetry Is Not Magic*]. New Delhi: Vani Prakashan.

Kristeva, J. (1969) 'Word, dialogue and novel' (trans. A. Jardine, T. Gora and L. S. Roudiez). In Moi, T. (Ed.) (1986) *The Kristeva Reader*. Oxford, UK: Blackwell Publishers Ltd.

Kristeva, J. (1980) *Desire in Language: A Semiotic Approach to Literature and Art*. Edited by Roudiez, L. S. Translated by Gora, T., Jardine, A. and Roudiez, L. S. Oxford, UK: Blackwell Publishers Ltd.

Kumar, A. (2009) *Poetry, Politics and Culture: Essays on Indian Texts and Contexts*. New York: Routledge.

Locke Swarr, A. and Nagar, R. (Eds.) (2010) *Critical Transnational Feminist Praxis*. New York: Sunny Press.

Lorde, A. (1977) 'The transformation of silence into language and action'. In Lorde, A. (Ed.) (1984) *Sister Outsider: Essays and Speeches*. Trumansburg, NY: The Crossing Press.

Lorde, A. (1979) 'An Open Letter to Mary Daly'. In Lorde, A. (Ed.) (1984) *Sister Outsider: Essays and Speeches*. Trumansburg, NY: The Crossing Press.

Lorde, A. (1984) 'Poetry is not a luxury'. In Lorde, A. (Ed.) (1984) *Sister Outsider: Essays and Speeches*. Trumansburg, NY: The Crossing Press.

Martínez Alfaro, M. J. (1996) 'Intertextuality: Origins and development of the concept'. *Atlantis* (1–2): 268–285.

Meena, G. S. (2014) *Adivasi Sahitya Vimarsh*. New Delhi: Anamika Publishers and Distributors. 61–68

Monnickendam, M., Yaniv, H. and Geva, N. (1994) 'Practitioners and the case record: Patterns of use'. *Administration in Social Work*, 19(4): 75–87.

Murray, S., Malone, J. and Glare, J. (2008) 'Building a life story: Providing records and support to former residents of children's homes'. *Australian Social Work*, 61(3): 239–255.

Nayak, S. (2015) *Race, Gender and the Activism of Black Feminist Theory: Working with Audre Lorde*. London: Routledge.

Nelson, K. and Fivush, R. (2004) 'The emergence of autobiographical memory: A social cultural development theory'. *Psychological Review*, 11(2): 486–511.

Putul, N. (2003) *Apne Ghar ki Talash Mein [In Search of One's Own House]*. New Delhi: Ramanika Foundation.

Putul, N. (2005) *Nagade ki Tarah Bajte Shabd [Words Resounding as Drums]*. New Delhi: Bharatiya Jnanpith.

Putul, N. (2014a) 'Vaishvikaran ke Bhanwar mein Adivasi Bhasha-Sahitya' ['Adivasi Language and Literature in the Swirls of Globalisation']. Adivasi Sahitya Vimarsh.

Putul, N. (2014b) *Beghar Sapne [Homeless Dreams]*. Panchkula: Aadhaar Prakashan.

Putul, N. (2017) *Adivasi Sanskriti Evam Parampara Bilkul Alag Hai: Nirmala Putul Se Baatcheet* (Interview). Edited by Gyanodaya, N. and Mandloi, L. New Delhi: Bharatiya Jnanpith.

Raghuvanshi, N. (1997) *Ghar Nikaasi [Exiting Home]*. New Delhi: Kitaab Ghar.

Rao, A. (2003) *Issues in Contemporary Indian Feminism: Gender and Caste*. New Delhi: Kali for Women.

Robbins, R. (2013) 'Stories of risk and protection: A turn to the narrative in social policy education'. *Social Work Education*, 32(3): 380–396.

Rose, R. and Philpot, T. (2006) *The Child's Own Story: Life Story Work with Traumatised Children*. London: Jessica Kingsley.

Ryan, T. and Walker, R. (2007) *Life Story Work: A Practical Guide to Helping Children Understand their Past*. London: BAAF.

Sangari, K. (1990) 'Mirabai and the spiritual economy of Bhakti'. *Economic and Political Weekly*, 25(27): 1464–1475.

Sangtin Writers and Nagar, R. (2006) *Playing with Fire: Feminist Thought and Activism Through Seven Lives in India*. Minneapolis, MN: University of Minnesota Press.

Shotton, G. (2010). 'Telling different stories: The experience of foster/adoptive carers in carrying out collaborative memory work with children'. *Adoption & Fostering*, 34(4), 61–68.

Shotton, G. (2013). '"Remember when . . .": Exploring the experiences of looked after children and their carers in engaging in collaborative reminiscence'. *Adoption & Fostering*, 37(4): 351–376.

Singh, S. (2013) *Swapn Samay [Time of Dreams]*. New Delhi: Rajkamal Prakashan.

Singh, S. (2017) *Humen Rashtravaad Ke Andheron Ko Bhi Dekhna Chahiye: Savita Singh Se Baatcheet (Interview) Naya Gyanoday*. Edited by Mandloi, L. New Delhi: Bharatiya Jnanpith.

Spivak, G. C. (1988) 'Can the Subaltern Speak?' In Nelson, C. and Grossberg, L. (Eds.) (1988) *Marxism and the Interpretation of Culture*. Basingstoke, UK: Macmillan.
Spivak, G. C. (1998) *In Other Worlds*. New York: Routledge.
Takbhaure, S. (2011) *Shikanje ka Dard [The Pain of Being in Clutches]*. New Delhi: Vani Prakashan.
Takbhaure, S. (2013a) *Tumne Use Kab Pehchana [When Did You Recognize Her]*. New Delhi: Swaraj Prakashan.
Takbhaure, S. (2013b) *Yeh Tum Bhi Jaano*. New Delhi: Swaraj Prakashan.
Takbhaure, S. (2015) *Dalit Kavyitriyon ki Kavita mein Stree Chetna [The Female Consciousness in the Poetry of Dalit Women Poets]*. Samkaleen Bhartiya Dalit Mahila Lekhan Vol. 2 (Kavita Khand). Edited by Tilak, R. New Delhi: Swaraj Prakashan.
Tilak, R. (2011) *Samkaleen Bhartiya Dalit Mahila Lekhan Vol. 1*. New Delhi: Swaraj Prakashan.
Varma, M. (2003) *Links in the Chain*. Translated by Sohoni, N. K. New Delhi: Katha.

2 Returning home

Intersectionality, social work and violence against BME women and girls in the UK

Hannana Siddiqui and Ravi K. Thiara

This chapter examines the utilisation of intersectionality within the UK Government and social work responses to violence against Black and minority ethnic (BME)[1] women and girls. Black feminists in the US and the UK, including those in Southall Black Sisters (SBS),[2] were already challenging additive 'double' or 'triple' oppression models when Crenshaw coined the term 'intersectionality' in 1989/1991. Since then the concept has expanded to analyse marginality more generally, but current applications have shifted from its original concern with racialised structural inequalities experienced by BME women and girls, thus displacing its focus on race (Lewis, 2013) in particular contexts and historical moments. We use the 'intracategorical' approach (McCall, 2005) to intersectionality to explore the manifestations of violence against women and girls (VAWG); the dynamics of abuse of power in VAWG; and access to services by women with multiple and transnational identities. We emphasise the mutually constitutive nature of social categories, which are continually re/produced through processes of rupture, contestation and re/negotiation. By using examples of immigration, forced marriage and honour-based violence (HBV), it is argued that intersectionality is crucial for theorising multiplicity and understanding how intersectional discrimination impacts the lives of marginalised women in both shaping their experience of violence and the policy and practice responses they receive.

We conclude that that recognition of the concepts of 'mature multiculturalism'[3] (Mike O'Brien, Parliament Debates, 1999) and 'mature multi-faithism'[4] (Siddiqui, 2013 and 2014) within human rights, intersectional, secularist and Black Feminist Theory frameworks enable a resolution of conflict of rights by simultaneously addressing inequalities based on race, gender, class, poverty and religion. We insist that these frameworks need greater prominence in concrete settings such as social work policy and practice in order to make the state more responsive to and accountable in meeting equalities obligations, due diligence in safeguarding and addressing gendered violence.

Intersectionality and Black feminist thought

The emphasis on power/marginality, interdependence, multiplicity, complexity and relationality within intersectional analysis has had far reaching appeal and been widely used by scholars and activists, leading some to focus on clarifying what intersectionality is and what it does to further sharpen its analytic value in the examination of power and marginality (Cho et al., 2013; Davis, 2009; Lewis, 2013; Mehrotra, 2010). Arguing that the intersecting axes of power and 'difference', which operate simultaneously to re/inscribe marginality and privilege, cannot be 'layered onto each other in an additive or hierarchical way' (Mirza, 2013: 6), intersectional theorising centred the lives and experiences of Black/marginalised women (Dill-Thornton and Zambrana, 2009). The later incorporation of nation, dis/ability, sexuality, religion and other markers of difference within the concept demonstrate its capacity to theorise 'difference'. Mehrotra argues that 'experiences of fluid and hybrid identities and multiplicity' within diasporic communities requires 'a continuum of different intersectional theories with potentially varying epistemological bases' (2010: 418) to address the contexts of different groups or practice settings. This is important in the UK context which is characterised by 'the experience of diaspora, nationality, and migration as salient oppressions, identities, and processes in women's lives' (Mehrotra, 2010: 425).

Mirroring the lived experience of 'difference', it has been argued that the concept of intersectionality 'allows endless constellations of intersecting lines of difference to be explored' (Davis, 2009: 77). Lewis also asserts that the popularity of intersectionality demonstrates that knowledge produced by Black women at the margins can go beyond this and form 'part of a more generalizable theoretical, methodological and conceptual toolkit' (2013: 871). Cho et al. (2013) underline the importance of intersectionality as an analytic tool to examine structural-racialised power structures, rather than diverse identities. It is also our view that 'identity' must be located in the unequal social structures and dynamics that construct identity in the first place, because 'intersectionality primarily concerns the way things work rather than who people are' (Cho et al., 2013: 923).

Given the plurality of ways in which the concept is used, McCall (2005) argues that intersectional theories comprise an 'epistemological continuum', namely: intercategorical approaches that emphasise discrete social categories of race, class and gender, produced by structural inequalities that construct individual identities. Here, the intersectional project highlights inequality between social groups; intracategorical approaches interrogate the essentialised nature of discrete social categories, whilst recognising the utility of strategic essentialism (for instance, emphasising the unique experiences of violence for Black women located at the intersection of multiple oppressions, to deconstruct the social category of gender); anticategorical (poststructuralist) approaches challenge the idea of fixed and inevitable social categories altogether, seeing them as constructed by language and discourse.

The importance of considering the intersection of systems of power and discrimination that shape the experiences of violence among BME women, rather than merely describing experiential diversity, is increasingly emphasised by some (Siddiqui, 2014; Thiara and Gill, 2010). This reinforces the need to consider diverse cultural contexts whilst centring intersectional discrimination based on race, gender, nation, immigration and sexuality. As noted by Lewis (2013), race, and indeed Black women, are being displaced from feminist discussions of intersectionality in Europe, even though race remains central to political and policy discourses. Concurrently, the displacement of race by culture, religion and ethnicity as the marker of essentialised difference situates the problem with 'othered' groups/communities/women themselves. This is reflected in discourses on violence against BME women and girls in the UK where harmful practices are seen to result from 'othered' cultures and religions (Chantler and Thiara, 2017). We argue that race and racialised power must be central to intersectional analyses. The focus on subjectivity and identity within intersectionality studies should not displace the emphasis on racialised structural inequality.

Furthermore, we argue that in some contexts, gender is also displaced in relation to BME women and girls. Anti-racist movements, due to the prevalence of hierarchy of oppression theories, often displace gender by silencing women about sexual oppression within BME communities, for fear of racist or an Islamophobic backlash. Equally, cultural relativist, or 'religious relativist' approaches ignore gender inequality in favour of respecting cultural and religious difference to promote good race or faith relations. For Black feminists, intersectionality recognises that oppression 'is always constructed and intermeshed in other social divisions' (Yuval-Davis, 2006: 195). Indeed, it is the 'inter-relationship of the elements in concrete settings that enable us to fully understand their impact on particular women at specific historical moments' (Thiara and Gill, 2010).

Application of intersectionality and Black women activism

Two of the most challenging issues that social work must address in safeguarding are immigration status and harmful practices in relation to BME women and girls, particularly forced marriage and honour-based violence. Immigration status, including the poverty caused by 'no resource to public funds' (NRPF), represent failures of the state, including social work policy and practice, to take account of the intersection of gender, race, poverty and class. While relativist, non-interventionist approaches to forced marriage and HBV deny BME women and girls protection in the name of promoting good race (or rather cultural) and faith relations, immigration policy can result in institutionalised racism and economic discrimination.

Black feminists' challenges of these views and responses remain only partially heard by government and practitioners. Black feminists have repeatedly called for an intersectional practice approach, and only under pressure by Black feminists, like Southall Black Sisters, did state policy regarding forced marriage incorporate 'mature multiculturalism' in the late 1990s/early 2000s.[5] The Home Office Minister, Mike O'Brien, took an unprecedented step in establishing the Forced Marriage Working Group, stating that, 'multi-cultural sensitivities are not an excuse for moral blindness', and advocated mature multiculturalism (Parliamentary Debates, 1999). Southall Black Sisters argued that mature multiculturalism recognised that gender oppression and other human rights abuses within BME communities had to be addressed with race inequality (Siddiqui, 2014). This policy ensured that the needs of BME women and girls facing forced marriage were not sacrificed to cultural relativism. Prior to this, and influenced by Southall Black Sisters, Mike O'Brien reformed immigration and domestic violence laws to allow victims on spousal visas the right to remain indefinitely in the UK. Acknowledging intersectionality, although not named as such, was instrumental in these policy reforms.

Mature multiculturalism challenged social work practices in a context where non-interventionist multicultural practices and institutionalised racism were deeply ingrained. For example, forced marriage was not seen as child abuse, but a cultural practice which had to be respected or policed by the BME community itself. Multiculturalism framed minority communities as homogenous entities with no internal power structures. This amounted to allowing powerful, self-styled, predominately conservative, male community and religious leaders ('gatekeepers') free reign, without interference from wider society and the state. This colluded with the oppression of BME women and other powerless sub-groups within minority communities, in return for harmonious race/cultural relations (Sahgal, 1990; Brah, 1996; Patel, 2003; Siddiqui, 2003; Thiara, 2003; Yuval-Davis, 1997).

Under multiculturalism, the culturalisation of domestic violence and harmful practices within BME communities has produced the sensationalising 'othering' of minority cultures; and in post-2000, rising awareness of harmful practices has increasingly collapsed all forms of gendered violence into HBV. This meant violence against BME women and girls was framed through cultural (and by extension race) rather than gender inequality. The exoticisation of forced marriage in particular became examples of 'backward' foreign value systems that undermine 'British values'; best tackled through restrictions on marriage migration. This logic was fastened to ideas of social cohesion, particularly post-9/11 when the 'war on terror' constructed Muslim extremism as a state priority. Multiculturalism was blamed for breeding religious fundamentalism. Conversely, 'multi-faithism' became the new state approach to religious difference. This reproduced cultural relativism with regard to BME women's rights in the name of 'religious sensitivity'.

Multi-faithism has reinforced power differentials within communities and faith groups where women's rights are denied by religious forces within communities. The right to worship (or not), without religious discrimination or privilege, should not only be protected by a secular state and within secular spaces, but state intervention should address human rights abuses justified by faith within all communities. Religious relativism that ignores gender-based violence within minority religious groups must be resisted by the recognition of a mature multifaithism approach.

Immigration, no recourse public funding, race, gender, poverty and class

Women with no recourse to public funds (NRPF) face intersectional discrimination that enslaves them to abusive relationships. Under British law, unless entitled under EU or other regulations, people with an insecure immigration status are subject to NRPF, which means they are unable to claim most forms of social security benefits and council housing. Migrant women on spousal or dependent visas in abusive relationships are economically dependent on a violent partner or family member/s. Migrant women have a stark choice: leave and face destitution or stay and experience domestic violence.

Black feminists, led by Southall Black Sisters, have campaigned since 1992 to free migrant women from this impossible choice. In 1999, Southall Black Sisters won a concession from the Home Office allowing women, on spousal visas, the right to permanent settlement if their marriage broke down due to domestic violence. Prior to this, women faced deportation if they left abusive partners, as their right to remain in the UK was dependent on a subsisting marriage to a British national or settled partner for a probationary period of one year. In 2002, the concession became part of the immigration rules and is known as the 'domestic violence rule'.

Southall Black Sisters argued that the 'domestic violence rule' was undermined by unrealistic burdens of proof which required criminal convictions (despite low conviction rates) or civil court injunctions, even though many proceedings did not result in full court orders because of a practice of settling cases by perpetrators giving undertakings. The standard of proof also ignored the intersectional barriers of accessing services and/or reporting abuse, such as lack of knowledge of the English language, fear of racism and cultural pressures to stay within their marriage. Two other developments diminished the effectiveness of the domestic violence rule. Firstly, the probationary period was extended to two years. Southall Black Sisters argued against this extension as it meant that it took longer for migrant women to report abuse, as many attempt to save their marriage until there is a crisis, often near the expiry of their visa. They also warned about the escalations of abuse resulting in more homicides and suicide, which were already disproportionally higher among BME and migrant women (Mayor of London, 2010; Raleigh, 1996). Secondly, although demanded by Southall Black Sisters, the government failed to remove the NRPF requirement. The fear or experience of destitution either prevented women from leaving an abusive relationship or forced a return to the abusive situation due to homelessness and poverty.

Research by Southall Black Sisters showed that there were about 600 women in the UK suffering domestic violence, immigration and NRPF problems (Amnesty International and Southall Black Sisters, 2008). Many of these women had young children, and although the spousal visa rules gave the right to work, they were unable to find or take up employment. Unable to pay rent, women and their children could not access women's refuge. Refuges are dependent on rental income to survive, and even when they agreed to house women for free, they were unable to pay for their living expenses. Refuges complained of high debt and 'bed blocking' because women and children could not be re-housed through public or private sector accommodation until their immigration status was resolved. Regularisation of status often involved lengthy delays, particularly if subject to appeal against refusal. As a result, many women and children faced life on the streets, dependent on religious institutions such as temples, mosques and churches where they may be blamed for the breakdown of the marriage and pressured to reconcile with abusive husbands. Women complained of being exploited as 'domestic servants' in the home of strangers who offered board and lodging, while some were driven to prostitution and sexual slavery.

Although vulnerable women or those with dependent children were entitled to help from social services under the Children Act 1989 (amended 2004) and community care legislation (much of which was incorporated in the Care Act 2014), most reported inadequate or inconsistent responses from local authorities. Women were deterred from seeking their support when told that the councils' only obligation was to protect children and threatened to put them in care or return them to the abusive father or in-laws, even when, in some cases, they lived overseas. Women were reported to the Home Office and sometimes social services offered to pay their travel fare back to their countries of origin, even without their children. Most women could not return to their home countries for fear of being social outcasts and subjected to harassment and violence from extended families and communities as divorced or separated women, often justified under cultural and religious codes of honour and shame. While groups like Southall Black Sisters helped women to threaten or take legal action against local authorities which failed to meet their obligations, many women were too afraid of being separated from their children or being reported to the Home Office as 'illegal immigrants'.

While successful legal challenges and lobbying helped to reduce the standard of acceptable proof in the domestic violence immigration rule to a more workable level, Southall Black Sisters campaigns for reform on NRPF faced stiff resistance from national government. Reform on NRPF did not come until 2012 when the Tory-led coalition government introduced the Destitution Domestic Violence (DDV) concession following a pilot scheme set up in 2009 by the outgoing Labour Government. The pilot paid the victim's housing and subsistence costs for a short period while they resolved their status. Surprisingly, the DDV concession went further than the pilot by allowing victims to access benefits and council housing for three months while they applied for settlement under the domestic violence immigration rule.

The reforms on domestic violence, immigration and NRPF are major victories for Black feminists where the conflict between race, gender and poverty/class was resolved to protect BME migrant women. The DDV concession was remarkable considering it took place under a Conservative-controlled Government in a context where they were imposing draconian restrictions on migration generally and specifically on migrant rights to benefits. Together with cuts in legal aid, this has made it more difficult for people to enter or remain in the UK and obtain welfare support or justice.

These victories were achieved for a number of reasons, including the momentum for reform created by Southall Black Sisters over a 20-year period, which in the latter years of the NRPF campaign also had the support of 30 leading women and human rights groups. They also both happened at a juncture where there was political change centred on general elections, where, at first at least, there was a desire to act on issues that may be popular. Mike O'Brien introduced the domestic violence immigration rule following the election of the Labour Government in 1997, and Theresa May, in her role as Home Secretary, established the DDV concession after the 2010 general election. In both cases, the need for the state to tackle domestic violence, and later, also VAWG, was demanded by an increasingly stronger women's sector. Southall Black Sisters had long argued that excluding migrant women from protection afforded to other women facing gender-based violence undermined the government's own strategy on domestic violence or VAWG and amounted to multiple discrimination. The need for reform, however, for the government was not due to an understanding of intersectional discrimination, but as a response to pressure for change to address gendered violence by Black feminists. However, it did indicate how the 'mature multiculturalism' approach had been used to resolve the conflict between race, gender and class by recognising the need for cultural sensitivity, tackling poverty and for state intervention to protect BME women's rights.

Due to the displacement of race, however, in 2012, the government increased the probationary period for spousal visas to five years, prolonging the period some women would have to stay in an abusive situation before they can regularise their status. The state has, so far, also failed to meet Black feminist demands to extend the DDV concession to those on non-spousal visas, such as women subjected to gender-based violence while on student visas and work permits. As a result, at a local level, social services continue to turn vulnerable women away, ignoring the need to provide a safety net for all women subjected to gendered violence or to tackle race discrimination. Indeed, recent trends have led some local authorities to have immigration officials based at their offices. This has increasingly made social services the agents of Home Office immigration control, which deter many from seeking their support. This policy has reinforced institutionalised racism, together with wider developments such as increased police and immigration official presence in local BME communities conducting stop and search, raids for illegal immigrants and driving Home Office sponsored vans with 'Go Home' slogans (now discontinued following protest). These have all added to a more tangible experience of 'everyday racism.'

Harmful practices, gender, race and religion

The battle against forced marriage and HBV is another example where intersectionality is not applied by many social workers in safeguarding practice. Since the publication of the Home Office Forced Marriage Working Group report, *A Choice by Right* (2000), we have had the establishment of the government's Forced Marriage Unit, forced marriage guidance for professionals and the Forced Marriage (Civil Protection) Act 2007. In 2014, forced marriage was criminalised, although there were differences within the BME women's movement on whether this would drive the problem underground and give the state an excuse to divert resources away from civil law remedies and welfare services.

However, since 9/11 and the 2001 race riots in northern UK cities, positive developments on forced marriage have been hindered through culturalist, racist and Islamophobic responses. The need to promote social integration in the 'war on terror', for instance, has been used to justify greater immigration controls while multiculturalism has been blamed for breeding racial segregation and religious fundamentalism, particularly Muslim extremism. In this context, restrictions on marriage migration were introduced, which, argued the state, ensured that men, particularly Muslims, with little knowledge of English and 'backward' cultural values which accepted forced marriage would not be able to enter the UK. The culturalisation of forced marriage, and the consequent 'othering' of BME communities was then used to argue that these controls would prevent undermining of social cohesion through the adoption of common shared 'British values'; which were assumed to be inherently liberal. Indeed, an age-related policy introduced in 2003, which required a minimum age of 18 (later increased to 21 in 2008) for overseas spouses was justified on these grounds. It was argued that BME women living in Britain would be protected from forced marriage under this policy as it reduced pressure on them to sponsor men into the UK,[6] and in any case, limits on marriage migration encouraged people to find partners within this country where shared British values made them more compatible (Home Office and UK Border Agency, 2008). Black feminists like Southall Black Sisters, however, argued that immigration controls not only failed to protect victims from forced marriage as the practice primarily aims to control female sexuality and autonomy, but they also denied the right to family life for those in BME communities. Ironically, the state was using Black feminist demands for gender equality to introduce more racist immigration laws (Siddiqui, 2013 and 2014), and ignored the reinforcement of intersectional discrimination based on race and gender.

The forced marriage and immigration debate highlights the intersectional discrimination faced by BME women. Furthermore, BME women's rights were pitched against race equality; a position that anti-racist movements have used to silence Black feminists' demands for gender equality for fear of fuelling racism. Since the Rushdie Affair in 1989, draconian anti-terror security measures and an increase in race and religious hate crimes, the race backlash fears now extend to religion and to Islamophobia in particular. Southall Black Sisters and other feminists, such as those in Women Against Fundamentalism, have been criticised for promoting Islamophobia, even though their critique has focused on fundamentalist ideologies in all religions or of conservative and orthodox forces in the UK and elsewhere in regard to oppressing women and stirring up communal hatred.

In recent years, Southall Black Sisters and others have expressed strong concerns about the increasing use of religious arbitration tribunals or Sharia courts within minority communities to settle family matters such as divorce. In 2008, the Muslim Arbitration Tribunal (MAT) even claimed to resolve problems related to forced marriage and domestic violence, diverting Muslim women away from pursing civil or criminal justice remedies. MAT also claimed that their ruling could be upheld by the state under the Arbitration Act 1996 (Taher, 2008).[7] Black feminists argue that religious law discriminates against women by denying them equal rights to divorce, custody and financial settlements. These tribunals become mediation forums, placing Muslim women under pressure to reconcile to abusive situations at home. Even though a minority of women exercise agency by choosing to use religious tribunals to obtain religious divorce, the wider context of intersecting racialised gendered structural inequalities, growth of religious fundamentalism and reduced state support through cuts in legal aid and services, cannot be ignored. These contexts limit choices for the majority of women, pressuring them into resorting to religious arbitration tribunals. Similar pressures apply where women are also expected to conform to other religious dictates such as the wearing of the veil, attending single-sex religious schools or sex segregation in schools/universities.[8]

While multiculturalism has been held responsible for the racial (or cultural) fragmentation of British society, the state has increasingly adopted a contradictory approach by accepting segregation in the name of religious sensitivity, under 'multi-faithism'. The state has accommodated demands for separate existence by faith groups through a range of provisions from state funding of religious schools to faith-based services. The government's Preventing Extremism initiative has placed a duty on local authorities to promote social cohesion, which has led to funding of faith-based Muslim organisations, including those for Muslim women, with little checks and balances on their record in the promotion of women's rights or of equalities generally. The 'racialisation of religion' (Sahgal and Yuval-Davis, 1992: 15) conflates race with religion, leaving little state support for secular anti-racist work across the religious divide. Secular, anti-racist and feminist BME organisations now receive reduced levels of or no local state funding. These groups have also been undermined by new competitive commissioning processes which favour larger, more generic providers as well as general cuts in services and rights (such as those for legal aid) resulting from austerity measures.[9]

The shrinking of these progressive secular spaces makes it harder for BME women from all religions and none, and for Black feminists to find common ground to fight VAWG and intersectional discrimination. While national government (from 2010 in Conservative-led governments, although the proceeding Labour-controlled governments had some similar policies) has stated its commitment to support gender equality for Muslim women, it has fails to provide sufficient support to secular, feminist BME women's organisations that have led the way in fighting extremism and for women's rights within their own communities. Instead, the government is focusing on using Muslim women/mothers to prevent radicalisation among children, especially young men.[10] Increasingly, extremism is linked to men's violence against women, particularly harmful practices.[11] For Black feminists, this linkage denies VAWG within BME communities as a cause and consequence of gender inequality that requires the wholesale eradication of patriarchy. It denies support for BME women's self-empowerment, rather than simply targeting extremist elements, which may use VAWG and sexual oppression as a tool to achieving specific political goals.

Extremists could not take advantage if patriarchy, and conservative cultural and religious value systems, which justify VAWG as a means of men's control over women, did not already exist to allow them to do so.

Even moderate community and religious leaders, which the state depends on to engage with BME communities, are often, male, self-styled and largely only interested in maintaining the status quo for preserving their own power base. Hence, the current review of Sharia Councils, established in May 2016 by the Tory Government which has a panel involving clerics,[12] may have an outcome which only regulates rather than ends state recognition of parallel religious law and rulings. This does not serve the interests of Muslim or BME women and girls, particularly as there are also pressures in BME communities for religious tribunals to be extended to other faith groups. The review is therefore unlikely to address intersectional discrimination BME women and girls face due to their gender, race and religion.

Forced marriage, HBV and other forms of harmful practices, including female genital mutilation (FGM), remain ignored based on the logic of cultural or, increasingly, religious sensitivity under multi-faithism. Due to the activism of Black feminists like Southall Black Sisters and FORWARD, current safeguarding policy now recognises these harmful practices as a form of child abuse. It is recognised that forced marriage, for example, can involve a continuum of intersecting violence including: threats, assaults, emotional blackmail, abduction, false imprisonment and rape by their parents, husbands and/or extended family or community members. Former cultural relativist approaches to forced marriage meant that social workers ignored or accepted informal mediation by family elders and community/religious leaders as a solution to forced marriage, at least it kept the family together and deflected allegations of racism and intolerance. Southall Black Sisters criticised this approach because the underlying problem of abuse remained unchallenged; and mediation and reconciliation left girls and young women vulnerable to further abuse. In extreme cases, returning home led to murder or suicide. More recently, this problem has intensified where culturalisation has re-categorised all other forms of abuse, including forced marriage and domestic violence, against BME women and girls as HBV (Siddiqui, 2013 and 2014). This re-categorisation may lead to some social workers ignoring violence against BME women and girls in the name of cultural sensitivity; thus disregarding best practice procedures on safeguarding.

Other practices, if justified by faith through, for example, a process of 'Islamisation' may also not be regarded as child abuse, particularly for 16–18-year-olds. These include girls and young women coming under pressure to conform to religious or traditional dress; forbidden interaction with friends, especially those from a different race and faiths; to live in polygamous households; marriage within the same race and religious groups;[13] avoid 'sinful' same-sex relationships; and to have religious marriages instead of civil ceremonies in the UK. Indeed, it would take a very brave social worker or social services department to challenge practices justified in the name of religion; and most are reluctant. Social work's lack of intervention may be legitimated by other agencies, such as the police and the courts, where 'experts' such as priests and scholars are sought to give evidence on religious belief and practice about acceptable female behaviour. Even women's more liberal spiritual or religious interpretations are sidelined in favour of those expounded by the more powerful religious leaders or experts with conservative views on gender roles. In such cases, religion is remembered, but the intersection with gender is displaced and forgotten.

Conclusion

Intersectionality provides a versatile conceptual tool, which although developed to include a wider marginality, was initially advocated by Black feminist activists and scholars to highlight the multiple, overlapping discrimination experienced by BME women and girls. At a concrete level, however, intersectionality is rarely understood or applied by practitioners, such as social workers.

Mature multiculturalism and mature multi-faithism are concepts which help to resolve conflicts of rights by tackling inequalities of race, gender and religion simultaneously in concrete settings within intersectional, secularist and human rights frameworks. While intersectionality acknowledges these and other inequalities and that BME women's experience of discrimination is amplified at the intersection of multiple axes of power, human rights and secularist frameworks can be used to resolve conflicts of rights. These concepts and frameworks help us to return home, so to speak, from the distance travelled away from the roots of intersectionality; and thus BME women and girls are made visible once again.

Notes

1 The term BME refers to people from a range of ethnic minority groups. Although people from BME backgrounds can include white ethnic minorities, we are using BME in relation to non-white groups.

2 SBS is a leading progressive secular, Black feminist organisation, founded in 1979, to address violence against BME women and girls. It provides direct services and undertakes campaigning and policy advocacy to change attitudes and practices within BME communities, including social/legal policy and practice reform regarding gendered violence. SBS empowers BME women and girls within equalities, intersectional, secularist and human rights frameworks.

3 Mature multiculturalism accepts that in a multicultural society, ethnic minority groups should be free of racial injustice, but also recognises power divisions and illiberal practices within minority communities that require greater state intervention to protect the vulnerable. See Siddiqui (2014) on how mature multiculturalism helps to resolve contradictions.

4 Mature multi-faithism accepts that in a multi-faith society, minority religious groups should be free of religious discrimination, but also recognises power divisions and illiberal practices within minority religious groups which require greater state intervention to protect the vulnerable. See Siddiqui (2014) on how mature multi-faithism helps to resolve contradictions.

5 Recently, for the first time, central government's strategy on violence against women and girls (HM Government, 2016) acknowledged the concept of 'multiple discrimination'. However, not only did the strategy fail to provide sufficient measures to address the problem, their stated intentions were also undermined by other policies

to prevent extremism, which linked requirements to learn the English language with the right to remain in the UK for Muslim women (Siddiqui, 2016).

6 In 2003, the Home Office introduced immigration regulations requiring spouses to be 18 years old before a British or settled spouse could be joined by their overseas spouse in the UK; this age requirement was increased to 21 in 2008. The state rationale for this new rule was that this would prevent British or dual national women being forced into marriage overseas in order to sponsor men into the UK, particularly as maturity, education and economic independence enabled victims to become more assertive. However, even prior to the extension of the age requirement to 21, research evidence showed that the rule for 18-year-olds have not been effective in tackling forced marriage (Hester et al., 2007). Black feminists such as SBS had argued that as forced marriage primarily aimed to control female sexuality and autonomy, this policy would not prevent forced marriage to overseas partners, but rather lead to more victims being married and/or abandoned abroad for longer periods of time. Even if they came back to the UK to sponsor their husbands, they would still be under greater, not less, surveillance and control by families determined to use them to sponsor men into the UK when they turn 21. This 21-year age-related policy was overturned by the Supreme Court for contravening the right to family life in the cases of *Quila and Bibi*, 2011.

7 Also see www.thesun.co.uk/news/2080998/womens-rights-group-accuses-sharia-law-court-of-sabotaging-cases-of-men-facing-domestic-violence-charges/ (Accessed 31/10/16).

8 See more information at www.secularism.org.uk/opinion/2014/03/gender-segregation—universities-and-student-representatives-continue-to-fail-their-students-miserably (Accessed 31/10/16).

9 See Patel and Siddiqui (2010) for a detailed discussion of SBS's successful legal challenge against Ealing Councils (2008). This challenged the closure of specialist domestic violence services for BME women run by SBS, using a secular, anti-racist and feminist framework in favour of generalist services, and at the same time, offering funding for a Muslim women's service under its social cohesion strategy.

10 In January 2016, the government announced that migrant Muslim women had to learn English or face deportation; the aim being that social integration could prevent radicalisation. See www.theguardian.com/politics/2016/jan/18/david-cameron-stigmatising-muslim-women-learn-english-language-policy and www.huffingtonpost.co.uk/2016/01/18/english-lessons-muslim-women-radicalisation_n_9008418.html (Both accessed 31/10/16).

11 See, debates in parliament where the government links extremism with harmful practices: https://hansard.parliament.uk/commons/2016–06–13/debates/1606133000017/ExtremismAndRadicalisation (Accessed 31/10/16).

12 Secularists and Black feminists have protested about the make up the panel for the review. See www.independent.co.uk/news/uk/home-news/sharia-courts-review-branded-a-whitewash-over-appointment-bias-concerns-a7128706.html (Accessed 31/10/16).

13 A recent example includes increased raids of wedding ceremonies in Sikh temples by Sikh extremists to prevent mixed faith marriages. See www.telegraph.co.uk/news/religion/11836456/Religious-protesters-force-mixed-faith-couples-to-abandon-wedding-ceremonies.html (Accessed 31/10/16).

References

Amnesty International and Southall Black Sisters (2008) 'No Recourse, No Safety: The Government's Failure to Protect Women from Violence'. London: Amnesty International and Southall Black Sisters. [Online]: Available from: www.refuge.org.uk/cms_content_refuge/attachments/0803-No%20Recourse-No%20Safety.pdf (Accessed: 8/1/16).

Brah, A. (1996) *Cartographies of Diaspora: Contesting Identities*. Oxford, UK: Routledge.

Chantler, K. and Thiara, R. K. (2017) 'We are still here: Re-centering the quintessential subject of intersectionality', *Atlantis: Critical Studies in Gender, Culture & Social Justice*, 38 (1): 82–94.

Crenshaw, K. (1989) 'Demarginalizing the intersection of race and sex: A black feminist critique of antidiscrimination doctrine, feminist theory and antiracist politics', *The University of Chicago Legal Forum*, 139–167.

Crenshaw, K. (1991) 'Mapping the margins: Intersectionality, identity politics and violence against women of color', *Stanford Law Review*, 43: 1241–1299.

Cho, S., Crenshaw, K. W. and McCall, L. (2013) 'Toward a field of intersectionality studies: Theory, applications and praxis', *Signs: Journal of Women and Culture in Society*, 38 (4): 785–810.

Davis, K. (2009) 'Intersectionality as buzzword: A sociology of science perspective on what makes a feminist theory successful', *Feminist Theory*, 9 (1): 67–85.

Dill-Thornton, B. and Zambrana, X. (2009) 'Critical thinking about inequality', in B. Dill-Thornton and X. Zambrana, *Emerging Intersections: Race, Class and Gender in Theory, Policy and Practice*. New Brunswick, NJ: Rutgers University Press.

Hester, M., Chantler, K., Gangoli, G., Devgon, J., Sharma, S. and Singleton, A. (2007) 'Forced marriage: The risk factors and effects of raising the minimum age for a sponsor, and leave to enter the UK as a sponsor or a fiance(e)'. Bristol, UK: University of Bristol. [Online]: Available from: www.bristol.ac.uk/media-library/sites/sps/migrated/documents/rk6612finalreport.pdf (Accessed: 31/10/16).

HM Government (2016) *Ending Violence Against Women and Girls, Strategy 2016–2020*, London: HM Government.

Home Office (2000) *A Choice by Right: The Report of the Working Group on Forced Marriage*. London: Home Office Communications Directorate.

Home Office and UK Border Agency (2008) *Marriage Visas: The Way Forward*. London: UK Border Agency.

Lewis, G. (2013) 'Unsafe travel: Experiencing intersectionality and feminist displacements', *Signs: Journal of Women and Culture in Society*, 38 (4): 869–892.

Mayor of London (2010) 'The way forward: Taking action to end violence against women and girls. Final strategy 2010–13'. London: Mayor of London. [Online]: Available from: www.london.gov.uk/sites/default/files/the_way_forward_-_strategy.pdf (Accessed: 8/1/16).

McCall, L. (2005) 'The complexity of intersectionality', *Signs*, 30: 1771–2002.

Mehrotra, G. (2010) 'Toward a continuum of intersectionality theorizing for feminist social work scholarship', *Affilia: Journal of Women and Social Work*, 25 (4): 417–430.

Parliamentary Debates (Hansard 1999) 'House of Commons adjournment debate on human rights (women)', 10 February. London: House of Commons 325, 8 February 1999–16 February 1999.

Patel, P. (2003) 'Shifting terrains: Old struggles for new?', in Gupta, R. (ed) *From Homebreakers to Jailbreakers: Southall Black Sisters*. London: Zed Books.

Patel, P. and Siddiqui, H. (2010) 'Shrinking secular spaces: Asian women at the intersect of race, religion and gender', in Thiara, R. K. and Gill, A. K. (eds) *Violence Against Women in South Asian Communities: Issues for Policy and Practice*. London: Jessica Kingsley.

Raleigh, V. S. (1996) 'Suicide patterns and trends in people of Indian sub-continent and Caribbean origin in England and Wales', *Ethnicity and Health*, 1 (1): 55–63.

Sahgal, G. (1990) 'Fundamentalism and the multi-culturalist fallacy', in Southall Black Sisters (eds) *Against the Grain: Southall Black Sisters 1979–1989*. London: Southall Black Sisters.

Sahgal, G. and Yuval-Davis, N. (eds) (1992) *Refusing Holy Orders*. London: Virago Press.

Thiara, R. K. (2003) 'South Asian women and collective action in Britain', in Andall, J. (ed) *Gender and Ethnicity in Contemporary Europe*. London: Berg.

Thiara, R. K. and Gill, A. K. (2010) *Violence Against Women in South Asian Communities: Issues for Policy and Practice*. London: Jessica Kingsley.

Siddiqui, H. (2003) 'It was written in her kismet: Forced marriage', in Gupta, R. (ed) *From Homebreakers to Jailbreakers: Southall Black Sisters*, London: Zed Books.

Siddiqui, H. (2013) '"True honour": Domestic violence, forced marriage and honour crimes in the UK', in Rehman, Y., Kelly, L. and Siddiqui, H. (eds.) *Moving in the Shadows*. London: Ashgate.

Siddiqui, H. (2014) *Violence Against Minority Women: Tackling Domestic Violence, Forced Marriage and 'Honour' Based Violence*. Warwick, UK: University of Warwick.

Siddiqui, H. (2016) 'What will it take to end honour based violence in the UK', 28 November, Open Democracy. [Online]: Available from: www.opendemocracy.net/5050/hannana-siddiqui/lasting-change-to-end-honour-based-violen (Accessed: 3/2/17).

Taher, A. (2008) 'Revealed: UK first official Sharia courts'. 14 September. *The Sunday Times*.

Yuval-Davis, N. (1997) *Gender and Nation*. London: Sage Publications Ltd.

Yuval-Davis, N. (2006) 'Intersectionality and feminist politics', *European Journal of Women's Studies* (13): 193–209.

3 The detachment of intersectionality from its Black feminist roots

A critical analysis of social service provision training material based in Ontario

Edward Hon-Sing Wong

There is growing recognition of the relevance of Black feminist thought and the intersectional framework across academic disciplines. The Canadian social service sector reflects this, with intersectional analysis increasingly incorporated in training and practice (Walton, 2010; FCJRC, 2015; Simpson, 2009; Samuel, 2002). In this chapter, I engage in a close reading of three texts produced by Ontario-based social service[1] agencies that incorporate Black feminist thought, and intersectionality, in particular. The training texts include: Rainbow Health's *Training for Change: Practical Tools for Intersectional Workshops* (Walton, 2010); FCJ Refugee Centre's *From Youth to You* (FCJRC, 2015); and Canadian Research Institute for the Advancement of Women's *Everyone Belongs: A Toolkit for Applying Intersectionality* (Simpson, 2009). Created for organisations that serve a range of communities, these training tools are centred on a variety of social identities, including: the LGBT+ communities, women, and migrant youth. While there are variations in application, the stated purposes of all texts are to apply an intersectionality framework in the context of social services. Deidre Walton (2010: 1) expresses a desire to train service providers to 'relate successfully to our communities in their totality'. Joanna Simpson (2009: 6) also expresses that the broader goal of intersectionality is to 'strive for a world in which everyone, regardless of who they are or where they live, can live violence-free, access safe housing, have their voice heard and enjoy freedom from discrimination'. The FCJ Refugee Centre (FCJRC, 2015: 5) produced their toolkit with the stated purpose of helping newcomer and migrant youth 'feel more valued and included in various services across the City of Toronto'. While these training texts set out to provide an intersectional approach to addressing oppression, critical analysis reveals a disconnect between their interpretations of intersectionality and the radical roots of Black feminist thought.

This chapter begins with a review of Black feminist literature to contextualise key concepts relevant to the analysis of social service training texts. I consider how Black feminist thought and the intersectional framework emerged out of collective Black feminist resistance, against the erasure of Black women's voices in daily life and within the specific contexts of Black liberation and feminist struggles. Accompanying aspects to the intersectionality framework within Black feminist thought are also explored: historicisation and interlocking oppression. The analysis of the social service training texts reveals that these two accompanying aspects are problematically absent, resulting in a depoliticised analysis that fails to uncover the root causes of oppression. This absence may also have serious implications for social work practice, fostering a rush to practice, historical amnesia, and stereotyping approaches. The most significant discrepancy lies in the premise of applying intersectionality to individualised social service provision, in that the reformism of individualised social services is diametrically opposed to the goal of substantive social change through collective action integral to Black feminist thought.

Collective struggle as an incubator for black feminist thought and the intersectionality framework

Intersectionality was first coined by Kimberlé Crenshaw (1989: 139) in *Demarginalizing the Intersection of Race and Sex: A Black Feminist Critique of Antidiscrimination Doctrine, Feminist Theory and Antiracist Politics*, a critique of how antidiscrimination doctrine, feminist theory, and antiracist politics often fail to consider Black women, whose experiences are 'theoretically erased'. Crenshaw (1991) elaborates on the concept in *Mapping the Margins: Intersectionality, Identity Politics, and Violence Against Women of Color*, an examination of how violence against women is experienced by women from different social positions. Crenshaw examines how immigrant women may be prevented from accessing services for survivors of violence due to immigration status or a lack of proficiency in English. Crenshaw (1991: 1249) states, 'these examples illustrate how patterns of subordination intersect in women's experience of domestic violence. . . . the imposition of one burden . . . interacts with pre-existing vulnerabilities to create yet another dimension of disempowerment'. Intersectionality allows for recognition that multiple processes of subordination overlap to form unique experiences of oppression.

Crenshaw's work remains a crucial analytical tool in political struggle, but it should be recognised that intersectionality builds on a history of Black feminist activist engagement in collective struggle and imagination (Carastathis, 2014). The development of the concept of intersectionality can be attributed to the work of various activist intellectuals and collectives – including: Angela Davis (1981), The Combahee River Collective (1982), Audre Lorde (1984), Sojourner's Truth (1851), Mary Ann Weathers (1969), and hooks (1984) – a body of work identified by Patricia Hill-Collins (2000) as Black feminist thought. Black feminist thought emerged as a collective political movement for self-definition in the context of interlocking/intersecting oppressive social processes. Maria Stewart was as an early torch bearer for this political movement in the 19th century (Collins, 2000: 1). Not content to simply name the forms of oppression faced by Black women, Stewart sought to dismantle oppression through a prefigurative politics that could build self-sustaining communities. A component of this prefigurative politics is recognition that knowledge creation should be a communal process. This recognition is apparent in Stewart's championing of 'Black women's relationships with one another in providing a community for Black women's activism and self-determination' (Collins, 2000: 2). Black feminist thought is not the work of the solitary scholar, but the accumulation of the collective knowledge of a community of Black women engaging in activism.

Black feminist activists produce knowledge 'by using their experiences as situated knowers' (Collins, 2000: 19). The centring of Black women experiences by activists like Truth 'laid the foundations for what we would now recognize as intersectional analyses and methods'. Crenshaw (1984) cites Truth's speech given at a Women's Convention in 1851, as an early example of intersectional analysis and an attempt to challenge racism within the women's movement. While Truth (1851) highlights Black women's experiences of physical toil as a means of challenging the notion of women's weakness, another major objective of the speech was to compel white women in the crowd to reject racist discourses that presented Black women as 'less than real women' (Crenshaw, 1989: 154). The reasoning was that this rejection was requisite, if white women were to take on Black women's experiences in their own critiques of patriarchy.

Intersectional analysis as emerging in the context of social movements is also reflected in the work of Black feminist activists almost a century later (De Veaux, 2004). The Combahee River Collective (1977) statement was the product of a collective process, the culmination of a series of meetings by Black lesbian feminists, with the goal of clarifying their political stance and addressing the relationship between Black feminists and other progressive movements (De Vaux, 2004; The Combahee River Collective, 1977). In the statement, Black feminist thought was considered a response to frustrations from 'Black, other Third World, and working women' (The Combahee River Collective, 1977) in their attempts to participate in the American feminist movement in the late 1960s. It was felt that these attempts were thwarted by 'both outside reactionary forces and racism and elitism within the movement itself' (The Combahee River Collective, 1977).

Echoing this critique of broader social movements and societal processes, hooks (1984: 15) explains that: 'Black men may be victimized by racism, but sexism allows them to act as exploiters and oppressors of women. White women may be victimized by sexism, but racism enables them to act as exploiters and oppressors of black people.' hooks suggests that this dual role, the exploited and exploiter, is reflected in the constitution of liberation movements that fail to acknowledge issues faced by Black women. Instead, these liberation movements champion the interests of Black men and white women in ways that reinforce the oppression of other groups. While Black men and white women have often resisted calls to address sexism and racism within liberation movements ('But Some of Us', 1996), only wishing for their own equality with the ruling class, hooks (1984) argues that this resistance to Black feminist critiques undermines their own desires for liberation as it represents a failure to challenge the core logic of oppression. Intersectional critique is tied to desires to build mass liberatory movements that aim to dismantle oppression at its roots, and not the individualised social service provision promoted by the training texts examined.

Any comprehensive application of the intersectional framework should consider other aspects integral to Black feminist thought, such as the historicisation of social categories and oppression. Crenshaw (1989: 157), in elucidating the distinctions between Black women and white women's experiences to demonstrate the need for intersectional analysis, relies on 'the development of a historical critique'. For example, Crenshaw (1989: 156) examines the history of Black women involvement in the workforce as a critique of the generalised feminist notion of women being excluded from the public sphere.

This use of historical analysis in Crenshaw's (1989) intersectionality framework is consistent with Davis's (1971: 82) contention that an accurate assessment of Black women's experiences must 'attempt to illuminate the historical matrix of her oppression'. While intersectionality complicates constructions of social categories, historicising oppression allows for acknowledgement that these social categories emerge from specific social and political processes, shaping people's experiences. Processes that have shaped the experiences and identities of Black women include Western discourses and history (Collins, 2000; Lorde, 1984), capitalism (Amott and Matthaei, 1996; Collins, 2000), slavery (Collins, 2000, Davis, 1971), and the denial of legal and political rights (Collins, 2000).

Revealing the nuances of intersectional theory, Collins (2000) is careful not to imply that historical processes deterministically produce homogenous experiences for people placed within a social category. Collins (2000: 28) concludes:

> There is no essential or archetypal Black woman whose experiences stand as normal, normative, and thereby authentic. . . . Since Black feminist thought both arises within and aims to articulate a Black women's group standpoint regarding experiences associated with intersecting oppressions, stressing this group standpoint's heterogeneous composition is significant.

Collins (2000) suggests that the goal of Black feminist thought is not to create new categories. Instead, people should uncover how common challenges were constructed through historical processes and acknowledge that while common struggles related to various forms of oppression may exist, these processes do not operate in a deterministic or rigid manner. Any exploration or historicisation of identity categories need to recognise that there is a diversity of responses to these common struggles.

In addition to an emphasis on historicisation of oppression, the concept of interlocking oppression – or matrix of domination – is a major aspect within Black feminist thought. The Combahee River Collective introduces the concept of interlocking oppression in their general statement of politics (1977). The Collective describe how systems of racism, sexism, heterosexism, and classism intermesh with one another to produce the present conditions. While intersectionality can be understood as a challenge to understanding groups as internally homogenous, interlocking oppression represents the idea of interconnectedness between systems of oppression. The Combahee River Collective (1977) draws on the work of Black women activists, like 'Sojourner Truth, Harriet Tubman, Frances E. W. Harper, Ida B. Wells Barnett, and Mary Church Terrell, and thousands upon thousands unknown' to illustrate interlocking oppression. The Collective highlights the work of these activists in drawing awareness to how sexual identity intersects with racial identity in shaping their experiences and struggles. For example, The Collective cites the use of rape by white men against Black women as a means of political repression. An analysis that 'separates race from class from sex oppression' (Combahee River Collective, 1977) results in the erasure of context and contributing factors of rape.

Collins (2000: 18) expands the idea of interlocking oppression with the concept of 'matrix of domination'. Collins (2000, ibid.) considers the matrix of domination as an integral companion concept to intersectionality, as 'the matrix of domination refers to how these intersecting oppressions are organised. Regardless of the intersections involved, structural, disciplinary, hegemonic, and interpersonal domains of power reappear across quite different forms of oppression.' The matrix of domination refers to how various forms of oppression intermesh and are organised in specific sites and aspects of social order (e.g. housing discrimination, racial profiling, stereotyping media representations, or everyday racism). While the broader concept of intersectionality focuses on 'micro-level processes' (Hulko, 2009: 47), the matrix of domination emphasises the macro-level connections that create the social positions, categories like race, gender, and class. Engaging in social analysis with an interlocking oppression or matrix of domination framework is crucial as it allows for a more complex reading of oppression, rejecting flawed interpretations of intersectionality that presents oppressive systems as additive or separate. Instead, race, class, gender, and other identity categories are understood as intermeshed to form the daily experiences within a society.

Application of the intersectionality framework to social services

All three social service training texts profess to engage in and apply intersectional analysis. The FCJRC (2015: 10) defines intersectionality in terms of how 'Intersecting social identities such as age, gender, gender identity, ethnicity, class, social status, immigration status, sexual identity, experiences with authority, violence, etc. shape our individual uniqueness and inform our complicated relationships with power, privilege and oppression.' Simpson (2009: 6) also posits that an intersectional approach considers 'how different kinds of discrimination work together' to assess 'the full range of identities and circumstances facing people' (2009: 10). Finally, while Walton (2010) does not include an explicit definition of intersectionality, a similar definition to intersectionality revolving around how experiences are shaped by the interactions of multiple social identities is implicit within the text. This is apparent as many of the included training exercises focus on examining how multiple identity categories intersect to shape social service user experiences.

Aspects of intersectionality as articulated by Black feminist thinkers can be identified in the various definitions provided in the training texts. However, further analysis of the training texts reveals that their application of the intersectionality framework is not comprehensive. Two of the major accompanying concepts discussed – the historicisation of identities and oppression; and interlocking oppression – are absent, with serious implications to social work practices.

In a section on accessibility policies, Simpson (2009: 14) states,

> A widely held understanding of 'disability' and 'accessibility' places the emphasis on the way society is organized, rather than on particular impairments that the individual may have. People with disabilities may be challenged more by systemic barriers and inadequate accessibility within the community than by their own circumstances. It is not the disability, but the way society is organized (barriers to accessing activities of daily living) which determines the life experience of people with disabilities.

Superficially, this definition of disability appears consistent with the social constructionist perspective espoused by Black feminist thought. However, without contextualisation, social practices and perceptions of disability may appear arbitrary and disconnected from specific political and economic interests. This representation of identity categories serves to depoliticise as it ignores the political basis of processes that shape society's treatment of certain people.

Discussion of disability should consider how historical processes have shaped contemporary understandings of disability and pathology. In the Canadian context, a significant historical process is eugenics, 'the first cohesive ideas about a class of disabled people' (Withers, 2012: 13), introduced by Galton in 1865. Galton explained that eugenics was 'the science of improving inherited stock, not only by judicious mating, but by all the influences which give more suitable strains a better chance' and as a way 'to give the more suitable races a better chance of prevailing speedily over the less suitable' (cited in Withers, 2012: 13). Eugenics, then, was the science of improving the genetic quality of a population by preventing the procreation of certain people and by encouraging the procreation of white non-disabled people. The eugenicist theories took hold because it emerged in the context of colonialism, influenced by and reinforcing an imperialist logic (Levine, 2010). It did so by presenting people of the colonised world as less-abled, child-like, and sub-human, intertwining the concept of ability with race. Colonialism through a eugenicist lens was understood as justifiable since the subjugation of 'subhumans' was not considered a moral transgression but, simply a natural phase within human evolution (Levine, 2010).

The eugenics movement influenced public policy in Canada, through the intertwining of nationalist and eugenicist discourse. The Canadian state engaged in forced sterilisation and immigration policies that restricted non-white and disabled people (Wong, 2012; 2016). Based on the construction of disability as unproductive and burdensome in the context of Canadian colonial capitalism, these policies marked people with disabilities as undesirable. These policies were both a product of and acted to reinforce Canada's foundation as white (Thobani, 2007). Simpson's (2009) dehistoricised examination of disability is certainly problematic in terms of failing to address identity categories in a comprehensive manner. But, it is also problematic in that this dehistoricisation can lead to presumptions that identity categories and the policies or practices targeting these categories are the result of arbitrary actions or deterministic 'indicators of social structures' (Foucault, 1995). Instead, Foucault (1995: 23) argues that identity categories and associated practices are 'political tactics', forming a reciprocal and intertwining relationship with broader social and economic processes.

This decontextualised consideration of social categories echoes throughout all three training texts. Another example is the FCJRC's (2015: 31) discussion of intersectionality as 'step[ping] back and reflect[ing] on our privileges, the multiple identities that shape us, and the different ways we have faced oppression and discrimination'. In this definition, intersectionality is understood as focused on the idea that identities and social categories play a meaningful role in our lives, as indicated by the call for self-reflection. However, there is again little critical examination of how these identities emerged. Similarly, Walton (2010) emphasises the importance of acknowledging identity categories. An exercise entitled Rainbow Spectrum involves strips of paper containing gender and sexual identities, alongside their definitions. Participants are asked to place each identity category on a gender identity spectrum, ranging from cis to trans, or a sexual identity spectrum, ranging from hetero to homo. The stated purpose of the exercise is to provide participants with the language to talk about LGBTQ+ identities. While Walton (2010) may give an impression that identities are fixed by presenting identities as defined social categories on a spectrum, Walton (2010: 18) does qualify that 'identity and sexual orientation are both fluid, and may change, or not fully encompass the range of that persons [*sic*] gender or sexual behaviour'. Walton's (2010) qualification is limited to how gender and sexual orientations may not correspond to definitive categories, and how people's identifications may not stay consistent throughout their lifespan. This limited qualification fails to emphasise or acknowledge that these identity labels are historically constructed (Butler, 1988). Instead of considering how these social categories were constructed, Walton (2010) 'responded to marginalization by creating new marginal categories' (Kwan, 1997: 1276).

Simpson (2009: 8) also explains,

> So then, a big part of intersectionality is about taking into account people's experiences and identities without placing them into fixed categories . . . [and] to reveal meaningful distinctions and similarities in order to overcome discriminations and put the conditions in place for all people to fully enjoy their human rights.

Simpson (2009) cautions against accepting identities presented in these training materials as fixed. This caution is important; however, Simpson and the other authors do not go far enough in their interrogation of social categories, failing to consider how categories emerge and are reinforced. While Simpson (2009: 5) does include processes like capitalism, historical forces, and the legal system as 'larger forces and structures that work together to reinforce exclusion', they do not suggest that the emergence of these very categories may have served as components of political tactics linked to and been predicated on these processes.

Other than lacking historicisation, the training tools also made no mention of the term 'interlocking' or 'matrix of domination', nor is the interlocking oppression framework explicitly applied in their examination of oppression. The training literature emphasises a narrow definition of oppression that focuses on individual acts of discrimination, or more explicit forms of systemic discrimination, but does not consider these through the lens of interlocking oppression. The FCJRC (2015: 46) states, 'Leave your assumptions at the door! Each member of our group is a dynamic rainbow, and cannot be judged by any single aspect of our identities.' The FCJRC (2015) suggests that intersectional theory informs people to avoid stereotyping and making assumptions in relation to others' social identities. Without the concept of interlocking oppression, the FCJRC (2015) is unable to allude to the notion that the act of stereotyping is transformed by the interlocking of various forms of oppression based on multiple social identities. Nor is the FCJRC (2015) able to consider that these multiple social identities are themselves resultant from interlocking oppression. The emphasis of these training tools should not be limited to understanding how stereotyping reduces people into a single narrative. This focus within social service training literature on individual identity is problematic as it fails to consider collective identities – identities as tied to a group, and practices predicated on the notion of 'collective'.

Walton (2010) also holds a similar perspective. For example, an exercise asks participants to explore how stereotypes change when a LGBTQ label is attached to people of varying social identities (racial identities, immigration status, religious identities, etc.). The implication is that there is a need to be aware of how multiple overlapping social identities can change perceptions and lived experiences of people. Intersectionality is brought up as a critique of stereotyping, characterised as binary thinking that posits that 'people of colour are not queer, or queerness is a "white thing"' (Walton, 2010: 8), that queer people are 'non-religious [and] . . . can't maintain a religious affiliation after coming out because communities of faith are not welcoming' (Walton, 2010: 8), or that 'queerness is a white/Canadian thing and doesn't exist in other cultures/parts of the world' (Walton, 2010: 8). The primary underlying issue addressed by the exercises is how binary stereotyping does not allow for people to take up multiple social positions; but, the author does not consider that multiple forms of oppression intermesh to produce distinct stereotypical narratives. For example, a gay Chinese man may certainly be affected by stereotypes that fail to consider the possibility of racialised people being gay; however, a stereotypical notion of being Chinese is also linked to emasculation that is rooted in sexist ideas of women being weak. A gay Chinese man can also be affected by ideas of Chinese people as inherently pathological, with 'Chinese-ness' defined through disablist discourses (Wong, 2016). These different forms of oppression interlock to constitute representations of 'the gay Chinese' man.

Without an interlocking oppression framework, only one component of stereotyping – binary thinking – is examined, while the notion of stereotypes as constituted by the totality of multiple forms of oppression is omitted.

Also missing from the training literature, given the lack of an interlocking oppression framework, is the notion that the construction of privilege exalts identity categories (i.e. white, male, able-bodied) in a process that is predicated on the existence of subjugated categories. In other words, oppression is not only about harm or disadvantage; oppression, through the deprivation of certain people, also produces privileged identity categories and their related discourses. Razack (1998: 13) elaborates:

> Analytical tools that consist of looking at how systems of oppression interlock differ in emphasis from those that stress intersectionality. Interlocking systems need one another, and in tracing the complex ways in which they help to secure one another, we learn how women are produced into positions that exist symbiotically but hierarchically. We begin to understand, for example, how domestic workers and professional women are produced so that neither exists without the other.

Drawing on the example of domestic workers and professional women, Razack traces how colonial policies have led to the impoverishment, and thus, creation of the conditions that led to emergence of domestic workers. At the same time, these colonial policies enable women to 'pursu[e] . . . middle-class respectability in the First World' (Razack, 1998: 13) as First World women (Razack, 1998) access greater autonomy with domestic and childrearing tasks assumed by working-class women from the Global South. The lack of analysis on how social categorisation as a political process privileges certain people also leads to depoliticisation, naturalising the existence of group privileges.

Implications for social work practices: Tensions and contradictions

The failure to historicise identity categories and to recognise interlocking oppression, other than being uncomprehensive, has negative implications within a social work and advocacy context. Critical social work scholars like Poon (2011), Pon (2009) and Hulko (2009) have acknowledged the importance placed on historicisation by Davis (1971) and other Black feminist activists. Pon (2009) makes a pointed call for historical understanding in social work practice, so that social workers can reject 'rushing to practice'. Pon (2009: 69) explains that rushing to practice is:

> often related to a refusal to engage with learning about social violence, such as colonialism, racism and slavery, which can cause intense difficulty for learners [as it] often entails the challenging work of self-knowledge, including acknowledging how we are all implicated in contradictory relationships of oppression.

Chapman (2004) provides an example of rushing to practice when, in the role of social worker, participated in the restraining of Indigenous children with disabilities at a group home in Canada. Chapman (2004: 5) describes how the social service training regime had replaced their commitment to social justice 'with concern about my ability to 'set limits', 'establish boundaries' and generally discipline and control'. Chapman (2004) had accepted restraints as a necessary response to 'misbehaviours' from the residents. This acceptance was predicated on a failure to recognise the colonial violence that had brought these children to the group home and that children's 'misbehaviours' may be a response to the violence perpetrated by social workers and broader society. A failure to recognise the political implications, or rushing to practice, allows for the perpetration of violence without question or challenge. Today, violence against Indigenous children and their communities by the Canadian social welfare sector continue to occur in what Sinclair (2007) calls the 'millennium scoop', whereby Indigenous children have been taken into the care of the state in disproportionate numbers, rushing to practice at a systemic level.

Rushing to practice and surface-level examinations of identity are examples of what Lorde (1984) calls historical amnesia. Lorde (1984: 117) describes historical amnesia as the process by which the past is ignored, resulting in mistakes being repeated. This past does not only refer to the historical processes by which oppression and identity categories emerge, but also of the contributions, in analyses and direct action, of Black feminist thinkers. Lorde (1984: 117) attributes historical amnesia to a generation gap rooted in ageism, whereby the young view the old with contempt, failing 'to join hands and examine the living memories of the community, nor ask the all-important question, 'Why?'. Jordan (1989) and Nayak (2015) argue that resisting historical amnesia is a crucial task, in that the very 'recognition (or not) of the existence (or not) of Black women, their experience and what they produce' (Nayak, 2015: 37) depends on it.

While the acknowledgement of uniqueness stemming from intersections allows for added nuance, the decontextualised approach taken by the authors of these social service texts can lead to social work practices that remain essentialising and based on stereotypes. This perspective can lead to social work practices like cultural competency. In its definition of cultural competency, the National Association of Social Work (2015: 14) (NASW) states, 'Social workers should have a knowledge base of their clients' cultures and be able to demonstrate competence in the provision of services that are sensitive to clients' cultures.'

Cultural competency frameworks have been critiqued for relying on absolutist notions of culture (Pon, 2009), for failing to consider the role of power relations (Sakamoto, 2007), and for presenting whiteness as a standard by which 'others' are differentiated (Sakamota, 2007). For instance, Seipel and Way (2006: 5) recommend that in response to Latinx communities' apparent emphasis on interpersonal relationships, social workers should make 'Some modifications . . . include[ing] an increased amount of self-disclosure, accepting gifts (often food), and more physical contact (e.g. handshakes, pats on the back), as well as being closer spatially.' As Pon (2009) argues, this simply replaces essentialising notions of race based on biological differences with essentialising notions based on culture, with little consideration about the role of whiteness or racism. As Collins (2000) warned, the creation of more numerous social categories is a problematic interpretation of the intersectionality framework. Based on this problematic interpretation, social workers may presume that a move from the reliance on broader stereotypes of Latinx people to the reliance on more specific categories – such as that of Latinas or of queer Latinas – is sufficient. While the social service training texts examined urge social workers to refrain from stereotypes, its adoption of an intersectional approach that does not sufficiently deconstruct social identities can lead to this very mistake of stereotyping, albeit with greater specificity as more social categories are introduced.

It is unsurprising that a central proposition within Black feminist thought is that substantively addressing problems of discrimination and marginalisation requires challenging underlying social processes. It is for this reason that the premise of applying Black feminist thought and the intersectionality framework to individualised social service provision is problematic. Many of the core aspects that are central to the intersectionality framework were 'defined in a social movement context . . . as the target of integrated political struggle' (Carastathis, 2014: 306). Many of the Black feminist theorists cited here were either community activists or, in the case of the Combahee River Collective, an activist grouping. Collins (2000: xi) considers her theoretical work as organically linked to 'Black feminism as a social justice project'. hooks (2000: 3) also argues that 'radical freedom struggles awakened the spirit of rebellion and resistance in progressive females and led them towards contemporary women's liberation'. It was through participation in radical mass movements that contemporary feminist thought emerged.

Unlike the works of prominent Black feminists like hooks (2000) and Collins (2000), the emphasis of these intersectionality framework-based social service training resources is not on mobilising and building social movements. Instead, the focus is on developing 'inclusive' social service provision and reformist social policy. Simpson (2009: 83) defines intersectionality as 'a tool for analysis, advocacy and policy development that addresses multiple discriminations and helps us understand how different sets of identities impact on access to rights and opportunities'. While advocacy is mentioned, these tend to be reformist in nature or emphasise adaptation to the existing systems, rather than substantively changing the systems. For example, Simpson (2009) describes an initiative conducted by the Saskatchewan Intercultural Association that concluded that the primary need was education for young people and the raising of awareness for social issues with the public. There is no mention of addressing root causes of these social issues. In Walton (2009), multiple exercises revolve around examining barriers and improving access. It is believed that understanding the LGBTQ community as a diverse group made up of differences in terms of race, class, ability, gender, religion, etc. allows service providers to begin developing strategies for change. Thus, the focus is more on individual experiences of exclusion and marginalisation versus broader collective processes. Finally, the FCJRC (2015: 33), in defining intersectionality as 'invit[ations] to value and strive to understand the individualism of those around us rather than make assumptions', also emphasises individualised interactions. Though the FCJRC does not specifically define its use of individualism beyond implications around the role of social identities in shaping 'individual uniqueness', this Western notion of understanding individualism is situated in the context of service provision. This suggests a move away from notions of collective struggle that may emphasise a shared legacy of challenging social structures.

Critiquing reformist interpretations and applications of feminist theory, hooks (2000) suggests that reformist approaches failed to substantively benefit women of colour and did not challenge the fundamental logic of the system rooted in sexism and white supremacy. In fact, hooks (2000) contends that this avoidance of challenging the fundamental logics, was what made reformist demands more palatable to policy-makers.

Considering the origination of intersectionality in Black feminist activist movements, whose 'legacy of struggle against the violence that permeates . . . social structures is a common thread' (Collins, 2000: 26), the attempt to redirect intersectional theory and Black feminist thought towards service provision over mass movement building can be perceived as deviating from the original intentions of Black feminist theorists. Collins (2000: xiii) concludes, 'social injustice is a collective problem that requires a collective solution'. Explicit in this argument is a demand that social service providers move beyond a narrow focus on individualised service provision or reformist advocacy and towards an emphasis on collective action directed at substantive social change.

This repurposing of Black feminist thought from mass movement building to social service provision and reformist advocacy can be understood in the context of the growth of the non-profit sector and its associated funding models. In *The Revolution Will Not be Funded*, INCITE! Women of Color Against Violence, a feminist women of colour collective, presents the concept of the non-profit industrial complex (NPIC) (Smith, 2007). In the introduction, Smith (2007) suggests that the mass movements from the 1960s have been co-opted by funding mechanisms that emerged in the 1970s, echoing Robert L. Allen's warnings regarding co-option of the Black Power movement by the Ford Foundation as early as 1969. Of significance is Smith's (2007: 3) contention that the NPIC has served to shift attention to 'career-based modes of organizing [or professional social service provision,] instead of mass-based organizing capable of actually transforming society'.

Elaborating on the critique of professional social service provision, Kivel (2007: 1) contends that while 'social change work challenges the root causes', social service work only focuses on addressing individual needs. Kivel (2007) does not suggest that the two are mutually exclusive, citing the historic Black Panther Party and the Zapatistas as examples of movements that have provided social services while engaging in political change. However, Kivel (2007: 2) believes that most forms of service provision 'serve . . . to mask the inadequate distribution of jobs, food, housing, and other valuable resources'.

The specificities of the social service and non-governmental sectors in Canada have some differences from their American counterparts. Nevertheless, there are still parallels between the two. Similar arguments around the stifling of mass-based organising can be made of government regulations related to organisations operating under charitable statuses and the defunding of dissenting organisations (LRWC, 2014). The removal of intersectional theory from the context of mass movement building in the training literature reflects Smith's (2007) concerns and is in opposition to the Black feminist political projects that have long sought to build mass movements capable of radical societal change.

Conclusion

Black feminist thinkers have long challenged the oppression and marginalisation that exist within social justice movements and the broader society through collective struggle. Out of these struggles came the intersectionality framework, alongside a focus on historicisation and interlocking oppression, that sought to destabilise essentialising notions of social identity and their underlying social processes. However, thinkers from within Black liberation movements and their allies have long warned of the potential for misappropriation and the neutering of radical political thought (Allen, 1969). I suggest that these warnings have come to fruition, contending that the various social service training literature examined detaches the concept of intersectionality from its radical political roots. This detachment is apparent with the failure to historicise social categories and oppression, and to recognise oppression as interlocked. This absence has potential negative implications for social work practices, in that it can lead to rushing to practice, historical amnesia, and stereotyping procedures. But most importantly, in emphasising service provision over mass movement building, the authors fail to advocate for substantive societal changes in the spirit of Black feminist thought and the liberation movements from which this thought emerged.

Note

1 Social services in an Ontario context refers to a wide range of public services, provided by a variety of governmental and non-governmental agencies, including: mental health, child welfare, housing and homelessness, immigrant support services, disability services, lgbt+ services, and women's shelters.

References

Allen, R. L. (1969). *Black Awakening in Capitalist America: An Analytic History*. Garden City, NY: Doubleday.

Amott, T. L., and Matthaei, J. A. (1996). *Race, Gender, and Work: A Multi-cultural Economic History of Women in the United States*. Boston, MA: South End Press.

Butler, Judith (1988). 'Performative Acts and Gender Constitution: An Essay in Phenomenology and Feminist Theory', *Theatre Journal*, 40(4), 519–531.

Carastathis, A. (2014). 'The Concept of Intersectionality in Feminist Theory', *Philosophy Compass*, 9(5), 304–314.

Chapman, C. (2014). 'Becoming perpetrator: How I came to accept restraining and confining disabled Aboriginal children', in B. Burstow, B. A. LeFrançois, and S. Diamond (Eds.),

Psychiatry Disrupted: Theorizing Resistance and Crafting the (R)evolution (pp. 16–33). Montreal: McGill-Queen's Press.

Collins, P. H. (2000). *Black Feminist Thought: Knowledge, Consciousness, and the Politics of Empowerment.* New York: Routledge.

The Combahee River Collective (1977). *The Combahee River Collective Statement.* Retrieved on June 1, 2016, from www.circuitous.org\\scraps\\combahee.html.

The Combahee River Collective (1982). 'A Black feminist statement', in G. T. Hull, P. B. Scott and B. Smith (Eds.), *But Some of Us Are Brave* (pp. 13–22). Westbury, NY: Feminist Press.

Crenshaw, K. (1989). 'Demarginalizing the Intersection of Race and Sex: A Black Feminist Critique of Antidiscrimination Doctrine, Feminist Theory and Antiracist Politics', *University of Chicago Legal Forum*, 1, 139–167.

Crenshaw, K. (1991). 'Mapping the Margins: Intersectionality, Identity Politics, and Violence Against Women of Color', *Stanford Law Review*, 43(6), 1241–1299.

Davis, A. (1971). 'Reflections on the Black Woman's Role in the Community of Slaves', *The Black Scholar*, 3(4), 2–15.

Davis, A. (1981). *Women, Race and Class.* New York: Random House.

De Veaux, A. (2004). *Warrior Poet: A Biography of Audre Lorde.* New York: W. W. Norton & Company.

FCJRC (2015). *From Youth to You.* Retrieved on February 1, 2016, from www.fcjrefugeecentre.org/wp-content/uploads/2014/03/TOOLkit_FinalPrezied.pdf.

Foucault, M. (1995). *Discipline and Punish: The Birth of the Prison.* New York: Random House.

hooks, b. (1984). *Feminist Theory: From Margin to Center.* Boston, MA: Southend Press.

hooks, b. (2000). *Feminism is for Everybody: Passionate Politics.* Cambridge, MA: Southend Press.

Hulko, W. (2009). 'The Time and Context Contingent Nature of Intersectionality and Interlocking Oppressions', *Affilia: Journal of Women and Social Work*, 24(1), 44–55.

Jordan, J. (1989). *Moving Towards Home: Political Essays.* London: Virago Press, Ltd.

Kivel, P. (2007) 'Social service or social change?' in Incite! Women of Color Against Violence (Eds.), *The Revolution Will Not Be Funded: Beyond the Non-Profit Industrial Complex* (pp. 129–150). Cambridge, MA: South End Press.

Kwan, P. (1997). 'Jeffrey Dahmer and the cosynthesis of categories', *Hastings Law Journal*, 48(6), 1257–1292.

Levine, P. (2010). 'Anthropology, colonialism, and eugenics', in A. Bashford and P. Levine (Eds.), *The Oxford Handbook of the History of Eugenics* (pp. 43–61). Oxford, UK: Oxford University Press.

Lorde, A. (1984). *Sister Outsider: Essays and Speeches.* New York: Quality Paperback Book Club.

LRWC (2014). *The Shrinking Space for Dissent in Canada.* Retrieved on June 1, 2016, from www.lrwc.org/ws/wp-content/uploads/2014/05/Online-Copy-Canada.Shrinking-Space-for-Dissent.LRWC_.25.May_.2014.pdf.

National Association of Social Work (2015). *Standards and Indicators for Cultural Competence in Social Work Practice.* Retrieved on August 20, 2017, from www.socialworkers.org/practice/standards/NASWCulturalStandards.pdf.

National Collaborating Centre for Determinants of Health and National Collaborating Centre for Healthy Public Policy (2016). *Public Health Speaks: Intersectionality and Health Equity.* Antigonish and Montreal: Author.

Nayak, S. (2015). *Race, Gender and the Activism of Black Feminist Theory: Working with Audre Lorde*. Oxford, UK: Routledge.

Pon, G. (2009). 'Cultural Competency as New Racism: An Ontology of forgetting', *Journal of Progressive Human Services*, 20(1), 149–167.

Poon, M. K. L. (2011). 'Writing the Racialized Queer Bodies: Race and Sexuality in Social Work', *Canadian Social Work Review*, 28(1), 145–150.

Razack, S. (1998). *Looking White People in the Eye: Gender, Race, and Culture in Courtrooms and Classrooms*. Toronto: University of Toronto Press.

Samuel, M. (2010). *Peel District School Board School Services and Staff Development – Support Documents for the Implementation of the Future We Want*. Retrieved on February 1, 2016, from www.gobeyondwords.org/documents/IntersectionalityFull Discussion_000_000.doc

Seipel, A., and Way, I. (2006). 'Culturally Competent Social Work: Practice with Latino Clients', *The New Social Worker*, 13(4), 4–7.

Simpson, J. (2009). *Everyone Belongs: A Toolkit for Applying Intersectionality*. Retrieved on February 1, 2016, from www.criaw-icref.ca/sites/criaw/files/Everyone_Belongs_e.pdf.

Sinclair, R. (2007). 'Identity Lost and Found: Lessons from the Sixties Scoop', *First Peoples Child & Family Review*, 3(1), 65–82.

Smith, A. (2007). 'Introduction: The revolution will not be funded, by Andrea Smith', in Incite! Women of Color Against Violence (Eds.), *The Revolution Will Not Be Funded: Beyond the Non-Profit Industrial Complex* (pp. 1–20). New York: South End Press.

Thobani, S. (2007). *Exalted Subjects: Studies in the Making of Race and Nation in Canada*. Toronto: University of Toronto Press.

Truth, S. (1851). *Ain't I a Woman?* Retrieved on January 25, 2017, from www.nps.gov\\wori\\learn\\historyculture\\sojourner-truth.htm.

Walton, D. (2010). *Training for Change: Practical Tools for Intersectional Workshops*. Retrieved on February 1, 2016, from www.oaith.ca\\assets\\files\\Publications\\Intersectionality\\Practical-tools-intersectional-workshops.pdf.

Weathers, M. A. (1969). 'An Argument for Black Women's Liberation as a Revolutionary Force', *No More Fun and Games: A Journal of Female Liberation*, 1(2).

Withers, A. J. (2012). *Disability Politics & Theory*. Winnipeg: Fernwood Publishing.

Wong, E. H. S. (2012). 'Not Welcome: A Critical Analysis of Ableism in Canadian Immigration Policy from 1869 to 2011', *Critical Disability Discourse*, 4.

Wong, E. H. S. (2016). '"The Brains of a Nation": The Eugenicist Roots of Canada's Mental Health Field and the Building of a White Non-disabled Nation', *Canadian Review of Social Policy*, 75.

4 The politics of intersectionality as location

Andrew Hollingworth

This is a critical reflective analysis of two journeys of international social work that I undertook in 2016. One journey was to a refugee camp in Calais, France, called 'the Jungle'; a name steeped in colonialism, conveying danger and dislocation. The Calais journey was undertaken with fellow students from the University of Salford's Student Social Work Network. The other journey involved one-month volunteer work in Fort Portal, Uganda, including the Kyaka II refugee camp. Throughout reflection I relocate the reader, without warning, across borders. I give no apologies for this dislocation, because the theme of displacement across socially constructed borders is fundamental to the intersectional experience of refugees. Intersectionality is a theory about borders (Nayak, 2015a), and my experience of borders in these locations reveals 'ideological and political currents' (Crenshaw, 1989:160) that deny multiple injuries of subjectivity and movement. Butler (2004) reminds me that deconstructing psychic borders is painful. This reflection demonstrates how sensitive I/we are to threats to location, even when those threats are from the relative safety of these pages.

I offer a critical reflection of the experience using Crenshaw's (1989) intersectional gaze to embrace, rather than rationalise with causalities, the murky contingencies of subjectivity. Intersectionality is a methodology to navigate the pitfalls of dividing embodiment, emotion and cognition as distinct realms of human experience. I offer an intersectional gaze to reveal the simultaneous and mutually contingent experience of subjectivity, embodiment and agency. Bilge cautions how intersectionality's potential as a tool for promoting radical social justice is diluted I/we fall into the trap of seeing social interaction as the dominion of 'individual social entrepreneurs' (Bilge, 2013: 407).

My reflexivity is constituted of the 'psychic life of power' (Butler 1997), whereby 'injurious interpellations' are internalised and politically regulated social identities become self-subjugated lived experiences. This doxic formation of subjectivity (Oliver, 2004) requires the unconscious to be understood as psychosocial. Lacan's statement (1966–1967: 205) that the 'unconscious is political' contributes to my intersectional scrutiny of both journeys by offering the political unconscious as a site of the (Lorde, 1980: 123) 'oppressor within'. Re-reading the political unconscious as a site where the oppressor operates sees it as a site that constrains my/our intersectional gaze. Lorde warns that revolutionary change begins with that 'piece of the oppressor, which is planted deep within each of us' (Lorde, 1980: 123). Addressing the political unconscious requires making connections between and within experiences of multiple privilege and oppression. Making such connections is difficult irrespective of how frequently they have been encountered, as the political unconscious ensures that I/we have a myopic vision of the experience; our intersectional gaze is clouded by rhetoric of individual ability and pathology. In this way, privileges and oppressions become an *unknown familiar*.

The formation of the unconscious is the perpetual political formation of an embodied subject (Oliver, 2004) whose subjectivity develops in language and always in relation to politics (Parker and Pavón-Cuéllar, 2014). Thus, my colonised psyche is the product of dividing practices (Foucault 1975, 1982) that locate pathologies within those experiencing oppressions and keeps my white patriarchal privilege hidden (Ahmed, 2007). I am grappling 'whether intersectionality is a theory of marginalised subjectivity or a generalised theory of identity' (Nash, 2008: 7). Directing an intersectional gaze towards privilege is to question my tacit entitlement as identity.

The early summer flight from Dubai to Entebbe mistakenly felt like the last leg of a long journey. Absence and presence is fundamental to critical reflection (Nayak, 2015a) and as a student of Black feminist theory I have begun to appreciate the power of absence. I disembarked the plane at Entebbe International with excitement and without fear at the imminent encounter with border control. My hand movements for the passport in my bag subconsciously displayed and were implicitly recognised as the confident orientations of a multiply privileged subject. As a middle-aged, white, middle-class, heterosexual male able-bodied Western European this border presented no real resistance. Ahmed (2006) argues that bodies are oriented in the world towards objects that appear within reach, as well as away from other objects. These orientations, however, are influenced by a discursive turn or cultural understandings that govern the position of the subject in relation to those objects. Thus, Ahmed argues that bodies inherit 'sticky impressions' at birth, that are moderated through encounters with social others and objects: 'what sticks "shows us" where the object has travelled through what it has gathered onto its surface, gatherings that become part of the object, and call into question its integrity as an object' (Ahmed, 2004: 91).

My inherited colonial privileges intersect to produce a sense of fluidity where I can pass unnoticed to those accustomed to privileged social shape. My privilege is located in the intersection of language and an embodied positionality. The discursive and embodied orientations towards multiple, accessible and affirmative hospitalities, simultaneously positions the privileged subject away from more distant authoritarian processes such as police stop and checks, benefit sanctions, social work section 47 enquiries and, in this instance, immigration refusal at border control. My confidence was confirmed by a habitual micro-concession; a privileged subject invested in not seeing, as the officer called me forward with an unknown but familiar smile.

There was anxiety as I waited for further instructions. Sitting in the parked white transit van made me feel vulnerable because of dislocation from privilege. The way the foreign uniformed police observed us was alien to me. There was an obvious distrust. My first experience of this dislocation had occurred several hours prior as we approached the UK border to access the Eurotunnel to Calais. The British police have been known to use terrorism legislation (Schedule 7) to question volunteers crossing this border. When they learned we were part of the Social Work Action Network convoy to Calais they asked us to pull over for further checks. We had to surrender passports and disclose our home addresses and wondered if our names were being added to a database that would impact on our future movements. Of course, represent musings of privilege; I was confident that this encounter alone would not stick anything of significance to our embodied selves. This inhospitality was more designed to stick further impressions of 'Other' to those refugee bodies gathering in the Calais camp. A traveller's movements challenge implicit assumptions of what belongs where. Politics of location fortified the inhospitality to social work movements towards refugees in Calais and this was re-affirmed by the comparative hospitality as I boarded summer flights to Dubai and Entebbe. The in/hospitalities were an attempt to re-align social work activism with the implicit assumption that refugees belong on another Continent, they do not belong in Europe.

My work in Uganda was twofold: to help the UK charity, which sent me, to scale up their production of a hand sanitiser and develop a business plan for the product. I was also seconded to work with YAWE (Youth and Women Empowerment) in Fort Portal to provide social care to the community who are living with HIV or disability. The UK-based charity called 'Knowledge for Change' currently supplies the hand sanitiser at cost to local maternity wards within Fort Portal's clinics and hospitals. Their work has reduced instances of sepsis but needed to find a profitable private market in order to continue. My first career as a director of a chemical firm and my associated position and connections were put to use here. Fort Portal is a town in the Western Region of Uganda and is the seat of both the Kabarole District and the Toro Kingdom. HIV prevalence in Kabarole is 11.6%, which is significantly higher than the national average at 6.4% (Alibhai et al., 2010). A male colleague at YAWE explained the higher rate was due to Congolese sex-workers, an explanation that appeared more rooted in patriarchal opinion than research. Many women who had fled the first and second Congo Wars in 1996–1997 and 1998–2003 respectively had settled in Western Uganda and sold their bodies, the male colleague argued, for a price equivalent to a cup of Ugandan tea. It was interesting to note how blame was positioned with the woman rather than the men who refused to wear a condom (Bukenya et al., 2013).

Nash (2008) suggests the differences between Black women are masked by the frequent presentation of 'Black women' as a category in intersectional scholarship. The Black women engaging with YAWE in Fort Portal certainly had a lived experience that was distinct from other Black women in Kabarole. A diagnosis of

HIV is stigmatised in Uganda and those living with the disease are more likely to be unemployed, socially isolated and living in poverty.

The experience of race in Uganda is rooted in colonisation. British colonial administration in Uganda from 1894 to 1962 employed the divide and rule system (Doyle, 2009) and this still plays a role in the construction of the Ugandan psyche. Post-independence Kampala Governments have sought to silence the divisions between North and South, between religions, between urban and rural and between classes in order to realise national unity. Any questioning of these differences is labelled divisive and politically dangerous; it exposes the psychic attachment to colonial 'injurious interpellations' (Butler 1997). The problem is that when we are talking about language 'we are really dealing with power' (Jordan, cited in Nayak, 2015a: 36) whose discursive turn orientates the Ugandan subject to a 'historical amnesia' (Lorde, 1980: 117) of identity and difference. Failure to define the intersectional self and reach across 'difference as equals' (Lorde, 1980: 115) ensures social interactions are constrained by a colonial discourse that positions the privileged white body as the authentic, even on Black land.

Social interactions are constituted by passing glances and bodily movements that are influenced by an internalised language of the master (Lacan, 1972), which masks the intersectional self and encourages genuflection to the hegemonic. This produces a plethora of micro-aggressions for oppressed subject and micro-concessions for the privileged subject that moderate embodied sticky impressions (Ahmed, 2004) inherited at birth and influence our movements towards and position in relation to objects. Intersectionality exposes the contingencies and murkiness of agency. Hall (1990) has suggested that a new politic of difference must assist rethinking difference as agency.

An embodied inheritance that includes HIV shapes the location of the Black women of YAWE in relation to 'positive' identities and moderates their movements. By virtue of the intersection of gender and disease, bodies are oriented away (Ahmed, 2004) from the affirmative and towards poverty and isolation. Each Saturday morning men, women and children living with HIV came together at YAWE to talk, eat and provide support. During these discussions, some women spoke of their challenges. The intersectional experience of being Black, working-class, HIV positive and female located and oriented these women away from identities such as mother, lover and worker. Their location, orientation and movement in relation to isolation and destitution, however, make such identities probable, as they require only a short and fluid movement to achieve. The movements are fluid since the journey to isolation and destitution is facilitated by mutual expectation. On several occasions I drove my colleague from YAWE around the District as he dispensed antiretroviral medication and these deliveries were always made in discrete packages that were given to nervous family members and the handover frequently had the feel of a covert manoeuvre. In order to resist the stigma, the support offered by YAWE included training those with HIV in vocations that are in demand in the wider community. YAWE themselves employ several women as sewing machinists and are looking to open a bakery on site. They have also successfully helped several young men with HIV train and gain employment as mechanics. The assistance to achieve sustainable independence was augmented by group social support.

The instructions on how to distribute aid that were given earlier at the warehouse prepared us for a military-style operation once we reached the camp. We were told the refugees 'are desperate' and we were given clear instructions that were delivered in such a way that ominous consequences of failing to comply were implied and understood. The two smallest volunteers were assigned to be in the back of the van handing out food parcels. The largest male volunteers were to hold either rear van door, arms outstretched with the other volunteers forming two lines from these men by linking arms. The refugees were to queue in between this liberal tunnel and be quickly moved on once their food parcel was collected. As we began to approach the camp from the Care4Calais warehouse to the Jungle two young male refugees stopped us and asked for water. As all the aid was in the back of the van we handed the two our own half-empty bottles of water and re-joined our particular convoy of three transit vans. The inconspicuous roads that led to the outskirts of the Jungle were marked by several police vans whose occupants stood outside and presented the only air of menace we were to witness that day. For those who haven't been to the Calais camp before, its deconstruction began on 25th October 2016; it was situated on a flood plain and this particular morning was especially wet and very cold. There was no obvious organisation to the camp at first glance yet the squalor, sewage and open litter were palpable as we made our way deeper into the camp towards the distribution point.

It is a very peculiar experience for a white Western city-dweller delivering goats. Our colleagues from YAWE asked us to part from their company while they negotiated prices with the herder as the rate would increase dramatically if he saw Mzungus. Mzungu is a term used in the African Great Lakes region that dates back to the 18th century to describe a white subject of European descent and its possessive translates, almost as an early foretelling of a theory of performativity, as 'behaving rich'. Delivering goats is part of the Goats4Life program run by YAWE. They provide a doe free of charge to the families they work with who, after 2 years, need to either return it or a different nannie, which is then given to another family with the same conditions attached. In those 2 years, the family breeds the goat and uses it as an invaluable source of income by selling some of its offspring while at the same time growing their herd and thus their source of income. The YAWE projects were consistent with the principles of international social work by looking to 'promote . . . social cohesion, and the empowerment and liberation of people' (IFSW, 2014) rather than fostering an individualistic colonial charitable approach. Once loaded onto the back of the pick-up I drove out to the isolated villages in the mountains so the goats could be handed over to their new owners who turned out to be four young children, each with cerebral palsy cared for by their grandmothers. The people in the respective villages were helping each of the grandmothers and it was inspiring to witness community social work. Neoliberalism has eroded the UK's sense of intersectional collective community working (Turbett, 2014) and this experience showed me that collectivity is a powerful site of resistance to social injustices.

Intersectionality is a theory of borders (Nayak, 2015a: 100) and can bring into vision those phantom barriers that are not available as objects. The refugees who queued for aid had fled conflict and possessed fear of prosecution due to their nationality, race, gender, sexuality or political opinion. The intersectional experience of tens of thousands of men, women and children attempting to reach Europe in the 21st century has resulted in dehumanised deaths and disenfranchised grief. Any willful resistance and call for recognition as a human is interpreted as a threatening uninvited '*guest*' and I am here reminded of Sojourner Truth as the uninvited guest at the 1851 Women's Convention in Ohio (Nayak, 2017: 206). To date, domestic populism has orchestrated a reply that has acknowledged the diaspora as the ungrievable and unworthy of shelter, trust or compassion.

Spivak (2013: 3) observes that 'globalization takes place only in capital and data. All else is damage control'. The existence of the Jungle refugee camp and the global rise of nationalism in 2016 can be understood by challenging any assumptions of homogeneity amongst the privileged group. Intersectionality insists on a deconstruction of the impact of difference in the unequal distribution of privileges by those invested in not seeing their privilege. Intersectionality reveals the motivation and necessity for the divide and rule strategy (Freire, 2000) employed by the hegemonic privileged subject. This subject belongs to a corporate '*aristocracy*' who are privileged by race, nationality, class and wealth to such an extent that the incredible difference of their intersectional experience of privilege is incomprehensible to other privileged subjects. By virtue of shared colonial privileges of race, gender and sexuality the privileged subject who is oppressed by class, for example, can assume a false reciprocated attachment to the hegemonic. The deceit of this reciprocity can be found in numerous policies in the name of austerity, from public sector pay caps, benefit sanctions to a lack of regulations for the 'gig economy'. The assignment of the hegemonic is to feed the deceit of this attachment through the dehumanising of the colonial Other and the construction of this Other as a threat to the distribution of resources, which in reality are dominated by the hegemonic (Dorling, 2014). These resources of capital and data transcend national borders without resistance from domestic populism; in December 2016, for example, 82,000 miles of gas pipeline, a significant portion of the UK's National Grid infrastructure, was sold to Chinese and Qatari investors for £13.8 billion (Independent, 2016). Furthermore, an agreement in 2007 has allowed the USA to keep 'unminimised' private data on UK citizens (Guardian, 2013).

On Saturday morning I drove to YAWE to meet Dr Rita, a volunteer from 'Knowledge for Change' working in a local health clinic. We were meeting to take a Congolese couple and their three-week-old baby back to Kyaka II refugee camp. The couple had presented at the clinic two weeks earlier with the baby dangerously underweight but Dr Rita had managed to put a care plan in place where the baby was strong enough for the family to go back to the refugee camp. My only prior experience of a refugee camp was the Calais camp so I was nervous what to expect, considering Uganda was sheltering many more refugees per capita than the UK with a significantly lower GDP. If the lack of hospitality and squalid conditions in Europe for refugees was due to austerity and lack of resources as some media and politicians claim, then I was expecting the conditions in a Ugandan camp to be desperate. My expectations, my comparative framings and my desperation to find ways in which to mitigate my psychic defenses serve to highlight the extent of my *unknown familiar*.

As we turned onto the track leading to Kyaka II there was a road sign stating its name. To be explicitly prohibited is better than implicitly proscribed and the camp in Calais had not been acknowledged with an official name. The purposeful refusal of identity for the Calais gathering and the persistent misrecognition of those in the camp as migrants rather than refugees was in stark contrast to the sign on the red dust road declaring Kyaka II the home of 27,000 refugees. There were many other differences on the journey to Kyaka; there was an absence of resentment by the Ugandan driver and in the surrounding villages we stopped at for fuel and refreshment towards the refugees in the camp or towards those volunteers supporting them. There was an absence of discourse around resources being stolen – in fact, the driver proudly advised that the refugees in the camp are each given a parcel of land to grow food on. This brought to mind questions of belonging and not belonging that were so fundamental to the experience of the diaspora across Europe. The hospitality shown in Europe and Africa to the refugee seemed in stark contrast to the resources available to share.

There was still a long line when the last of the food parcels had been collected. The more experienced volunteers shouted 'Finished! Finished!' and those in the queue moved on without complaint. This had obviously become a well-practiced routine for the camp's inhabitants. We got back into the emptied vans and made the short journey past the watchful French police back to the warehouse to help sort clothing donations into type, gender and size. One of the volunteers (Jack) stopped to buy some cigarettes en route to the warehouse so we pulled over at a petrol station. Jack jumped out of the van and made his way into the shop. He came back out moments later looking a little embarrassed. The shop owner had refused to serve him as he was wearing a Care4Calais vest and those helping the refugees were not welcome. Natacha Bouchart, the mayor of Calais, has stated she wants policies to prevent the distribution of food to those refugees sleeping in hedges or ditches around the now demolished camp (*Guardian*, 2017). These micro-aggressions seem intent on orienting social work activism away from refugees on European land.

As we drove deeper into the vast Kyaka II there appeared little difference between the standard of the infrastructure inside the camp to that on the outside. The borders around quality of life, around what is valued as life, were not so clearly defined between refugee and host as they seemed to be in Europe. There were markets, homes with gardens in which laundry hung, schools, churches, mosques, clinics and shops. Outside the family planning clinic was a volleyball court and small playground. When we arrived at the couple's home a group of children quickly surrounded the car to welcome back the family. The two older children, who had been staying with a nearby family, were quite emotional to see the safe return of their mother, father and baby sister. We were invited into the family home and this was well built, dry and clean.

When we returned to the camp we had the opportunity to explore. We had been warned, however, to stick together. Revisiting and re-reading Ahmed's (2004: 91) concept of 'sticky impression', it seemed the instruction to stick together was as if to ensure we would not 'gather or incorporate anything that would call into question our integrity as a white privileged body' as we moved through the Calais camp. Destitution is normalised in the *Jungle* and this serves as both a deterrent to Others and a confirmation to those present that they do not belong. The simultaneous oppressions of race, gender, sexuality, physicality, nationality and displacement is represented in Calais by a refugee experience of tents on a flood plain where the cold and wet quickly seeps through to clothes, belongings and bodies. The lack of an official health and social care response means that disease and death in the camp are a daily reality.

We accompanied the Congolese mother and newborn to the refugee hospital, which is in the centre of the camp. There we spoke to a nurse who took notes from Dr Rita. On the drive back to the family home we stopped by the market. I learnt that Saturday is market day for Kyaka II and we made our way through a huge gathering of colourful stalls and boda boda taxis. The vibrant feel around Kyaka II refugee camp could not be more distant from the conditions on the flood plains in Calais. However, a camp is a camp and any hierarchy of oppression construction of which is the better camp is dangerous and reminds me of the ways in which UK social work is structured on the logic of a hierarchy of oppression (McDonald and Coleman, 1999) As dusk approached in Calais a middle-aged man who was holding the hand of his five-year-old daughter approached us. In spite of surviving conflict and the horrific journey to Europe, this Afghan man introduced himself as a former teacher and told us he did not want his daughter to suffer the Jungle any longer and tearfully asked us to take her to the UK. When we told him we could not he nodded and slowly walked away.

Returning to the Ahmed's (2006) concept of bodies and 'sticky impressions' allows this father's movements to be recognised. The father's birth as a Black, Muslim, Afghan man provided an inheritance of bodily impressions that influence his movement and oriented him in the world towards objects that appear within reach, as well as away from other objects. These orientations have been influenced by a discursive turn or cultural understandings that govern the position of the father in relation to those objects. The failure of the negotiations between US-based Unocal and the Taliban in 1998 to build a pipeline to transport gas reserves in Turkmenistan through Afghanistan, Pakistan and India (Kleiner, 2006) contributed to a discursive turn that positioned this Black, Muslim, Afghan father closer to identities of freedom-fighter/terrorist, refugee or casualty and away from family, teacher or lover. The father's inherited impressions and movements have been moderated by his lived experience of micro-aggression or micro-concession with social Others and objects. The incessant micro-aggressions of European inhospitality shaped his acceptance of another refusal and framed his movements as he retreated back into a camp besieged by psychosocial borders. Like him, so many 'Others' in Calais are trapped in the indeterminate border between two of Europe's wealthiest economies and in this shared space it is clearly constituted who are host and who are unwelcome.

The smiles and hospitality at border controls at Entebbe, Dubai and Manchester International placed deserving refugees and valued international social work on continents other than Europe. The forensic-type van search and individual checks coming back from Calais caused us to miss our booked space on the Eurotunnel. The orientation of social work activism towards refugees in Europe is not welcomed and these micro-aggressions at the border are to re-align psyches and orient bodies away from hospitality on European soil.

My journeys increased my awareness of anti-intersectional processes of dislocation. In Western Africa, for example, the political dangers of intersectional self-definition for the Ugandan subject function through labels of deviance. Intersectional self-definition for refugees is prohibited through double diasporisation (Hall, 1990). The politics of location is a politics of intersectionality where location becomes a verb, a process (Nayak, 2017) and an orientation for connection or disconnection. A politics of intersectionality as location offers a space to resist the colonised psyche. If 'the space and place we inhabit produces us' (Probyn, 2003: 294) then intersectional locations are vital.

If the politics of intersectionality as location is employed as a social work methodology and intervention, then social work would be more effective in challenging oppressive border constructions. This requires situating social work activism in those locations that question the policies of Natacha Bouchart, that protest against the Home Office guidance that offers the security of false borders to the intersectional experience of being a gay, Afghan asylum seeker deported to Kabul. The politics of intersectionality as location offers a model of critical social work reflexivity pivotal to a human rights-based social work profession. The politics of intersectionality as location offers a model of critical social work solidarity that challenges fragmented, dislocated, individualistic social work approaches. The politics of intersectionality as location says, 'let's face it we're undone by each other' (Butler, 2004: 23).

References

Ahmed, S. (2004) *The Cultural Politics of Emotion*. Edinburgh, UK: Edinburgh University Press.

Ahmed, S. (2006) *Queer Phenomenology: Orientations, Objects, Others*. Durham, NC: Duke University Press.

Ahmed, S. (2007) 'A phenomenology of whiteness', *Feminist Theory*, 8(2): 149–168.

Alibhai, A., Kipp, W., Duncan Saunders, L., Senthilselvan, A., Kaler, A., Houston, S., . . . and Rubaale, T. (2010) 'Gender-related mortality for HIV-infected patients on highly active antiretroviral therapy (HAART) in rural Uganda', *International Journal of Women's Health*, 2: 45–52.

Bilge, S. (2013) 'INTERSECTIONALITY UNDONE: Saving intersectionality from feminist intersectionality studies', *Du Bois Review: Social Science Research on Race*, 10(2): 405–424.

Bukenya J., Vandepitte J., Kwikiriza M., Weiss H., Hayes R. and Grosskurth H. (2013) 'Condom use among female sex workers in Uganda', *AIDS Care*, 25(6): 767–774, DOI: 10.1080/09540121.2012.748863

Butler, J (1997) *The Psychic Life of Power: Theories in Subjection*. Stanford, CA: Stanford University Press.

Butler, J. (2004) *A Precarious Life the Powers of Mourning and Violence*. London: Verso.

Crenshaw, K. (1989) 'Demarginalizing the intersection of race and sex: A Black feminist critique of antidiscrimination doctrine, feminist theory and antiracist politics', *The University of Chicago Legal Forum. Feminism in the Law: Theory, Practice and Criticism*, 139–167.

Dorling, D. (2014) *Inequality and the 1*. London: Verso.

Doyle, S. (2009) 'Immigrants and indigenes: The Lost Counties dispute and the evolution of ethnic identity in colonial Buganda', *Journal of Eastern African Studies*, 3(2): pp. 284–302.

Foucault, M. (1975) *The Birth of the Clinic: An Archaeology of Medical Perception* (trans. A. M. Sheridan Smith). New York: Vintage.

Foucault, M. (1982) 'The Subject and Power'. In Dreyfus, H. L. and Rabinow, P. (eds.) (1993) *Michel Foucault: Beyond Structuralism and Hermeneutics*. 2nd ed. Chicago, IL: University of Chicago Press.

Freire, P. (2000) *Pedagogy of the Oppressed*. 30th ed. New York; London: Continuum.

The Guardian (2013) 'US and UK secret deal on surveillance of personal data'. Retrieved February 27th 2017 from www.theguardian.com/world/2013/nov/20/us-uk-secret-deal-surveillance-personal-data.

The Guardian (2016) 'Migrant death toll passes 5000 as two boats capsize'. Retrieved February 27th 2017 from www.theguardian.com/world/2016/dec/23/record-migrant-death-toll-two-boats-capsize-italy-un-refugee.

The Guardian (2017) 'Calais Mayor bans distribution of foods to migrants'. Retrieved March 2nd 2017 from www.theguardian.com/world/2017/mar/02/calais-mayor-bans-distribution-of-food-to-migrants.

Hall, S. (1990) 'Cultural Identity and Diaspora'. In Ruthford, J. (ed.), *Identity: Community, Culture, Difference*. London: Lawrence.

IFSW (2014) 'International Federation of Social Work Global definition of Social Work'. Retrieved 29th September 2017 from http://ifsw.org/get-involved/global-definition-of-social-work/.

The Independent (2016) National Grid sells shares to China and Qatari investors. Retrieved 28th February 2017 from www.independent.co.uk/news/business/news/national-grid-sells-shares-china-qatar-investors-a7463256.html.

Kleiner, J. (2006) 'Diplomacy with fundamentalists: The United States and the Taliban', *The Hague Journal of Diplomacy*, 1(3): 209–234.

Lacan, J. (1966–1967) *The Seminar of Jacques Lacan, Book XIV: Logic of Phantasy* (unpublished translation by C. Gallagher from unedited French manuscripts).

Lacan, J. (1972) ''Du discours psychanalytique'. ' In Contri, G. B. (ed.), *Lacan in Italia 1953–1978. En Italie Lacan*. Milan: La Salamandra, 32–55.

Lorde, A. (1980) 'Age, Race, Class, and Sex: Women Redefining Difference'. In Lorde, A. (ed.) (1984) *Sister Outsider: Essays and Speeches*. Trumansburg, NY: The Crossing Press.

McDonald, P. and Coleman, M. (1999) 'Deconstructing hierarchies of oppression and adopting a 'multiple model' approach to anti-oppressive practice', *Social Work Education*, 18(1): 19–33.

Nash, J. (2008) 'Re-thinking intersectionality', *Feminist Review*, 89: 1–15.
Nayak, S. (2015) *Race, Gender and the Activism of Black Feminist Theory: Working with Audre Lorde*. London: Routledge.
Nayak, S. (2017) 'Location as method', *Qualitative Research Journal*, 17(3): 202–216.
Oliver, K. (2004) *Colonization of Psychic Space: A Psychoanalytic Social Theory of Oppression*. Minneapolis, MN: University of Minnesota Press.
Parker, I. and Pavón-Cuéllar, D. (eds) (2014) *Lacan, Discourse, Event: New Psychoanalytic Approaches to Textual Indeterminacy*. Oxford, UK: Routledge.
Probyn, E. (2003) 'The Spatial Imperative of Subjectivity'. In Anderson, K., Domosh, M., Pile, S. and Thrift, N. (eds.) (2003) *Handbook of Cultural Geography*. London: Sage.
Turbett, C. (2014) *Doing Radical Social Work*. Basingstoke, UK: Palgrave Macmillan.

5 Gendered Islamophobia

Intersectionality, religion and space for British South Asian Muslim women

Rashida Bibi

The focus of this chapter is British South Asian Muslim women in Oldham, and an analysis is employed which navigates intersectional identities within spaces and social structures. Located North East of Manchester, Oldham is a post-industrial town with a sizeable Pakistani and Bangladeshi community. In the 2011 census Muslims accounted for 1 in 9 of the population, with nearly 14,000 Pakistanis, and the highest number of Bengalis outside London's Tower Hamlets. In 2016, Oldham was characterised as the most deprived town in England, having below the national average rates for employment, education, housing and health (ONS, 2016). Oldham has been the site for various policy initiatives, including community cohesion and integration, a consequence of the 'race riots' that hit the town in the summer of 2001. This chapter focuses on the complexity of intersectionality, attending to the way power relations in society affect representations of the 'other', as well as how individuals emphasise or relate to aspects of their identity within different situations and spaces. This analysis asserts the discursive practises of embodiment and space, imperative to the intersectional experiences of British South Asian Muslim women.

At the heart of intersectionality is the complex interplay of race, ethnicity, gender and class and how these feed into, inform and influence the multiple ways in which they are experienced (Crenshaw, 1989). Intersectionality features not only as a lens to analyse multiple identities and discriminations, but how these identities are performed, valued or subordinated across sites (Collins and Bilge, 2016). At its broadest, intersectionality is a concept which centralises a post-modern, poststructuralist concept of the 'self' (Oleksy, 2011). Key to intersectional theorisation is the notion of 'lived experiences', shifting the focus from considering discrimination as operating along a single axis to one that considers overlapping lived experiences of inequalities (McKinnon, 2013). Intersectionality remains a critique of structural and social inequalities which explores personal identities in a complex way. An intersectional analysis necessitates attending to systems, inequalities and structures which support, produce and maintain notions of difference and othering (Grzanka, 2014). Though individual identity narratives 'provide an important contribution to fleshing our understandings of how people experience and construct identities within intersecting systems of power' (Collins, 2000: ix), nonetheless, this 'inward turn' should not replace criticisms of social inequalities, institutional prejudices or discriminatory policies. Understanding *how* groups become marginalised, precisely through unequal social hierarchies, political and social exclusion is a crucial step in challenging these injustices. This chapter, in focusing on 'how' British South Asian Muslim women are marginalised situates their experiences of discrimination within everyday spaces, and as derivatives of wider political and social exclusion.

In positing intersectionality studies as remaining aware of both identity and structure, it follows that the two are 'deeply intertwined facets of social life and inquiry' (Grzanka, 2014: 69). As Taylor (2010: 43) notes, '"intersection" is not an abstract concept; it is something that lives, breathes and moves'. This chapter focuses on intersectionality as an embodied, lived reality, where interlocking systems of oppression are experienced in ordinary spaces. Marginalisation and social 'othering' rely on a corporeal dimension upon which to pin differences, and as such intersectional analyses should pay attention to the ways in which 'macro' societal discourses function within micro-embodied practises experienced in the minutiae of everyday spaces. This presents the challenge of resisting essentialisation and 'flattening differences' (Luft, 2009: 102) and reduction of the individual to merely a 'body', through an effort to remain vigilant to 'human creativity and autonomy' (Yuval-Davis, 2011: 153).

Embodied intersectionality and space

The embodied experiences of British South Asian Muslim women in public spaces across Europe and the UK have received increased attention from the state, media and wider public discussions on social media. In bringing discourses of space, intersectionality and embodiment together it is possible to better understand how narratives of the 'Muslim other' are impacting upon British South Asian Muslim women's experiences of everyday spaces. Under the lens of intersectionality, embodied or inscribed differences of gender, race and religion are axes of difference which cannot be disentangled. The racialised representations of Muslim women across Europe, and the embodied otherness she represents in the national subconscious are reflected here in the experiences of British South Asian women in Oldham and are detailed through the empirical data below (Mirza, 2013). This chapter analyses the everyday encounters in Oldham and how representations of veiling practises as alien, challenging or threatening to a 'British way of life' are being enacted in public spaces (Moore et al., 2008).

Considering the embodied experiences of British South Asian Muslim women who veil and their negotiation of public spaces in Oldham necessarily brings us into the micro-level, of the everyday. In these spaces and encounters the category of 'Muslim woman' is constructed, and racialised. The 'body' is read as a site upon which differences, anxieties and gendered violence can be enacted. The body also represents the value of an individual, and the extent to which that body is characterised as 'same/different' is a part of the lived experience. The 'hypervisiblity' of the Muslim community, in the post 9/11 and 7/7 London bombing contexts, is experienced differently by Muslim men and Muslim women.

Pathologised within discussions across Europe, the Muslim man appears as intolerant, a potential extremist and sexually deviant, whilst the Muslim woman appears as both an aberration and a victim of a backward culture (Rashid, 2014). Muslim women's bodies have become a symbol of concerns over national identity, fear of the 'other', terrorism and immigration (Yunis and Husband, 2013; McGhee, 2008). Muslim women in public spaces have increasingly become a site of state intervention and control. In the name of liberalism, and protection of 'traditional', nationalistic values, the approach to Muslim women is, on the one hand, to make them hypervisible through discourses of difference and belonging, or, on the other hand, to render them invisible by denying them access to public spaces (Ryan, 2010). In seeking to save Muslim women from their backward patriarchal religion, they are treated as 'not quite up to the mark, abnormal, or downright sub-human' (Delphi, 2015: vii) and as such must unveil, or face being excluded. Muslim women have become subsumed in narratives on forced marriage, gender violence and of course veiling and are thus understood through neat cultural icons (Abu-Lughod, 2002), that present them as essentialised, homogenous subjects. Analysis of the data in this chapter shows how individual experiences are situated within and against the 'pathologisation' of the 'veiled Muslim woman' and how, as 'embodied-sentient beings', Muslim women are 'both spatially and ontologically displaced' (Lewis, 2013: 881).

The analytic lenses of embodiment and intersectionality show how social structures and oppressions come to be experienced by and through the intersectional identities of Muslim women. Additionally, as 'embodied identities', bodies become 'marked', and these marked differences function as illustrative boundaries between those who do/do not belong (Ahmed, 2000). Differences should not be merely read from these 'marked bodies', but understood relationally, in the form of encounters. These 'relational encounters' between one body and another are situationally connected, contextually configured through power relations and affected by the space in which they occur. Crucially, these power relations are never fixed. In these spaces, the processes of power constituted in and through binaries are never equal or linear, but form a 'relational web' (Pedwell, 2010) and are dependent on who has the power to accord difference, or to name the 'other'. Embodiment is also partly constituted by our view of the world (Leder, 1990) and it is the result of how we are located in the world, our relationship to the spaces we enter and the way we perceive or are perceived (Crossley, 2007). If we consider the body as an 'inscriptive surface' contributing to the ways of 'being in space' (Grosz, 1994), we can see how social relations and structures exclude Muslim women due to their 'embodied differences'. The same social structures are designed and maintained to perpetuate the Islamophobic construction of the barbaric, repressed Muslim in need of enlightenment and reform.

The juxtapositioning of discourses of embodiment with intersectionality enables us to better understand and thereby better challenge the relation between macro and micro of multiple, intersecting discriminations. Seeing space as something that is reproduced and experienced unevenly across groups enables us to understand the 'intimate connections between the production of space and the systematic productions of power' (Valentine, 2007: 91). Combining discourses of space, embodiment and the everyday allows us to see through the 'intersubjective micro-politics of everyday action' (Villa, 2011: 177).

There is an increasing and established Black feminist scholarship which focuses on the place of religion and feminism (Zine, 2004; Brown, 2006; Ali et al., 2008; Badran, 2009; Ramazanoglu, 2012). This chapter proposes that the tricky position religion occupies in feminism produces a reluctance in accepting nuanced perspectives on women and religion, with Muslim women considered as willing participants in their own subjugation. The reluctance to include religion or faith within anti-racism or feminist movements is attributed to the way in which religion, and particularly Islam, is considered as premodern, unchanging, misogynistic and discriminatory. It also feeds into Western hegemonic hierarchical binaries between secularism and religion.

However, religious affiliation and being visibly Muslim is an aspect of British South Asian Muslim women's everyday lives, which are articulated through processes of racialisation, discrimination and contemporary understandings of identity and belonging. Intersectionality calls for new understandings of anti-racism and feminism. The inclusion of discrimination based on religion, gender and ethnicity is essential to this understanding. Without negating the importance of race or gender, intersectionality can be reconceptualised in a way that includes faith and religion with an emphasis on lived practises and 'how it is lived and 'made' in ever changing ways' (Weber, 2014: 23). The use of an intersectional lens also highlights the complex way collective identities are transmitted and maintained amongst subsequent generations. This chapter focuses on second- and third-generation British South Asian Muslim women, as the issue of generation is yet another vector in the intersectional experience, as differences in aspirations, expectations and lived experiences between this and previous generations affect issues of identity and belonging (Franceschelli, 2017).

Affiliation to a Muslim identity is a factor in discrimination faced by Muslim women in Britain, as statistics show victims of anti-Muslim attacks are generally female and significantly 'wearing distinctively Muslim dress at the time of the attack' (Littler and Feldman, 2015). The theological roots of wearing the hijab can be conceived as an embodied practise. The act of veiling can be articulated as a visual representation of faith and adhering to this practise as part of that faith (Zempi, 2016). Bilge (2010) argues for an approach to the 'veiled woman' as one that looks beyond arguments of either 'subordination or resistance'. Nonetheless, given the continuing power of Islamophobic images of the hijab (Haddad, 2007) as the analysis shows, Muslim women inevitably reflect on the hijab's visibility and how it could be read by others (Hopkins and Greenwood, 2013; Hopkins, 2016).

The research process

The empirical research discussed here formed the basis for a PhD thesis, which explored the everyday lives of British South Asian Muslim women living in

Oldham, examining the embodied intersections of race, ethnicity, religion and gender within local everyday interactions. The concept of Muslim women's bodies as intersectional subjects considered 'in place' and 'out of place' and the complexity of 'in' or 'out' as mutually dependent and co-productive narratives was the theoretical framework which underpinned the research. Thirty second and third-generation women were recruited and interviewed in face-to face interviews between October 2015 and July 2016. The women were of similar socio-economic status but varied in age, as well as life stages, from unmarried women, to mothers; they were employed and unemployed, in education, housewives or living with family. The interviews featured semi-structured questions which focused on the notion of community, belonging, interactions and the sense of 'self' and perceived 'Muslimness'. The semi-structured interview is a verbal interchange, and allows the interview to unfold in a conversational manner. In feminist research practises, the semi-structured interview is deemed a useful method for generating data, especially if conducted with a conscious effort to minimise the hierarchical relation between researcher/researched.

The narratives that emerged provided material for considering questions of the nature of 'self', and, the extent to which being perceived as inside/outside a sense of national belonging affected their everyday interactions. Religious identity and the ways in which Muslim women's bodies become inscribed with meanings *for* them rather than *from* them featured in almost all the narratives, with women's bodies emerging as an anxiety marker, a source of ambivalence, threat or resistance. Names of women who have taken part in the research are anonymised and the extracts featured here are from Muslim women who 'veil' – either wearing the hijab, head covering, or niqab, the face veil.

Muslim women's daily negotiations

An intersectional approach which explores the complex interplay of social economics, migratory history, ethnicity and religion can be used to disrupt singular or stereotypical understandings of British South Asian Muslim women and to challenge homogenous notions of 'a Muslim community'. The relationship between spaces of Oldham and embodied intersectionality of the Muslim women who negotiate these spaces requires us to consider specificity. Doing so means seeing each space as made up of different categories, complicated by what is both tangible and intangible, of individuals and groups, of self and the other, of being and being seen (Philo, 2000). Foucault (1980) considers this as 'interconnectedness', whereby the nature of spatial relations exists along a plane, upon which histories, social otherness, locality and power over and knowledge of the other operates in the space of and between bodies. Collins (2000: 228) articulates this as the 'matrix of domination', whereby 'intersecting oppressions originate, develop and are contained'.

Through Foucault's 'interconnectedness' analogy, it becomes possible to see how representations of Muslim women inform and affect encounters in Oldham, as 'knowledge of' Muslim women as the 'other' dominates in the space between bodies shaping understandings of bodies which belong, and those which do not. Considering how communities function, how and which spaces are created and which meanings drive social interactions are all aspects which merit intersectional thinking and give rise to the following questions: Which embodied differences cause ripples in spaces? How are meanings attributed to the racialised, gendered and religious 'othering' of Muslim women, and with what effect? Which meanings are being inscribed onto Muslim women's bodies and within which spaces? How do these inscribed meanings then de/value the Muslim woman?

Zainab, a 29-year-old, mother of one, moved from Manchester to Oldham after her marriage in 2010, and was immediately struck by what she considered the 'sheer amount of hostility' she encountered there, such as during trips to the town centre:

> sometimes if I'm going out especially with the little one in the pram, if we're in Primark or whatever, we're waiting for the lift, you'll see like some white, young mums with their kids in tow, I hate to be stereotypical, but they just really look down at us. It's that impression they give, like as if to say, we've got more rights here than you, so I just wander round until the lifts clear or whatever, or if the space is empty, so I'll think yeah, now we can go . . .

Here, the everyday activity of shopping is imbued with an almost subconscious understanding of social hierarchies and inequality and how they position people in space. For Zainab, the access to this particular space is denoted by intersectional differences, with 'white young' women placed higher on the social hierarchy than someone of a different ethnicity. 'Having more rights than you' is a deeply ingrained lack felt by Zainab, articulated as being outside belonging. The 'here' relates not only to the space of the lift, or even the town, but also to the more symbolic national space. As such, it is an example of the macro structures of social practises and divisions impacting on the micro of everyday lives. Spaces are interwoven with complex intersections of race, ethnicity, nationalism and religion. The initial hostility Zainab felt and her subsequent acquiescent behaviour, which, significantly, also speaks of resilience and survival, is telling not only of nationalist discourses that mark the other, but also of how they operate within this space of a shopping centre in Oldham. As a space marked with multiple deprivation, a history of racial unrest and contradictory politics, Zainab's worth is devalued within Oldham's public spaces. This is because, as a veiled Muslim woman, she embodies the concerns over national identity, belonging and fear of 'other'. The Muslim woman's body is one that is perceived and marked as inferior, or unwanted. Savage et al. (2005: 12) remind us that belonging is a contested term, a socially constructed process by which 'people reflexively judge the suitability of a given site as appropriate given their social trajectory'. The ability to reflexively judge spaces is a daily feature of British South Asian Muslim women's everyday lives.

> When we're going out, in public settings, I don't think . . . for the first week or so wearing the niqab after the Paris attacks it did worry me, then I thought as long as I'm being reasonable, as long as I'm careful . . .
>
> (Naima, 34)

> I mean with park, yeah maybe on weekends, or family gatherings I would go, or maybe if I had a man with me I would go, but not at certain times, like early in the morning I wouldn't go, probably in the afternoon . . .
>
> (Hanifa, 25)

We can employ the concept of habitus to explain this reflexive process. Bourdieu (1984) considers habitus as the internalised embodiment of social structures, which then shapes the body's propensity to think, feel or behave a certain way (Wacquant, 2004). Because expectations of the way bodies should look or behave are culturally conditioned and therefore deeply embodied (Wise, 2009), Zainab not only *feels* 'looked down upon' but she then acts upon this feeling to modify her own behaviour, to only enter a space when it becomes empty of other bodies. In this sense, British South Asian Muslim women portray an awareness of the representations and Islamophobic discourses which determine the way they are seen. This then translates into a feeling, of lack, fear or caution, which is then accompanied by a performative action; to avoid particular places at certain times and to give way.

Cultural and national differences situate those who are seen to be outside belonging, and these boundaries are enacted in social interactions. Consequently, British Muslim women's embodied habitus becomes a symbol of their cultural and national difference. Thus, Muslim women experience their bodies as being 'othered' and 'out of place', which then informs their interactions in public. In the example below, Jamila, a new mother of one who has lived in Oldham all her life, spoke of a recent interaction:

> I was waiting for the bus when an elderly white male told me to move my f>ing pram and how people like me assumed we owned the country. I wanted to laugh, but felt rather intimidated.
>
> (Jamila, 30)

Being told to move the pram, and the remark regarding 'owning the country' is significant to note in this exchange, and indicative of how even the next generation of Muslims are cast as a threat and outside belonging. As Yuval-Davis (1997: 38) notes, women's membership in the collective national is that of being cast as 'biological reproducers of the nation'. In this encounter Jamila and the pram represent a threat to the national ideal; as the re/producer of cultural, ethnic and religious otherness, Jamila is seen not only as the unwelcome 'other', but as the primary source through which that 'other' may multiply and contaminate the national collective.

Spaces are not neutral, and within certain structures the modes of habitus presented by Muslim women are replete with notions of disruption, which leads to such pronouncements of 'them' taking 'over' or 'owning the country'. Such notions are nationalistic and invoke some the specific ways in which the majority align with a claim of belonging through intersecting fields of gender, religion and race over the lesser Muslim woman (Abdel-Fattah, 2016). Spaces are constructed in part through popular and political discourses which construct the Muslim 'as a social, economic, physical and/or moral threat' which is particularly heightened when the 'other' comprises groups racialised and visibly different, and constructed as an intrusive presence (Mohammad, 2013: 1804). The British South Asian Muslim woman's body, particularly one that pushes a pram, is denoted as a body, through its sexual and reproductive biology which can reproduce an undesired difference. As such, Jamila and the pram become the embodiment of disruption, a visible example of ethnic and cultural otherness, and, therefore, corruption to the mythical sameness produced in the national ideal.

If the ideal representations of the national ideal are those whose bodies 'fit', in other words, 'those who are not marked by their body, and who are, in an embodied sense, invisible' (Puwar, 2004: 58) then the veiled Muslim woman is clearly marked by her otherness through the clothes she wears. This marking is multi-directional (Crenshaw, 1991), the veil functions symbolically as Other, and Muslim women are Othered because of the veil. This process becomes mutually constitutive as the veil becomes the physical embodiment of otherness. It is in the public space where collective social norms and values are legitimised and negotiated through (in)visibility. If that visibility is deemed problematic, or as an intrusion, then a contestation for 'ownership' or the national ideal becomes a part of encounters in public spaces (Mohammad, 2013). There is a tendency for the cultural majority to conflate nation and race as a homogenously contained singularity, whereby 'Britishness' is conventionally associated with 'whiteness', and national identity is associated with a 'mythical sameness'. Jamila's veiled otherness personifies a fissure in this 'mythical sameness' thus acting as a marker for the basis of discrimination (Alexander, 1998).

Encounters in public, shared spaces, however brief, can have deep, lasting effects on an individual (Dirksmeier and Helbrecht, 2015). Even in these fleeting encounters people carry with them pre-formed ideas of 'others' based on negative racial or religious attitudes. As such these dispositions, when brought into contact with the 'other', can result in rejection, hostility or aggression (Amin, 2002). The seemingly mundane act of shopping, waiting for the lift or visiting the local supermarket can become fissures in the sense of 'self', especially when the encounter is negative or ambivalent. The use of intersectionality can highlight and challenge these fissures.

Interviewed after the Paris attacks of 2016, Khadija, aged 33, a full-time mother of three children, who wears hijab, recounted a frightening experience that took place in a supermarket. This encounter exemplifies the extent to which Muslim women embody difference, and the extent to which this makes them targets of gendered violence.

> Because I had Islamic attire on, this jubba and headscarf on, he didn't even see my face! He was screaming at me whilst looking at my back! He didn't even see my face . . . this is the worst thing, when he went past me saying you fucking bastard paki, my back was to him, he hadn't even seen my face. I had a scarf and jubba on and that was enough for him.

Muslim women feature heavily in statistics of racial or religiously motivated attacks, as 'stereotypes about veiled women's subservience coupled with the assumption that their Muslim identity cannot be mistaken, denied or concealed' makes them ideal targets of gendered and racialised violence (Chakraborti and Zempi, 2012: 269). Bodies matter; bodies which are of a particular gender, clothed in a certain way and situated in particular spaces present contradictions and conflict. Fears over 'what looks different' have been inscribed on Muslim women's bodies, and this 'visibility' is 'vital to how race and gender operate in the social world to allocate roles and to structure interactions' (Alcoff, 2006: 103). Crucially, what the abusively racist encounter that Khadija experienced signifies is the extent to which religion intersects with gender and codified signifiers such as the veil (Selod, 2015). Khadija's attacker did not see her face, he could not assert her race or ethnicity, yet within the everyday space of a supermarket the clothes she wore, her embodied intersectional identity, marked her out in the eyes of the man in question as 'other', leading to his violent outburst.

The result of such victimisation is that veiled Muslim women must then employ a constant renegotiation in their use of everyday public spaces and showing reflexive judgement of personal safety is an essential aspect of such negotiations. Veiled Muslim women have, increasingly in a post-9/11, and post-7/7 context, internalised feelings of threat and insecurity (Spalek, 2002). Many report being unable to walk unnoticed in public spaces (Kapur, 2002), as well-being reluctant to visit certain spaces due to being conspicuous because of dress. Negotiations of public spaces such as shopping centres, local parks or supermarkets involve deep introspection on the part of Muslim women. Their intersectional identities, of which 'Muslimness' is clearly visible, mark them as both outside and unwelcome, while their gender confirms them as 'easy targets'. Within certain spaces Muslim women do not feel safe, changing their behaviour and even their body language to offset any potential danger. Nabila, a 30-year-old woman who recently began to wear niqab, describes her negotiation of public space as one characterised by awareness of her surroundings and a projection of her embodied identity:

> I thought if I put on . . . if I give out that vibe or that body language of 'I'm nervous or scared' then it's going to attract the wrong attention, so I just have to force myself to be confident in walking past. I have to make that conscious effort, stand taller, walk firmer on the ground, not cower away, so it is sometimes quite nerve wracking . . .

Bodily practices, such as 'standing taller', 'walking firmer' and not 'cowering away' exemplify how Muslim women's embodied experiences become a reaction to the spaces and social structures of the world around them, whereby 'both consciousness and action are directed at the world' and the spaces in which they are acting (Crossley, 2007: 83). The unequal nature of power relations which govern social life are experienced in everyday spaces, and structure relationships between people and places. Learning the 'correct' behaviours and body languages to negotiate spaces is a facet of everyday life. For Muslim women, this learning involves managing gendered Islamophobia, which simultaneously casts the body of the veiled Muslim woman in contradictory terms as the subservient, yet dangerous other. Muslim women encounter stigmas in their everyday lives, and in doing so they must negotiate negative powerful signifiers, through making self-conscious, deliberate and reflective choices about spaces, as well as how their 'self' is perceived by the collective majority. What could be regarded as innocuous spaces, such as supermarkets, are not considered the same for all individuals. For Muslim women who visibly embody the 'other', they become spaces of anxiety and exclusion. Our relationship with the spaces we occupy is shaped by the gaze of others, as certain characteristics, ethnicity, gender and religion represent factors by which people are included or excluded from the social policy.

Muslim women, however, are employing new strategies of resistance to misrepresentations and defining their right to veil in ways which are unique and representative of their own interpretation of veiling:

> I'm just choosing to cover myself, 'cause I don't want to give in to the stresses of daily life about the right makeup or clothes, or living up to people's expectations in society. I choose to take myself out of that and wear what I want so I don't have to live up to your expectations, I don't have to keep up with other people. I think niqabi women are judged for doing that, stepping away from those pressures.
>
> (Saima, 29)

Social hierarchies are influenced and sustained by social norms, which means certain bodies become privileged over others. Managing intersectional identities in everyday spaces is a necessary part of 'normal' life. For Muslim women, such as Hanifa (35), gendered Islamophobia may remain a prominent part of that everyday negotiation, nevertheless they choose not to allow such oppressive discourses to define them:

> Life doesn't stop, you have to go out, you have to pay your bills, you have to buy your groceries, you can't stay at home locked behind closed doors, because somebody has to do the jobs. It does make you aware of your surroundings, I've always been aware . . . if you yourself . . . if you know you've not done anything wrong then there's no reason to hide away. Why should we hide away?

Conclusion

Understanding embodied intersectionality highlights the ways in which multiple oppressions are acted upon the body. Considering how bodies become 'othered' and in which spaces allows us to contextualise the situatedness of political, economic and social structures, and how these are constituted and lived (Mirza, 2013). Intersectionality highlights unequal structures and goes deeper to understand what effect these inequalities have on individuals. However, as Staunaes (2003) has argued, what risks being lost in intersectionality studies is the 'subject': as intersectionality 'travels' and is adapted by institutions globally, the framework for intersectionality risks becoming a purely 'theoretical practise'. This is contrary to Crenshaw's (1991) original conceptualisation of intersectionality, which she saw as rooted in experience. In other words, there is no disconnect between intersectionality as theory and as embodied practise, it is not simply a heuristic tool. Intersectionality is a strategy for doing social justice (Collins and Bilge, 2016). Muslim women face discrimination within and exclusion from almost all aspects of social and political institutions. Muslim women in the UK and Europe occupy an 'outsider' status, thus intersectionality becomes central to an empowered political discourse (Goswami, et al., 2014), especially given that Black feminism has and continues to emerge 'out of a cultural-historical context that positions, represents and constitutes Black women as outsiders' (Nayak, 2015: 7). Given its importance in anti-racism work, intersectionality has long been considered vital in the politics of liberation. In combining considerations of spatial dynamics within intersectionality and space in the production of inequalities we can understand how power dynamics function within space to include or exclude. The discourses of embodiment and spaces in 'everyday' life, with all its mundane, banal and seemingly ordinary routines, is where micro-practices, interactions, emotions and relationships connect with that of 'macro' – social practices, institutions, forces, structures and divisions. Incorporating embodiment and 'space' into intersectional analysis presents an essential tool through which to recognise how intersectional identities are lived in and across spaces, thus crucially returning intersectionality to its roots, emancipation.

The voices of Muslim women are frequently absent or misrepresented in public debates, reinforcing perceptions of a subjugated or disengaged group (Bilge, 2010). Given that differences such as clothing and religion are not 'fixed' or 'capacity endowed', the inclusion of such differences, it can be argued, is less likely to be considered in Western discourses of anti-racism or feminism. However, as illustrated in this chapter, the bodies of veiled Muslim women clearly carry less value in public spaces. A complex interplay of national identity, othering and gendered racism has placed Muslim women outside of the 'norm'. Thus, British South Asian Muslim women come to represent not only the biological reproducers of ethnic difference (as indicated by Jamila's experience and the reference to the pram) but a visible threat against which to enact violence, othering, physical or verbal abuse. The experience of embodied intersectionality within spaces is vitally important in understanding racialised and gender-differentiated experiences for

Muslim women. It is these embodied differences, operating on intersectional levels within spatial and social structures, which need to be included in intersectional discourse. Though the subjectivity of Muslim women presents a complexity to contemporary understandings of intersectionality, representing these voices is a challenge that should not be ignored.

References

Abdel-Fattah, R. (2016) '"Lebanese Muslim": A Bourdieuian "Capital" Offense in an Australian Coastal Town', *Journal of Intercultural Studies*, 37 (4).

Abu-Lughod, L. (2002) 'Do Muslim Women Really Need Saving? Anthropological Reflections on Cultural Relativism and Its Others', *American Anthropologist*, 104 (3).

Ahmed, S. (2000) *Strange Encounters. Embodied others in Post-Coloniality*. London: Routledge.

Alcoff, L.M. (2006) *Visible Identities: Race, Gender and the Self.* Oxford, UK: Oxford University Press.

Alexander, C. (1998) 'Re-imagining the Muslim Community', *The European Journal of Social Science Research*, 11 (4).

Ali, SR; Mahmood, A; Moel, J and Hudson, C. (2008). 'A Qualitative Investigation of Muslim and Christian Women's Views of Religion and Feminism in their Lives', *Cultural Diversity and Ethnic Minority Psychology*, 14 (1).

Amin, Ash. (2002) 'Ethnicity and the Multicultural City: Living with Diversity', *Environment and Planning A*, 34 (6).

Badran, M. (2009) *Feminism in Islam: Secular and Religious Convergences*. London: OneWorld Publication.

Bilge, S. (2010) 'Beyond Subordination vs Resistance: An Intersectional Approach to the Agency of Veiled Muslim Women', *Journal of Intercultural Studies*, 31 (1).

Bourdieu, P. (1984). *Distinction: A Social Critique of the Judgement of Taste*. London: Routledge.

Brown, W. (2006). *Regulating Aversion: Tolerance in the Age of Identity and Empire*. Oxford, UK: Princeton University Press.

Chakraborti, N. and Zempi, I. (2012) 'The Veil under Attack: Gendered Dimensions of Islamophobic Victimization', *International Review of Criminology*, 18 (3).

Collins, P. H. (2000) *Black Feminist Thought*. New York: Routledge.

Collins, P. H. and Bilge, S. (2016) *Intersectionality*. Cambridge, UK: Polity Press.

Crenshaw, K. W. (1989) 'Demarginalising the Intersection of Race and Sex: A Black Feminist Critique of Antidiscrimination Doctrine, Feminist Theory and Antiracist Politics', *University of Chicago Legal Forum*, 140.

Crenshaw, K. W (1991) 'Mapping the Margins: Intersectionality, Identity Politics, and Violence Against Women of Color', *Stanford Law Review*, 46.

Crossley, N. (2007) 'Researching Embodiment by Way of Body Techniques', *The Sociological Review*, 55 (1).

Delphi, C. (2015) *Separate and Dominate: Feminism and Racism after the War on Terror*. London: Verso.

Dirksmeier, P. and Helbrecht, I. (2015) 'Everyday Urban Encounters as Stratification Practices'. *City*, 19 (4).

Foucault, M. (1980) *Power/knowledge: Selected Interviews and Other Writings, 1972–1977*. New York: Pantheon Books.

Franceschelli, M. (2017) *Identity and Upbringing in South Asian Families: Insights from Young People and Their Parents in Britain*. London: Palgrave McMillan.

Goswami, N., O'Donovan, M. M, and Yount, L. (eds) (2014) *Why Race and Gender still Matter: An Intersectional Approach*. London: Routledge.

Grosz, E. (1994) *Volatile Bodies*. London: Routledge.

Grzanka, P. (2014) *Intersectionality: A Foundations and Frontiers Reader*. Boulder, CO: Westview Press.

Haddad, Y. (2007). The Post-9/11 Hijab as Icon. *Sociology of Religion*, 68: 253–267.

Hopkins, P. (2016) 'Gendering Islamophobia, Racism and White supremacy: Gendered Violence Against Those who Look Muslim', *Dialogues in Human Geography*, 6 (2).

Hopkins, P. and Greenwood, R. M (2013) 'Hijab, Visibility and the Performance of Identity', *European Journal of Social Psychology*, 43.

Kapur R (2002) 'The Tragedy of Victimisation Rhetoric: Resurrecting the 'Native' Subject in International/Postcolonial Feminist Legal Politics', *Harvard Human Rights Journal*, 15 (1).

Leder, D. (1990) *The Absent Body*. Chicago, IL: University of Chicago Press.

Lewis, G. (2013) 'Unsafe Travel: Experiencing Intersectionality and Feminist Displacements', *Signs: Journal of Women in Culture and Society*, 38 (4).

Littler, M. and Feldman, M. (2015) 'Tell MAMA Reporting 2014/2015: Annual Monitoring, Cumulative Extremism, and Policy Implications', June 2015.

Luft, R. E. (2009) 'Intersectionality and the Risk of Flattening Difference: Gender and Race Logics, and the Strategic Use of Antiracist Singularity'. In Berger, M. T. and Guidroz, K. (eds) *The Intersectional Approach: Transforming the Academy Through Race, Class, & Gender*. Chapel Hill, CA: North Carolina University Press.

McGhee, D. 2008. *The End of Multiculturalism? Terrorism, Integration and Human Rights*. Maidenhead, UK: Open University Press.

Mirza, H. S. (2013) '"A Second Skin": Embodied Intersectionality, Transnationalism and Narratives of Identity and Belonging Among Muslim Women in Britain', *Women's Studies International Forum*, (36): 5–15.

Mohammad, R. (2013) 'Making Gender Ma(r)king Place: Youthful British Pakistani Muslim Women's Narratives of Urban Space', *Environment and Planning A*, (45): 1802–1822.

Moore, K., Mason, P. and Lewis, J. (2008) *Images of Islam in the UK: The Representation of British Muslims in the British national Print News Media 2000–2008*. Cardiff, UK: Cardiff School of Journalism, Media and Cultural Studies.

Nayak, S. (2015) *Race, Gender and the Activism of Black Feminist Theory: Working with Audre Lorde*. Oxford, UK: Routledge.

Office of National Statistics (ONS) Towns and Cities analysis, England and Wales, March 2016. [online] Available at: www.ons.gov.uk/peoplepopulationandcommunity/housing/articles/townsandcitiesanalysisenglandandwalesmarch2016/2016–03–18.

Oleksy, E. (2011). 'Intersectionality at the Crossroads', *Women's Studies International Forum*, 34 (4): 1–132.

Pedwell, E. (2010) *Feminism, Culture and Embodied Practise*. London: Routledge.

Philo, C. (2000) 'Foucault's Geography'. In Crang, M and Thrift, N. (eds) *Thinking Space*. London: Routledge.

Puwar, N. (2004) *Space Invaders: Race, Gender and Bodies Out of Place*. Oxford, UK: Berg.

Ramazonoglu, C. (2012) *Feminism and the Contradictions of Oppression*. London: Routledge.

Rashid, N. (2014) 'Giving the Silent Majority a Stronger Voice? Initiatives to empower Muslim Women as part of the UK's "War on Terror"', *Ethnic and Racial Studies*, 37 (4): 589–604.

Ryan, L. (2010) 'Muslims in Britain: Race, Place and Identities, Peter Hopkins, Edward Gale', *Political Geography*, 29 (1): 55–56.

Savage, M., Bagnall, G. and Longhurst, B. J. (2005) *Globalization and Belonging*. Nottingham, UK: SAGE Publications.

Selod, S. (2015) 'Citizenship Denied: The Racialization of Muslim American Men and Women Post-9/11', *Critical Sociology*, 41 (1): 77–95.

Spalek, B. (2002) 'Hate Crimes Against British Muslims in the Aftermath of September 11th', *Criminal Justice Matters*, 48 (1): 20–21.

Staunaes, D. (2003) 'Where Have All the Subjects Gone? Bringing Together the Concepts of Intersectionality and Subjectification', *Nordic Journal of Feminist and Gender Research*, 11 (2): 101–110.

Taylor, Y. (2010) 'Complexities and Complications: Intersections of Class and Sexuality'. In. Taylor, Y., Hines, S. and Casey, M. E. (eds) *Theorizing Intersectionality and Sexuality*. Basingstoke, UK: Palgrave.

Valentine, G. (2007) 'Theorising and Researching Intersectionality: A Challenge for Feminist Geography', *The Professional Geographer*, 59 (1): 10–21.

Villa, P. I. (2011) 'Embodiment is Always More: Intersectionality, Subjection and the Body'. In Lutz, H., Vivar, M. T. H. and Supik, L. (eds) *Framing Intersectionality: Debates on a Multi-Faceted Concept in Gender Studies*. Farnham, UK: Ashgate.

Wacquant, L. (2004) 'Habitus'. In Beckert, J. and Zafirovski, M. (eds.) *International Encyclopedia of Economic Sociology*. London: Routledge.

Weber, B. M. (2014) 'Gender, Race, Religion, Faith? Rethinking Intersectionality in German Feminisms', *European Journal of Women's Studies*, 22 (1): 22–36.

Wise, A. (2009) '"It's Just an Attitude that You Feel": Inter-ethnic Habitus before the Cronulla Riots'. In Noble, G. (ed.) *Lines in the Sand: The Cronulla Riots and the Limits of Australian Multiculturalism*. Sydney: Institute of Criminology Press.

Yunis, A. and Husband, C. (2013) 'Islamophobia, Community Cohesion and Counter-terrorism Policies in Britain', *Patterns of Prejudice*, 47 (3): 235–252.

Yuval-Davis, N. (2011) 'Beyond the Recognition and Re-Distribution Dichotomy: Intersectionality and Stratification'. In. Lutz, H., Vivar, M. T. H. and Supik, L. (eds) *Framing Intersectionality: Debates on a Multi-Faceted Concept in Gender Studies*. Farnham, UK: Ashgate Publishing.

Zempi, C. (2016) 'It's a Part of Me, I Feel Naked Without It': Choice, Agency and Identity for Muslim Women Who Wear the Niqab', *Ethnic and Racial Studies*, 39 (10): 1738–1754.

Zine, J. (2004). 'Creating a Critical Faith-Centered Space for Antiracist Feminism: Reflections of a Muslim Scholar–Activist', *Journal of Feminist Studies in Religion*, 20 (2): 167–187.

6 State building in Kosova

An intersectional analysis

Kaltrina Kusari

Introduction

After 18 years of peacebuilding and state-building efforts, Kosova continues to struggle with high levels of poverty and low levels of integration among ethnicities. Many of these practices have been unsuccessful and have led to an increase in the marginalisation of certain social groups. The peacebuilding and state-building process in Kosova is an example of how a top-down approach disregards local knowledge (Lemay-Hebert, 2011). Analysis of Kosova's state-building practices illustrates that they are built upon monolithic views of culture, ethnicity, religion, gender and other identity categories. One way to challenge these oppressive practices is through using intersectionality to problematise the definition and application of social and identity categories.

Social work, with its commitment to social justice and anti-oppressive practice, is well suited to contribute towards state-building practices which reject homogenous views of identity categories. Social workers need to recognise the multiple realities which characterise both individuals and societies, and create space where such realities can be expressed. This chapter draws on intersectional analysis, grounded in postcolonial theories, to discuss state-building practices in Kosova. The chapter aims to highlight that social work has a professional duty to address state-building practices, placing primacy on intersectional theorising to approach contemporary global issues.

The framework presented adopts a postcolonial lens. A postcolonial perspective is essential in analysing Kosova's state-building process, as it examines the Global North-South power dynamics and can help explain why the international community retains executive powers in Kosova's institutions. Juxtaposing an intersectional framework with a postcolonial lens produces a contextualised analysis of Kosova's state-building efforts. In doing so, it helps social workers better understand the power dynamics in Kosova and encourages them to remain vigilant about not replicating these in practice.

An intersectional lens contributes to advancing feminist theory. The term was coined by Crenshaw (1989) when she argued that mainstream feminism failed to recognise intersecting intragroup differences and constructed gender and race on a single axis. Many intersectional theorists (Dei, 2016; Patil, 2013; Stasilius,

2016) have looked at the intersection of various identity categories, advancing intersectional theory and contributing to the evolution of feminism.

I use Bogdandy et al.'s (2005: 583) definition of state-building. State-building 'means the establishment, re-establishment, and strengthening of a public structure in a given territory capable of delivering public goods'. I begin by providing an analysis of the armed intervention in Kosova, then present an intersectional framework, which focuses on the intersection between ethnicity, gender, and citizenship to explore Kosova's state-building process. My analysis will interweave personal experience and examples from literature (e.g. Carton, 2008; Mulaj, 2008) – both highlight the multiple identities which exist in Kosova, and the efforts of the international community to silence those voices which do not fit their agenda. The international community, in this case, refers to the United Nations and European Union (EU) troops and staff that have been present in Kosova since the end of the 1999 war. To conclude, I discuss how the theoretical framework contributes to both intersectional theorising as well as the advancement of social work literature.

Contextualising Kosova

On March 24th, 1999, the North Atlantic Treaty Organization (NATO) started an air strike campaign against former Yugoslavia. The United Nations Security Council approved NATO's military intervention because of concern for 'the excessive and indiscriminate use of force by Serbian security forces and the Yugoslav Army which have resulted in numerous civilian casualties and . . . the displacement of over 230,000 persons from their homes' (United Nations Security Council, 1998: 1). This military intervention was justified on the premise that the ethnic cleansing of Albanians by the Yugoslav Army violated human rights and imposed an ethical requirement for military intervention (Uberti, 2013).

As an eight-year-old, I was thankful to the international community for deciding to intervene and stop the ethnic cleansing of Albanians. My experiences in Kosova and my studies since the end of the war have changed my position. I became aware that the intervention placed primary emphasis on ethnicity in a way which has increased the divisions which led to war. Further, my gratitude was a result of the power imbalance between Kosovars and Westerners. I am more critical of the approach adopted by the international community in Kosova because, despite claims that they support the country's development and the creation of a multi-ethnic society, Kosova remains the poorest country in Europe, lacking integration amongst ethnicities.

Using human rights discourses to justify the involvement of NATO and other international organisations essentialised ethnicity. At the Dayton Agreement, which sought to promote peace and stability in Bosnia and Herzegovina in particular, and the Balkan region in general, the discrimination of Albanians in Kosova was completely ignored. Consequently, 'political exclusion of the Kosovo [sic] question accelerated radicalization of Kosovo Albanians. The key lesson that they learned from Dayton was that peaceful resistance would not win Albanians rights. Instead, violence pays' (Mulaj, 2008: 1109). Indeed, until the Dayton Agreement took place, Kosova's political elite, headed by Ibrahim Rugova,[1] used non-violent resistance against the Serbian regime. Some have argued that this non-violent resistance was purposefully not recognised by the international community because it did not fit the stereotypical perception of the Balkans – a place of uncivilised peoples who need to be civilised by Western powers (Mulaj, 2008; Uberti, 2013). It took the massacre of the Jashari family, whose house was a main KLA stronghold, and the massacre in Reçak to mobilise international support, evidencing that there was an 'interdependent relationship between international responses to the conflict and events in Kosovo [sic] themselves' (Mulaj, 2008: 1113).

Kosova was a UN protectorate under the administration of United Nations Mission in Kosova (UNMIK) until it declared independence in 2008 (Uberti, 2013). Since 2008, the main international factor in Kosova had been the EU Rule of Law in Kosova (EULEX) which assured Kosova's alignment with EU policies and the establishment of rule of law in the country (European Union External Action, 2016). Despite receiving the second largest amount of development aid from the EU and the Organization for Economic Cooperation and Development (OECD) countries, Kosova continues to suffer from a high rate of poverty and political instability (Mulaj, 2008; Uberti, 2013). Poverty and instability persist as problems, partly because 80% of the foreign aid invested in Kosova 'was spent in capacity building and consultancy, which means that 3200 million [euros] went back to the base' (Lemay-Hebert, 2011: 191).

Many elements contribute to Kosova's current socio-economic and political hardships. However, I argue that UNMIK and the EU have used ethnicity as an explicating tool for post-war problems – a practice which has contributed to the marginalisation of Kosovars. A single-cause solution has created a hierarchy of oppression in Kosova, which has placed discrimination based on gender, socio-economic class, and citizenship, secondary to ethnic discrimination. The UN and EU's discursive tendency to exclude multiple entry points into addressing oppression continues to negatively impact Kosova by: silencing and excluding Kosovars who are subject to forms of oppression such as sexism and classism; intensifying the division between ethnicities; and allowing international organisations to assume a 'helper' role, which increases their exertion of power over Kosova.

The form of humanitarian intervention carried out in Kosova relates to social work practice because much like UNMIK and EULEX, Global North social workers tend to assume a 'savior' role when working in Global South countries (Deepak, 2012). Social workers often lack 'consciousness about the postcolonial and post-developmental critiques of the established western development discourse' (Jönsson, 2010: 399) and perpetuate the belief that Western models of development are the sole way towards modernity. As such, an intersectional analysis of Kosovo's peacebuilding and state-building practices is important in challenging superficial attempts at social justice, both in international development and within social work practice.

An example of a superficial attempt to establish justice through creating a multicultural society is the term Kosovar itself. Prior to the 1999 war, all those who lived in Kosovo identified themselves by their ethnicity – Albanian, Serbian, Roma, Ashkali, Egyptian, Turk and so forth, although they were often referred to as Yugoslav by those outside Kosova. After Kosova declared its independence in 2008, to create a common identity, the term Kosovar was adopted to represent the citizenship of all those who live there. In my experience, most people in Kosova continue to place primacy on their ethnic identity, and rarely identify as a Kosovar. For example, when asked where I am from, I say Kosova, but when asked about my nationality, I identify as Albanian. It is artificial for me to say that I am Kosovar seeing that my native language is Albanian and that I grew up learning Albanian history and celebrating Albanian traditions. Beyond my experiences, the trivial nature of the term Kosovar becomes apparent in reports published by international organisations, such as the Organization for Co-operation and Security in Europe (OSCE), which write about Kosovar-Albanians and Kosovar-Serbs, but never just Kosovars.

There are two different interpretations of the term Kosovar. While some local analysts believe that Kosovar signifies citizenship and recognises Kosovo as an independent country, others believe that Kosovar also refers to one's nationality and are grounded in the belief that with Kosovo's independence, a new nation was also created. The important issue is that Kosovar is a contested identity category. This term is just one manifestation of the superficial post-war intervention that has taken place in Kosova.

Theoretical framework

A single-cause solution to conflict – centering ethnic divisions – is a concern for social work as it silences individuals who are not solely defined by ethnicity; this silence creates an oppressive erasure to considerations of gender, socio-economic class, and citizenship. An intersectional framework is useful in understanding Kosova's state-building process because it rejects a hierarchical view of oppressions (Dei, 2016). Instead of blaming the current socio-political and economic stagnation on ethnic hatred, intersectionality encourages the exploration of how various identity and social categories intersect with each other to contribute to Kosova's culture, economy, politics, and the general well-being of its citizens.

Intersectional theorising seeks to contextualise the impact of identity and social categories (Stasiulis, 2016), thus facilitating the analysis of Kosova's current challenges. This Kosova-specific intersectional framework focuses on an analysis of the intersection between ethnicity, gender, and citizenship. Intersectional theorists such as Dei (2016) suggest that our academic work is most significant when grounded in our experiences. Personal experiences make us aware of how power operates and equips us with tools to examine the intricacies and intersections of the oppressions which exist. A personal narrative has inherent tensions, because it can prevent us from noticing the ways in which we are implicated in the processes we seek to examine. Of importance to me as a social worker is that my subjective contexts are brought to the forefront so that I remain aware of how my interpretation of the situation is informed by previous experiences. As I am acquiring social work as part of my identity, I must remain committed to a reflexive practice which challenges oppressive practice within social work. Intersectionality will facilitate my critique of the dichotomous way of thinking which places social workers and service users in opposition.

I am an Albanian woman, belonging to the Kosovar middle class, and have completed all my secondary and higher education in North America. Until recently, my socially constructed hypersensitivity to my ethnic identity kept me from seeing other forms of oppression, such as sexism. Completing my social work education in Canada allowed me distance from the dominant discourses in Kosova. Critical theories of liberation have given me insight into how my ethnicity and gender have been largely constructed by the war and its aftermath. I use ethnic/national identity as an entry point into an intersectional analysis because, until now, they have been powerful tools in constraining this multiple axis approach.

Because of the international intervention in Kosova, which created a dichotomy between Western democracy and Balkan governance structures, my ethnicity and gender have become sites of oppression, whereas my Western education gives me privileges when in Kosova. For example, I could secure a social work practicum at a UN agency in Kosova because I completed my education at a Western university. Of the six practicum students that were at the agency, none had completed their education in Kosova. Foreigners or those who attended a Western university in Kosova were given priority over local students. Such unjust practices deny local students the opportunity to intern at an elite agency, such as the UN. This places them at a disadvantage when applying for jobs, continuing the division between those with a Western and Kosovar education. I have noticed that employers are impressed that I was able to secure a UN practicum. No regard is given to the fact that I could only intern with the UN because I completed my education in Canada.

Considering the power that Westerners enjoy in Kosova, my intersectional analysis is grounded in postcolonial theory. Postcolonial theory examines how new colonial mechanisms of oppression continue to shape today's global relations. In Kosova, the involvement of Western organisations in the state-building process is justified through an approach which deems human rights to be 'both natural and universal, leading to the belief that it is the duty of the world's powerful to guarantee that they are respected everywhere' (Carton, 2008: 6). Attempting to ensure human rights in Kosova, the UN and EU interventions have promoted democracy and guided the state-building process (UN General Assembly, 2005). This involvement, however, is problematic because the universal human rights discourse is often used to impose dominant Global North practices without regard to the context of a country (Deepak, 2011).

Postcolonialism helps to posit the country and the social work profession within the increasing divisions between the Global North and South. Even though Kosova is rarely mentioned as a Global South country, its current political, social, and economic situation is similar to countries which are usually thought as constituting the Global South (United Nations Development Programme, 2012: 13). This makes Kosova vulnerable to Global North influences. Global North countries have political, economic, and social power over Global South countries because '. . . far from weakening the nation-state, globalization is seen as a new form of imperialism, designed to reinforce the power of core Northern states, their ruling classes and multinational corporations which they serve' (Castles, de Haas, and Miller, 2009: 33). The representation of Kosova's global position requires a more complex intersectional and postcolonial approach which challenges the binary split of the world into the Global North and South.

A postcolonial lens is important to social work theorising because 'the lives of an increasing number of individuals can no longer be understood by looking only at what goes on within national boundaries' (Levitt and Gluck-Schiller, 2004: 1003). As someone from Kosova who has completed her entire post-secondary education in North America, I have a transnational identity. As such, I am aware of the importance of finding social work tools which take into consideration the challenges and opportunities that arise along with these identities. Deepak (2012: 779) suggests that social work as a field needs to develop an 'analysis of globalization as historical, gendered and complicated by cross-cutting power dynamics from the personal to the national to the global'.

Similar developments are needed in intersectional scholarship. Intersectional studies are often limited to the race-gender-class triad (Purkayastha, 2012) which fails to account for identity categories, such as ethnicity, religion, sexual orientation, and citizenship that are more salient in the Global South (Stasiulis, 2016). To advance intersectional theory, I use postcolonial theories to move beyond the domestic realm and address axes of domination that arise out of the Global North-South power imbalance.

Applying intersectionality to Kosova

A postcolonial, intersectional analysis suggests that the state-building process in Kosova is akin to 'the creation of political entities accountable to the international community, and in line with dominant economic and social policies' (Carton, 2008: 6). Programs such as the Stabilisation and Association Process (SAP) aim to hold Kosovar institutions accountable to the EU, but do not establish reciprocal accountability measures for the EU (Carton, 2008). Development has been 'reduced to adopting strings of 'European standards, and writing self-congratulatory donor reports' (Uberti, 2013: 385). These practices have neocolonial undertones because 'the partnership between the EU and Kosovo is one between uneven partners, "with only one party [the EU] being the judge of whether the conditions of the contract are met and in a position to coerce the other"' (Chandler, 2006 cited in Carton, 2008: 10).

EU power is evident in its freedom to draft Kosovar policies and the fact that most Kosovar 'courts of law are presided over by English-speaking foreign judges from EULEX, while some positions in key bodies such as the constitutional court or the privatisation agency are reserved, by law, to "internationals"' (Uberti,

2013: 282). Such practices place the assumed objectivity and moral prowess of international personnel in opposition to the assumed hate-inspired nature of Kosovars. They also construct foreigners as experts and give them immunity 'from the laws they help to draft' (Uberti, ibid.).

Analysis of power relations between Westerners and local Kosovars is relevant to social work because although social workers intend to use their power 'in ways that are enabling and productive for those needing protection, there are continual dangers of using expert knowledge, and legal and organizational status, in order to construct oppressive, excluding or patronising forms of professional *power over*' (Tew, 2006: 47). Social workers have often replicated oppressive state-building practices which neglect to consider the importance of internationalised social problems. Jönsson (2010), researching empowerment projects in southern India, found that social workers often focus on the micro-level of practice and end up blaming individuals for the lack of development in their society. In doing so, social workers perpetuate hierarchies of whiteness and citizenship and continue to support a system they would like to overturn. My critique of the state-building practices is not limited to the Kosovar context, but raises a more general issue about the position and function of social work in development projects.

Much like Global North social workers who are privileged in the Global South, EU personnel enjoy certain rights in Kosova because both have something that Global South citizens and Kosovars desire. Kosova hopes to eventually join the EU and its political leaders are eager to meet European standards (Uberti, 2013). Western ideals are perpetuated because the EU can threaten to use sanctions against Kosova in case its government does not fulfill EU expectations. The use of sanctions is a neocolonial practice because it is used to punish countries which oppose Western domination (El-Lahib, 2015).

Social workers have often used sanctions to penalise service users. Social workers monitor service users who do not have the right to question the approach used by the practitioner (Lens, 2008). Such practices strengthen the idea that failure is a result of the service users' inability to learn. In similar manner, the EU conditionalities on Kosova suggest that the country is incapable of meeting EU standards, and place the blame on Kosova without calling into question whether these standards are the adequate ones for Kosova to aspire to. EU power and position are configured to locate the failure within Kosova, just as social workers have used their power to locate failure within the service user.

Operation of power through discourse

Although the EU requires Kosova to work towards a multi-ethnic society to be eligible for EU membership, EU involvement has created further divisions between the Albanian and Serbian populations in Kosova. As I write, the EU is encouraging Kosovar politicians to implement the Association of Serb Majority Municipalities (the Association hereafter), which would separate the Serbian population living in Kosova into their own municipalities (European Union External Action, 2015). It is puzzling to understand how this segregation contributes to a multi-ethnic society. Kosova's Constitutional Court, upon reviewing the proposal for the establishment of the Association, stated that several principles of the agreement did not fully comply with Kosova's constitution (Popova, 2015). It asked for revisions of the agreement before implementing the Association. Yet, the EU continues to support this physical segregation, perpetuating the idea that the two cannot co-exist in peace, and justifying the involvement of the EU as a mediator in the state-building process.

Looking at the UN intervention immediately after the war suggests that essentialising ethnicity enabled UNMIK to delegitimise old governance structures and request the eradication of such structures based on the premise that they belonged 'to the terrible years of 'ethnic hatred'' (Blumi, 2003: 216). This allows the UN to consider racism as a phenomenon of the past, while simultaneously understating their own racist practices.

UNMIK and the EU, have 'asserted mastery over Kosova's population' through taking agency away from Kosovars in 'asserting collective guilt for criminal acts conducted by individuals' (Blumi, 2003: 226). Blumi states:

> Characterizing Kosova's tragedy along lines of 'ethnicity' has thus reduced the capacity of individuals, and the communities they make, to act outside the conditions set by UNMIK which only recognizes its constituents in ethnic terms: Albanian, Serb, Roma or Goran.
>
> (2003: 216)

While the ethnic cleansing of Albanians by Serbian forces cannot be denied, concealing the multiple oppressions which shape the lives of Kosovars often silences those who experience these oppressions. Silencing is a social justice issue and implicates social workers, whose ethical standards require them to promote social justice and challenge marginalisation.

I recently returned to Kosova, where I plan to practice as a social worker. Already, I have noticed that, as an Albanian, international NGOs consider me as incapable of working with the Serbian 'other' without a mediator because of the assumed hatred between us. For example, I am an alumna of the OSCE Dialogue Academy for Young Women, which brought together women from Kosova and Serbia to discuss our role in reconciliation and peacebuilding. The discussions were mediated by OSCE personnel, who placed emphasis on our gender identity, but did so in a way that moved attention away from the current tensions which exist between our countries. The fact that Serbia does not recognise Kosova's independence was never discussed, but it was avoided because of its 'sensitive' nature. Without critical engagement with issues which are deemed too 'sensitive' neither reconciliation nor peacebuilding will be sustainable. The fact that the Academy took place allows the OSCE to take pride in its efforts to mediate the collaboration of Albanian and Serbian young women. By selecting Academy participants based on where they live (Kosova or Serbia), the OSCE sends a subtle cue that ethnicity continues to remain a dividing factor.

A recent poll suggests that only 5% of Kosova's population report experiencing discrimination based on ethnicity. Instead, according to survey participants, discrimination based on gender, age, and (dis)ability is more prevalent in Kosova (UNDP, 2012). These findings support the argument that an analysis of Kosova's state-building process cannot be limited to ethnic divisions. The international intervention in Kosova has neglected to address its role in maintaining the Albanian-Serbian division in Kosova. Instead, it has perpetuated a dichotomy between Albanians and Serbians as well as that between Kosovars and Europeans, constructing Europeans as modern, leading to feelings of inferiority among Kosovars.

This dichotomous way of thinking, which differentiates between Westerners and locals, is crucial for social workers to challenge, seeing that practice is often impacted by the division between 'us' (social workers) and 'them' (service users) (Jönsson, 2010). Kosovars who accept EU's conditionalities are seen as Western-oriented and, therefore, cultured, whereas those who want to develop local forms of democracy are considered primitive. Likewise, social workers are seen as educated and capable while service users as uneducated, passive, deviant, manipulative and so forth (Jönsson, 2010). I am often met with shock from relatives and friends when I say that I have been educated in the West, but am critical of their intervention in Kosova. It is almost inconceivable for most in Kosova to meet someone who has lived in the West, but has chosen to return to Kosova and prefers local approaches to education, social work practice and so forth. This expression of shock is a testament to the binary way of thinking that exists in Kosova. Although I have a hybrid transnational identity, most people in Kosova limit me to either my Kosovar or Canadian identity; I cannot exist at the intersection of Canada and Kosova because they are assumed to have no similarities.

The intersectional postcolonial framework helps to understand that such divisions resemble colonial and imperialising practices which rely on 'othering' discourses built upon monolithic constructions of identity. Said (1978) argues that Western texts purposefully construct the Orient as the 'traditional' other to justify Western domination which, presumably, brings about civilisation and modernity that is lacking in non-Western societies. Similarly, biased literature which portrays people from the Balkans as 'savages' who need to be 'civilised' allows the international community in Kosova to exert power over the local population.

Because divisions between ethnicities continue to exist, it remains that 'what has changed in Kosova since June 1999 is the nature of rule, not the discursive relationship between power and subject' (Blumi, 2003: 219). Like the current international community practices in Kosova, the pre-war Serbian media and government also worked to create the impression that all dissatisfaction and uprisings in Kosova were nationalistic in nature and driven by ethnic hatred. When referring to uprisings in rural parts of Kosova, Blumi (2003: 220) explains:

> These uprisings, however, were not nationalistic in nature, but distinctively local, emerging from communities that resisted state conscription and tax

> collection . . . While the nature of the resistance to the state has changed, it would be a mistake to suggest rural Kosovars' resistance to Serbia's colonial state was driven by 'ethnic hatred'.

As someone who grew up in Kosova, I can attest that the main discourses used to explain these uprisings continue to be centred along ethnic lines.

Mulaj (2008) attempts to challenge the monolithic construction of ethnicity by pointing out the differences of opinion which existed within the Albanian population. Highlighting the heterogeneity of ethnicity is important within social work because social workers have often imposed their own knowledge through using mainstream discourses of development as a superficial approach of addressing the complexities of any given society. Related is the lack of attention that social workers have paid to structural inequalities which result from colonial pasts. According to Moosa-Mitha (2014: 203), observing international social work education, there are 'universalizing tendencies of consultant social work educators from the Global North advising on the development of social work education to universities located in the Global South'. In doing so, social workers perpetuate the dichotomies between the Global North and South.

Operationalisation of power through gender mainstreaming practices

State-building practices in Kosova embody colonialist paternalism, as have other state-building practices carried out by Global North countries in Global South countries and 'reaffirms notions of Northern paternalist beneficence and makes invisible ongoing relations of power' (Patil, 2013: 861).

The attempt of the UN and EU to obscure power can be detected in the approach to gender equality in Kosova. The establishment of the quota system has contributed to sexism and other forms of hegemonic oppression, while allowing the international community to pride itself in facilitating gender equality in a patriarchal society. Relying on a quota system does not reflect the complexity of women's involvement in the state-building process because it 'reinforces static conceptions of both peacebuilding and gender' (Cole and Norander, 2011: 41). That is, the quota system allows 'development initiatives [to] often position women's participation as add-ons to existing methods rather than as part of a radical revision of the central concepts of peacebuilding' (2011: 30). Until recently, the state-building process in Kosova assigned women leadership positions in domestic affairs, while limiting their engagement with international structures, thus perpetuating the idea that 'local peacebuilding initiatives are a feminine space while global negotiations remain a masculine space' (ibid.).

The Kosovo Women's Initiative (KWI) reflects this superficial attempt to establish gender equality. The main aims of KWI were to 'promote the recovery of traumatised women, and to redress gender equalities within Kosovo [sic]' (Kalunga-Banda, 2004: 31). However, the planning process for KWI programs was led by the UNHCR, which consisted mostly of international staff, and did not involve any of the Kosovar women who were to benefit from such programs. As a result, most of the KWI beneficiaries reported that 'the projects were not adequately addressing their needs' (2004: 35). The leadership role taken by the UNHCR in KWI perpetuated 'differences between local women and foreigners' (ibid.). None of the initiatives aimed to bring women from both ethnicities together. Such practices do not contribute to a multi-ethnic and inclusive society.

The inadequacy of UN and EU projects which aim to further gender equality becomes most apparent when compared to the work of smaller international organisations. Looking at effective practices pushes us to find ways to challenge the status quo, instead of merely criticising the current system. It is also important not to portray the work of the international community in Kosova as homogeneous.

Kvinna till Kvinna (KtK) is a Swedish-based NGO that partners with women's organisations in post-conflict areas and aims to facilitate partnerships among local feminist movements involved in the state-building process (Cole and Norander, 2011). The organisation embodies feminist practices in several ways. First, KtK does not impose a prescribed list of steps to women's involvement, but instead allows local communities to determine their mode of engagement. Second, KtK focuses 'on the micro-practices of peacebuilding work, including relationship building and attention to women's everyday needs' (2011: 39). Third, KtK sees women's empowerment in Kosova as inseparable from reconciling tensions between Serbian and Albanian women. Fourth, KtK is aware of the importance of involving men when addressing gender issues. In taking these steps, KtK is successful in 'engage[ing] in gender-sensitive post-conflict work that is more complex than simply adding women to the mix . . . the goal in doing this is to create a more inclusive peace that acknowledges the complexities of gender relations' (2011: 40).

In allowing local women to determine their terms of engagement in the state-building process, KtK recognises that 'a feminist approach to peacebuilding reckons with the fact that "human experience is diverse, multi-vocal, and infused with disparate power relations of class, ethnicity and gender-based identities"' (Pollock, 2007 in Cole and Norander, 2011: 44). Such anti-oppressive practices do not impose a Western ideal of gender equality but instead facilitate the development of an 'autonomous [Kosovar] feminist perspective irrespective of ethnicity' (Jafa, 2002: 84). KtK could only do this work because it hired local women who understood the Kosovar context. In doing so, they could marry Western and local knowledges, creating practices that are authentic to Kosova.

The process used by KtK is not linear and has tensions that need highlighting. KtK continues to be present in Kosova 18 years since the war ended, suggesting that local women have not been able to take leadership of gender equality projects, and 'need' their Western counterpart at least financially. This posits Western women as more capable of furthering gender equality in Kosova because they can access resources. It also demonstrates that Western women are impacted by their need for employment, even when working in a sector that ideally requires them to move on.

Local women in Kosova are familiar with hierarchies of oppression because Kosova has been characterised by a hierarchical system which has always placed women's issues as subordinate to the national movement for freedom.

A similar hierarchical structure of oppressions is inherent in the state-building process in Kosova, which has created divisions between Albanian men and women as well as within the women's movement. Only those Kosovar women who support the EU agenda are given a voice, meaning that gender has come to represent 'a category of women only who are aligned by their [the EU's] common struggles (read: determined by donors)' (Cole and Norander, 2011: 31). As a result, women working in the grassroots level often struggle to secure funding. Local women working in the grassroots level cannot relate to local women who work in the decision-making level because the current political elite in Kosova is not representative of marginalised groups and their needs.

These divisions are like the tensions between social workers who work for the state and those who work in grassroots organisations. Those who work for the state have more consistent sources of funding but must abide by government agendas and are often constrained by bureaucracies which limit their engagement with service users; whilst social workers at the grassroots level often use alternative approaches when working with service users because they are less constrained by strict regulations. However, when struggling to find funding, grassroots social workers also must abide by donor preferences.

Conclusion

The practices and discourses used by the UN and EU interventions in Kosova have essentialised and institutionalised ethnicity as a way of erasing the multiple realities which exist in Kosova. Such practices are not limited to Kosova, but have existed and continue to exist throughout the Global South. It appears that current state-building practices are no longer interested in preserving state sovereignty, but on imposing Western ideas of democracy (Uberti, 2013). Westernisation of both Kosova and the Balkans has been justified based on the notion that this region is plagued by a savage nature that needs to be tamed. By blaming the war solely on ethnic hatred, the international community painted people from the Balkans as savages. This enabled the EU to maintain its power over both ethnicities, seeing that 'when individuals identify themselves according to their victimization as a member of an oppressed group, there is less ability for them to see their own agency and power to effect change' (Dei, 2016: 14).

It is possible that social workers have contributed to static notions of identity categories beyond the race-class-gender triad. Precisely, 'some of the new intersectional ways of viewing religious/ethnic/national women's particularity are also prone to cultural essentialism, ignoring the ways in which religious, ethnic, and national cultures are internally heterogeneous, have been constructed historically, and vary across time' (Stasiulis, 2016: 29). Essentialism has not only plagued the theoretical realm of social work, but is also reflected in practice. For example, Todd states:

> The gaze is outward onto classed, gendered, and racialized others who are in need of support, possibly even help, and through offering such help, community workers are able to imagine a space in which they can get outside of oppressive relations so as to avoid being implicated.
>
> (2012: 214)

Todd's observation is important as it draws links between past social work practice and the UN and EU discourses which have framed Balkan peoples as in need of help.

Failing to recognise the heterogeneity of identity categories, such as ethnicity, which are salient in the Global South, 'points to the ongoing myopia of hegemonic concepts of gender when it comes to the cross-border dimensions of gender dynamics, and the continued power of the geographies of colonial modernity' (Patil, 2013: 848). As such, without grounding intersectional analyses in a post-colonial lens, intersectional theorising losses its analytical power. Therefore, a postcolonial intersectional lens, 'which centers on the dialectical relationship between discourse and materiality' (Cole and Norander, 2011: 32), is necessary.

Note

1 Ibrahim Rugova was the first president of Kosova. He served from 1992–2000 and then again from 2002 to 2006. He was a prominent figure in Kosova's struggle for independence from Yugoslavia, and preferred the use of peaceful resistance.

References

Blumi, I. (2003). Ethnic borders to a democratic society in Kosova: The UN's identity card. In F. Bierber and Z. Daskalovski (Eds.), *Understanding the War in Kosovo*. Portland, OR: Frank Cass.

Bogdandy, A., Häußler, S., Hanschmann, F., and Utz, R. (2005). State-building, nation-building, and constitutional politics in post-conflict situations: Conceptual clarifications and an appraisal of different approaches. *Max Planck Yearbook of United Nations Law, 9*: 579–613.

Carton, W. (2008). Beyond the Kosovo status question: The limits to Europe's state-building efforts. *The Interdisciplinary Journal of International Studies, 5*(1): 1–22.

Castles, S., de Haas, H., and Miller, M. J. (2009). *The Age of Migration: International Population Movements in the Modern World*. Hampshire, UK: Palgrave Macmillan.

Cole, C. E. and Norander, S. (2011). From Sierra Leone to Kosovo: Exploring possibilities for gendered peacebuilding. *Women and Language, 34*(1): 29–49.

Crenshaw, K. (1989). Demarginalizing the intersection of race and sex: A Black feminist critique of antidiscrimination doctrine, feminist theory and antiracist politics. *University of Chicago Legal Forum, 40*(1): 139–167.

Deepak, A. C. (2012). Globalization, power and resistance: Postcolonial and transnational feminist perspectives for social work practice. *International Social Work, 55*: 779–793.

Dei, G. S. (2016). The intersectionality of race, class, and gender in the Anti-Racism discourse. In V. Zawilski (Ed.), *Inequality in Canada: A Reader on the Intersections of Gender, Race, and Class*. Don Mills, ON: Oxford University Press.

El–Lahib, Y. (2015). The inadmissible 'Other': Discourses of ableism and colonialism in Canadian immigration. *Journal of Progressive Human Services, 26*: 209–228.

European Union External Action. (2015). *Association/Community of Serb majority municipalities in Kosovo: General principles/main/elements*. Retrieved from: http://eeas.europa.eu/statements-eeas/docs/150825_02_association-community-of-serb-majority-municipalities-in-kosovo-general-principles-main-elements_en.pdf.

European Union External Action. (2016). *European Rule of Law in Kosovo*. Retrieved from: www.eulex-kosovo.eu/.

Jafa, S. (2002). Between identities: Women in post-communist Kosovo. *Indian Journal of Gender Studies, 9*(1): 81–87.

Jönsson, J. H. (2010). Beyond empowerment: Changing local communities. *International Social Work, 53*(3): 393–406.

Kalunga-Banda, A. (2004). Post-conflict programmes for women: Lessons from the Kosovo women's initiative. *Gender and Development, 12*(3): 31–40.

Lemay-Hebert. (2011). The 'empty-shell' approach: The set-up process of international administration in Timor-Leste and Kosovo, its consequences and lessons. *Academia.edu*. Retrieved from: www.academia.edu/676640/The_Empty-Shell_Approach_The_Setup_Process_of_International_Administrations_in_Timor-Leste_and_Kosovo_Its_Consequences_and_Lessons.

Lens, V. (2008). Welfare and work sanctions: Examining discretion on the front lines. *Social Service Review, 82*(2): 197–222.

Levitt, P. and Gluck-Schiller, N. (2004). Conceptualizing simultaneity: A transnational social field perspective on society. *International Migration Review, 38*(3): 1002–1039.

Moosa-Mitha, M. (2014). Using citizenship theory to challenge nationalist assumptions in the construction of international social work education. *International Social Work, 57*(3): 201–208.

Mulaj, K. (2008). Resisting an oppressive regime: The case of Kosovo Liberation Army. *Studies in Conflict and Terrorism, 31*: 1103–1119.

Patil, V. (2013). From patriarchy to intersectionality: A transnational feminist assessment of how far we've really come. *Journal of Women in Culture and Society*, *38*(4): 847–867.

Popova, E. (2015, December 24). Kosovo court approves Serbian municipal association. *Balkan Insight*. Retrieved from: www.balkaninsight.com/en/article/kosovo-constitutional-court-approves-the-association-agreement-with-serbia-12–24–2015.

Purkayastha, B. (2012). Intersectionality in a transnational world. *Gender and Society, 26*(1), 55–66.

Said, E. W. (1978). *Orientalism*. New York: Vintage Books.

Stasilius, D. K. (2016). Feminist intersectional theorizing. In V. Zawilski (Ed.), *Inequality in Canada: A Reader on the Intersections of Gender, Race, and Class*. Don Mills, ON: Oxford University Press.

Tew, J. (2006). Understanding power and powerlessness: Towards a framework for emancipatory practice in social work. *Journal of Social Work, 6*(1): 33–51.

Todd, S. (2011). 'That power and privilege thing': Securing whiteness in community work. *Journal of Progressive Human Services, 22*(2): 117–134.

Uberti, L. J. (2013). Depoliticising the Balkans? International intervention(s) and economic development in Kosovo [Review of the book *From Myth to Symptom: The Case of Kosovo*]. *Capital and Class, 52*(2): 379–385.

United Nations Development Programme. (2012). *Kosovo human development report: Private sector and employment*. Retrieved from: www.ks.undp.org\\content\\kosovo\\en\\home\\library\\human_development\\kosovo-human-development-report-2012.html.

United Nations General Assembly. (2005). *Resolution adopted by the General Assembly: 60/180, The Peacebuilding Commission*. Retrieved from: http://daccessdds.un.org/doc/UNDOC/GEN/N05/498/40/PDF/N0549840.pdf?OpenElement.

United Nations Security Council. (1998, September 23). *Resolution 1199*. Retrieved from: www.un.org/en/ga/search/view_doc.asp?symbol=S/RES/11999.

7 Reflections on the theory and practice of intersectionality

Immigration and health provision services in Brazil

Ilana Mountian and Elena Calvo-Gonzalez

Contextualising the debate: Intersectionality and difference

In this chapter, we discuss aspects of critical research on public health and immigration conducted in Brazil. These examples demonstrate the importance of considering the social context, as well as the impact that past colonial discourses on difference have had on how certain groups are taken as the 'Other'. We argue that an awareness of how these ideas about 'Otherness' intersect with gender, race, class, age and sexuality at a local, on-the-ground level, becoming entrenched within power relations, is central to an understanding of how immigrants are perceived in public policies and health care provision.

Intersectionality has already been established as fundamental for the social sciences, critical theory and social intervention (Crenshaw, 1989, 1991; Burman, 2005; Berger and Guidroz, 2009).[1] There are, however, numerous ways to approach intersectionality, particularly in its practical, on-the-ground uses, producing tensions and debates within and between academic forums and social interventions. Nonetheless, these tensions and debates often destabilise taken-for-granted notions, reproduced both within the sciences, as well as in everyday life.

Intersectionality has long been important to critical feminism, as the traditional understanding of social categories as universal and neutral were seen as functioning in ways that reproduced power relationships, maintaining inequality (Haraway, 1991; Butler, 1999). In contrast, intersectionality emphasises that social categories are situated and relational (Haraway, 1991; Chantler, 2007; Burman, 2005). Although the debate on intersectionality is prominent in the work of contemporary authors (Brah and Phoenix, 2004; Crenshaw, 1989, 1991), it is important to recognise that feminist scholars have long considered gender in relation to other social categories, such as class, race, sexuality, or age (Beauvoir, 1949/1993; Lorde, 1980/1997; Sedgwick, 1991, Benhabibb and Cornell, 1987; Yuval-Davis, 1997). These critical debates were central during the so-called second wave feminism, where essentialist views of the category 'women' were challenged.

While some feminist scholars asserted the importance of accounting for 'women' as a category in academic analyses, there were others, from within the academy and social movements, that questioned essentialist notions of woman (Harding 1986). Here, the debate focused on the importance of incorporating the discussion on gender in academic spaces, while critically questioning how the notion of woman was used. This provides a challenge for research and practice, that is, the importance of deconstructing mainstream understandings of what it is to be a 'woman', whilst keeping the inclusion and recognition of the specificity of gender according to the social context and local struggles, both within academic circles, as well as within public policies and social work.

The recognition, during second wave feminism, that 'woman' was a socially created category, and that 'women' were not inferior to men, had a crucial impact in a number of academic settings in several countries, such as the UK and the US (Berger and Guidroz, 2009; Saavedra and Nogueira, 2006). This dynamic was also present in social movements, during the 1970s both in European and US settings as well as some countries in the Global South, such as Brazil, with struggles towards women's autonomy, right to work and increased presence in politics. Nonetheless, a specific and restrictive understanding of the category woman was still at stake. This limitation was raised by Black Feminists (Lorde, 1980/1997; hooks, 1984/2005; Mohanty, 1994; Nayak, 2015), Marxist Feminists (Benhabib and Cornel, 1987; Federici, 1975), Post-Colonial and Subaltern studies (Spivak, 1988), and Queer studies (Butler, 1999), as well as by diverse social movements. The differences and the invisibility of the demands of diverse groups of women, were highlighted by these groups, producing important critiques on the universal understanding of the category 'woman', influencing how history, politics and science were understood.

In the case of Brazil, this process of contesting women's social position was linked to wider processes of political change, struggling for general political rights, as well as more specific demands from organised civil society segments such as: anti-racist initiatives from organised Black women movements, LGBTQI movements and grassroots organisations (Saffioti, 1969/2013; Alves and Pitanguy, 1991; Gonzales, 1984; Rohden, 2001). Debates around representation and identity politics have been seen in academic and activist settings in Brazil (Gonzales, 1984).

This is important for the Brazilian context, where there is still a lack of feminist, anti-sexist and anti-racist approaches in public policies, despite some initiatives developed in the past 10 years. These initiatives include: the development of projects to criminalise violence against women, programmes that aim to stop homophobia, transphobia, LGBTQIphobia and sexism in schools, and the implementation of racial quotas in some universities, among others. These initiatives, however, are not yet well established and still face opposition from certain political groups. For example, the implementation of anti-sexist and anti-LGBTQIphobia in schools has encountered several obstacles, particularly from religious Christian and Evangelical fundamentalist groups (Mountian, 2013b).

While there are various ways to approach intersectionality, a critical view of these inter-related categories is still necessary. We highlight how some of these debates have been put forward in postcolonial settings, and bringing another layer of analysis, we argue for the importance of considering the dynamics of colonial heritage. In particular, the specificities of how power relations operate within postcolonial contexts more precisely, to account for the colonial past and its contemporary discursive repetition, for critical analysis on the reproductions of power relations regarding the intersectionality of gender, race, sexuality and class.

To account for colonial history within the Brazilian context has proven to be a challenge for academic research and social movements alike. While a number of studies have pointed out the importance of taking into account Brazilian history for the analysis of how intersections between race, gender, and class operate within this context, revealing how discourses reproduce and maintain specific social positions (Carneiro, 2003; Gonzales, 1984; Nascimento, 2003; Santos, Schucman and Martins 2012), there is still a need for critical research on the intersectionality of colonial relations and their current discursive reproduction within the matrix of domination (Hill-Collins, 2000:18).

Contextualising the debate: History and discourse

Intersectionality has been seen to be central for critical research by showing how the categories of gender, race, sexuality, and class are intertwined. Nevertheless, there are still on-the-ground difficulties in accounting for these aspects in research. There remains a need to avoid falling for the analytical trap of separating them and presenting them in a hierarchical way: for example, presenting gender as being the main category for discrimination before race, or vice versa.

Intersectionality questions how social categories relate to one another in research and public policy. In these, once again, either gender or race or class is commonly neutralised, seen as yet one more category to add on, and not as a structural category that intrinsically operates through and is inextricably intertwined with other categories. This can be seen, for example, in the importance of a critical analysis of the work on gender and immigration, where discourses on 'culture' are at times used in a way that makes gender a natural trait and culture a fixed signifier (Mountian and Rosa, 2015; Philips, 2010). Burman, Smailes and Chantler (2004) highlight this in relation to debates on domestic violence in the UK. When violence is seen as having a 'cultural' origin, gender becomes invisible. On the other hand, when violence against women and girls' services focuses primarily on gender, the issue of racism for Black women becomes invisible or marginalised. A similar phenomenon happens when individuals requiring assistance from public services are 'Othered' within the services. This issue will be taken up in this chapter in regards to immigration and health services in Sao Paulo, Brazil, to illustrate how past colonial relations have contributed to shaping the landscape of contemporary experiences of oppression.

Power relations are expressed in different and diverse ways, and the deconstruction of power relations in 'postcolonial' settings are crucial for critical perspectives. Based on feminist critiques and anti-racist perspectives, amongst which postcolonial and recent decolonial studies (Ballestrin, 2013), we offer some examples and considerations regarding the importance of power relations within academic settings and social interventions. The argument presented is that the application of intersectionality must account for the context of past colonial relations.

In the case of Brazil, it is crucial to question how past colonial discourses still operate and influence power dynamics contemporarily. An intersectional lens, through which we can look at Brazil's history and the constitution of its power relations, helps explicate how the categories of gender, race, and social position were, from its early days, affecting the everyday making of the country. Brazil was colonised in the 16th century, after the arrival in 1500 of an expedition led by Portuguese Pedro Álvares Cabral. Implementing an extractionist colonial project, the Portuguese initially enslaved Indigenous people, with numbers dwindling up until its official abolition in the 18th century (Ramos, 1997). With the increase in Atlantic slave trade, Indigenous slaves were progressively substituted by the millions of enslaved African people to its shores, who were forced to work on its sugarcane plantations, gold and diamond mines, as well as acting as domestic slaves. In these first centuries of the colonisation of Brazil, the basis for contemporary racist and sexist dynamics, and moral and religious values were constituted, inextricably linked and interdependent. As Freyre (1946) explains in '*The Masters and the Slaves*', these relationships were based on the absolute patriarchal-based power of the Master, who ruled and exerted his will over all the other members of his family (women and children), as well as over slaves. According to Freyre, this was done through an ambiguous and balanced equilibrium of dichotomies such as closeness and distance, and of love and violence.

The slavemaster's rule became, for Freyre (1946), the basis on which Brazilian society was established. The interplay of hierarchical social categories is foregrounded. On the one hand, the Portuguese slavemasters incorporated not only some of the habits of these enslaved people into their customs, affecting cultural practices, but also, and more crucially, they also incorporated into their households some of the offspring they had with enslaved women. The slave-master held absolute power over white women, their children, and enslaved Black women and men. While this power was deemed to be absolute, in practice it led to certain instances of accommodation, in strategies for slave survival that included, for instance, the acceptance of the incorporation of enslaved Black women into the masters' house as domestic slaves and at times as 'illicit' sexual partners. This planted the seed for the process of admixture and miscegenation that Freyre described as Brazil's defining characteristic. However, as Freyre points out, despite this incorporation, Portuguese male slavemasters maintained a hierarchical and violent control over enslaved African women and men. This illustrates the importance of incorporating the temporal and local context of colonial relations into the analysis and application of intersectionality in the Brazilian context. Considering the importance of historical power relations in all contexts enables an analysis of the inherent tensions and complex contradictions of subjugated subject positions. Inclusion of the colonial context in intersectionality pushes against a reductionist binary or hierarchical formulation.

The Catholic Church played an important role in the process of legitimising the position of the Portuguese slavemasters in the colonisation of Brazil, particularly through the catechisation of Indigenous people by the Jesuits (Fausto, 1996). During the years of 1808 to 1821 the King Dom João VI moved the Portuguese court to Brazil, fleeing Napoleon's invasion and forming the United Kingdom of Portugal, Brazil and Algarves (since 1815), and in 1822, Dom Pedro I, his son and regent prince, declared independence from Portugal, instituting the Empire of Brazil.

In 1888 Brazil abolished slavery, the last country to officially end it in the Americas. A year later Brazil became a republic, but few people had the right to vote: women and the illiterate (the majority of the population) could not vote. During this period, while the sugar plantations entered into decline, the boom of coffee plantations in the Southeast of Brazil, and rubber extraction in the North, in the Amazon region meant that there was still a strong need for labour force. However, the Brazilian elites did not consider that the ex-enslaved Black population was well suited for paid labour, given that they were seen as idle, indolent, and not given to work unless forced. This initiated a process of official State promotion of European immigration, deemed to be more suited to paid labour, and a progressive criminalisation of idleness that contributed to the disenfranchisement of the recently freed enslaved population. In the late 19th century, under the influence of scientific racism doctrines, and the desire of Brazilian elites for a 'whitened', European future, these State programs were increased, resulting in over 4.5 million European immigrants arriving to the country. Their arrival, however, did not result in the 'whitened' country its elites had dreamt of: in the last Brazilian census more than half of its population declared themselves to be 'non-whites'.

Alongside the initial European immigration waves directed towards recruiting labour for the coffee plantations, later immigration directed itself more to the cities, particularly of the Southeast. At the beginning of the 20th century a strong process of industrialisation affected particularly Southeastern cities such as Sao Paulo. From 1930 to 1945 Getúlio Vargas ruled Brazil, under military support, with full dictatorship powers, while he also ruled the country from 1951 to 1954 as a democratically elected president. From 1964 to 1985 Brazil lived under a military regime. After the military dictatorship, the country started a process of democratisation through direct political vote, a period in which feminism, anti-racist movements and other social movements became progressively more active and organised.

Despite the actions of social movements, as well as the implementation of public policies and legislation aimed at reducing inequalities, there is still a resistance within Brazilian society in admitting the effects of colonisation and slavery. Intersectionality supports an understanding of how in contemporary Brazilian society, there are still reduced socio-economic opportunities for women, LGBTQI people, Indigenous and non-white people, particularly 'Black' and 'brown' women, and a lack of awareness of how sexism and racism is reproduced and operates socially. This is exemplified by public polls[2] that deny the existence of racism in

Brazil, or the widespread opposition to decriminalising abortion. Denying these power relations not only invisibilises several types of violence, but helps to perpetuate them, for example, through the type of public policies approved or legislations passed.

Inequality amongst intersectional social categories is seen in all levels in society. While Brazil has one of the strongest economies worldwide, the 7th largest in 2011 (IMF and IBGE), it is still marked by huge inequalities in terms of income and social welfare. In terms of Gini index parameters, Brazil stands for one of the ten worst patterns of income distribution (0,549) among countries analysed by PNUD (United Nations Programme for Development) in 2011 (Mountian, 2013a). Currently, Brazil is one of the most violent countries in the world; the Ministry of Health reported 59,080 homicides in Brazil in the year of 2015 (Cerqueira et al. for IPEA and FBSP, 2017), particularly of Black people (Waiselfsz, 2016), and amongst these, of young, poor, and Black males (Waiselfsz, 2011). Brazil is often cited as a country with the highest numbers of homicide of women (Waiselfsz, 2015) and transgender people (TGEU, 2016), followed by high numbers of violence against LGBTQI people, and violence and displacement of Indigenous people (CIMI, 2015).

Taking this context into account, this chapter argues that an intersectional approach needs to be conceptualised and applied in and through a rigorous understanding of how the historical colonial experience of Brazil affects contemporary contexts, and how it features in current processes of 'Othering' certain population segments. Using a case study about how contemporary immigration appears in the implementation of public policies for this group, we highlight how these power relations are reflected in health services.

Putting theory into practice: Public policies and intersectionality

In this section we will look at intersectional dynamics of social categories in the case study on immigration in Brazil, as such it will be seen how these categories overlap and operate in the production of Othering processes. It is important to highlight that these dynamics are structural and reproduced through power relations within institutions and social interactions.

Gender, race and sexuality are categories that are often naturalised and invisibilised in discourse, and to question how and when they become visible is vital to social work (Burman, Smailes and Chantler, 2004). When do we find their absence normalised and their presence pathologised (Phoenix, 1987)? We provide some examples from the research on immigration, gender and public health in Sao Paulo, Brazil (Mountian, 2016). In 2016 Mountian participated as coordinator of a city council project named '*Política de saúde para imigrantes e refugiados no município de Sao Paulo*' (Health policy for immigrants and refugees in the city of Sao Paulo) in partnership with PAHO/WHO (Pan American Health Organization/World Health Organization). The project entailed workshops conducted by the immigrants and refugees themselves, aimed at health practitioners. There were around 30 public health units and four hospitals in Sao Paulo visited by the group that Mountian coordinated and participated, where three workshops were conducted in each of these institutions. The objective of this project was to sensibilise health workers around issues of xenophobia, racism, and sexism and to promote a health network. These workshops provided debates, information, and materials for the health practitioners and for the refugee and immigrant populations to access health services. The case study here is primarily based on Mountian's observations of the workshops.

It is worth noting that these health workers were actively engaged in providing adequate services to immigrants, in many instances having to make use of creative strategies to overcome deep institutional structural problems and lack of resources. In spite of this eagerness to provide their best service possible, some shortcomings were observed, shortcomings that are related to unspoken issues about the power dynamics in which the work of these professionals was set. While we observed individuals in our research, our target gaze was not them as individuals *per se*, but the structural discourses reproduced within health care provision in which these individuals were immersed.

First, it is relevant to consider how xenophobic discourses operate differently according to the groups that are being considered as 'minority'. In the analysis of the results of this research, we found a specific reproduction of racism within the discourse of who is considered 'immigrant' in Brazil: often they were Black people coming from African countries and Haiti, and Indigenous people, mainly from Bolivia and Peru. This is related to the continuing presence of historical discourses from the 19th and 20th century that valued Europeanness as a desired trait for Brazil's future, favouring the immigration of these Europeans and blocking or not seeing with good eyes the immigration of people from countries seen as not having a 'white' population. Looking at these issues through the lens of intersectionality, giving consideration to their position at the intersection between race, ethnicity, gender, and class, the reproduction of Brazilian colonial discourses is interrogated. Those coming from European countries and the United States of America were commonly referred to as *gringos*, with a more positive reception. This reproduces racialised and racist relations firmly rooted in the history of Brazil, such as the belief that 'Blacks' are less inclined to work, or the hierarchical ideas of beauty that put European facial features and white skin tone at the top, which many immigrants face and denounce in the encounter with the Brazilian population.

Second, many health services felt that were not prepared to receive immigrants, with stated concerns ranging from the lack of translators, to the lack of appreciation of differences relating to beliefs and values, impacting directly on the way that health and the body is understood. The health practitioners tended to show their frustration at the lack of adherence to prescribed health treatments. Several issues are raised here, such as the lack of adequate funding of the public health services in Brazil, and the lack of awareness by the health practitioners of the immigrant population's needs. Chronic understaffing issues within the public health service sometimes had consequences in regards to understanding and engaging with the patient, for example: not enough attention was paid to listening to the patient; failure to pick up the specificities of the personal history of the patient; failure to understand how the patient situation in their social, economic, political and geographical contexts affects their lived experience of health; and failure to understand the patient's complex and problematic relationship with the health system. Further, the effects of the hardships faced by immigrants were not always considered, risking naturalising exceptional circumstances. This was seen in other research projects (Mountian and Rosa, 2015) when practitioners tend to resort to quick mental health diagnosis.

Third, it is important to challenge racist and xenophobic beliefs found in health institutions and to identify how they impact health care provision and treatment. For example, in the workshops conducted, some medical practitioners stated their belief that immigrants brought tuberculosis into Brazil, rather than considering the possibility that they most probably acquired the disease after they arrived. Tuberculosis is a disease commonly associated with poverty and inadequately cramped living and working conditions, all of which historically in Brazil, since colonial times, are associated with poverty and non-white populations. In the case of Bolivians, not only do many live in inadequate housing, but they are also exposed to the disease in overcrowded, irregular sweatshops that do not meet labour laws. Some of these sweatshop owners enact within them slave relationships that, although different from historical colonial slavery by being outside the legal framework, are nevertheless influenced by power relations that can be traced back to the slave system. These working conditions could also be seen in past colonial contexts of slavery times: workers often were not allowed to leave their working/living quarters, had their passports confiscated by the sweatshop managers or owners, and worked long hours without a break.

These working conditions that reproduce historical Brazilian colonial relations, meeting at times the modern legal definition of slave-work within Brazil's contemporary labour laws, intersected with another issue that affected healthcare provision for Bolivians: that of ideas about gender, class, femininity, and the place of women in the workforce. These ideas affected how Bolivian mothers were seen as responsible for exposing their children to tuberculosis. The practices of Bolivian mothers having to keep children with them while they are at work, due to the lack of accessible childcare, fear, and the extreme length of their working days, were often blamed by health professionals either directly or indirectly for their children's ill health. This is an example of how historical colonial discourses may have impacted these contemporary structural power relations, as dominant discourses were placing minoritised groups in particular oppressive positions. In the case of the Bolivian mothers and their children, the intersection of discriminatory gendered and racialised viewpoints have been seen to have an impact on the ways that their health and work were considered, as an idealised image of motherhood is present, affecting how some healthcare professionals are oblivious to social living conditions of Bolivian mothers and their children.

There are other medical conditions, such as sexually transmitted infections (STIs), that are also gendered and sexualised in everyday medical discourses. Teles (2007) highlights the risks of sexual and domestic violence suffered by Bolivian women who work under these conditions, who may have their passports removed by their landlords, and do not feel safe to seek medical help. Teles (2007) highlights the increase in STIs in immigrant women in the region where immigrants work. There is a need to recognize intrinsic classist, racist, xenophobic, and sexist views within health services, which is also a claim from LGBTQI communities and Black and poor women in Brazil. This recognition is important to improve health services and provisions as well as working towards a decolonised approach to minoritised groups.

Fourth, a range of issues regarding the intersection of gender, religion, race, and culture is often not recognised. This lack of recognition is reflected in service provision. For example, in the research, it became apparent that some Muslim women did not want to be seen by male doctors. Issues of domestic violence were at times taken to be part of 'cultural' differences: it was common to hear the idea that women from other Latin American, particularly Bolivian women, were more submissive than Brazilian ones (Mountian, 2016). Critically analysing this discourse, it becomes clear that the patriarchal context in which women are placed is not taken into consideration. Further, it is relevant to look at how this discourse was employed, as it seems to describe immigrant women as the 'Other', not as 'modern', as 'Us' (McClintock, 1995). It is crucial for social work and health services to consider past colonial discourses and the patriarchal context that both immigrant and Brazilian women are positioned in.

Finally, issues regarding sexuality were hardly mentioned by health practitioners in the research conducted, and the understanding of how LGBTQIphobia impacts on immigration and health was not recognised. This can be set within a patriarchal context that feeds off a historical continuity from colonial gender relations. This ranges from the need of people to leave their countries because of persecution for their sexual identities and practices, to the lack of an adequate environment and practices in health institutions to attend to these subjects. This example demonstrates how social categories must be considered in intersection.

This lack of recognition of how LGBTQIphobia and sexism are present and affect peoples' lives is seen not only in health policies for immigrants, but also in how public policies overall take into account these issues in their services and initiatives. This includes the need to consider not only the effects of LGBTQIphobia and sexism on individuals and the LGBTQIphobia that many subjects suffer in health provisions, but also how sexuality and gender intersect with other social categories such as class, race, or country of origin. Previous research (Mountian, 2013b) showed that in some cases the transphobia that *travestis* (a local category in Brazil) and transsexual women suffer in Brazil contributed to their migration out of Brazil. Moreover, this research (Mountian, 2015) highlighted that specific demands of older transgender women and *travesties* such as, for example, the health consequences of non-medical industrial silicone applications, or of the use of hormones bought over the counter and without medical supervision, were hardly taken into account by public policies in Brazil.

Intersectional considerations

This chapter has presented reflections on the importance of intersectionality for public policies and social interventions with specific reference to health care provision. These reflections arise not only out of observation of how these policies are implemented, but also out of academic research in this area. The examples in this chapter argue for the importance of considering power relations to account for intersectional analysis. We have used the social context of Brazil to demonstrate how past colonial discourses are reproduced in the contemporary exclusion and marginalisation of specific groups.

Intersectionality is key for critical social work and theory, as it implies a continuous reflexivity on how social categories appear in discourse. Crucially, the position of the researcher also has to be considered (Mountian, forthcoming). Intersectionality for social work practice provokes a debate on the limits and tensions of historically constructed power relations, which are seen here as constitutive of the process of producing the 'Other'. At the same time, it is within this deconstruction that other possibilities of discourses are envisaged.

The tensions and debates explored point to the need to consider power dynamics within the social context for analysis of the intersectional social categories. There is a need for further research that accounts for these elements, including how their historical development affects contemporary practices. A view on how power operates in postcolonial contexts was also highlighted and points out to us the need to identify and challenge how colonial discourses are reproduced in research and institutions. The experience of immigrants in Brazil, considered part of a 'minority', has implications in terms of psychological and institutional violence that reveal intersecting dynamics of race, gender, sexuality, age, and class.

Past discourses are present, albeit in a reconfigured way, in the construction of the 'Other'. The ways in which social inequality and its distribution across race, gender, sexuality, and class lines feeds from past power configurations that are then renewed in contemporary terms needs to be considered, with Brazil standing as one of the countries with higher levels of social inequality.

The tensions and debates discussed here aim to open an area for critical perspective, as specific strategies and an ongoing process of reflexivity on power relations are required. There is still a need to challenge the construction and reproduction of the 'Other' in discourse, and how this alterity affects everyday life, including public service provision and public policy design.

The examples in this chapter demonstrate how intersectional social categories have to be accounted for. Social workers and researchers must consider the reproduction of past colonial discourses to recognise the 'Othering' process. The studies highlighted (Mountian, 2015) a number of invisibilised or over-visibilised intersections between social categories which impact health provision, such as the category of immigrant in mainstream discourses; the need to acknowledge the immigrants' background and different understandings on the health and the body; the need to consider the social conditions where immigrants live and work and the risks that women and their children might encounter; and the effects of LGBTQIphobia on the immigrants trajectory and in health care.

Intersectionality challenges researchers and social workers to keep a continuous critical view on the colonial characteristics of research practices and social interventions, from the design to the implementation of public policies. A socially and historically contextualised view on intersectionality is a strategic tool towards decolonising processes.

Notes

1 These debates, based mainly though not restricted to the work of authors based in Europe and North America, as well as other authors from South America, had a wide circulation in different academic areas in Brazil.

2 See http://csbh.fpabramo.org.br/o-que-fazemos/editora/teoria-e-debate/edicoes-anteriores/sociedade-discriminacao-racial-e-preconceit and http://congressoemfoco.uol.com.br/noticias/vox-populi-82-da-populacao-e-contra-aborto/.

References

Alves, B.M. and Pitanguy, J. (1991). *O que é Feminismo*. São Paulo: Editora Brasiliense.

Ballestrin, L. (2013). 'América Latina e o giro decolonial'. *Revista Brasileira de Ciência Política*, 11 (May–August): 89–117.

Beauvoir, S. (1949/1993). *The Second Sex*. London: Everyman's Library.

Benhabib, S. and Cornell, D. (1987). *Feminismo como crítica da modernidade*. Rio de Janeiro: Rosa dos Tempos.

Berger, M.T. and Guidroz, K. (2009). *The Intersectional Approach: Transforming the Academy through Race, Class and Gender*. Chapel Hill, NC: The University of North Carolina Press.

Brah, A. and Phoenix, A. (2004). 'Ain't I a woman? Revisiting intersectionality'. *Journal of International Women's Studies*, 5 (3): 75–86.

Burman, E. (2005). 'Engendering culture in psychology'. *Theory & Psychology*, 15 (4): 527–548.

Burman, E., Smailes, S. and Chantler, K. (2004). '"Culture" as a barrier to service provision and delivery: Domestic violence services for minoritized women'. *Critical Social Policy*, 24 (3): 332–357.

Butler, J. (1999). *Gender Trouble – Feminism and the Subversion of Identity*. London: Routledge.

Carneiro, S. (2003). 'Mulheres em movimento'. *Estudos avançados*, 17 (49): 117–133.

Cerqueira, D., Lima, R.S., Bueno, S., Valencia, L.I., Hanashiro, O., Machado, P.H.G. and Lima, A.S. (2017). *Atlas da violência*. Brasília: Instituto de Pesquisa Econômica Aplicada (IPEA) and Fórum Brasileiro de Segurança Pública (FBSP).

Chantler, K. (2007). 'Border crossings: Nationhood, gender, culture and violence'. *International Journal of Critical Psychology*, 20: 138–166.

Conselho Indigenista Missionário (CIMI, 2015). *Violência contra os povos indígenas no Brasil*. www.cimi.org.br/pub/relatorio2015/relatoriodados2015.pdf.

Crenshaw, K.W. (1989). 'Demarginalising the intersection of race and sex: A Black feminist critique of antidiscrimination doctrine, feminist theory and antiracist politics'. *University of Chicago Legal Forum*, 140: 139–167.

Crenshaw, K.W. (1991). 'Mapping the margins: Intersectionality, identity politics, and violence against women of color'. *Stanford Law Review*, 43: 1241–1299.

Fanon, F. (1952/2008). *Black Skin White Masks*. New York: Grove Press.

Fausto, B. (1996). *História do Brasil*. São Paulo: EDUSP.

Federici, S. (1975). *Wages against Housework*. Bristol, UK: Falling Wall Press Ltd.

Freyre, G. (1946). *The Masters and the Slaves: A Study in the Development of Brazilian Civilization*. New York: Knopf.

Gonzales, L. (1984). 'Racismo e sexismo na cultura brasileira'. *Revista Ciências Sociais Hoje*, ANPOCS (ed.), pp. 223–244.

Harding, S. (1986). 'Is there a feminist method?' *Feminism and Methodology*, Harding, S. (ed.), pp. 1–14. Buckingham, UK: Open University Press.

Haraway, D. (1991). *Simians, Cyborg and Women – The Reinvention of Nature*. London: Free Association Books.

Hill-Collins, P. (2000). *Black Feminist Thought: Knowledge, Consciousness, and the Politics of Empowerment*. 2nd ed., London: Routledge.

hooks, b. (1984/2005). 'Black women: Shaping feminist theory'. *Feminist Theory: A Philosophical Anthology* Cudd, A. and Andreasen, R.O. (eds). Oxford, UK: Blackwell.

Lorde, A. (1980/1997). 'Age, race, class and sex – Women redefining difference'. *Dangerous Liaisons: Gender, Nation and Postcolonial Perspectives*, McClintock, A., Mufti, A. and Shohat, E. (eds), pp. 374–380. Minneapolis, MN: Minnesota University Press.

Lorde, A. (1984/2007). 'The master's tools will never dismantle the master's house'. *Sister Outsider: Essays and Speeches*, Lord, A. (ed.), pp. 110–113. Berkeley, CA: Crossing Press.

Mbembe, M. (2001). 'As Formas Africanas de Auto-Inscrição'. *Estudos Afro-Asiáticos*, 23 (1): 171–209.

McClintock, A. (1995). *Imperial Leather: Race, Gender and Sexuality in the Colonial Contest*. London: Routledge.

Mohanty, C.T. (1994). 'Under Western eyes: Feminist scholarship and colonial discourses'. *Colonial Discourse and Post-Colonial Theory. A Reader*, Williams, P. and Chrisman, L. (eds), pp. 196–220. New York: Columbia University Press.

Mountian, I. (2013a). *Cultural Ecstasies: Drugs, Gender and Social Imaginary*. London: Routledge.

Mountian, I. (2013b). *A critical analysis of public policies on education and LGBT rights in Brazil*. Sussex, UK: Sussex University Institute of Development Studies https://opendocs.ids.ac.uk/opendocs/bitstream/handle/123456789/3614/ER61.pdf?sequence=1.

Mountian, I. (2015). 'Aspectos sobre travestilidade e envelhecimento: História, corpo e imigração'. *Quaderns de Psicologia*, 17 (3): 31–44.

Mountian, I. (2016). *Interseccionalidade e alteridade: Trajetórias de imigrantes e redes de apoio*. Post-doctoral research, funded by CAPES/PNPD.

Mountian, I. (forthcoming). 'Reflexões sobre metodologias críticas em pesquisa: Interseccionalidade, reflexividade e situacionalidade'. *Revista Psicologia Política*.

Mountian, I. and Rosa, M.D. (2015). 'O outro: Análise crítica de discursos sobre imigração e gênero'. *Revista Psicologia USP*, 26 (2): 152–160.

Nascimento, E.L. (2003). *O sortilégio da cor: Identidade, raça e gênero no Brasil*. São Paulo: Selo Negro.

Nayak, S. (2014). *Race, Gender and the Activism of Black Feminist Theory: Working with Audre Lorde*. London: Routledge.

Phillips, A. (2010). *Gender & Culture*. Cambridge, UK: Polity Press.

Phoenix, A. (1987). 'Theories of gender and black families'. *Gender Under Scrutiny: New Inquiries in Education*, Weinger, G. and Arnot, M. (eds), pp. 50–63. London: Open University Press.

Ramos, André RF. (1997). 'A escravidão do indígena, entre o mito e novas perspectivas de debates.' *Revista de Estudos e Pesquisas*, 1 (1): 241–265.

Rohden, F. (2001). *Uma ciência da diferença: Sexo e gênero na medicina da mulher*. 2nd edition. Rio de Janeiro: Editora FIOCRUZ, Antropologia & Saúde collection.

Saavedra, L. and Nogueira, C. (2006). 'Memórias sobre o feminismo na psicologia: Para a construção de memórias futuras'. *Memorandum*, 11, 113–127.

Saffioti, H. (1969/2013). *A mulher na sociedade de classes: Mito e realidade*. Sao Paulo: Expressão Popular.

Santos, A.O., Schucman, L.V. and Martins, H.V. (2012). 'Breve histórico do pensamento brasileiro sobre relações étnico raciais'. *Psicologia, Ciência e Profissão*, 32: 166–175.

Sedgwick, E.K. (1991). *Epistemology of the Closet*. Los Angeles, CA: University of California Press.

Spivak, G.C. (1988). 'Can the subaltern speak?'. *Marxism and the Interpretation of Culture*, Nelson, C. and Grossberg, L. (eds), pp. 271–313. Basingstoke, UK: Macmillan.

Teles, M.A.A. (2007). 'As imigrantes bolivianas em São Paulo: O silêncio insuportável!'. *Tráfico de Pessoas e Violência Sexual*, Leal, M.L.P., Leal, M.F.P. and Libório, R.M.C. (eds), pp. 35–43. Brasília: Grupo de Pesquisa sobre Violência, Exploração Sexual e Tráfico de Mulheres, Crianças e Adolescentes – VIOLES/SER/Universidade de Brasília.

Transgender Europe Monitoring project (2016). http://transrespect.org/wp-content/uploads/2016/05/TvT_TMM_IDAHOT2016_Map_EN.pdf.

Waiselfisz, J.J. (2011). *Mapa da Violência: Os Jovens do Brasil*. Brasília: Ministério da Justiça, Instituto Sangari.

Waiselfisz, J.J. (2015). *Mapa da Violência: Homicídio de mulheres no Brasil*. Brasília: Flacso.

Waiselfsz, J.J. (2016). *Mapa da Violência: Homicídios por armas de fogo no Brasil*. Brasília: Flacso.

Yuval-Davis, N. (1997). *Gender & Nation*. London: Sage.

Part 2

Realisations of the activism of intersectionality

8 Revolutionary spaces?

[Re]imagining and transforming work to end violence against Black women and girls

Dorett Jones and Marai Larasi

Introduction

This auto-ethnography seeks to [re]imagine non-statutory social work practice as a critical site for transformation in work to end violence against Black women and girls. We draw on our experiences as Black women working, in the Black women-led, ending violence against women and girls sector in the UK. We reflect on the tensions and constraints that have emerged in the context of mainstreaming.

We also begin a journey of [re]imagining, and ask questions such as: 'Is it possible for us to [re]claim social work practices which operate outside of the domain of 'casework'?' 'How can we build collective Black women spaces of recovery and accountability, while disrupting the impact of white, patriarchal, colonial social work practices?' 'Is it possible to DEcolonise social work?' 'What would those spaces look like, and would we survive the psychic ruptures and practical challenges of removing the 'walls' of Social Work?' As Gray et al. state:

> Decolonizing Social Work requires that the profession acknowledge its complicity and ceases its participation in colonizing projects, openly condemns the past and continuing effects of colonialism, collaborates with Indigenous Peoples to engage in decolonizing activities against public and private colonizing projects, and seeks to remove the often subtle vestiges of colonization from theory and practice.
>
> (Gray et al., 2013: 7)

> Our focus is the experiences of African-Caribbean women and girls in an attempt to, as Back states, 'point to those things that cannot be said . . .' as 'It is in silence that inequitable relations and gross political complicities are hidden'.
>
> (Back, 2007: 166)

Excavating Blackness

We use the contested term 'Black'. While it has political utility amongst many anti-racist activists, 'Black' is not always claimed by those very 'communities' it seeks to connect with and describe. Increasingly the terms 'Black and minority ethnic' (BME) or 'Black, Asian and minority ethnic' (BAME), which emerged in the context of race relations thinking and policy, are used to describe people who are minoritised based on ethnicity. These terms focus primarily on people originating in the 'Global South',[1] also referred to as 'people of colour'.[2] Both BME and BAME are often used as homogenous terms that fail to address differences of experience, patterns of migration and treatment within race relations policy. The term 'minority ethnic' also disavows the processes of minoritisation, a legacy of colonisation (Burman, 2005: 533).

Many of us use terminology, despite our reservations, as shorthand, and to avoid engaging with the contestations around who is 'Black'. This site of tension relates to how we are named / called and known. Although this is one of the ways that we 'survive' racism, it does harm to 'self'. We participate in language that feels subordinating, coping with a sense of being less than; and thus, as with all survival strategies, there is a cost.

We use the term Black politically, 'as a phenomenon of assertive decolonisation' (Gilroy, 2002: xiv). We assert Blackness as a site of connection and resistance allowing the excavation and telling of journeys without the silencing. As British, African-Caribbean women, we are rooted in the struggles and strengths of Black women and girls; a place of deep political and psychic connection to our Black Sisters everywhere.

The landscape: Contextualising work to end violence against women and girls in the UK

Over the last two decades, violence against women and girls[3] (VAWG) has received increasing attention within public policy, mainstream media and within society more broadly. Information about high-profile figures accused of, or implicated in sexual harassment and abuse has forced the issue of VAWG into public consciousness in an unprecedented way. In the last ten years, inquiries into child sexual exploitation, sexual harassment and sexual violence in schools (Berelowitz et al., 2012)[4] highlight the failures of society to respond appropriately. Research conducted in 70 countries including the UK highlight that this shift is the result of the activism and advocacy of feminist movements and associated organisations and services which have pushed for legislative and other changes (Htun and Weldon, 2012). Yet the specialist ending VAWG sectors, at the forefront of these changes, are marginalised[5] within a neo-liberal, market-driven context. Ironically, this dynamic mirrors the power relations at play in VAWG. The State exercises its power and control over women's social justice organisations, through restrictive funding regimes, silencing, exclusion of dissenting voices and forced closure of services. Feminist demands for State accountability, including the resourcing of independent ending VAWG provision, have been misused to legitimise State control. Critically, despite the centrality of Black feminist activism, advocacy and service provision, in the development of ending violence against Black women and girls work in the UK, we remain 'othered' and on the fringe.

To understand how service responses to VAWG have developed in the UK, it is important to acknowledge the way that violence is framed in Western societies. What is defined as violence is constituted by power: 'First, the interpretation of any given act as "violent" lies not within the act itself but in how powerful groups conceptualize it' (Hill-Collins, 2013: 190).

Policy, programming and practice priorities reflect which lives and bodies matter, which attitudes and behaviours are deemed harmful and who is doing what to whom. VAWG is defined in the realm of the 'individual' and the 'interpersonal' based on 'incidents' of violence at the hands of a known perpetrator (usually a male partner) or a stranger (a predatory individual operating outside of the agreed norm). Ideas of state-led or state-sanctioned violence, for example the violence meted out through colonisation, is largely absent from understandings of perpetration and victimisation. The brutality of racism and homophobia/heteronormativity is often absent from discourses on VAWG. Policy, programming and common-sense narratives around VAWG have been dominated by domestic violence,[6] limited to the idea of 'wife battering'.

UK, non-statutory services which focus on responding to VAWG are funded largely by the State or by charitable foundations. Services designed to operate independently of the State are often forced to engage with restrictive State commissioning structures that involve high levels of monitoring and scrutiny. Notions of independence are limited because the autonomy of funded organisations is curtailed and controlled. This 'structural violence' (Sanders-McDonagh et al., 2016), through State control over women's organisations, mirrors the power dynamics in VAWG. Providers of support are trapped in structures and systems that heavily influence or dictate the work that they are able to do with women and girls. This means a woman seeking support, from a local organisation whose conditions of funding demand a certain process and a pre-defined set of outcomes, is effectively only one step away from the State. In addition, independence from the State is complicated in the interaction between feminist practice and the criminal justice system. Demands for State action around VAWG, contextualised in human rights framings, have consistently included the importance of 'holding perpetrators to account'; an accountability that in the Eurocentric feminist imagination is located mainly within the criminal justice system. The State's effectiveness around addressing VAWG is partly measured through the way women and girls are treated as victims and witnesses, the numbers of men charged and punished through incarceration and the length of prison sentences. While there is wide acceptance that women and girls often have no interest in engaging with, or faith in, the criminal justice system, critiques of the system rarely move beyond suggestions of reform. There is an ongoing tension between the desire for independence from the State, reliance on the State for survival and investment in the State as site of justice and accountability.

One impact of this dynamic is that services which were developed based on liberatory practice are mutating into adaptations of statutory social work. Elements of the day-to-day practice may differ, but much of the structure (referral, assessment, casework, case closure, risk management, case conferencing) is the same. Resistance to these models, especially by Black women's organisations, can result in services being framed as bastardised versions of accepted practice, and therefore not appropriately qualified for State and charitable foundation support.

By and for, Black women's ending VAWG organisations present a significant challenge to the dominant social work model. These organisations develop holistic responses which value Black women's experiences, ways of knowing and practice expertise. This expertise navigates a range of cultural nuances, is mindful of, and alert to, multiple intersecting oppressions, and provides support which responds to a broad range of needs. However, Black women practitioners grapple with the internal (psychic) tensions that occur with the requirements of 'casework' which sets parameters of 'appropriate' and 'ethical' that diminish, dismiss and vilify anything which falls outside of those frameworks.

In order to survive, 'by and for' organisations need to demonstrate their 'professionalism' and their credibility (to the State and their white feminist and non-feminist counterparts). In order to remain viable, they are forced to subscribe to the very models that they have sought to disrupt. In practice this has meant the shrinking of autonomous spaces provided 'by and for' Black women's organisations.

Surviving the collisions: Black women resisting violence

While some of the challenges faced by Black women-led organisations are linked to broader neo-liberal agendas and the shrinking of the welfare state, others are directly linked to academic and policy approaches to 'race relations'. Race relations theory and policies, building on legacies of colonisation and empire, were instrumental in [re]establishing how whole groups of people are known and understood in the UK. At the heart of ''race relations' are concepts which have sought to address the perceived social problems arising from the post-Second World War, Black migrant presence in Britain.[7] African-Caribbean communities have been constructed as the 'bastardised' children of the British Empire, lacking specific cultural identity (cultural deprivation), 'tribal' connections, and plagued with insecure, unstable family structures (matrifocal families).

> the West Indians . . . no longer have the tribal associations and native language which can still provide some fundamental security for the disillusioned African. The West Indian disillusioned with Britain is deprived of all sense of security. He [sic] becomes, quite understandably, the most sensitive and neurotic member of the coloured community, and may be inclined to drift into bad ways.
>
> (Lawrence, 1992: 69)

Conversely, South Asian communities have been constructed as rigid and culturally intact. Children born in the UK to South Asian parent(s) are seen to inevitably find themselves at the mercy of a specifically racialised form of intergenerational conflict and struggling 'between two cultures' (Lawrence, 1992).

Constructions of 'culture' as homogenous, static, rigid, clearly marked and all enduring produce essentialist racist representations:

> There is a collapse between the categories of 'culture' and those of 'race': this serves not only to homogenise a range of different ethnic groups, origins, migration histories, family circumstances and personal histories, but also to reduce everyone to a baseline of black identity constructed around a stereotype of 'the black family', which is actually itself a (discredited) stereotype of the African Caribbean family.
>
> (Alexander, 2008: 15)

Thus, when, in the 1980s services began to utilise 'culture' to secure funding for specialist services, Mama (1989) warned against the 'muddled thinking' that rests on ideas of cultural specificity and difference, rather than autonomy and self-determination. While 'by and for' spaces were responses to racism, sexism and class discrimination, arguments based on 'culture' provided more leverage and were more palatable. The impact on service and organisational development was painful. African-Caribbean women were perceived as having no specific cultural or language needs and therefore no requirement for specific services, whereas services for South Asian women were funded on the basis of cultural need and difference. In both situations, Black women's rights to organise, and to define their/our intersectional experiences and resist violence autonomously, was denied. The lack of acknowledgement, within the broader feminist movement of racism as a cultural product of white Britishness, resulted in a failure of many white women to position themselves as a) beneficiaries of racism and b) allies to Black women in the struggle for autonomous Black women's spaces.

In the last decade, Black women's activism and campaigning have pushed issues such as forced marriage (FM), 'honour-based' violence (HBV) and female genital mutilation (FGM) into the public policy agenda. 'Cultural needs' have become synonymous with specific forms of violence, resulting in reductive problematic narratives surrounding violence against Black women. These forms of violence framed as 'cultural' rather than manifestations of inequality are now defined as 'extreme' and included in policies such as the Counter-Extremism Strategy (2015). Black women are either 'pigeon-holed' by strategies to address 'harmful practices' and 'terrorism', or excluded, if they do not identify with these experiences. We have listened to African-Caribbean women describing an invisibility in government strategies and local commissioning and questioning where they fit in such a landscape. As practitioners and activists, we believe that a deeper, structural shift is required which goes to the core of how we work to end violence against Black women and girls.

Working socially at the intersection

Murphy et al. (2009) discuss self-reflexivity through intersectionality, drawing on Heron's theories (2005), which explore social worker self-examination for addressing power relations; the social position of the client within power dynamics;

and social work efficacy in disrupting systems of oppression. Their analysis has relevance to ending VAWG practice, and in particular, the difficulty, resistance and pain that can be encountered by social workers attempting self-reflection.

Although we recognise self-reflexivity as essential across social contexts, as a practice it remains inconsistent. In ending violence against Black women and girls work, here in the UK, positive encounters with statutory social workers will often be on an individual basis depending on the level of knowledge, self-awareness of difference, privilege and power. A recent pilot[8] in London on preventing female genital mutilation (FGM) through early intervention and collaborative working with statutory sector social workers and maternity services highlighted the challenges of applying 'text book' social work knowledge when working with Black communities, who have been framed through the lens of violence, such as the case with FGM.[9] The lead statutory social workers, involved in the pilot, formed partnerships with Black women working in community organisations at a 'grassroots' level, who held leadership and knowledge and links within community structures for women and girls. The project, through effective co-production with Black women community groups, enabled social workers to initiate conversations around their roles as social workers; and begin to address their own power in these interactions. Conversations eventually led onto FGM, the impact, support and service provision and associated legislation. The social workers involved learnt some basic principles around difference, such as the importance of ways to step into someone's home, and over time built a level of trust with Black women on the pilot. This pilot led to a revision of assessment processes and the forming of a new framework designed with Black women's organisations. While this way of working arguably disrupted everyday practices within statutory social work, the power imbalances within the relationships remain intact because of embedded structural differences; and the universal structures of social work practice remain. The pilot provides one illustration of the gaps between the textbook knowledge of social workers and the lived experience of their clients (Murphy et al., 2009), highlighting the extent of the challenges of integrating intersectionality, beyond the theoretical, into social work practice.

Practitioners working socially within the ending VAWG sector and statutory social care sector are faced with the failure to address whiteness as an axis of power and privilege. Reflexive theories that focus on the individual need to shift from categories of ethnicity, sexuality, gender, class, age and disability in reference to either client or social worker. An ongoing scrutiny of whiteness that contextualises post-coloniality and the socio-historical, ontological and epistemological impact on Black communities (how whiteness operates individually and systemically) is urgently needed. Transformative social work practice is only possible when white supremacy is dismantled individually and collectively.

Defining space: Transformational encounters

In our practice, space is a constant theme, expressed through nostalgia, longing, gratitude and even regret. As Black women, defiant postcolonial subjects, we seek and long for an [imagined] whole herstory that has been appropriated and re-codified. As British African-Caribbean women, impacted by the ruptures of colonisation and post-Second World War migration, we hear echoes of this space from mothers, tantie/taanta[10] and grandmothers. This knowledge could not have remained fully intact on that journey across the Atlantic during the slave trade, nor could it have entirely survived the hostility of the plantation or the trauma of arrival to Britain during the 'Windrush'[11] period. Many of us clutch at tiny, fragile fragments from our barely known past in an attempt to [re]claim and [re]build what was lost. Black women speak of needing space, often with each other, to heal, to organise, to resist and even just be. This is the significance of space as conceptual, experiential and providing something.

It is this something then, within the [re]claimation of space, that is intrinsic to the reimagining of Black women working together to address, recover from and end violence against us. Working socially with each other, outside the dominant social work construct, suggests an undetermined 'new' way of working; however, it is important to note that despite fragmentation and ruptures, creating space and work have been constant in Black women's journeys. As part of our herstories of gathering, sharing and speaking tongues, from the Indigenous tribes of Guyana's Amazon and the mountain people of Jamaica, through the terrorist breaches of colonisation and migration pathways, to womanist spaces developed in England, we have always sought ways to create safe space. Thus, we assert that reimagined space is more than a composite or response to the socio-political landscape of the day, but rather a transformative encounter which provides many things, including pause. The pause gives room to work our herstory, resilience, commonalities, resistance, recovery, voice, silence and lived experience. The concept of an imagined space and our work is neither mutually exclusive nor reliant on an absolutism of space, but rather provides: 'A space longed for, rare and often unfamiliar; we are left with ourselves and each other in the space' (Nayak, 2015: 95).

This longing is reiterated by the numerous women we have encountered and worked with over the decades, and most significantly once they have occupied and experienced safe space. We assert that the creation and provision of space for Black women brings forth a myriad of internal and external encounters; known and unknown, as women attempt to balance the safety of speaking, along with the collisions and ruptures experienced through everyday violence of hetero-patriarchal white supremacy and the discomfort of the unfamiliar [space]. Having space is not utopian but provides an intersectional site for the emergence of new and reclaimed ways of working as Black women that build recovery and collective accountability.

However, Black women and the spaces we occupy in the UK have been homogenised, with a one-size-fits-all approach, which fails to fully apply intersectional practice.

In 'About My Rights' (1989) Jordan speaks of being constructed as 'wrong'. To understand and interrogate the experiences of African-Caribbean women subjected to violence, we must recognise the impact of being 'wrong' on women's ability to access safety and justice even within the ending VAWG sector. We must recognise that the narratives around VAWG in the UK tend to note only one aspect of this 'wrongness', i.e. sex/gender. We must recognise and deal with the invisibility of Black African-Caribbean women within the discourse of ending VAWG. The apathy within the ending VAWG sector regarding the needs of African-Caribbean women has resulted in a total shrinking of space for us, with the assumption that the need for specialism and space rests elsewhere with others.

We recognise the will to redefine spaces of connection and innovative responses to VAWG, whilst critiquing how those spaces are created, and how the work is done. For example, London-based organisation, Women and Girls Network (WGN), provides services to support women to heal and recover from violence. They note: 'The aim of our work is to create a safe, non-judgemental and non-directive space . . . providing a holistic, integrated, healing journey that involves the diverse aspects of the self: Mind, body and spirit . . .' (Women and Girls Network, 2013).

Community-based models developed by Imkaan have established ways of working with diverse Black women within accountable community structures: 'Imkaan's community engagement models seek to ethically collaborate and form partnership which address the multiple inequalities and oppressive power dynamics experienced by racialised communities in their responses to VAWG' (Imkaan, 2014). The development and holding of safe and accountable community spaces is central to Imkaan, and women involved in these dedicated spaces report:

> Sharing of this space was so precious, being with other black women made a positive difference to me.
>
> (Imkaan Community Champion, 2015)

> Having the space to talk about things that impact me everyday has been so important, I have felt safe here . . .
>
> I have never been taught by another Black woman and this has made such a difference.
>
> (Imkaan Peer Educators, 2016)

However, the provision of space is beyond the realm of services by Black women for Black women.

Writing about English-speaking Caribbean domestic violence complainants, Lazarus-Black refers to 'cultures of reconciliation' that 'influence the choices people make regarding what to do about the violence in their lives'. Lazarus-Black speaks of reconciliatory norms intrinsic to family, gender and work spaces that are separate to the law and criminal justice systems (Lazarus-Black, 2008: 25–51). These spaces, which may not necessarily be Black feminist spaces, sites of risk and threat, may also offer psychic safety, reprieve, 'being known', retrieval and recognition. Black feminists must engage with the intersecting complexities of women and girls' lives by connecting the conceptual to everyday practices.

Without space, no one can hear you

As [both] survivors and practitioners, we witness the ways narratives of violence against Black women have focused on our communities and men being more dangerous and prone to violence, or more radicalised and extreme behaviours. As Gilroy notes,

> the view of the blacks as innately criminal, or at least more criminal than the white neighbours whose deprivation they share, which became 'common sense' during the early 1970s, is crucial to the development of new definitions of the black problem and new types of racial language and reasoning.
>
> (Gilroy, 1987: 140)

Racist representations of 'the African' by European Enlightenment white male philosophers[12] are foundational to contemporary discourses of African-Caribbean-ness as threat and danger, lawless and criminal. In this context, the criminal justice system is placed as the only option, for African and African-Caribbean woman, who are, for example, disproportionately represented in Metropolitan Police statistics on sexual and domestic violence (MBARC, 2016). All Black women are under pressure as mothers and partners as upholders of law and order, and to demonstrate their commitment to 'punishment' of the perpetrator, and/ or notions of [British] 'justice'. For example, the 'War on Terror' involved a range of UK 'counter-extremist' programmes including Prevent,[13] including specific activities targeted at women. The government has explicitly stated that women are 'safe friends' for the government (Center for Human Rights and Global Justice, 2012). One critic of Prevent noted 'the skills of Muslim women are being built up to spy on their families rather than participate fully in society and overcome the barriers they face' (Gohir, 2009: np). This deployment of Black women's experiences in the interest of oppressive, neo-liberal, State security and surveillance, often overlooked within broader feminist rhetoric, are rarely a priority for the wider ending VAWG sector. When Black women's concerns are noted, the default response is one of reform, rather than meaningful challenge to the State.

Given the depth and breadth of challenges facing Black women and girls, we sometimes 'down tools' in utter frustration, as the inadequacies of best intentions deny Black woman's autonomy. Yet, we have, ourselves, experienced that something magical happens when we get to 'show up' as our whole selves and experience being seen, understood and 'gotten'. Our experiences of community work, and of working in a Black feminist organisation [re]affirms for us the need for space; and desperation we feel for affirmation, knowing and connection.

We acknowledge that as practitioners we have been part of, and continue to be, complicit in the 'professionalisation' of ending VAWG work in the UK. To ensure survival many Black women's organisations, have employed strategies that have included 'playing the game'. Our/your journey of [re]imagining is not a diminishing of the critical line that Black women's organisations struggle to hold in order to provide safe spaces which support Black girls, women and their children. [Re]imagining is a pushing beyond the current constraints.

As we started the process of this [re]imagining, we confronted the idea that invoking Black feminist notions of space involved a willingness to move outside of the established 'professionalised' client-work paradigm. Stripping away how we have constructed our work identities, and how we have been trained to question knowledge that does not comply. As postcolonial subjects, carrying within our very bodies and psyches, the legacies of colonisation, we are trained to think of Western scientific knowledge (including social science) as superior and reliable. We have been taught to trust, while also fearing Eurocentric social work frameworks. Trust, because we are the insider-outsider 'professionals'; fear, because we are Black African-Caribbean women who have been raised with an instinctive distrust of systems which constructed us, African-Caribbean women, as social problems. There is a daily psychic violence that is done to self in holding this paradoxical position, and there is a violence that is done in the deconstructing of our professional selves.

We also began a process of [re]call of that which has always been there in Black women's rituals, healing and connections. We reflected on women's healing circles,[14] women's business,[15] and the balm yard.[16] We noted the importance of consciousness-raising[17] groups in many feminist struggles. We shared journeys, memories, tears and food. We spent days with each other and with our Black feminist Samoan Sistah, Betty Siō, from Aotearoa, talking through 'the work'. Our [re]imagination has taken us, not to a place of solution, but to one of inquiry. We have started rather than ended with, what for us are, building blocks, critical elements, of [re]constructing space; our [re]construction, at its very essence, demands push, upheaval, nurture and ongoing excavation.

[Re]constructing space

To [re]imagine, we must [re]call, [re]claim and [re]connect in order to [re]construct space. As African-Caribbean women have become more invisibilised within ending VAWG work; space, for us, must be dynamic and solid. Space must be [re]created that acknowledges all forms of violence we experience as African-Caribbean women, including State violence.[18] [Re]constructing requires a centring of our work in DEcolonised Black feminist practice, which includes work around intersecting sites of multiple trauma. This recognises the connections of body, and the emotional, mental and psychic (our being), to the economic, political and social, as healing. This is both restorative and transformative healing from interpersonal and broader violence and injustices perpetrated on our beings.

Let us [re]imagine women in a conversation, 'as women' where the 'survivor' is woman; and where the 'practitioner' is allowed to be a woman who is surviving the colonisation of her practice. This is a space, where the practitioner is able to 'show up' as Black, African-Caribbean, woman and survivor, and is there, as a practitioner, with responsibilities, boundaries and mindfulness of power, not dominating space, but speaking from the place of connection and truth telling, as survivor, here the work and conversations are those which heal, challenge and resist subjugation.

In such a 'service', yes, the crisis is responded to – for example a woman who needs to be relocated, can be relocated in an emergency – but 'casework' is not the thing; the thing is an ongoing 'conversation', about who she is and what she wants. The 'service' becomes space, for a woman or girl to [re]claim herself through voice, companionship, sharing with others and reflection. The service and the work become synonymous with the subjective and space develops around the individual.

Thus, when we:

> have been raped
> be-
> cause I have been wrong the wrong sex the wrong age
> the wrong skin the wrong nose the wrong hair the
> wrong need the wrong dream the wrong geographic
> the wrong sartorial.
>
> (Jordan, 1989)

and carry the shame of being 'wrong', we are able to connect with others who understand this shame and are able to 'intervene', through recognition and deconstruction. A holistic approach is not about 'holistic' casework, but a bringing and responding to the whole self, so pathways and connections, albeit those that may seem circular, always lead back to the reclamation of 'self'. Practice remains dynamic, subjective and ever changing, as we are, rigorous in accountability to all in the process. Woman and girls are not 'clients', but authors of their own narratives. These narratives are not framed by brokenness and the specificities of the violence, but framed in relationship to her whole self, as a Black woman: lesbian, older, younger, queer, disabled, trans and so forth. Narratives rooted in resilience and strength.

To avoid the overwhelm that a woman may experience, she may need a sense of safety. Safety means different things for different girls, women and their children. Meaningful, transformative work around safety engages with and disrupts the different systems of harm that we encounter, including the harms of racism, and other intersecting forms of oppression. In practice this also recognises the need for respite and time; not in the sense of time passed but more time given, as she takes up space, so too must she take up time. This is not about ignoring or de-prioritising her practical needs, but rather creating space for those needs to be responded to within the context of her whole self. For example, housing options for women need to simultaneously prioritise safety from the perpetrator(s) of the interpersonal violence, as well as a location that actually feels safe for Black women.

[Re]constructing the ways Black women work with one another emerges as a 'choosing': choosing the 'specialism', the conversations, our locations and choosing the space. We may not always be able to name the 'thing', as it may live in the realm of the intangible. For practitioners rooted in statutory social work theory and practice, this will involve constant unlearning and deconstructing. For all practitioners, this will involve a level of reflexivity that challenges every aspect of social work practice with a view to decolonising self.

Final words

When Black women encounter a safe re-created space, there are opportunities for healing. We can share in ways that acknowledge the socio-historical context of empire, as a site of ongoing devastation. We can speak about the different ways that we have been, and continue to be, impacted by this devastation; but we can also invoke our [re]imagined herstories and evoke commonality, connection and resistance. We are able to [re]treat and [re]cover from the violence done to us by men, by families, by the State and by the society that we live in. For African-Caribbean women, working socially to end violence against all Black women and girls, we who have offered our backs to be walked on, our shoulders to be stood on, and voices to be spoken through, the need for this space which is by us, for us and with us, is now urgent.

Notes

1 'Global South' in international policy refers to countries located in the Southern Hemisphere, defined as 'developing' by institutions such as the World Bank.
2 The term 'people of colour' is used in the United States of America to describe people who are not white, who are subjected to racism.
3 The United Nations definition: 'any act of gender-based violence that results in, or is likely to result in, physical, sexual or psychological harm or suffering to women, including threats of such acts, coercion or arbitrary deprivation of liberty, whether occurring in public or in private life' (General Assembly Resolution 48/104 Declaration on the Elimination of Violence against Women, 1993).
4 www.parliament.uk/business/committees/committees-a-z/commons-select/women-and-equalities-committee/inquiries/parliament-.
5 www.unrisd.org/unrisd/website/newsview.nsf/(httpNews)/FF586794AC3EE1E0C1257E1B004FDB3B?OpenDocument.
6 The UK definition is: 'any incident or pattern of incidents of controlling, coercive, threatening behaviour, violence or abuse between those aged 16 or over who are, or have been, intimate partners or family members regardless of gender or sexuality'.
7 This 'wave of immigration', largely as a direct result of the British call to its Commonwealth subjects to rebuild the 'motherland', very quickly became a challenge to (white) British society. Responses to these 'problems' included successive pieces of legislation restricting the numbers of Commonwealth migrants. By the same token, weak legislation, initially framed within a civil context, was introduced to address 'racial discrimination', demonstrating the State's unwillingness to address racism in (white) British society.
8 The Department for Education funded The London Mayor's office for Policing and Crime to lead a pilot project on the Prevention of FGM using a social work and maternity model across five London boroughs.
See www.london.gov.uk/what-we-do/mayors-office-policing-and-crime-mopac for the project evaluation report.

9 Commonly associated with some communities from African nations, Somalian and Sudanese communities in London are often disproportionately highlighted in media. FGM is also known to be practised within some Middle Eastern, East European and South East Asian communities.
10 Words used in many Caribbean countries for biological Aunt, or for elder women within the family, close circle or community.
11 The 'Windrush' period refers to the 'mass' arrival of Caribbean migrants to the UK, which commenced in 1948 with the arrival of the SS Empire Windrush at Tilbury Dock, Essex, in England.
12 Kant, Hume, and historians such as Long, linked skin colour with intelligence, particularly in the case of Africans: dark skin equalled an indication of intellectual and emotional inferiority. Even anti-enlightenment thinkers such as Herder were known to make connections between physical characteristics of Africans and a propensity to sensuality.
13 See www.ltai.info/what-is-prevent/.
14 Women's healing circles are associated wit' Indigenous practice and women's gathering throughout Aotearoa, the Pacific Islands, Australia, Africa, the Caribbean and Asia.
15 'Women's business' are private sacred gatherings, conversations and healing spaces that are important aspects of Indigenous Australian cultures and other Indigenous cultural contexts. Although they are called by different names, such sacred circles are commonplace in many Black cultures.
16 'Balm yards' are sacred places in Jamaica where healing practices are performed by women who have received the power of healing as a sacred gift (Wedenoja, 1989).
17 Consciousness-raising groups were an important part of Western feminist practice popularised in the places such as the UK and USA in the 1960s.
18 Violence represents a spectrum which includes: immigration control, stop and search and death in custody.

References

Alexander, C. (2008) *(Re)Thinking Gangs*. London: The Runnymede Trust.

Back, L. (2007) 'Live Sociology'. In Back, L. (ed.) *The Art of Listening*. Oxford, UK: Berg.

Berelowitz, S., Firmin, C., Edwards, G. and Gulyurtlu, S. (2012) *'I Thought I Was the Only One. The Only One in the World'*. London: The Office of the Children's Commissioner.

Brah, A. and Phoenix, A. (2004) 'Ain't I a Woman? Revisiting Intersectionality', *Journal of International Women's Studies*, 5 (3): 75–86.

Brooks, R. L. (2012) 'Cultural Diversity: It's All About the Mainstream', *Monist*, 95 (1): 17–32.

Bryan, B., Dadzie, S. and Scafe, S. (1985) *The Heart of the Race: Black Women's Lives in Britain*. London: Virago Press.

Burman, E. (2005) 'Engendering Culture in Psychology', *Theory and Psychology*, 15 (4): 533.

Center for Human Rights and Global Justice (2012) *Women and Preventing Violent Extremism: The U.S. and U.K. Experiences*. New York: NYU School of Law.

Crenshaw, K. (1991) 'Mapping the Margins: Intersectionality, Identity Politics, and Violence against Women of Color', *Stanford Law Review*, 43 (6): 1241–1299.

Crenshaw, K. (1995) 'The Intersection of Race and Gender'. In Crenshaw, K., Gotanda, N., Peller, G. and Thomas, K (eds) *Critical Race Theory: The Key Writings that Formed the Movement*. New York: New Press.

Gilroy, P. (1987) *There Ain't No Black in the Union Jack*. London: Hutchinson.

Gilroy, P. (2002) *There Ain't No Black in the Union Jack*. London: Routledge.
Gohir, S. (2009) *Submission from Muslim Women's Network UK for the Inquiry into the Preventing Violent Extremism Programme*. Birmingham, UK: MWNUK.
Gray, M., Coates, J., Yellow Bird, M. and Hetherington, T. (2013) *Decolonizing Social Work*. New York: Routledge.
Hill-Collins, P. (2000) *Black Feminist Thought: Knowledge, Consciousness and the Politics of Empowerment*. New York: Routledge.
Hill-Collins, P. (2012) *On Intellectual Activism*. Philadelphia, PA: Temple University Press.
Htun, M. and Weldon, S. L. (2012). 'The Civic Origins of Progressive Policy Change: Combating Violence against Women in Global Perspective, 1975–2005', *American Political Science Review*, 106: 548–569.
Imkaan (2015) *State of the Sector: Contextualising the Current Experiences of BME Ending Violence against Women and Girls' Organisations*. London: Imkaan.
Imkaan (2016) *Capital Losses: The State of the Specialist BME Ending Violence Against Women and Girls Sector in London*. London: Imkaan.
Imkaan, Rape Crisis England and Wales, Positively UK (2015) *Women's Mental Health and Wellbeing: Access to and quality of Mental Health Services*. London: Imkaan.
Jones J. (1999) 'The Caribbean Community in Britain'. In Owusu, K. (ed.) *Black British Culture and Society*. London: Routledge.
Jones, D. and Ng, P. (2014) 'Supporting and Working with the Needs of Black, and Minority Ethnic Women Survivors of Violence Within the UK'. In Kutálková, P. and Kobová, L. (eds) *Sexual Violence in Social Work*. Prague: Iustitia.
Jordan, J. (1989) 'A Poem About My Rights'. In Jordan, J. (ed.) (2005) *Directed By Desire: The Collected Poems of June Jordan*. Port Townsend, WA: Copper Canyon Press.
Larasi, M. (2013) 'A Fuss About Nothing?: Delivering services to Black and Minority Ethnic Survivors of Gender Violence – The Role of the Specialist Black and Minority Ethnic Women's Sector'. In Rehman, Y., Kelly, L. and Siddiqui, H. (eds) *Moving in the Shadows: Violence in the Lives of Minority Women and Children*. Farnham, UK: Ashgate.
Larasi, M. and Jones, D. (2017) *Tallawah: A Briefing Paper on Black and 'Minority Ethnic' Women and Girls Organising to End Violence against Us*. London: Imkaan.
Lawrence, E. (1992) 'Just Plain Common Sense: The 'Roots' of Racism'. In Centre for Contemporary Cultural Studies (ed.) *The Empire Strikes Back: Race and Racism in 70s Britain*. London: University of Birmingham.
Lazarus-Black, M. (2008) 'Vanishing Complainants: The Place of Violence in Family', *Gender, Work and Law in Caribbean Studies*, 36 (1): 26–46.
Lieberman, M. and Bond, G. (1976) 'The Problem of Being a Woman: A Survey of 1,700 Women in Consciousness-raising Groups', *The Journal of Applied Behavioural Science*, 12 (13): 363–379.
Mama, A. (1989) *The Hidden Struggle: Statutory and Voluntary Sector Responses to Violence Against Black Women in the Home*. London: London Race and Housing Research Unit.
Mama, A. (1995) *Beyond the Masks: Race, Gender and Subjectivity*. London: Routledge.
MBARC (2016) The London Sexual Violence Needs Assessment 2016 for MOPAC & NHS England (London).
McCracken, K., Priest, S., Fitzsimons, A. and Torchia, K. (2016) 'The Mayor's Office for Policing and Crime Female Genital Mutilation Early Intervention Model: An Evaluation'. Opcit Research with University of Central Lancashire, UK.

Murphy, Y., Hunt, V., Zajicek, A. M., Norris, A. N. and Hamilton, L. (2009) *Incorporating Intersectionality in Social Work Practice, Research Policy and Education*. Washington, DC: NASW Press.

Nayak, S. (2015) *Race, Gender and the Activism of Black Feminist Theory: Working with Audre Lorde*. New York: Routledge.

Reddock, R. (2007) 'Diversity, Difference and Caribbean Feminism: The Challenge of Anti-Racism', *Caribbean Review of Gender Studies*, 1.

Sanders-McDonagh, E., Neville, L. and Nolas, S. (2016) 'From Pillar to Post: Understanding the Victimisation of Women and Children Who Experience Domestic Violence in an Age of Austerity', *Feminist Review*, 112 (1): 60–76.

Tuck, E. (2009) 'Suspending Damage: A Letter to Communities', *Harvard Educational Review*, 79 (3): 409–427.

Voice4Change England and NAVCA Specialist Services: A Guide for Commissioners (2012) www.navca.org.uk/news/view-article/equalities-new-report.

Walter, M., Taylor, S. and Habibis, D. (2011) 'How White is Social Work in Australia', *Australian Social Work* 64 (1): 6–19.

Wedenoja, W. (1989) 'Mothering and the practice of Balm in Jamaica'. In Shepherd-McClain, C. (ed.) *Women as Healers: Cross-Cultural Perspectives*. Sydney: Rutgers University Press.

9 Understanding the macroaggressions underscoring the invisibility of Black female victims of police violence within Black Lives Matter protests

Kamaria Muntu

Representations of young white female vulnerability have been historically and disingenuously used in the service of inciting racialised fear when it comes to the criminalisation of Black males, particularly for rape. Yet the idea of shining a light on a vulnerable population at added risk for certain kinds of violence need not be a reactionary strategy for protecting that population. In fact, it has served to acknowledge, even as a limited construct, one identifier of white female experience (a non-racialised rape culture) that has enabled an understanding and empathy for their victimisation. For Black women, gender as well as other delineators of lived experience, functioning as oppressive constructs, are often marginalised or rendered invisible. Hence, in private and public spheres, Black women are generally contextualized through the optics of race, or as is the case with poor Black women, race and class. How this plays out with the escalation in excessive force and death at the hands of law enforcement (which has seen a perilous trajectory in the Black community for men and women) is that Black women's experience of repressive state violence continues to be marginalized or erased. Though Black men constitute the majority of deaths by extrajudicial killings, alarming numbers of Black women and girls have been harassed, brutalised and killed in encounters with the police. These women are rarely the focus of sustained public outrage – and the major women organisers of the Black Lives Matter Movement have been unable to locate them successfully within their organising initiatives. A female member of Millennial Activists United (MAU), pointed out: 'The media is excluding the fact that the police brutality and harassment in our communities impacts the women just as much as the men. They're highlighting Black male lives and pushing the Black female lives lost to police violence to the side' (Jemmott, 2016: online).

In searching for underlying reasons for the androcentric response to the killings of Black people in America, microstructural macroaggressions are posited as a means of impeding Black women's liberatory agency, thereby nullifying their victimisation. The microstructural macroaggressions submitted are either perpetuated by, or are the result of, aggressive cultural narratives like 'Missing White Women Syndrome', or theorised as intra-racial cultural narratives, as in 'the Willie Lynch Letter'; both function as deterrents to the social comprehension of the conditions facing Black women. Black women navigate between racial allegiance and their own, often, suppressed identities, identities central to their victimisation. Investigations into the complex realities of Black women's lives have been largely limited to academic spheres, therefore the prevailing intersecting oppressions and biases that render them vulnerable to the criminal justice system are obscured by singular, racialised narratives of injustice. By critically analysing the underlying barriers to implementing intersectionality in movement building, not only will Black women be de-marginalised in their fight for justice, but it is the only way that understanding of all the factors instigating police and other forms of violence targeting Black communities can be redressed.

Reasserting an intersectional episteme

The absence of intersectional approaches in tackling problems of oppression results in a weakening of the collective power of exploited groups. Lorde's axiom, 'There is no such thing as a single issue struggle because we do not lead single issue lives' (Lorde, 1982: 138), explains how an elite hegemony marginalises and renders entire populations invisible, particularly when they eschew the interdependent nature of their issues as potential sites of solidarity. Within Black communities, Black women's precarious position (subjects under objectified men), and the adjunct marginalisation of that position, is both sanctioned and assumed, despite the inherent danger such intragroup disregard presents. Suggesting episteme as one way of dissecting Black female resistance, I loosely affirm Foucault's assertion, that 'power is everywhere; not because it embraces everything, but because it comes from everywhere' (Foucault, 1978: 92). Such power deriving from an emergent knowledge system is in keeping with the postcolonial praxis that presumes a hidden knowledge within Black women's lived experience. As Nanny in Zora Neale Hurston's prescient novel opines:

> Honey, de white man is de ruler of everything as fur as Ah been able tuh find out. Maybe it's some place way off in de ocean where de black man is in power, but we don't know nothin' but what we see. So de white man throw down de load and tell de nigger man tuh pick it up. He pick it up because he have to, but he don't tote it. He hand it to his womenfolks. De nigger woman is de mule uh de world so fur as Ah can see.
>
> (Hurston, 2004: 17)

With this, Hurston outlined the intersections of race, class, gender and work, long before intersectionality theory appeared for deconstruction. The character's ability to locate herself, *multidimensionally*, within a system that perceives her as less than human, supports the Foucauldian notion that power need not be exclusively structuralised or institutionalised, but as he contends, 'where there is power, there is resistance' (Foucault, 1978: 95), and that resistance lay in the *power-knowledge* relationship, revealing a hidden reality, that of the poor Black woman as mule of the world, and bringing it into a reality of being. 'We must not imagine a world of discourse divided between accepted discourse and excluded discourse, or between the dominant discourse and the dominated one; but as a multiplicity of discursive elements that can come into play in various strategies' (Foucault, 1978: 100). Discourse is a way of transgressing a previously fixed social materiality that renders Black women either peripheral or invisible – in this case one that would see its way into contemporary discourses more than 50 years on, and one that also continues to be contested.

In a chapter on *Intersectionality and Social Work Practice*, under the heading of diversity, the authors state, 'Since the 1950's, Blacks, persons with disabilities, women, gays and lesbians have begun calling attention to their experiences of oppression' (Murphy, 2009: 41). In this well-intentioned attempt to dismantle the paradigm of anti-intersectional practice when it comes to diverse groups, the authors reinforce the classic fault line of which Black women are particularly sensitive. The explanatory title of the anthology, 'All the Women Are White, All the Blacks Are Men, But Some of Us Are Brave' (Hull, Bell-Scott, and Smith, 1982) remains illustrative of that fault line and underscores the need for critical education imperatives within client advocacy sectors seeking to address service users spaced in the margins. Although written decades ago and cited voraciously, the title warrants restating because of its sustained revelatory impact and grassroots accessibility. For many Black women struggling at that time with the concomitant invisibility of an *either/or* ascription, the title represented not only a fresh opening in Black feminist discourse, but a precise descriptor for activist women outside the academy seeking to construct intersectional frameworks. While the chapter on Intersectionality and Social Work Practice does address Black feminist practice as an ante categorical solution (Murphy, 2009), the disconnect in language is an indicator of a kind of cognitive dissonance that, intentionally or not, perpetuates an unconscious erasure of a separate Black female identity. This stripping of dimension continues to exempt Black women from either the universal feminine or their ethno-national identity as it applies – limiting an understanding of the multiple ways in which they experience oppression (Smith, 2016).

While this may be quite familiar to those with an engagement in Black feminist research and analyses – in terms of the Black Lives Matter movement – we have embarked upon a new phase of liberation politics and therefore are addressing masses of activists, organisers and affected communities of whom many have little knowledge or who are oppositional to Black feminist praxis. In using 'All the women are white. . .' as example, Gail Lewis (2000: 158) defends: 'That this has been said for some time now, neither detracts from the fact that it still needs saying nor, more importantly, that some very hard work is required to undo both the common sense of this position and its re-articulation in analyses of the every-day of social life.' Amongst the activist vanguard, an incremental enlightenment should be the tangible outcome of any broad-based movement for transformative change. Non-exclusionary ways of thinking and being should be assiduously

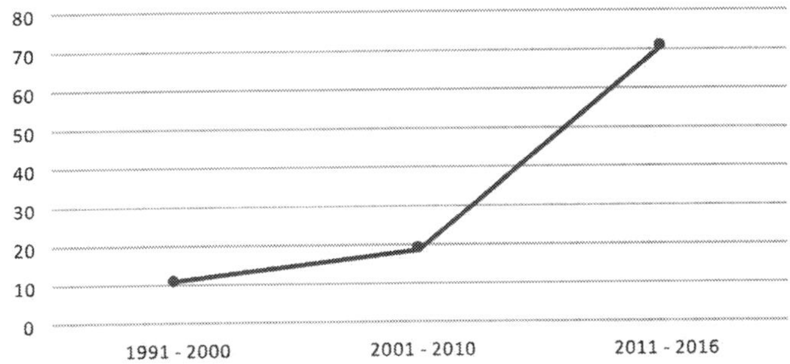

Figure 9.1 Rise in extrajudicial killings of women of colour over the past 25 years.[1]

imagined – and these ontologies should enable the oppressed to defend against violent repression, emerging as practical as well as ethical. In the past 25 years, there have been over one hundred public cases of Black women having been killed at the hands of corrupt law enforcement as shown in Figure 9.1.

The repetitious claims that police departments across America are acting in their own defence when they murder innocent Black men as a by-product of fear could in all practicality be contested by raising the visibility of the upsurge in killings of non-threatening women and girls. By disabling androcentric tendencies in Black ethos and citing a landscape of injustice inclusive of those most vulnerable, the public may be better able to contextualise injustices levelled at the Black community. Vivian May (2015: 5) notes, '. . . intersectional concepts of liberation approach the world's possibilities pragmatically, in the here and now, and idealistically, with an eye toward more utopian goals of eradicating inequity, exploitation, and supremacy, both at the micropolitical level of everyday life and at the macropolitical level of social structures, material practices, and cultural norms'. Any broad-based movement for social justice must be multi-dimensionally understood, not only to chart its own trajectory for strategic aims, but to foster far reaching alliances.

Microstructural macroaggressions

Microagressions are defined as: 'subtle, cumulative, mini assaults' (Yosso, Smith, Ceja, and Solórzano, 2009). Expanding on that concept, macroagressions are loosely defined as participation in large, oppressive systems (Gorski, 2014). They may not always be registered as such participation but can be covert ways of exacting the damage of brutal systemisations like racism, sexism, classism, homophobia and transphobia (Donovan, Galban, Grace, Bennet and Felicie, 2012). It is suggested that these macroaggressions can be devised externally (Table 9.1) (outside the oppressed group) or internally (Table 9.2), and they may have corresponding or reciprocal elements.

Table 9.1 External macroaggressions enabling the marginalisation of Black women and women of colour

Device	*Description*	*Literature*
Missing white woman syndrome	A neologism used by social scientists, media commentators and pundits as a descriptor of preoccupation with missing young upper-middle class white women and girls to the exclusion of others.	Conlin and Davie, 2015; Maynard, 2016
Moynihan report	Among other racist scripts, this report cited Black matriarchal patterns of dominance as a destabilising factor in the Black family. 'The Negro Family: The Case for National Action, completed in March, 1965', by Moynihan would become one of the most controversial documents of the twentieth century.	Social Service Review, 1966; Geary, 2015
Misrepresentation of Black women's history	A misrepresentation of Black women's historical reality that reduces them to submissive counterparts to patriarchal leadership – invalidating them as change agents in liberation struggles. 'Parks (Rosa) was not an apolitical, middle-aged lady whose fatigue kept her seated. Both shy and militant, she was a committed activist enmeshed racial politics – and their class and gender in complications – wherever she lived'.	Painter, 2014
Androcentric social initiatives	Paula Giddings elucidates the problem with male centred governmental initiatives like 'My Brother's Keeper'. Reifying poverty and violence as men's issues, Giddings suggests that separating men and boys from the people in their lives 'perpetuates a misogynist episteme'.	Giddings, 1984; Gilman, 2012
Eurocentric/ white beauty standard	Reinforces the notion of a white beauty aesthetic by submitting a 'white idealised femininity' leading to lower self-esteem in Black women and girls, and creating a normalised expectation of abuse.	Gray, 2015
Myth of Black female invulnerability	The myth of Black women's invulnerability inhibits effective contextualising and processing of Black female victims of violence.	Bell and Mattis, 2000
Angry Black woman stereotype	Stereotypes of Black women are varied, many, and cumulative – this one serves to silence Black women's ability to articulate their oppression.	Griffin, 2012
Partus Sequitur Ventrem Act	While this Act was part of the macro-repressive institution that was chattel slavery (the offspring will follow the condition of the mother) – the present socio-economic system 'blames Black women for allowing men to impregnate them without benefit of marriage or money.' Hence, the poverty that renders a Black woman and her children vulnerable to violence is her fault for not being cared for or valued by Black men.	Omolade, 1994

Table 9.2 Internal (intra-racial) macroaggressions enabling the marginalisation of Black and women of colour

Device	*Description*	*Literature*
Willie Lynch letter	Debunked letter supposedly written by English slave-owner outlining how to maintain slave system by exploiting difference – often used to nullify Black women's particular post-colonial experience.	Cobb, 2003
Myth of Black female privilege	The myth that Black women enjoy 'advantaged status' in the workforce as well as in other exclusionary and discriminatory spaces, further delegitimises their stresses as oppressed persons.	Sanchez-Hucles, 1997
Black male protectionism	Defensive reaction to extreme oppression experienced by Black men, particularly in their historical criminalisation for rape – and the 'myth of the bestial black man'. Serves to diminish the centrality of Black women's need for protection.	Patton and Snyder-Yuly, 2007
Sexism in Black male leadership	Patriarchal leaders and androcentric leadership initiatives like 'The Million Man March' – (wherewomen were told to 'stay at home' by Nation of Islam leader Minister Louis Farrakhan) underscores the notion that Black women are superfluous to Black advancement and that the real victims of injustice are Black men who should dominate the progression of Black people.	Salaam and Brown, 1996
Romanticised patriarchal Africa	The tendency to romanticise and mythologise precolonial history in a way that perpetuates a patriarchal hegemony, and shames Black women who do not subscribe to that hegemony for 'embracing western values'.	Farmer, 2014
Black male exceptionalism	The idea that Black men are more oppressed than any other group – and therefore a justification to be less concerned with the impact oppression has on Black women and girls.	Butler, 2013
Pastoral patriarchy in Black cinema	Thematic tendencies in independent or (Black oriented) cinema to uphold religiosity, patriarchy and male dominance in Black female/male cinematic interactions.	Wilson, Gutiérrez and Chao, 2013
Lesbian baiting	A gendered (woman) hating macroaggression designed to shame or frighten women identifying as cis-gendered and heterosexual who embrace feminist politics and feminist sisterhood.	Lorde, 2007

Missing white women syndrome (MWWS)

To have a thorough understanding of how racism and sexism as brutal systemisations inform the overall efficacy of client advocacy sectors, the ways in which racial dynamics are gendered must be conceptualised. In a geography of explicit bias, the methodology by which challenges to interlocking pathways of oppression are contended must be considered from the perspective of political resistance. With a mainstream narrative regaling a major shift in racial dynamics following the election of the first Black president, 'The [Black Lives Matter] movement shattered what remained of the notion of a 'post-racial' America and reoriented the entire national conversation on anti-Black racism' (Petersen-Smith, 2015). The gap in knowledge delineating the cross-pollination of racial and sexual oppression in Black women's experience can only be filled by understanding how political resistance can disrupt an oppressive status quo. 'The civil rights revolt, for example, cracked open the Cold War conservatism of the McCarthy era and inspired more than a decade of mass social struggle on many other fronts' (Petersen-Smith, 2015). An awareness of the *boots on the ground* struggle for women's rights is the *sine qua non* in developing a response to the needs of Black women and girls in social work. As Lewis (2000: 82) points out, while framing race and class differentiation, 'Gender, despite women being the vast majority of recipients and deliverers of social services, is absent from this analytical frame.' Likewise, the painful reality of Black female life is often circumscribed by a negligible focus on cultural and social apparatuses that enable her easy exploitation. This diminished focality leads to her inability to describe, understand or be conscious of her own victimisation as something outside herself. Hence, the needs of a young Black female service user could be lost on a service deliverer who may not separate her from what may appear to be a consensual affiliation with a culture of normalised sexism. For example, young Black women invested in misogynist rap music may not readily appear as victims of a sexist and oppressive patriarchy. Yet it is important to note the position that Black feminist activism has taken on the subject from its inception,

> vulgar rap has become a form of pornography passed off as Black male rage and free speech which contributes to the abusive behaviour of young Black men toward young Black women. For Black women in America who live in the midst of a population of young men who listen to a daily diet of vulgar rap, the connection between sexualised violence portrayed in rap videos, and the sexual behaviour and violence in everyday life is troubling.
>
> (Omolade, 1994: 237)

How Black feminist activism has sought to resist and reshape the narrative that has led to the suppression of the Black female voice amidst her own reality of violence is critical to dissecting the silence surrounding the violence Black women suffer. Reemphasising that there has been a stymying rise in state repression against women and girls – engendering a landscape of fear and endangerment –

noted are three cases of Black female brutalisation: the case of the slight 18-year-old Black girl, Genele H. Laird, who was repeatedly punched in the chest and face, and then tazed with a bag over her head by police in Madison, Wisconsin (Cartwright, 2016); the case of the 26-year-old Hispanic woman, Carolinmar Torres, who was punched in the chest and called a 'f**king b>h' (Konstantinides, 2016) by police in Providence, Rhode Island; and the case of 31-year-old Mayra Martinez, also Hispanic, who was repeatedly punched in the chest by police before being left on the side of an alley doubled over in pain in Jacksonville, Florida (Day, 2016). These are only a few incidents from 2016.

While there is a wealth of well-established Black feminist research and theory from which to draw insight, it is also reasonable to assume that social work practitioners as well as the community at large have differing levels of familiarity with Black feminist scholarship, specifically where macro/micro-aggressions may intersect. The erasure of Black women as victims of violence by macro aggressions like MWWS have a knock-on effect in Black life where the well-being of males is thought to be more essential to the well-being of the *race*. This is often interwoven with the micro aggressive mythos that Black women are not as victimised by the power structure as Black men, and in many instances are thought to be privileged (Jackson, 1971). Submitting that microstructural macroaggressions in contemporary usage act to mute the Black female voice as she raises objection to her unique, individualised oppression lends insight into oppressive cultural instruments designed to silence Black women's experience with a violence that does not occlude girls.

Death of Aiyanna Stanley Jones

Aiyanna Stanley Jones was seven years old when she was shot in the head by a heavily militarised police unit known as Detroit's Special Response Team (Hackman, 2015). Responding on a 'No Knock' warrant, they stormed the home of Aiyanna's grandmother in Michigan – a home where children's toys were visibly strewn on the front lawn, and where Aiyanna lay sleeping next to her grandmother on the sofa. They also tossed a flash grenade through the front window, causing Aiyanna's blanket to catch fire. During the invasion, the child was shot in the head by a swat team officer, and on the 16 May 2010 the death of the seven-year-old amounted to another racialised statistic. The paradoxical photo released by the family afterwards, of a smiling Aiyanna beneath an image of Snow White, did little to engender her preciousness to a corporate media and race-obsessed white public, as well as some Blacks buying into class assumptions. Their main concern appeared to be the alleged criminality of her father, which somehow rendered the circumstances of the child's death less horrific (Lambertz, 2014). 'Often the assumption is that the white girls are quote-unquote innocent victims whereas with poor children or children of colour, there's some nefarious activities involved' (Maynard, 2016). Aiyanna's killing did not spark sustained and major protests in the BLM movement, nor was it used to repudiate the narrative that law enforcement feared for their lives. The adventuresome mission was commandeered by a police officer who stars in a reality TV programme where he routinely carries out such exploits in neighbourhoods like Aiyanna's (Saulny, 2014). Aiyanna's death as a casualty of a police search for her father was emphatically a safeguarding issue – as the chairman of the Justice for Aiyanna committee lamented: 'Surely, the death of a baby by a well-trained police force must be deemed unacceptable in a civilized society' (Abbey-Lambertz, 2014).

Owing to the further disregard for Black female life is the incommensurate lack of concern the media has for Black female victims of violence. Yet, so disproportionate is the media attention given to white female victims of violence as opposed to women of colour and both Black and white men, it has facilitated the neologism Missing White Women Syndrome (MWWS) (Conlin and Davie, 2015). According to Maynard (2016) media interest in the syndrome 'exploded' after the intense exposure given to the disappearance of Natalee Holloway in Aruba in 2005. Natalie fit the prototype of the kind of victim the media and, by suggestion, the dominant white society is most obsessed with: young, attractive by Anglicised standards and middle class.

When 4-year-old Rilya Wilson disappeared from Foster Care in 2007, she didn't fit the typical criteria for children characterised as victims in the media. She was poor, Black, and without parents. Yet, despite her obvious vulnerability, outrage over her disappearance was non-existent (Maynard, 2016). Though Black children represent 35% of those missing (Molla, 2016), the lack of media coverage diminishes the chances of their being returned home safely (Stovall, 2016). Frequently judicial bodies choose to ignore missing Black children (as the criteria for Amber alert requires confirmation by law enforcement that the child is missing, which is sometimes difficult for Black women to obtain, due to macroaggressions such as MWWS, class assumptions or the *angry Black woman* stereotype).

To be clear, MWWS, in my view, is not a *pure* descriptor of a racialised phenomenon, but a microstructural macroaggression allowing for the erasure of Black women and girls – and a devaluation of their lives. Understandably, there has been some refutation of MWWS as a misnomer, as its limited criteria does not consider such factors as age, class, size, ableism, and non-standardised physical

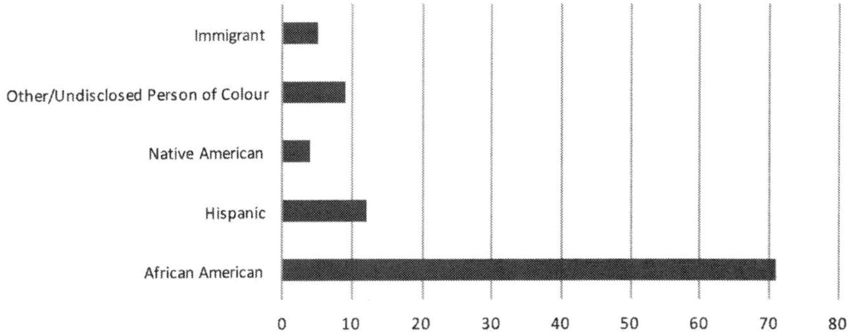

Figure 9.2 Ethnic distribution of the 101 cases of extrajudicial killings. Black (African American) women constitute the majority.

beauty – even for women identified as white (Liebler, 2010). Therefore, the ongoing dialogue and struggle between white women spaced in the margins who share intersections with women of colour based on oppressions outside of race remains critical, particularly in these times when the elite structures of power erected by men continue to oppress women of all races, lesbian and straight – as well as gay men and those designated as other. In accordance with their biology, white and Black women's oppressions are intersecting, and the erosion of their rights are once again under extreme threat. Although white women experience privilege, it is only insofar as white male supremacy will allow, and those margins may intersect with the limited powers of Black women under patriarchy. Yet, unlike white women for the most part, the reality for Black women and girls in an increasingly repressive state is to be under siege by forces not only within an intimate patriarchal landscape, but also under violent governmental siege. Mainstream media and BLM's negligible coverage of their murders and disappearances is especially dangerous in this unrelenting climate of injustice. The self-care and self-esteem of Black women and girls is compromised when the land they call home does not believe their lives matter. The fact that the government is moved to action when white women are killed and there is relative silence when Black women are murdered or disappear will continue to engender divisive terminology like Missing White Woman Syndrome until Black female lives command visibility and are no longer superfluous. As in the case of LaToya Figueroa, the young pregnant woman of African-American and Hispanic descent who went missing, she was later found dead: her disappearance received virtually no media attention (Associated Press, 2005). Stephanie Brzuzy and Amy Lind (2008) recount how the cases of missing white women, in addition to garnering greater media coverage, has also transformed the legal landscape, as did the Scott Peterson case that gave way for Laci's Law, or the Unborn Victims of Violence Act (McQueeney, 2005) where the law makes it double homicide to murder a pregnant woman (Lind and Brzuzy, 2008).

Microstructural microaggression and the transfiguration of Willie Lynch

In slave folklore *High John the Conqueror*, the son of an African King (Wilson, 1948), was a trickster who bamboozled the plantation master in order to make slave life more tenable. High John, in myth, embodied the collective consciousness of the enslaved Black community yearning for freedom (Sanfield, 2006). The latent emergence of *The Willie Lynch Letter* could be regarded as a kind of perverted inversion of the *High John the Conqueror* myth, as its sexist tone is used as a microstructural macroaggression to justify limiting the Black female voice – the letter states:

> Because she [the Blackwoman] has become psychologically independent, she will train her FEMALE offsprings to be psychologically independent. What have you got? You've got the nigger WOMAN OUT FRONT AND THE nigger MAN BEHIND AND SCARED.
>
> (Lynch, 1970)

Willie Lynch, a purported English plantation owner, is said to have made a speech in 1712 giving instruction to fellow slave owners on maintaining chattel slavery (Morrow, 2003). Having been featured in major cinema where its reified by high-profile Black celebrities, the letter has extensive reach. Despite being debunked as a hoax (Ashanti, 2001), academicians, public intellectuals and politicians continue to subscribe to Willie Lynch. Some site it metaphorically rather than actually, yet masses of Black people embrace its legitimacy. The contention in the Black community that the pathology espoused in this letter is at the crux of the destabilised Black family is not only ahistorical, but xenophobic in scope. Throughout the letter, differences among the enslaved population framed as exploitable are often used as a justification for exorcising healthy difference, and the agency of differentness in the present day. Granted that in the colonial slave *plantocracy* every exploitable thing that could be exploited *was* – but among the many and varied problems with this suspicious document is its socially matricidal tendencies. On enslaved motherhood, Lynch (1999) writes:

> Therefore, if you break the FEMALE mother, she will BREAK the offspring and when the offspring is old enough to work, she will deliver it up to you, for her normal female protective tendencies will have been lost in the original breaking process.

Billingsley attests to the erroneousness of the Lynch attack on Black motherhood:

> At the beginning of the slave trade families were more defined by blood ties [sanguinity] than by marital ties [conjugality], while in the seventeenth century European culture, it was just the opposite. Among women, who are the primary culture bearers for the group, it often happens that if a choice be

> made between allegiance to blood relatives, including, siblings, parents, *or children*, or to marital partners, *the latter allegiance must give way*.
>
> (Billingsley, 1994: 28)

The accusation that Black mothers have lost their 'protective tendencies' conjures images of the Black mammy, who was historically rare (Wood, Clinton, Kemble, and Clinton, 2002).

This internal macroaggression is staggering in its similarity to the dominant cultural narrative that villainises poor Black mothers who find their children and existence jeopardised by a depressive socio-economic reality. Unlike *High John the Conqueror* who was tricking *ol' massa* at every turn, desirous of liberty for his people in the midst of bondage, the supposed intra-racial pathology of Willie Lynch seeks to shame African descendants, particularly Black women into an acceptable homogeneity. Further, it positions Black women as obstacles to Black progress.

Death of Sandra Bland, a Black Lives Matter activist

Unlike other Black women killed by state aggression, the media visibility of Sandra Bland's death was high, a fact standing in stark contradiction to the timidity of proactive community response to her killing. Sandra was on her way to a job interview at her alma mater when she was pulled over by police for failing to signal a turn (Lai, Park, Bauchanan, and Andrews, 2015). In a climate of law enforcement's tendency to wield power punitively over citizens of colour, a situation already fraught with tension worsened when the officer asked her to put her cigarette out. Sandra responded by saying she was in her car and did not have to put it out, which was true. It could be surmised that her refusal agitated him, as he then asked her to get out of her vehicle. Sandra understood her rights – she did not have to leave her vehicle unless she was under arrest. She was told that she was under arrest, but when she queried more than once as to what the charges were, there was no answer given. The dashcam recordings further attest to the officer's mounting anger, as he orders Sandra from her car, shouting, drawing his stun gun, and threatening to 'light her up' (Dart, 2015). At some point, he yanks the 28-year-old woman from the car and slams her to the ground. From her prone position on the ground, Sandra could be heard screaming that she couldn't hear and her back was hurting (Dart, 2015). On the 13th of July 2015, the BLM activist was found hanged in her prison cell, a plastic rubbish bag tied tightly around her neck (Dart, 2016).

Bland's recalcitrant posture in the face of danger is by no means unique to women resisting the violence of subjugation. As one of the NAACP's most intractable field organisers, Rosa Parks' tireless pursuit of justice has been all but obfuscated by the parable of the sweet old lady who just wanted to sit down (Painter, 2014). This perception of the passive Black female actor during the precedent Civil Rights movement is germane to how activists like Sandra Bland and Black female resistors of state aggression are viewed today. The misrepresentation of Black women's agency in their own pursuit for liberation inhibits a clear understanding of their position within this present-day matrix of imputative domination. For the masses of Black women seeking to change their subordinate condition this leads to a misunderstanding about how radical change occurs. Throughout Jeanne Theorharis's history, 'The Rebellious Life of Mrs. Rosa Parks', Parks' radicalism in opposition to the prevailing white power structure and the more docile Black community is underscored. In Parks' own community she was labelled an 'agitator and troublemaker' (Theoharis, 2013).

Within contemporary society, Black women continue to be viewed as invulnerable, particularly those who appear to be uncensored and non-submissive. 'Sandra's murder dramatically drives home the ever-present dangers of not just being Black in a culture of normalized anti-Blackness, but the vulnerabilities associated with being a Black activist and especially a Black woman activist' (Baraka, 2016). Moreover, what is not interrogated when mainstream media and others insist that Bland should have complied, is the precarious predicament of being Black and female in a climate of codified racial and gendered violence. As Sandra herself predicted in her video-blogs, 'In the news that we've seen as of late, you could stand there, surrender to the cops, and still be killed' (Rogers, 2015). This supposes that aside from being resolute, Sandra may have been frightened to leave the vehicle that served as her only protection from fate she had seen too often in the headlines. In the panic of coming to terms with the nightmare that was unfolding, her car and her curses may have been the only buffer she had between her

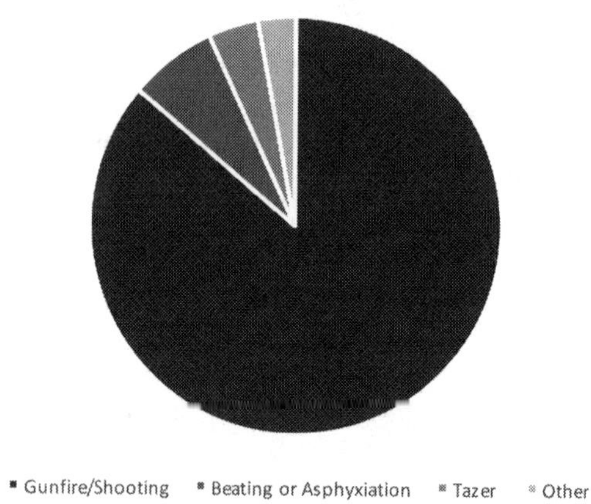

Figure 9.3 Method of death. Most women were killed by guns, but there were other methods of killing such as tasing and a woman who was thrown from a roof.

Source: *New York Times*, 1997.

vulnerable female body – enraged maleness, and weaponry. As Black women are subsumed by sadistic landscapes both intimately and publicly, it is unsurprising that Sandra would act defensively – with a simultaneity of ferocity and uncertainty for her survival. It is the muting of this reality that leads to a misunderstanding of the ways in which Black women protect the body and female psyche. 'Many characteristics of the angry Black woman stereotype, including hostility, rage, aggressiveness, and bitterness may be reflective of survival skills developed by Black women in the face of social, economic, and political oppression. This trifecta of oppression is all encompassing and creates a pervasive environment of injustice. A climate of constant danger or threat can significantly affect neural arousal and subsequent processing' (Ashley, 2014: 28).

Socially working grassroots activism: Successes in synergism

The violence Black women experience presents a challenge for social work. Social workers in the public sector may be viewed as extensions of the state. Given that state authorities are not protecting Black women from being killed extra-judicially, judicially or from entrapment by the carceral state practice is fraught with its impasses. A woman asking for help if she is a victim of domestic or intra-community violence can set off a chain of events that could jeopardise her life. As Monica Yorkman (2016), a Black transgendered woman activist imparts: 'I've had situations where I called the police, and the police ended up accusing me of things . . .' The question as to whether social workers see themselves as empaths and equals in their provision of service to diverse client populations is critical to service delivery. Understanding fissures in cultural competencies can be reconciled with the awareness that 'all groups need to see how their views of truth remain limited by the workings of unjust power relations' (Collins, 1998: xv). This then will enable a greater understanding of how Black women define their existence in accordance with the many strata of their identity, as well as the uniqueness of their circumstance: Black, ethnic, female, workers, mothers, immigrants, impoverished and sexual beings.

The Civil Rights movement transformed the American landscape with groundswells of legislation, institutions and policies that gave voice to those previously located outside empowered spaces. Even on smaller scales, ordinary citizens have felt called to action and advocacy. In San Francisco, in the 1960s, a social work initiative that spawned the National Association of Black Social Workers (NABSW) was inspired by their identification with the objectives of the Civil Rights Movement. Their common goal was Black liberation, racial equity and self-determination and improved social work practice and service delivery ('Mission Statement – National Association of Black Social Workers NABSW', 2016). Grassroots efforts inspired by the spirit of social justice movements influence social work practice, and often develop into organisations capable of impacting policy on an institutional level. The southern-grown National Black Women's Health Project used Civil Rights leader Fannie Lou Hamer's canonical maxim 'I'm sick and tired of being sick and tired' as a rallying chant for Black

Women's Health Justice (Springer, 1999). Additionally, the Black Panther Party of the 1960s and 70s was an organisation viewed by many in the mainstream as extremist, yet their advocacy and administration of free breakfasts for school-aged children remains an invaluable feature of American life (Heynen, 2009). In the school year of 2014–2015, over 54 low-income children received a school breakfast for every 100 who participated in school lunches; that school year saw 11.7 million students with eligibility for free and reduced meals receive a school breakfast (*School Breakfast Scorecard: 2014–2015*, 2016). Different from the Civil Rights and Black Power Movements, BLM has arrived at a moment where activists can not only reprocess their language to suit intersectional discourse, but have embraced intersectional theory as a modality for building social justice movements with the possibility of positive change for heterogeneous communities.

We must continue to be mindful of hierarchal and hegemonic obstacles to building such communities. As one human rights activist imparts:

> Despite decades of persistent activity . . . the intergenerational efforts of Black feminist women, like Black lives generally, still don't seem to matter much. In recent public conversations aimed at the reclamation and rebuilding of Black Liberation, political activists and writers seem to be largely committed to retrieving only those political ideas and projects in which the systemic effects of patriarchy have been ignored and underestimated.
>
> (Iverson, n.d.)

In summary

Theorising why there hasn't been a spontaneous eruption of support for Black women and women of colour brutalised and killed at the hands of police is attributable to the adoption and maintenance of an androcentric ethos that remains pervasive in the Black community, and in Black community activism. The macroaggressions forwarded serve to not so much explicate why new political movements remain sexist, but rather why it's not important to *not be* sexist. External macroaggressions, such as MWWS, relegate Black women and girls to the margins as non-victims: and internal macroaggressions such as the Willie Lynch Letter enable the Black community to say it's better if they remain there. The macroaggressions presented are by no means exhaustive and are discourses in themselves; and I suggest these *intra*-racial macroaggressions to be a dangerous refutation of the wise admonition, 'The Master's Tools Will Never Dismantle the Master's House' (Lorde, 1979). The Black Lives Matter Movement augurs tremendous hope for social, political and cultural activism on a wide berth of inclusion, yet the fact that the movement is still grappling with a devaluation when it comes to the lives of Black women is sobering, suggesting deeply rooted hetero-patriarchal philosophies foddering that devaluation. As such, realisations for powerful and inclusive social justice, structures and social work initiatives arising out of the movement are arrested, as Black women activists and their allies are consistently forced to break old ground.

Note

1 275 cases of Black women and women of colour named in the press who were killed by police were examined from 1991 to 2016 for instances of aggression toward black women and women of colour. Cases in which the death was arbitrary (due to police or medical negligence/neglect); domestic (between couples or those who were acquaintances), which constituted three cases; or murder while Black women and women of colour were incarcerated in prison (more than 60 cases) were excluded as overt aggression couldn't be determined. In-custody deaths, such as those in the case of Sandra Bland, were also excluded, as the cause of death, though highly suspicious, was deemed police neglect. Cases where policing policies that directly resulted in higher death rates among people of colour, such as 'No Knock' warrants (Kraska and Cubellis, 1997) remained, as their existence makes vulnerable populations of Black women and women of colour especially susceptible to police aggression. Cases of in-custody deaths, such as those of Natasha McKenna who was tased four times and subsequently died in custody (Funke and Susman, 2016), or Alexia Christian who was shot in the back of a patrol car (Boone, 2016), remained. Three of the 101 women were trans-women of colour. Two were shot and one died after tasing (Moore, Demarco and Hall). The youngest Black girl shot and killed was Aiyana Stanley-Jones, who was 7 years old at the time of death (Abbey-Lambertz, 2014), and the oldest Black woman was Pearlie Golden, 93 (Associated Press, 2014). Both were killed as the result of 'No-Knock' warrants. The final analysis was 101 extrajudicial killings between 1991 and September 2016.

References

Abbey-Lambertz, K. (2014) Manslaughter Charge Dropped For Cop Who Fatally Shot 7-Year-Old. *The Huffington Post*. Retrieved 15 August 2016, from www.huffingtonpost.com/2014/10/06/joseph-weekley-manslaughter-charge-dismissed_n_5940534.html.

Ashanti, K. F. (2001) *Psychotechnology of Brainwashing: Crucifying Willie Lynch*. Durham, NC: Tone Books.

Ashley, W. (2014) The Angry Black Woman: The Impact of Pejorative Stereotypes on Psychotherapy with Black Women. *Social Work in Public Health*, 29(1): 27–34.

Associated Press (2005) Police: Remains of LaToyia Figueroa found. Msnbc.com. Retrieved 10 October 2016, from www.nbcnews.com/id/9016541/ns/us_news/t/police-remains-latoyia-figueroa-found/.

Associated Press (2014) Cop Fatally Shoots 93-year-old Woman. *Mail Online*. Retrieved 15 August 2016, from www.dailymail.co.uk/news/article-2622997/Cop-history-fatal-shootings-guns-93-year-old-woman-home-brandished-firearm.html.

Baraka, A. (2016) The Assassination of Sandra Bland and the Struggle against State Repression. Ajamu Baraka. Retrieved 24 July 2016, from www.ajamubaraka.com/the-assassination-of-sandra-bland-and-the-struggle-against-state-repression/.

Bell, C. and Mattis, J. (2000) The Importance of Cultural Competence in Ministering to Black Victims of Domestic Violence. *Violence Against Women*, 6(5): 515–532. http://dx.doi.org/10.1177/10778010022182001.

Billingsley, A. (1994) *Climbing Jacob's Ladder: The Enduring Legacies of African-American Families*. New York: Simon and Schuster.

Boone, C. (2016) No Charges for Atlanta Officers Who Shot Woman in Back of Cop Car. *Myajc.com*. Retrieved 15 August 2016, from www.myajc.com/news/news/crime-law/no-charges-for-officers-who-shot-woman-in-back-of-/nry6Q/.

Butler, P. (2013) Black Male Exceptionalism? *Du Bois Review: Social Science Research on Race*, 10(02), 485–511. http://dx.doi.org/10.1017/s1742058x13000222.

Cartwright, Z. (2016) Police Savagely Punch and Tase Black Girl, Then Put a Bag Over Her Head (VIDEO) U.S. Uncut. Retrieved 1 October 2016, from http://usuncut.com/black-lives-matter/wisconsin-madison-police-brutal-video/.

Cobb, W. J. (2003) Willie Lynch is Dead (1712?–2003) *Retrieved from the Internet*, 3(15): 2011.

Collins, P. H. (1998) It's All in the Family: Intersections of Gender, Race, and Nation. *Hypatia*, 13(3): 62–82.

Conlin, L. and Davie, W. R. (2015) Missing White Woman Syndrome: How Media Framing Affects Viewers' Emotions. *Electronic News*, 9(1): 36–50.

Crenshaw, K. (1989) Demarginalizing the Intersection of Race and Sex: A Black Feminist Critique of Antidiscrimination Doctrine, Feminist Theory and Antiracist Politics. *University of Chicago Legal Forum*, 1: 141.

Dart, T. (2015) Sandra Bland Dashcam Video Shows Officer Threatened: 'I Will Light You Up'. *The Guardian*. Retrieved 05 May 2016, from www.theguardian.com/us-news/2015/jul/21/sandra-bland-dashcam-video-arrest-released.

Dart, T. (2016) Sandra Bland's Family Settles Wrongful Death Lawsuit Against Texas for $1.9m. *The Guardian*. Retrieved 15 August 2016, from www.theguardian.com/us-news/2016/sep/15/sandra-bland-family-settles-wrongful-death-lawsuit-million.

Day, H. (2016) Shocking Moment Florida Police Officer Punches Woman in Chest. *Mail Online*. Retrieved 1 October 2016, from www.dailymail.co.uk/news/article-3565235/Shocking-moment-Florida-police-officer-repeatedly-punches-woman-chest-handcuffs-cops-stand-watch.html.

Donovan, R., Galban, D., Grace, R., Bennett, J., and Felicie, S. (2012) Impact of Racial Macro- and Microaggressions in Black Women's Lives: A Preliminary Analysis. *Journal of Black Psychology*, 39(2): 185–196. http://dx.doi.org/10.1177/0095798412443259 from http://samples.sainsburysebooks.co.uk/9781136497551_sample_888352.pdf.

Farmer, A. (2014) Renegotiating the 'African Woman': Women's Cultural Nationalist Theorizing in the Us Organization and the Congress of African People, 1965–1975. *Black Diaspora Review*, 4(1): 86.

Foucault, M. (1978) *The Will to Knowledge: History of Sexuality*. London: Penguin.

Funke, D. and Susman, T. (2016) From Ferguson to Baton Rouge: Deaths of Black Men and Women at the Hands of Police. *Latimes.com*. Retrieved 1 October 2016, from www.latimes.com/nation/la-na-police-deaths-20160707-snap-htmlstory.html.

Giddings, P. (1984) *When and Where I Enter*. New York: W. Morrow.

Gorski, P. (2013) Consumerism as Racial and Economic Injustice: The Macroaggressions That Make Me, And Maybe You, A Hypocrite. *Understanding and Dismantling Privilege: The Official Journal of The White Privilege Conference and The Matrix Center for the Advancement of Social Equity and Inclusion*, IV(1): 4–5.

Gray, E. (2015) When the Streets Run Red: For a 21st-Century Anti-Lynching Movement. *Metamute.org*. Retrieved 28 May 2016, from www.metamute.org/editorial/articles/when streets-run-red-21st-century-anti-lynching-movement.

The Great Debaters (2007) [film] Directed by Denzel Washington. The Weinstein Company, Metro-Goldwyn-Mayer.

Griffin, R. A. (2012) I AM an Angry Black Woman: Black Feminist Autoethnography, Voice, and Resistance. *Women's Studies in Communication*, 35(2): 138–157.

Hackman, R. (2015) 'She Was Only a Baby': Last Charge Dropped in Police Raid that Killed Sleeping Detroit Child. *The Guardian*. Retrieved 12 August 2016, from www.

theguardian.com/us-news/2015/jan/31/detroit-aiyana-stanley-jones-police-officer-cleared.
Heynen, N. (2009) Bending the Bars of Empire from Every Ghetto for Survival: The Black Panther Party's Radical Antihunger Politics of Social Reproduction and Scale. *Annals of the Association of American Geographers*, 99(2): 406–422.
Hull, G., Bell-Scott, P. and Smith, B. (1982) *All the Women Are White, All the Blacks Are Men, But Some of Us Are Brave*. Old Westbury, NY: Feminist Press.
Hurston, Z. (2004) *Their Eyes Were Watching God*. 1st ed. eBook Edition: Harper Collins.
Iverson, M. (n. d.) *On Patriarchy, Black Feminism and Radical Voice*. [online] OHR Democracy. Retrieved 7 February 2017, from www.ohrdemocracy.org/patriarchy-black-feminism-radical-voice/.
Jackson, J. J. (1971) But Where Are the Men? *The Black Scholar*, 3(4): 30–41.
Jemmott, Z. (2016) #FergusonFridays: Not All of the Black Freedom Fighters Are Men: An Interview with Black Women on the Front Line in Ferguson. *The Feminist Wire*. Retrieved from www.thefeministwire.com/2014/10/fergusonfridays-black-freedom-fighters-men-interview-black-women-front-line-ferguson/.
Konstantinides, A. (2016) Rhode Island Police Officer Caught on Video Punching Woman in the Face. *Mail Online*. Retrieved 1 October 2016, from www.dailymail.co.uk/news/article-3681392/Rhode-Island-police-officer-caught-video-punching-woman-face.html.
Kraska, P. B. and Cubellis, L. J. (1997) Militarizing Mayberry and Beyond: Making Sense of American Paramilitary Policing. *Justice Quarterly*, 14(4): 607–629.
Lai, K., Park, H., Bauchanan, L., and Andrews, W. (2015) Assessing the Legality of Sandra Bland's Arrest. *Nytimes.com*. Retrieved 15 August 2016, from www.nytimes.com/interactive/2015/07/20/us/sandra-bland-arrest-death-videos-maps.html?_r=0.
Lambertz, K. (2014) How A Police Officer Shot A Sleeping 7-Year-Old to Death. *The Huffington Post*. Retrieved 9 September 2016, from https://d.docs.live.net/04171726d4f2dc37/Final%20Daft%20BLMM%20NEW.docxh.
Lewis, G. (2000) *'Race', Gender, Social Welfare: Encounters in a Postcolonial Society*. Cambridge, UK: Polity Press.
Liebler, C. (2010) Me(di)a Culpa?: The 'Missing White Woman Syndrome' and Media Self-Critique. *Communication, Culture & Critique*, 3(4): 549–565. http://dx.doi.org/10.1111/j.1753–9137.2010.01085.x.
Lind, A. and Brzuzy, S. (2008) *Battleground*. Westport, CT: Greenwood Press.
Lorde, A. (1979) 'The Master's Tools Will Never Dismantle the Master's House.' In Lorde, A. (ed.) (2007) *Sister Outsider: Essays and Speeches*. Trumansburg, NY: The Crossing Press.
Lorde, A. (2003) The Master's Tools Will Never Dismantle the Master's House. *Feminist Postcolonial Theory: A Reader*, 25(27).
Lorde, A. (2007) *Sister Outsider: Essays and Speeches*. Trumansburg, NY: The Crossing Press.
Lynch, W. (1970) *Let's Make a Slave*. Black Arcade Liberation Library, Chicago, IL: Lushena Books.
May, V. (2015) *Pursuing Intersectionality, Unsettling Dominant Imaginaries*. New York: Routledge.
Maynard, D. (2016) Missing White Girl Syndrome – When a Child Dies. Journalism Center on Children & Families. *Journalismcenter.org*. Retrieved 29 June 2016, from http://journalismcenter.org/when-a-child-dies/missing-white-girl.html.
McQueeney, S. M. (2005) Recognizing Unborn Victims Over Heightening Punishment for Crimes Against Pregnant Women. *New England Journal on Crime & Civil Confinement*, 31: 461.

Mission Statement – National Association of Black Social Workers (NABSW) (2016) *Nabsw.org*. Retrieved 10 October 2016, from http://nabsw.org/?page=MissionStatement.

Molla, R. (2016) America's Missing Persons by Age, Race and Gender. *WSJ*. Retrieved 10 October 2016, from http://blogs.wsj.com/numbers/americas-missing-persons-by-age-race-and-gender-1814/.

Morrow, A. (2003) *Breaking the Curse of Willie Lynch: The Science of Slave Psychology*. St. Louis, MO: Rising Sun Publications.

The Moynihan Report (1966) *Social Service Review*, 40(1): 84–85. http://dx.doi.org/10.1086/641858.

Murphy, Y. (2009) *Incorporating Intersectionality in Social Work Practice, Research, Policy, and Education*. Washington, DC: NASW Press, National Association of Social Workers.

New York Times (1997) Hundreds Protest in Harlem, Saying a Death Wasn't Suicide. Retrieved 10 October 2016, from www.nytimes.com/1997/04/26/nyregion/hundreds-protest-in-harlem-saying-a-death-wasn-t-suicide.html.

Omolade, B. (1994) *The Rising Song of Black Women*. New York: Routledge.

Painter, N. (2014) 'The Rebellious Life of Mrs. Rosa Parks', by Jeanne Theoharis. *Nytimes.com*. Retrieved 3 May 2016, from www.nytimes.com/2013/03/31/books/review/the-rebellious-life-of-mrs-rosa-parks-by-jeanne-theoharis.html?_r=0.

Patton, T. and Snyder-Yuly, J. (2007) Any Four Black Men Will Do: Rape, Race, and the Ultimate Scapegoat. *Journal of Black Studies*, 37(6): 859–895. http://dx.doi.org/10.1177/0021934706296025.

Petersen-Smith, K. (2015) Black Lives Matter. [online] *Isreview.org*. Retrieved 21 December 2016, from http://isreview.org/issue/96/black-lives-matter.

Rogers, K. (2015) The Death of Sandra Bland: Questions and Answers. *Nytimes.com*. Retrieved 15 August 2016, from www.nytimes.com/interactive/2015/07/23/us/23blandlisty.html.

Sanchez-Hucles, J. (1997) Jeopardy Not Bonus Status for Black Women in the Work Force: Why Does the Myth of Advantage Persist? *American Journal of Community Psychology*, 25(5): 565–580. http://dx.doi.org/10.1023/a:1024678732098.

Sanfield, S. (2006) *Adventures of High John the Conqueror*. Atlanta, GA: August House Publishers.

Saulny, M. (2014) Tragedy in Detroit, With Reality TV Crew in Tow. *Nytimes.com*. Retrieved 15 August 2016, from https://d.docs.live.net/04171726d4f2dc37/Final%20Daft%20BLMM%20NEW2.docxh.

School Breakfast Scorecard: 2014–2015 (2016) Washington, DC. Retrieved from http://frac.org/pdf/School_Breakfast_Scorecard_SY_2014_2015.pdf.

Smith, S. (2016) Issues. *Isreview.org*. Retrieved 3 August 2016, from http://isreview.org/issue/91/black-feminism-and-intersectionality.

Springer, K. (ed.) (1999) *Still Lifting, Still Climbing: Contemporary Black Women's Activism*. New York: NYU Press.

Stovall, S. (2016) Why Do We Seldom Hear about Missing Black Children? *Denverpost.com*. Retrieved 1 October 2016, from www.denverpost.com/2013/02/14/why-do-we-seldom-hear-about-missing-black-children/.

Theoharis, J. (2013) *The Rebellious Life of Mrs. Rosa Parks*. Boston, MA: Beacon Press.

Wilson, C., Gutiérrez, F., and Chao, L. (2013) *Racism, Sexism, and the Media*. Thousand Oaks, CA: SAGE Publications.

Wilson, J. W. (1948) *High John the Conqueror*. Fort Worth, TX: TCU Press.

Wood, K., Clinton, C., Kemble, F., and Clinton, C. (2002) Fanny Kemble's Civil Wars. *The Journal of Southern History*, 68(3): 701. http://dx.doi.org/10.2307/3070190.

Yorkman, M. and Fisher, B. (2015) *The Global African: Repression in Egypt & Black Transgender Lives Matter*. The Global African with Bill Fletcher. Retrieved 11 May 2018, from www.youtube.com/watch?v=843w9w6OMxc.

Yosso, T., Smith, W., Ceja, M., and Solórzano, D. (2009) Critical Race Theory, Racial Microaggressions, and Campus Racial Climate for Latina/o Undergraduates. *Harvard Educational Review*, 79(4), 659–691. http://dx.doi.org/10.17763/haer.79.4.m6867014157m707l.

10 'They like you to pretend to be something you are not'

An exploration of working with the intersections of gender, sexuality, 'race', religion and 'refugeeness', through the experience of Lesbian Immigration Support Group (LISG) members and volunteers

Nina Held and Karen McCarthy

Introduction

> It is painful, I mean when you are saying something you know that you are speaking the truth and somebody is not believing you, you try to give all the evidences and then they are still like not believing you. It is painful, it is really painful, because you don't know how to express yourself again.
>
> (Lady Snarewell[1])

In this chapter, we explore the intersectional experience of gender, sexuality, 'race', religion and other oppressions in the lives of asylum-seeking women and discuss the tensions produced by the systematic failure of recognising refugee claims on grounds of sexuality as legitimate. We argue that 'refugeeness' troubles these intersections. 'Refugee' is a legal subject position defined by the Geneva Convention. One's legal status as a refugee is accepted if an asylum claim is successful. Many refugees are positioned as 'asylum seekers' for years in legal limbo, where their experiences are shaped by precarity and liminality through policies that prevent access to work, housing, social welfare and education. Hence, 'refugeeness' is a created subjectivity, determined by a process of becoming. This subjectivity is never fixed but constantly changing (Lacroix, 2004).

By drawing on research conducted with the Lesbian Immigration Support Group (LISG) in Manchester, we examine the complexities of the multiple structural oppressions experienced by Black, African and Asian lesbian asylum seekers and the tensions inherent in supporting them through the British asylum system. We base our analysis on our understanding of intersectionality.

Intersectionality, a term that was coined by American legal scholar Kimberlé Crenshaw (1989), evolved through earlier Black feminist writing (Nayak, 2015:

86), has become a buzzword in feminist scholarship (Davis, 2008). Applying Black feminist theory to anti-discrimination law, Crenshaw argued that gender and 'race' cannot be separated in Black women's lives but that Black women are subject to both sexism *and* racism. The term intersectionality expresses 'the multidimensionality of Black women's experience' (Crenshaw, 1989: 139). Intersectional thinking has been shaped by Black and Chicana lesbian feminists (The Combahee River Collective, 1982; Cade Bambera, 1970; Lorde, 1984a, 1984b; Smith, 1983; Moraga, 1983; Cornwall, 1983; Collins, 1990). Lorde wrote about the damage that is caused by having to neglect and reconcile different parts of her identity as a Black lesbian, describing how as a Black lesbian socialising in predominantly white lesbian environments in New York in the 1950s it was clear her experiences were different to that of white lesbians (Lorde, 1984b).

Whilst there is a vast amount of literature on intersectionality available, few studies exist that link intersectionality with asylum (Firth and Mauthe, 2013) and use the concept of intersectionality for the exploration of the lives of LGBT asylum seekers and refugees (Baillot et al., 2012; Lewis, 2014; Morgan, 2006). None of these studies include 'refugeeness' in the intersectional experience of structural oppressions. Studies on 'refugeeness', on the other hand, do not address sexuality nor intersectionality (Lacroix, 2004), with few exceptions (Lee and Brotman, 2011). This chapter aims to address this gap by examining LISG members' positions in a complex web of the social stratifications of gender, sexuality, ethnicity, religion, age and being an asylum seeker/refugee. As we will show, this position is complex, because of the predicament women find themselves in, of not only being unrecognised as refugees but also as lesbians, whilst in their country of origin being recognised as a lesbian meant being prosecuted, or persecuted.

Background and methodology

LISG grew out of a Manchester-based anti-deportation campaign for a lesbian asylum seeker in 2007. During the campaign, other lesbian asylum seekers contacted the women involved, seeking support. The campaign group, mainly white women, recognised there was a need for support for lesbian and bisexual women asylum seekers/refugees and created a support group. One of the authors (Karen McCarthy) was a founding member and the other (Nina Held) joined in 2009. The group currently consists of more than 20 active members, and nine volunteers, two of whom are refugee women. Over 60 members have passed through the group since 2007 and new women join regularly. Roughly half of the members of the group have been granted their status, but of these many have spent years in the limbo of the asylum process. Only three were granted refugee status at first application. Women come from a range of countries across Africa, Asia and the Caribbean. The group offers emotional, social and practical support, meeting monthly at a local women's centre. The group have lunch together, talk about cases, events and urgent business. Practical support for members includes: accompanying women to the United Kingdom Visa and Immigration Service (UKVI) in

Croydon/South London[2] to claim asylum, writing support letters, acting as witnesses in court hearings, accompanying women to solicitor appointments, substantive interviews (two hours away in Liverpool), and regular signing at the Salford Home Office Reporting Centre.

This chapter focuses on two group discussions that we facilitated in 2016 and draws on eight semi-structured interviews conducted by McCarthy in 2014/2015 as part of her MA dissertation. Eight women participated in the first discussion group, six of whom were asylum seekers, and two refugees, from various African, Asian and Caribbean countries. The need to protect the women's identities, due to the sensitivity of their cases, means that we use pseudonyms (mostly chosen by the participants) and do not provide any other identifying details.

We used a pre-prepared interview guide to help us focus the discussion, while remaining open and flexible to the flow of the group. This fluidity allowed women to express their intersectional experiences not just in response to the research questions but also to each other's contributions. This was important in avoiding focus on a single social identifier (such as lesbian) and allowed the women to move between their different lived experiences, as women, lesbians, Black women, asylum seekers and refugees, and other identities such as mother, single, Christian, Muslim and African, and various combinations of these. The response to each other's experiences and contributions created a space in which the participants were in relative control of defining themselves and their experiences as 'the synergistic relation between inequalities as grounded in the lived experience of hierarchy' (McKinnon, 2013: 1029). This reflected that analysis using intersectionality as a method allows us to see that 'the intersectional experience is greater than the sum' (Crenshaw, 1989: 140).

In a second group discussion, six women participated and discussed the first draft of this chapter. We went through quotations from the previous discussion which generated further debate. The women expressed their anger about their treatment by the UKVI. Discussing their experiences within the group appeared empowering for the women. Witney remarked, 'How lucky we are to be involved in such a book. Unusual to be asked to be involved in a book for intellectuals.' Her comment highlights the exclusion women feel from many parts of UK society, including academia, but also the different positions between the women and us as researchers.

The legal, social and economic position asylum-seeking lesbians find themselves in stands in contrast to the privileged lives of the white (European) volunteers. Whilst this research is shaped by many differences between the researchers and the participants – our different gendered, racialised, classed and sexualised subjectivities – it is also shaped by power inequalities which are reproduced through the system and through our interactions. For instance, it has been clear over the last ten years of LISG that the word of white volunteers (European nationals) is more respected, valued and deemed more credible than that of Black volunteers and asylum seekers/refugees by the members of the group as well as the 'authorities' (for instance, whose support letter and witness account carries weight in court). In addition, as Witney's remark demonstrates, our work as academics might be perceived in ways that add to the structural intersections of power. This reflects something that is common: white researchers conducting research on asylum seekers and refugees (so far, all requests LISG has received for members to be involved in research have been from white academics). Our main aim is to advocate for and raise awareness of the situation of lesbian and bisexual women claiming asylum in the UK, but this research will contribute to furthering our academic careers and further manifest structural inequalities. The research is shaped by the inevitable power relations between researchers and the researched. We tried to counter these power inequalities to some extent by actively involving the women in the process of writing and seeking their feedback. We also decided to use several interview quotations for the women's voices to be heard. Nevertheless, we are the producers of the knowledge presented in this chapter, and this knowledge production can only be partial and is dependent on our own situatedness (Haraway, 1991).

Asylum claims based on sexuality

Article 1A(2) of the 1951 Geneva Convention Relating to the Status of Refugees defines a refugee as a person who:

> owing to well-founded fear of being persecuted for reasons of race, religion, nationality, *membership of a particular social group* or political opinion, is outside the country of his nationality and is unable or, owing to such fear, unwilling to avail himself of the protection of that country. [emphasis added]

Asylum claimants need to provide evidence of political activity, ethnicity and so on, and in claims based on sexuality, evidence of persecution, or fear of persecution because of sexuality, or perceived sexuality. Claimants need to prove that they belong to a particular social group. Gender and sexual identity have been recognised as grounds to claim asylum in the UK since 1999. Since then it has been accepted that women, lesbians and gay men can form a 'particular social group' (Shah and Islam v Secretary of State for the Home Department, House of Lords, 2 A.C. 629, 1999). For an asylum claim based on sexuality to be successful, the asylum seeker must prove that s/he is lesbian or gay and needs to show a well-founded fear of persecution. A report by the UK Lesbian and Gay Immigration Group in London (UKLGIG 2010) found that whilst on average 73% of all initial asylum claims were refused by the Home Office, in LGBT cases this figure was 98–99%, indicating the difficulties of evidence.

There are currently 73 countries (and five entities) in the world with legislation in place that criminalises same-sex consensual acts between adults. In 13 of these countries these acts are punishable by death and in 15 by imprisonment up to life sentences. 40 of these countries are still using homophobic laws imposed during British colonial rule. The existence of such laws itself is not enough for asylum claims to be successful. Before a ruling by the Supreme Court in 2010, most claims were refused by the Home Office and the courts with the 'discretion argument', that is, the assumption that the person can go back to their country of origin and live their sexuality discreetly (UKLGIG, 2010). At LISG we had many cases where decisions were based on this argument (Held, 2016). With such decisions, the Home Office and the courts forced people back into the closet, and often into heterosexual relationships (Johnson, 2011).

The Supreme Court ruling of 2010 challenged this reasoning and made it more difficult for Home Office officials and courts to argue that claimants can go back and live their sexuality in secret. The ruling has been praised as progressive change and there is some indication of better decision-making since July 2010 (UKLGIG, 2013). However, courts are still required to identify how openly the claimant would live his or her sexuality if returned. Furthermore, negative decisions on grounds of 'credibility' have increased since the 2011 Supreme Court decision (UKLGIG, 2013). UKLGIG found that while before 2010 the majority of claims they looked at were refused by the Home Office, with the 'discretion argument' (UKLGIG, 2010), in most of the negative decisions made between 2010 and 2013 the claimant was not believed to be gay (UKLGIG, 2013).

Decisions on asylum applications are made using policies developed by the UKVI, the Home Office and the courts, where the asylum system is viewed through the lens of predominantly white and patriarchal organisational cultures. Intersections of gender, sexuality, 'race', age and religion and the structural oppressions experienced by applicants are not acknowledged in decision-making. Rather, decisions are based on a particular understanding of sexuality (one that is 'out and proud'), and based on a stereotypical white, male, middle-class gay identity (Morgan, 2006). This understanding of sexuality draws on a particular Western model of sexuality whereby gay identity and homosexual conduct are interchangeable and 'which presumes clarity of boundaries between heterosexual and homosexual identity and requires public expression of private and sexual behaviour' (Morgan, 2006: 151–152).

Many LGBT asylum seekers who are refused (and who have exhausted their appeal rights) as they cannot prove their sexuality become 'undocumented' and often destitute. They no longer receive aid from the state, other than the offer of a plane ticket to their country of origin, so are reliant on charity and friends. The impact of the UK asylum system, of being subject to intersected oppressions, limits their ability to be agents of their own lives and denies their reality and compromises their physical and mental health whilst exposing them to risk of abuse and exploitation. The danger of detention and deportation combine with the challenge to mental health of being disbelieved:

> when I was in detention I was, I don't know, I was like start, start crazy, it was very, very hard for me, it was very hard, very, very hard, I don't, sometimes I don't, didn't know where I am, I was like maybe the world the world is finished, so.
>
> (Sandra, in interview)

The lack of acknowledgement by the UK asylum system of the intersectional oppression and the cumulative effect of being forced into living a precarious and liminal life (a characteristic of 'refugeeness') has an impact on claimants' mental health. Shidlo and Ahola (2013: 10) list the mental health conditions experienced by asylum seekers and refugees, resulting from 'a life time of cumulative trauma' including 'recurrent depression, dissociative disorders, panic disorder, generalised anxiety disorder, social anxiety, traumatic brain injury and substance abuse'. People who are forced to migrate because of their LGBT identity may also experience post-traumatic stress disorders. The marginalisation of those with mental health conditions is well documented and adds another category to the oppressions that intersect in the experience of a Black, lesbian, asylum seeker.

Gaining refugee status does not suddenly relieve these oppressions. Once women get status they realise that they will never go back home, never see their family, or their mother before she dies, layers of loss that affect mental health. Added to this, they have to negotiate building a new life in a patriarchal, racist society while managing the mental, and other, health issues developed since they have been in the UK.

Intersections of gender, sexuality, 'race', age and religion in decision-making

> . . . believe me, be a lesbian, be a Muslim, be a woman, like you in the fire, fire, just in fire. Nobody can help you.
>
> (Razia, in interview)

From all the cases that we have supported over the years, only a small percentage (approx. 5%) were granted asylum in the first instance. Most other cases were refused on grounds of credibility, i.e., where it was not believed that the claimant was lesbian and, in a few cases, it was argued that there is not enough proof of the persecution of LGBT people in the claimant's country of origin. This can be in countries where (usually male) homosexuality is not illegal, or where the UKVI country of origin reports draw on Western gay magazines that say the country is safe for (Western) gay men to travel. The situation of lesbian and bisexual women is often different in these countries due to gender oppression, and is less likely to be documented.

Reports by the UK Lesbian and Gay Immigration Group (UKLGIG, 2010, 2013) have documented that delay in disclosure can negatively affect credibility assessment, and that decision-makers do not recognise the reasons behind that delay. Three of the women participating in the focus groups had their claims refused because of such delays. They explained the delay by saying they were 'still hiding' (Brown Honey; Favour); were 'scared' of someone finding out about their sexuality (Brown Honey; Kin); or did not know 'that they [LGBT people] have the right here to live in the country' (Favour).

Public expression of sexual behaviour is especially difficult for LGBT asylum seekers, who come from countries where such expression would have caused forced marriage, homophobic violence and potentially imprisonment, possibly death for the person and sometimes for their family and therefore 'you do everything in hiding' (Lady Snarewell), 'you have to fool everybody around you' (Witney), 'you have to live life in secret, a life in the closet' (Myself).

The women spoke about the pressures of coming out: 'you HAVE to come out, to prove your sexuality, in the UK, you have to prove your sexuality to certain people in the Home Office', and of feeling helpless because they do not know how to prove it when the UKVI do not accept their evidence:

> By the time you prove your sexuality they say that's not enough, they don't believe you.
>
> (Brown Honey)

> It's painful.
>
> (Lady Snarewell)

> Yeah, it's annoying, what proof do they want from me?
>
> (Brown Honey)

> They think everything is made up; I've done what I can do, I don't know what I need to do next to prove myself a lesbian.
>
> (Kin)

Some lesbian asylum seekers have experienced extreme trauma, because of the attitudes of others to their sexuality. All have lost/given up a lot to find safety and have invested a great deal in being believed, being seen to be lesbian. Not being believed then impacts on the women's experiences:

Nina: How does it make you feel if they don't believe you?
Kin: It's like painful, like in my case I don't know how to prove to them.
Hope: Back at home you are feeling very bad because you can't show it ['yeah'], you can't show it that you are a lesbian, you can't do action, you can't do action . . . but here you are allowed to do action, but how to prove it, because those people, Home Office, everything is 'no', you say this they say 'no, no that's a lie' so they make you to feel crazy.

Sandra explained in interview:

> you can't imagine, you tell people the truth, you tell people your story. You tell people all, all about you, how you're suffering, about your sexuality. But the thing they can't say to you is you're lying. It's not easy to hear that.

These statements highlight the importance of intersectionality as a (painful) lived experience as well as theoretical resource. This is echoed in Lorde's description: 'I find I am constantly being encouraged to pluck out some one aspect of myself and present this as the meaningful whole, eclipsing or denying the other parts of self' (Lorde, 1984a: 122). In the experience of LISG members, the UK asylum system picks out sexuality and focuses on that to the exclusion of all other facets of themselves. When the women's life experiences, both in their countries of origin and in the UK, are viewed through a Western, white, often male, heterosexual lens, the intersections of their subjectivity are marginalised and/or ignored. As the participants set out on their journey in life, in their countries of origin, their direction was controlled by the intersections of 'race', and imperial colonialism, gender, sexuality and sometimes class. The development of their *personhood* (Firth and Maute, 2013) is affected by the restrictions upon them resulting from these intersections. When because of this experience they have to change the direction of their journey, they are faced with a whole new arrangement of intersections that include the road works of the UK asylum system intersecting with their ethnicity, sexuality and gender. The women's status as refugees is controlled and compromised by the asylum system. Following the diversions and obstacles put in their way they navigate through the complicated intersections, developing their sense of themselves, their rights and their resilience until they reach a destination which may, or may not, be the one they had hoped and planned for. Their destination is controlled by their 'refugeeness', which prohibits them from working, studying beyond basic levels, marrying and travelling.

At the beginning of the group discussion we asked participants to write down words on sticky-notes to describe themselves and their identity. We gave them a list they could choose from (such as 'lesbian', 'asylum seeker'), as well as blank cards, and many women chose different descriptions (such as 'cute' and 'strong woman'). It is worth noting that only three women chose 'asylum seeker' as an identifier while four chose 'Christian' and four chose 'lesbian', three chose 'African' and three chose 'mother'. However, to navigate the roadworks and intersection of the asylum system they have to focus on lesbian, even if this is not a word they would previously have used for themselves, or an aspect of their identity they would have prioritised. Vervliet et al. (2014) highlight that 'migration policy clearly prioritises the category 'refugee' over the other categories in its approach to unaccompanied refugee mothers' and does not acknowledge the impact of the intersection of different 'categories' on the lived experience of those women. The same is true for lesbian asylum seekers, where proving their lesbian sexuality supposedly overrides any other consideration for the UKVI, and where intersecting aspects of their personhood, e.g. being a mother or being married, may be used to deny their sexuality, without recognising that these aspects may have been forced on them, or 'chosen' as means of surviving. Decision-makers often do not consider how the expression of sexuality is shaped by the intersections of other aspects of their lives.

In the group discussions, women referred to 'race', religion and age as affecting decision-making. Hope spoke of the intersections of 'race' and sexuality:

> At that time when they tell me that they don't believe me, I thought maybe the Home Office people are just discriminating. Kind of discrimination. This is what I am, that's nature, so when they are telling me they don't believe me

> this must be discrimination because of my colour. [G laughs and says 'sometimes it's like that'] Yeah because they are white people, these people must be discriminating.

Favour thought that she was refused because of her age:

> I think my solicitor thinks it's my age, he thinks because of my age, it's an age thing? Because of my age they don't think that I'm lesbian but in this country I've seen so many like me, older women like me, I wonder why they think that . . . [laughter]

We asked Favour how she felt at an event that was organised by a local lesbian group and attended by mostly older lesbians. She said that she was thinking, 'if the HO could come and see this. I was happy to see them [the older lesbians there], I have found many like that, like me.'

Giametta's (2014) research suggests that LGBT asylum claims might be even more difficult to prove when claimants 'confess' their religious beliefs which may be regarded as holding on to 'backward' beliefs, which contradicts the Western narratives of temporal progression in LGBT identity development that embraces the freedom of the West. This was expressed by Kin:

> They didn't believe me at all; I told them that I was a Muslim lesbian, and they say they don't believe me, everything, everything. If it's one thing or two things or three things that we need to focus, then it's OK but they deny me at all and say we don't believe that.

Having a faith was not always an easy path:

> So Yarl's Wood[3] was one big turning point where I really had to fight the right way, you're discriminated in church in the chapel you're not allowed cos you're lesbian.
>
> (Blessed, in interview)

The claimant faces the pressures of constructing their LGBT identity in a certain way (that is non-religious). Thus, gender, sexuality, religion and 'refugeeness' intersect in complex ways in this subject formation. Morgan (2006: 136), writing about the asylum system in the US, argues that decisions are based on racialised sexual stereotypes and culturally specific norms of sexuality. She identifies that 'it is not good enough for an asylum applicant simply to be attracted to people of the same sex; the applicant must be 'gay enough' for the government to find that they have met their burden of proof'. This seems to be similar in the UK. For instance, Bennett and Thomas (2013) argue that it is not only the claimant's sexual narrative that is taken as the basis for the decision-making but also her appearance in the court and whether she conforms to Western stereotypes.

In our second group discussion women expressed very strongly their anger about not being acknowledged as lesbians. There was a general agreement that some women are refused because of the way they look: 'but what does a lesbian look like?' (Witney); 'they like you to put on stereotypes' (Brown Honey); 'they like you to pretend to be somebody you are not' (Myself).

Two women who had recently got refugee status spoke about the changes they were going through and the relief of not having to 'prove' their sexuality anymore. Witney had gone through years of fighting for being accepted as a lesbian, as she had been refused by the UKVI and several judges:

> In court I was not believed, it was stress. What can I do? Now I have the freedom of whatever I chose. If I want to dress like a man I can. If I want to dress like a girl I can. No one can say because you want prove.

Both gave a very strong account of how they had felt as an asylum seeker: 'When I was an asylum seeker I was in bondage. I was captive. Something is holding you and want to strangle you to death. You are a walking corpse. The living dead' (Brown Honey); 'If I express myself it will not bring any gains. You are squashed, it is keeping you down. Whatever you say to yourself it comes back. Maybe it is like being hungry and food is there but you can't reach – if you eat it you are pushed back' (Witney); Brown Honey made the point, saying, 'only foreigners need to prove themselves'.

The asylum system asks for membership of a particular social group, and focuses on fixed social identities. The system requires evidence of sexuality and interprets this as evidence of an 'out' sexuality. Having a relationship, adopting a gay lifestyle including participating in lesbian and gay groups and Gay Prides and visiting the Gay Village, can form part of that proof that is expected to be produced (Morgan, 2006). However, over the years we have also seen decisions by the UKVI and the courts where judges have argued that going to the Gay Village is not necessarily proof of being gay as many heterosexual people also socialise in the Gay Village. Recently this has been part of the Home Office case against lesbian asylum seekers from Pakistan and Cameroon. Nevertheless, women are often questioned whether they have been to the Gay Village and to name bars and clubs they had been to, with any mistakes in names being seen as evidence of lying. It is also assumed that once LGBT people find 'liberation' and can live an openly gay lifestyle in the UK, they would do so (ignoring that many UK born LGBT people do not choose to live that way, despite change in public attitudes and laws). There is an assumption that they would 'immediately' start sexual relationships and if they do not then this damages their credibility (O'Leary, 2008: 90).

In McCarthy's research (2015), participants were clear that their lived sexuality was more about relationships than sexual activity. They expressed hope for building positive futures with families and partners: 'you got to go with your heart and you know, what you feel and it's not about sex, it's about having someone, that you love and care for you' (Jane). Some talked about the difficulties of meeting girlfriends: ''maybe you want a relationship with them and you like them, they like you and then you say, 'asylum seekers' and zooooom!!' (Brown Honey). As well as having the pressure to form a relationship to 'prove' sexuality, let alone out of attraction, there is the obstacle of the negative stereotypes of asylum seekers as being 'trouble' of some sort.

While most of the participants stated they enjoyed being able to be more open about their sexuality, and have opportunities to associate with others of a similar identity, living a 'Western' sexual lifestyle can be difficult for LGBT people who have been persecuted and /or prosecuted in their country of origin. They often experience internalised homophobia and a fear of talking about sexuality. Women often come from cultures where they have learned not to talk about sexuality. In addition, the terms 'gay' or 'lesbian' often do not exist in these countries, where constructions of gender and sexuality might be different, making it difficult for asylum claimants to identify as such when they come to the UK (O'Leary, 2008).

Conclusion

This chapter has shown that intersectionality is a useful framework for analysing the lived experiences of lesbian asylum seekers, illustrating the intersections of the structural oppressions of 'refugeeness', gender, class, religion and 'race'. Black feminist scholars, who developed the concept of intersectionality, were motivated by political activism, to trouble the categories of gender and 'race' and address 'the racialisation of gender and the gendering of race' (Fotopoulou, 2012: 20). By talking about and reflecting on their intersectional experience, LISG women highlight the structural oppression lesbian asylum seekers face is specific to the asylum process. They illustrate not only that gender and sexuality are racialised but also that these categories are shaped by being an asylum seeker. Lesbian asylum claimants face different structural oppressions than other members of the 'LGBT community'. Like other LGBT people, their experiences are shaped by the intersections of sexuality, gender, 'race', class, religion (and other social identifiers) but they experience these intersections in complex ways through the asylum system.

The asylum system not only shapes the experiences and subjectivities of LISG members but also those of BME and white volunteers. While volunteers at LISG work, with members, to raise awareness of the inherent racism, sexism and homophobia of the UK immigration system, they are often in the position of 'playing the game' by the rules of that system. For example, writing letters of support and acting as witnesses for members where any social status they may have, as professionals and academics, is invoked because this will carry more weight and make the member's case stronger. To choose not to use their status, the result of intersections of privilege, in this way would be to deny LISG members access to their power and to put their asylum cases at unnecessary risk. While volunteers acknowledge their power and privilege to make this choice, it compromises their personal and political convictions that the racism, sexism and classism of the UK asylum system must be challenged and changed. They must, and do, pursue other ways of challenging and working towards change. As UK and European citizens most of the volunteers at LISG are part of, and benefit from, the racist, Eurocentric society that created the UK asylum system, but they also experience the impact of gender oppression and heteronormativity. It is their own experience of the impact of the intersections of these structural oppressions, and privileges, that motivates them to work through the tensions inherent in differences in power and privilege and to use that power and privilege positively and productively to effect positive outcomes for individual women, and to work with those women to challenge that system. As of August 2017, in over 10 years no LISG member has been deported and over 50 have gained refugee status.

On arrival in the UK, lesbian asylum seekers may find that the homophobic oppression they experienced at home is alive and well, despite equality legislation and the possibility of a 'gay' marriage. Here the intersection of a range of oppressions and discriminations include that of the sexist, racist and homophobic UK asylum and immigration system. The asylum system is perpetuating imperial colonialism in the ways in which it defines what a lesbian looks like, and how a lesbian behaves, based on Western stereotypes.

Judgements that will affect the lives of lesbian asylum seekers, indeed may jeopardise their life if they are forced to return, will be based on Western stereotypes of sexuality and gender and underpinned by a 'culture of disbelief'. So, as women who most likely had to conceal their attraction to other women, including any sexual activity and/or relationships, from friends, family and community, whose life has been based on a deep, internalised level of secrecy will be expected to 'come out' in one huge leap and to live a life that includes socialising in gay venues, being in a relationship or at the least sexually active, to be 'out and proud'.

Hence, women like Brown Honey are not rejected by other women because they are Black lesbians but because they are Black lesbian asylum seekers. 'Refugeeness' shapes the experience of being a Black lesbian, letting other women perceive them in discriminatory and stereotypical way (as poor, uneducated, untruthful, 'needy').

Structural intersections affect us all. They can be lifelines, rungs on a social ladder, part of our social capital or they can be obstacles that trip us up, weights that weigh us down and make it far more difficult to achieve a fulfilling life. As demonstrated, for lesbian asylum seekers these structural oppressions are many and varied. Their experiences are shaped by something more than 'just' sexuality and 'race' and gender and religion. These categories of structural oppression cannot fully encapsulate the experiences of lesbian asylum seekers as their 'refugeeness' cuts across and troubles them in fundamental ways.

Notes

1 This is a chosen pseudonym by one of the participants of this study.
2 The borough of Croydon is the southernmost borough of London. The journey from Manchester can take at least half a day, involving many changes, and may necessitate an overnight stay.

3 Yarl's Wood Immigration removal centre (commonly referred to as a detention centre) is 'a fully contained residential centre housing adult women and adult family groups awaiting immigration clearance' (www.yarlswood.co.uk/). Issues such as sexual abuse, refusal of health care, e.g. lack of care for those with mental health problems, failure to call an ambulance when a woman was miscarrying) have been well documented (www.channel4.com/news/yarls-wood-immigration-removal-detention-centre-investigation (Accessed 10 June 2017)).

References

Baillot, H., Cowan, S. and Munro, V.E. (2012) '"Hearing the Right Gaps": Enabling and Responding to Disclosures of Sexual Violence within the UK Asylum Process', *Social & Legal Studies* 21 (3): 269–296.

Bennett, C. and Thomas, F. (2013) 'Seeking Asylum in the UK: Lesbian Perspectives', *Forced Migration Review* 42: 25–28.

Cade Bamber, T. (ed.) (1970) *The Black Woman: An Anthology*. New York: New American Library.

Combahee River Collective (1982) 'A Black Feminist Statement', in Hull, G.T., Scott, P.B. and Smith, B. (eds.). *All the Women Are White, All the Blacks Are Men, But Some of Us Are Brave: Black Women's Studies*. New York: The Feminist Press.

Cornwall, A. (1983) *Black Lesbian in White America (Essays)*. Tallahassee, FL: Niaide Press.

Crenshaw, K. (1989) 'Demarginalizing the Intersection of Race and Sex: A Black Feminist Critique of Antidiscrimination Doctrine, Feminist Theory, and Antiracist Politics', *University of Chicago Legal Forum* 14: 538–554.

Crenshaw, K. (1991) 'Mapping the Margins: Intersectionality, Identity Politics, and Violence against Women of Color,' *Stanford Law Review* 43 (6): 1241–1299.

Davis, K. (2008) 'Intersectionality as Buzzword: A Sociology of Science Perspective on What Makes a Feminist Theory Successful', *Feminist Theory* 9 (1): 67–85.

Firth, G. and Mauthe, B. (2013) 'Refugee Law, Gender and the Concept of Personhood', *International Journal of Refugee Law* 25 (3): 470–501.

Fotopoulou, A. (2012) 'Intersectionality Queer Studies and Hybridity: Methodological Frameworks for Social Research', *Journal of International Women's Studies* 13(2): 19–32.

Giametta, C. (2014) ''Rescued' Subjects: The Question of Religiosity for Non-heteronormative Asylum Seekers in the UK', *Sexualities* 17(5/6): 583–599.

Haraway, D. (1991): 'Situated Knowledges: The Science Question in Feminism and the Privilege of Partial Perspective', *Feminist Studies* 14: 575–599.

Held, N. (2016) 'What Does a *"Genuine Lesbian"* Look Like? Intersections of Sexuality and "Race" in Manchester's Gay Village and in the UK Asylum System*'*, in Stella, F., Taylor, Y., Reynolds, T. and Rogers, A. (eds.). *Sexuality, Citizenship and Belonging: Trans-national and Intersectional Perspectives*. London: Routledge.

Hill-Collins, P. (1990) *Black Feminist Thought: Knowledge, Consciousness and the Politics of Empowerment*. Crows Nest: Unwin Hyman.

Johnson, T. (2011) 'On Silence, Sexuality and Skeletons: Reconceptualizing Narrative in Asylum Hearings', *Social and Legal Studies* 20 (1): 57–78.

Lacroix, M. (2004) 'Canadian Refugee Policy and the Social Construction of the Refugee Claimant Subjectivity: Understanding Refugeeness', *Journal of Refugee Studies* 17 (2): 147–166.

Lee, O.J. and Brotman, S. (2011) 'Identity, Refugeeness, Belonging: Experiences of Sexual Minority Refugees in Canada', *Canadian Review of Sociology* 48 (3): 241–274.

Lewis, R.A. (2014) '"Gay? Prove it": The Politics of Queer Anti-deportation Activism', *Sexualities* 17 (8) 958–975.

Lorde, A. (1984a) *Sister Outsider. Essays and Speeches*. New York: The Crossing Press.

Lorde, A. (1984b) *Zami: A New Spelling of My Name*. London: Sheba Feminist Publishers.

McCarthy, K. (2015) 'What is the Experience of Lesbian Asylum Seekers of Living Their Sexuality In Their Home Countries and In The UK?' MA Dissertation. Unpublished.

McKinnon, C. (2013) 'Intersectionality as Method: A Note', *Signs: Journal of Women in Culture and Society* 38 (4): 1019–1030.

Moraga, C. (1983) *Loving in the War Years: Lo que nunca pasó por sus labios*. Boston, MA: South End Press.

Morgan, D. (2006) 'Not Gay Enough for the Government: Racial and Sexual Stereotypes in Sexual Orientation Asylum Cases', *Law & Sexuality: A Review of Lesbian, Gay, Bisexual, and Transgender Legal Issues* 15: 135–162.

Nayak, S. (2015) *Race, Gender and the Activism of Black Feminist Theory: Working with Audre Lorde*. Hove, UK: Routledge.

O'Leary, B. (2008) '"We Cannot Claim any particular Knowledge of the Ways of Homosexuals, Still Less of Iranian Homosexuals . . .": The Particular Problems Facing Those Who Seek Asylum on the Basis of Their Sexual Identity', *Feminist Legal Studies* 16 (1): 87–95.

Shidlo, A. and Ahola, J. (2013) 'Mental Health Challenges of LGBT Forced Migrants', *Forced Migration Review* 42: 9–11.

Smith, B. (ed.) (1983) *Home Girls: A Black Feminist Anthology*. New York: Kitchen Table; Women of Color Press.

UK Lesbian and Gay Immigration Group (UKLGIG) (2010) *Failing the Grade*. London: UKLGIG. Retrieved 8 April 2015, from http://uklgig.org.uk/wp-content/uploads/2014/04/Failing-the-Grade.pdf.

UK Lesbian and Gay Immigration Group (UKLGIG) (2013) *Missing the Grade*. London: UKLGIG. Retrieved 8 April 2015, from www.uklgig.org.uk/wp-content/uploads/2014/02/Missing-the-Mark.pdf.

Vervliet, M., De Mol, J., Broekaert, E. and Derluyn, I. (2014) '"That I Live, That's Because of Her": Intersectionality as Framework for Unaccompanied Refugee Mothers', *British Journal of Social Work* 44: 2023–2041.

11 Indian women on the margins of nation and feminism

Sonia Soans

In a bid to attract tourists the government of India in 2002 launched an international campaign, Incredible India (styled as Incredible!ndia), attempting to showcase the diversity of the subcontinent (Geary, 2013; Kant, 2009). The exoticness of the nation has never been underplayed. Carefully constructed images of unity without portraying conflict or poverty are part of how India is portrayed on screen (Saari and Chatterjee, 2009). The Incredible India campaign plays on a similar sentiment, portraying intrepid white travellers shy at first, then charmed by the hospitality and eventually falling in love with India (Chaudhary, 1996). Emphasising that the past is still a part of everyday life through images of yoga, temples and holy people, an illusion of tranquillity is established.

Stepping away from this commodified India lies a country that is divided and polarised. The carefully marketed past has become a source of nationalism in the present. Prosperity enjoyed by those in power seldom spills over into corners that are still subjugated along the lines of gender, caste, religion and ethnicity (Hardgrave, 1993). Social stratification in India is not new with tribal and lower caste people being at the bottom of this division (Mitra, 2008). The happy life portrayed in the tourism advertisements is a far cry from the reality of the oppressive social divisions. Income data is not collected by the Indian government. However, World Economic Forum figures estimate the Gini coefficient (a measure of wealth inequality) at around 50% and rising, indicating a high concentration of the country's wealth in the hands of millionaires (Corrigan and Di Battista, 2015). The brunt of this social stratification is borne by women, who are marked out not only because of their gender but also their caste, ethnicity and religion. Crime against women and the marginalised is disproportionally high, with the state often ignoring or colluding with the oppressors (TrustLaw, 2011).

Given the complex aspects of oppression these women's movements (Gulabi Gang, Red Brigade, Irom Sharmila) are fighting, it is not surprising that each one of them cannot be reduced to a single issue, dissected and discussed piece-meal. Intersectionality is a Black feminist tool that enables an understanding of subaltern women's struggles. Coined by Crenshaw in 1989, in response to issues Black women in the USA faced when it came to unequal employment issues, 'intersectionality' explained how race and gender affect Black women's lives (Crenshaw, 1989, 1991). Yuval-Davis (2006) highlights that the idea of multi-layered oppression was not alien to Black feminist struggles prior to the naming of the theory. Lorde (1984: 138) states that there is no such thing as a 'single issue'. Women activists in India know this to be true and have developed their own intersectional feminisms to address their grievances, claiming that oppression faced by them is not due to gender alone but other aspects of their identity that are inextricably linked.

Keeping intersectionality central, the issues presented in this chapter will focus on the various forms of feminism that exist in India with their nuanced understanding of feminism in India. Women in India are not a homogenous group. Feminist struggles in the country are based on structures that benefit those in power but prove to be a disadvantage to those whose caste, ethnicity and gender push them to the margins. Identity shapes access to resources in India, those who lack privilege are often denied their legal and social rights. Given that Indian women are not a homogenous group, feminism in India is not homogenous either. Criticism from marginalised groups claiming erasure of their cause is creating new feminist thought and activism.

Considering the failure of mainstream feminism in India and seeking common ground with Black feminism, Stephen proposes that Dalit feminism should be termed as 'Subaltern Indian Womanism' (2011). This proposal accounts for caste, region, ethnicity and spirituality. Dalit feminists seeking a new approach to empower Dalit women in areas they have historically been excluded from, such as political, economic, religious, social arenas, attempt to create a new consciousness.

An example of that exclusion is the violence suffered by women in the northeast region of India. On 10 July 2004 Thangjam Manorama, a 32-year-old Manipuri woman, was picked up from her home by the paramilitary unit Assam Rifles because of her alleged association with the People's Liberation Army. Her bullet-ridden corpse was found in a field. An autopsy of her mutilated body suggested rape and murder (Gaikwad, 2009). Failure to assign culpability for the crime led to widespread and extended protests. Manipur rarely features in national news, like most of the northeast region it has been forgotten and neglected since independence (Nag, 2002). Joined to mainland India by a thin strip of land, it has more in common (ethnically, linguistically and culturally) with its geographic neighbours Bangladesh, Burma and China. Reaction to this neglect resulted in protests, with some groups asking for freedom from India. The government's reaction has been to impose strict military rule, embodied in the Armed Forces (Special Powers) Act (AFSPA) of 1958, an Act of Indian Parliament that grants the Indian Armed Forces powers in 'disturbed areas' of the county (Kamboj, 2004). Some of the powers given to the army by this act include:

> To fire upon or otherwise use force, even to the causing of death, against any person who is acting in contravention of any law, against assembly of five or more persons, or possession of deadly weapons.
>
> To arrest without a warrant and with the use of 'necessary' force anyone who has committed certain offenses or is suspected of having done so.

To enter and search any premise in order to make such arrests.
No legal consequences will be met by these officers who act under the law.
(Francis, 2011)

For an area to be declared disturbed there must be a deterioration of the law and order situation, as judged by the governor who has the power to request the help of the central government. The power to determine a disturbed area is now also vested with central government.

Against this background lies a quiet protest staged by Irom Chanu Sharmila, a civil rights, political activist and poet known as the Iron Lady of Manipur. Protesting the death of ten people who died in the Malom Massacre, Irom Sharmila fasted as she always did for a day. However, this fast was different from the others – it began in 2000 and only ended in 2016 on 9 August. Arrested under section 309 of the Indian Penal Code[1] for attempt to commit suicide, she was held in a government hospital and force-fed for the duration of her fast. A similar form of torture was employed by the British government against the Suffragettes under the Cat and Mouse Act (Purvis, 1995). Irom Sharmila's arrest and forced feeding exposed the absurdity and cruelty of the law. A peaceful protest by a young woman against state-sanctioned violence has led to debate and questioning of how the northeast region is treated. Neglect and abuse from the state that allows atrocities to go unpunished has created apathy towards the government in the region. Sharmila's fast, drawing parallels to Gandhi's fast against the British, works to destabilise the notion that the northeast is violent and different from mainland India.

The north east of India, comprising of eight states (Arunachal Pradesh, Assam, Manipur, Meghalaya, Mizoram, Nagaland, Sikkim and Tripura), has been largely ignored by mainland India since independence (Nag, 2002). The spatial separation of the area from the rest of India has also resulted in it being cut off economically and culturally (Das, 2007). It is rare to see any news from this region, or see it represented in popular media, other than occasional reports of insurgency or the drug trade (Goswami, 2014). Government policies have disproportionate adverse effects upon women in this region, who have few means of survival (Palit, 2016). For example, the demonetisation drive of 2016 saw loss of livelihood of many women traders. Situated within the so-called 'Golden Triangle', an area known for its opium trade, these strong associations with drugs have led to unfavourable stereotyping of individuals. To a majority of Indians living in the mainland there is a lack of awareness of the northeast's socio-political history and it is not uncommon for racist language – including terms such as 'Chinky' – to be used to describe people of this region (Thounaojam, 2012). It was only in 2012 that the Ministry of Home Affairs ruled against the use of such derogatory language, with its use potentially leading to imprisonment up to five years (Sharma, 2012). Language used against the people of northeast India is not only racist but also misogynistic; women from the northeast are sexually harassed and often thought of as 'easy' in the rest of India (Golmei, 2013). This discrimination finds its way into everyday harassment and also into institutionalised neglect.

Women in India are subject to harassment on a daily basis, women from the northeast region are no exception to this, except in their case they are subject to additional harassment on the basis of their race and ethnicity. Their complaints are often ignored by the legal system, and are seldom registered (Golmei, 2015). Women from the northeast often become visible targets for misogyny and racism, they stand out as different in mainland India (Gohain, 2014; Niumai, 2016). Westernised in their appearance, northeast women experience discrimination on the basis of their gender and also for being 'the other'. Violence against them is not only misogynist in nature but also racist and casteist. This combination of subaltern identities makes women a target of male violence which seeks to attack their gender and their ethnic identity. These identities and the violence experienced cannot be compartmentalised.

While mainland Indian women (i.e. upper caste Hindu women) are presented as the norm, women from the northeast are presented as savage tribals, promiscuous and servile at best (Gohain, 2014). For over a century, the image of upper caste, domestic and middle-class woman has cast a spectre over Indian women who differ from her (Chatterjee, 1989). Women perceived to be foreign due to their different racial features often become targets of misogyny (Lozanskitourist, 2007). Northeast women are often discriminated against for not being Indian enough or being foreign based on how they look. The intersectional experience of racialised misogyny is an inextricable reality of northeast women's lives; they are victimised by society and state; both colluding to exclude them from accessing their basic rights. Feminist activism based in this region reflects these intersections of race and gender. It is precisely these fault lines that have caused divisions in how women in India have come to write their own feminisms.

Society in the northeast region allows women more autonomy, and a majority of the cultures are matriarchal and matrilineal; this differs from mainland India. Given this background it is not surprising that the struggle to end violence in the northeast is led by women (Das, 2007; de Lacy, 2014).

In another part of the country closer to the capital (New Delhi) lies the Hindi heartland, an area characterised by its deprivation and atrocities committed against women (Parker and Kozel, 2007). Within this area operates the women's group known as the Gulabi Gang. Their approach is described as follows on their bright pink website (Gulabi Gang, no date):

> The Gulabi Gang is an extraordinary women's movement formed in 2006 by Sampat Pal Devi in the Banda District of Uttar Pradesh in Northern India. This region is one of the poorest districts in the country and is marked by a deeply patriarchal culture, rigid caste divisions, female illiteracy, domestic violence, child labour, child marriages and dowry demands. The women's group is popularly known as Gulabi or 'Pink' Gang because the members wear bright pink saris and wield bamboo sticks. Sampat says, 'We are not a gang in the usual sense of the term, we are a gang for justice.' The Gulabi Gang was initially intended to punish oppressive husbands, fathers and brothers, and combat domestic violence and desertion. The members of the

> gang would accost male offenders and prevail upon them to see reason. The more serious offenders were publicly shamed when they refused to listen or relent. Sometimes the women resorted to their lathis, if the men resorted to use of force.

Recently there has been a surge of interest in the activism of the Gulabi Gang. Both a documentary Pink Saris and a Bollywood film (Gulab Gang) have been made capturing the activism this group engages in, with both being distributed worldwide (White and Rastogi, 2009). While the documentary generally follows the realities of the group, the Bollywood film takes artistic liberties with the story. Set in a village, but without the divisions seen in an Indian village, the characters are fictitious with little resemblance to the actual persons. Stylised rural costumes, exaggerated make up and melodrama lose the essence of what the movement stands for. Caste is erased from the film as are other marks of division that Sampat Pal Devi and her group fight for. Modified for cinema, this story takes liberties with the lived history of the movement. Critiquing the sensationalised narrative, Sampat Pal Devi opposed the screening of the film (Patcy, 2014). The documentary on the other hand follows the group more honestly, documenting their work in rural India (Longinotto, 2010). This erasure of caste is not an accidental omission but deliberate. Bollywood's focus on upper caste/class people is well documented. Erasing explicit references to caste, dark skinned actors are almost never portrayed as the main character (Rowena, 2012). Most Bollywood cinema depicts formulaic fantasies, which erase inter-caste, inter-religious interactions (Dwyer, 2006). Given this history of erasure not portraying the Gulabi Gang with accuracy is not exceptional. Representing the Gulabi Gang in its true form is not only threatening, as it exposes state negligence, but it makes for non-profitable cinema. Chatterjee describes realistic portrayals as 'full of platitude or, worse still, philosophical ramblings leading nowhere' (Saari, and Chatterjee, 2009, xviii). Roy (1994) points to another facet in portraying realism, portraying rape as a means of titillation. Women's resistance in Bollywood takes on a few formulaic forms to be palatable to the audience. Realistic portrayals are often reserved for unprofitable art cinema. Besides, to portray caste in all its complexity and ugliness, often leads to controversy and violence. Caste erasure in Bollywood is reflective of similar erasure in mainstream feminism and Indian society at large (Madhukar, 2015). Erasure of caste and dramatic altering of narratives are not minor issues when it comes to Dalit women's struggle. These lapses in memory are symptomatic of larger erasure in the Indian feminist movement.

Identity and intersectionality

Irom Sharmila's fast and the Gulabi Gang's activism, while geographically and ethnically diverse, do have a few features in common. These are areas of the nation that are deprived and through government corruption and mismanagement have seen growing discontent. Irom Sharmila is not just an Indian woman, she is from Manipur, her physical appearance different from those living in mainland India. Women from the Gulabi Gang are lower caste women, living in rural India, violence against them is often culturally sanctioned as a way of restoring 'honour'. While one can argue that both Dalit/northeastern men and women face violence, Dalit/northeastern women face an additional burden of being victims of culturally sanctioned sexual violence from upper caste men and their own families (Mrudula et al., 2013).

Reducing marginality to a single issue forces an individual to choose allegiances and also undermines the nature of the struggle against dominant forces. While the term has been in use since the 1980s, the idea of intersectionality goes further back and can be found in the writing of Black women such as Sojourner Truth (Painter, 1990) Audre Lorde (1984) and Angela Davis (1981). Challenging structural oppression involves the intersection of a multitude of factors, allowing for unique solutions that are tailor-made for different sections of society (Hill-Collins and Bilge, 2016). The universality of living within more than one marginalised identity is not unique to American or British Black feminists. Dalit feminists have similarly brought to attention intersectionality in their writing. Dalit feminism seeks its own identity from mainstream Indian feminism which often does not take caste or ethnicity into account (Rege, 1998).

Feminism in India, with its liberal and left-oriented value base, has over the years continued to marginalise Dalit women's lives and experiences from theorising and actions. It may even be said that the women's movement in India is in the grip of the Brahminical and casteist consciousness which totally obscures the role of caste oppression in the lives of the mass of underprivileged women in India (Stephen, 2011: 427).

Failures of postcolonialism

Postcolonial scholars often paint a picture of pre-colonial stability, ignoring the divisions in Indian society that have existed for centuries. Village life is imagined embodying tolerance and functioning on rigid caste hierarchies (Srinivas, 1956; Kakar and Kakar, 2009). Nandy (1994, 2007) claims that villages in India are not subject to communal violence and are tolerant of difference. Citing British rule and urbanisation as chief causes for communal violence in post-independence India, Nandy makes a case for returning to the pre-colonial past where divisions did not cause violence. Nandy does not mention caste or gender as issues of contention which lead to violence in villages. Silence on these issues is not merely an act of omission but complicity in caste-based violence. Dalit scholars challenge this notion of peaceful co-existence.

'His writings, starting from The Intimate Enemy clearly represent an Indianised version of Romanticism, the much-analysed trend of thinking which valourises pre-capitalist traditions, local cultures and subjectivities while critically opposing the rationalism and homogenizing values of industrial capitalism.' This is a perceptive observation of Mr. Nandy's academic romanticism. Such romaticisation of caste and culture has deeper scholastic roots (Ilaiah, 2013).

Ilaiah's (2004) critique of 'Buffalo Nationalism' challenges the version of Indian history and nationalism that is often assumed to be representative of the entire nation. Expanding on this term, Ilaiah describes this form of nationalism in India as 'spiritual fascism', which imposes upper caste narratives whilst mystifying lower caste roles. Opposition to these narratives by Dalits are met with violence from upper caste groups. In another conspicuous omission, Nandy fails to mention violence against women in villages, or that by its existence the caste system is violent. This erasure is twofold for Dalit women who are excluded on grounds of caste and gender. This omission has been challenged by Dalit feminists who critique the stance of upper caste academics in writing histories, which eliminate their voices as both women and Dalits.

Stephen (2013) challenges notions of tradition and its use to victimise Dalit women in everyday life and through festivals such as Holi where upper caste men are legitimately allowed to abuse lower caste women's bodies. While traditions are mystified as being part of an ancient line of continuity their propagation by upper caste men impinges on the rights of Dalit women. Stephen (2013) argues that the caste system is justified through religion and both collude to oppress Dalit women by exclusion from spiritual practises that would give them autonomy. However, upper caste men are given a free reign to interpret and impose their spiritual practises on Dalit women. These practises are often justified on the basis of culture thereby privileging cultural rights over women's rights.

The history of reforms in the colonial era are complex, in terms of how alliances were formed between the British government and upper caste men who sought reform. The alliances formed with colonial structures by Dalit women and men who benefited from colonialism are often written off as oppressive colonial practices that lead to a loss of culture. For example, the breast cloth, which was denied to lower caste women, was to be gained by the work of missionaries (Hardgrave, 1968). Similarly, the Devadasi system, which used lower caste women as temple prostitutes, and exclusion from education, were often revoked when bypassing upper caste channels and working with the British (Taneti, 2013). Reviewing these alliances and from a Dalit perspective, Roy (2014) claims they are revolutionary and defiant in the face of upper caste tyranny which prohibited lower castes from accessing the same privileges. Dalit feminism is borne out of several exclusions and oppressions over centuries; its challenges to the system are not one-dimensional but intersectional.

Questioning mythology and its use in mystifying misogyny, Stephen (2011) argues that postcolonial thinkers often erase the struggles of women at the margins of Indian society. Her proposal to combine the intersecting elements of Dalit women's struggle has led her to term this unique experience as 'Subaltern Indian Womanism'. According to Stephen this standpoint captures the intersectional nature of Dalit feminism in India. Violence in Indian villages is enacted upon women through a culture of 'honour'. Within such a system the woman is understood in terms of her community, her caste and her family and not as an individual. Punishing women for violations caused by male members of their family is often culturally (not legally) sanctioned in India. Women in such a system are targeted on the basis of both their caste and their gender. Their discrimination cannot be understood by dissecting each issue. Intersectionality provides the mechanism for understanding these issues as interconnected.

Post colonialism scholarship in India has been challenged on the grounds of erasure of caste and caste-based misogyny. While the role of the British in creating divisions in Indian society is thoroughly examined, pre-existing structures such as caste are rarely ever mentioned (Chakraborty, 2003; Heath, 2012). Since the system is deeply embedded in Indian society, with its beneficiaries in power, critiques of the system rarely seek to dismantle this form of oppression. Given how Dalit women are situated at the bottom of this hierarchy, Soundararajan goes so far as to say that caste culture by its very existence is rape culture (2014). This claim is not far-fetched in light of evidence of testimonies from Dalit women who are excluded from both mainstream feminism and Dalit activism (Rege, 1998).

Feminism and passivity

Feminist scholars advocate for ending violence, as a means of challenging long-held gender roles. hooks examines how domestic violence is not that different from war, in either rhetoric or nature (1981, 1996). Critical of all kinds of violence either perpetrated by the self or others, not excluding women as perpetrators, hooks advocates for a feminist society based on love. In contrast to hooks' stance, the actions of the women in the Gulabi Gang are violent. However, to dismiss the actions of the Gulabi Gang as re-enacting violence does the movement no justice, decontextualising the condition in which such violence is perpetuated. While Irom Sharmila's fast can be seen as an act of non-violence, the Indian state deems it otherwise. Sharmila's fast has been disruptive to state machinery which has had to react to a public fast/suicide attempt and under the eye of media. Yet in the context of women's struggle for liberation her fast is not new or exclusive to India. Both these forms of protest point to the intersectional nature of feminism in India and the diversity of activism that exists. Comparing these movements to each other does them an injustice as each form of activism is a response to specific forms of oppression. Their effectiveness lies in the unique way in which they address multiple issues.

Women employing violence is not a new phenomenon. The British Suffragette movement employed various violent tactics to prove women were not merely passive creatures (Pankhurst, 1913). Fasting (which led to force feeding), suicide and arson were routinely used as means of drawing attention to the cause of women. In post-independence India similar strategies represent the many forms feminism takes on in terms of ideology and action. In the case of the Gulabi Gang, carrying a stick and attacking violent men constitutes self-defence not violence, it disrupts violence against women. This action by village women challenges notions of their passivity in the face of violence.

Contextualising these actions in terms of self-defence as opposed to violence against men can help contextualise the inequality and injustice women face.

Crimes against women committed in the name of honour or tradition helps explain why these women have taken up arms in the region. These acts of self-defense have captured the public imagination and have sparked a debate about feminist activism. While the debate about the feminist nature of these acts will continue, they do highlight that feminist resistance can take on various forms depending on context.

When examined within the Indian context both passive and active protests constitute as acts of violence in the Indian state. In a nation where female passivity is valorised, activism of this nature challenges the notion of women as caring individuals. Much like their counterparts around the world who take up arms, female violence either enacted as self-defence or as a fast unto death challenges the notion of femininity as passive. McCaughey, in her analysis of self-defense as a means of feminist activism, argues that self-defense undertaken by feminists amounts to disruption of rape culture: 'As women embrace their power to thwart assaults and interrupt a script of feminine vulnerability and availability, they challenge the invulnerability and entitlement of men and, by extension, the inevitability of men's violence and women's victimization' (McCaughey, 1997: 177–178).

In the Indian context, these acts of self-defense mobilise women who are capable of stopping violence against themselves. Among many forms of protest this is one of them. These acts are a result of violence enacted due to multiple reasons. This disruption in the notion of women as the accepting victims of class/caste-based violence has led to the mobilisation of women who are working together to change policies that marginalise them. It must also be remembered that violence enacted by the Gulabi Gang has never led to death. In Sampat Pal Devi's own words: 'To face down men in this part of the world, you have to use force' (Prasad, 2008: 5).

Cultural context and abjectness of the women in India demands the use of violence in order to protect themselves from men and government forces that threaten to violate their safety. The use of physical force to protect oneself (as used by the Gulabi Gang) then becomes a means of resisting patriarchal forces that seek to dominate Dalit women.

Conclusion

Feminism in India is varied. It takes on many forms: pacifist, academic or vigilante justice and across these categories. This demonstrates the diversity of feminism and the reflexive nature of the movement. Diversity of feminist thought and action does not cancel out feminism but provides a more flexible way of understanding how feminism addresses issues of caste, violence, ethnicity and oppression by proposing solutions that are tailor-made for the situation. Intersectionality provides several feminist standpoints by expanding the space for more than one kind of feminism to exist. By extending itself reflexively it allows for a greater participation in the movement. Lombardo and Verloo (2009) point out that the strength of feminism lies in its coalitions.

A dynamic understanding of feminism hence not only offers better chances for hitting the moving target of gender inequality, but also enables wider sets of coalitions to profit from emerging political opportunities (Lombardo and Verloo, 2009: 110).

Dalit feminism does not render non-Dalit feminism null but allows non-Dalit women to broaden their understanding and to increase participation. By embracing the concept of intersectionality, feminism allows itself to acknowledge the many kinds of women who exist in India, whose needs and activism is varied.

In recent times India has gained notoriety for being the fourth most dangerous country in the world for women (TrustLaw, 2011). Discourse emerging from this revelation has often focused on the abjectness of Indian women as opposed to their resistance. While it is undeniable that women in India face oppression, erasing their activism does them no justice. To characterise Indian women only through their oppression colludes with the orientalist view of passive Asian women. Indian women of all classes and castes have participated in feminist struggles, pre- and post-independence (Anagol, 2005).

With their limited education and resources, women in remote areas of India have managed to challenge the state and make progress in bringing about the changes they have desired to see. Their lack of formal training or urban sophistication in dealing with the state and societal corruption is not a drawback, but needs to be understood in the context in which such movements take root. The intersectional nature of women's activism in India poses challenges to the homogenised idea of the nation state. Caste and ethnicity play an important role in shaping identity in post-independence India. These markers have been contentious issues as they have led to violence.

Note

1 Under section 309 the maximum sentence for attempted suicide was imprisonment for a year; the response by the police was just to release her at the end of the year and immediately re-arrest her. This was repeated annually, only ending with the decriminalisation of the Offence of Attempt to Suicide by the passing of the Mental Healthcare Bill on 8 August 2016.

References

Anagol, P. (2005) *The Emergence of Feminism in India, 1850–1920*. New York: Routledge.

Chakraborty, U. (2003) *Gendering Caste Through a Feminist Lens*. Calcutta: Popular Prakashan.

Chatterjee, P. (1989) 'Colonialism, Nationalism, and Colonialized Women: The Contest in India', *American Ethnologist*, 16(4): 622–633. [Online] [Accessed on 13th April 2013]. Available from: www.jstor.org/stable/pdfplus/645113.pdf?acceptTC=true.

Chaudhary, M. (1996) 'India's Tourism: A Paradoxical Product', *Tourism Management*, 17(8): 616–619.

Collins, P. H. and Bilge, S. (2016) *Intersectionality*. Cambridge, UK: Polity Press.

Corrigan, G. and Di Battista, A. (2015) '19 Charts That Explain India's Economic Challenge'. *World Economic Forum* [Online] 5th November [Accessed on 30th January 2017].

Available from: www.weforum.org/agenda/2015/11/19-charts-that-explain-indias-economic-challenge/.

Crenshaw, K. (1989) 'Demarginalizing the Intersection of Race and Sex: A Black Feminist Critique of Antidiscrimination Doctrine, Feminist Theory and Antiracist Politics', *University of Chicago Legal Forum*, 140: 139–167.

Crenshaw, K. (1991) 'Mapping the Margins: Intersectionality, Identity Politics, and Violence Against Women of Color', *Stanford Law Review*, 43(6): 1241–1299.

Das, S. K. (2007) 'Conflict and Peace in India's Northeast: The Role of Civil Society', *Policy Studies*, (42): I.

Davis, A. (1981) *Women, Race and Class*. London: Women's Press.

De Lacy, S. (2014) 'Life on the Border: LIBERALIZATION AND MILITARIZATION IN MANIPUR', *International Feminist Journal of Politics*, 16(2): 347–353.

Dwyer, R. (2006) *Filming the Gods: Religion and Indian Cinema*. Oxford, UK: Routledge.

Francis, G. (2011) *Armed Forces Special Powers Act*. SSRN. [Online] [Accessed on 26th December 2012]. Available from: http://ssrn.com/abstract=1854128 or http://dx.doi.org/10.2139/ssrn.1854128.

Gaikwad, N. (2009) 'Revolting Bodies, Hysterical State: Women Protesting the Armed Forces Special Powers Act (1958)', *Contemporary South Asia*, 17(3): 299–311.

Geary, D. (2013) 'Incredible India in a Global Age: The Cultural Politics of Image Branding in Tourism', *Tourist Studies*, 13: 36–21.

Gohain, M. P. (2014) '81% of Northeast Women Harassed in Delhi: Survey', *The Times of India*. [Online] 24th January 2014 [Accessed on 24th January 2014]. Available from: http://timesofindia.indiatimes.com/city/delhi/81-of-northeast-women-harassed-in-Delhi-Survey/articleshow/29270244.cms.

Golmei, A. (2013) 'Crimes against Northeast Women: Is the State Concerned Enough?', *Round Table India*. [Online] 12th February 2013 [Accessed on 13th February 2013]. Available from: http://roundtableindia.co.in/index.php? Option=com_content&view=article&id=6227:crime-against-northeast-women-is-the-state-concerned-enough&catid=119&Itemid=132.

Golmei, A. (2015) 'Beneath the Surface: Racism in India by Dr. Alana Golmei' [Online] 3rd October 2015 [Accessed on 30th January 2017]. Available from: https://alanagolmei.wordpress.com/2015/10/03/beneath-the-surface-racism-in-india-by-dr-alana-golmei/.

Goswami, N. (2014) 'Drugs and the Golden Triangle: Renewed Concerns for Northeast India', Institute for Defence Studies and Analyses. [Online] 10th February 2014 [Accessed on 27th March 2015]. Available from: www.idsa.in/idsacomments/DrugsandtheGoldenTriangle_ngoswami_100214.html.

Gulabi Gang (n. d.) Gulabi Gang Women Empowerment India – official website. Available from: http://gulabigangofficial.in/.

Hardgrave, R. L. (1968) 'The Breast-cloth Controversy: Caste Consciousness and Social Change in Southern Travancore', *Indian Economic & Social History Review*, 5(2): 171–187.

Hardgrave, R. L. (1993) 'India: The Dilemmas of Diversity', *Journal of Democracy*, 4(4): 54–68.

Heath, B. (2012) 'The Impact of European Colonialism on the Indian Caste System'. Available from: www.e-ir.info/2012/11/26/the-impact-of-european-colonialism-on-the-indian-caste-system/.

hooks, b. (1981) *Ain't I a Woman? Black Women and Feminism (Vol. 3)*. Boston, MA: South End Press.

hooks, b. (1996) *Reel to Reel: Race, Sex, and Class at the Movies*. New York: Routledge.

Ilaiah, K. (2004). *Buffalo Nationalism: A Critique of Spiritual Fascism*. New Delhi: Popular Prakashan.

Ilaiah, K. (2013) 'Caste, Corruption and Romanticism', *The Hindu*. [Online] 22nd March 2013 [Accessed on 22nd March 2013]. Available from: www.thehindu.com/opinion/lead/caste-corruption-and- romanticism/article4534892.ece.

Kakar, S. and Kakar, K. (2009) *The Indians: Portrait of a People*. New Delhi: Penguin Books India.

Kalota, R. (1948) 'A History of the Education of the Shudra Untouchables before and under the British Rule in India, circ. 2000 BC to 1947' (Doctoral dissertation, Durham University, UK).

Kamboj, A. (2004) 'Manipur and Armed Forces (Special Powers) Act 1958', *Strategic Analysis*, 28(4): 616–620.

Kant, A. (2009) *Branding India: An Incredible Story*. Noida: Harper Collins Publishers India.

Karthick, R. M. (2015) India's Patriotic Feminist Daughters. *Round Table India*. [Online] [Accessed on 7th March 2015]. Available from: http://roundtableindia.co.in/index.php?Option=com_content&view=article&id=8095:india-s-patriotic-feminist-daughters&catid=119:feature&Itemid=132.

Lombardo, E. and Verloo, M. (2009) 'Contentious Citizenship: Feminist Debates and Practices and European Challenges', *Feminist Review*, 92(1): 108–128.

Longinotto, K. (2010) *Pink Saris*. New York Women Make Movies. [Online] [Acessed on 22nd July 2016]. Available from: www.wmm.com/filmcatalog/press/psari_presskit.pdf.

Lorde, A. (1984) *Sister Outsider*. Berkeley, CA: The Crossing Press.

Lozanskitourist, K. (2007) 'Violence in Independent Travel to India Unpacking Patriarchy and Neo-colonialism', *Tourist Studies*, 7 (3): 295–315.

Madhukar, L. P. (2015) 'Silenced by Manu and "Mainstream" Feminism: Dalit Bhaujan Women and their History'. *Round Table India*. [Online] [Accessed on 7th April 2017]. Available from: http://roundtableindia.co.in/index.php?option=com_content&view=article&id=8177%3Asilenced-by-manu-and-mainstream-feminism-dalit-bahujan-women-and-their-history&catid=120&Itemid=133&tmpl=component&type=raw.

McCaughey, M. (1997) *Real Knockouts: The Physical Feminism of Women's Self-Defense*. New York: New York University Press.

Mentschel, B. N. (2007) 'Armed Conflict, Small Arms Proliferation and Women's Responses to Armed Violence in India's Northeast', Working Paper No. 33. Heidelberg: South Asia Institute, Department of Political Science, University of Heidelberg. [Online] [Accessed on 18th June 2016] Available from: www.sai.uni-heidelberg.de/SAPOL/ HPSACP.htm.

Mitra, A. (2008) 'The Status of Women among the Scheduled Tribes in India', *The Journal of Socio-Economics*, 37(3): 1202–1217.

Mrudula, A., Callahan, J. L. and Kang, H. (2013) 'Gender and Caste Intersectionality in the Indian Context', *Human Resource Management*, 6(9): 31–48.

Nag, S. (2002) *Contesting Marginality: Ethnicity, Insurgence and Subnationalism in North-East India*. New Delhi: Manohar.

Nandy, A. (1994) *The Illegitimacy of Nationalism: Rabindranath Tagore and the Politics of Self*. New Delhi: Oxford University Press.

Nandy, A. (2007) *An Ambiguous Journey to The City: The Village and Other Odd Ruins of The Self in The Indian Imagination*. New Delhi: Oxford University Press.

Niumai, A. (2016, July) 'Racial Discrimination: An Experience of North East Indians in the Metropolises'. Presentation at The Third ISA Forum of Sociology (10th–14th July 2016). Vienna.

Painter, N. I. (1990) 'Sojourner Truth in Life and Memory: Writing the Biography of an American Exotic', *Gender & History*, 2(1): 3–16.

Palit, M. (2016) 'Demonetisation Aftermath: Women, Children in Manipur Hard Hit due to Currency Ban'. *Firstpost*. [Online] 19th November 2016 [Accessed on 30th January 2017]. Available from: www.firstpost.com/india/demonetisation-aftermath-women-children-in-manipur-hard-hit-due-to-currency-ban-3113866.html.

Pankhurst, D. C. (1913) *The Great Scourge and How to End It*. London: E. Pankhurst.

Parker, B. and Kozel, V. (2007) 'Understanding Poverty and Vulnerability in India's Uttar Pradesh and Bihar: A Q-squared Approach', *World Development*, *35*(2): 296–311.

Patcy, N. (2014) 'Madhuri Has Never Met Me, I Will Stop Gulaab Gang No Matter What'. *Rediff.com*. [Online] Last updated on 5th March 2014. Available from: www.rediff.com/movies/slide-show/slide-show-1-madhuri-has-never-met-me-i-will-stop-gulaab-gang-no-matter-what/20140305.htm.

Prasad, R. (2008) 'Banda Sisters: In One of India's Poorest Regions, Hundreds of Pink-Clad Female Vigilantes are Challenging Male Violence and Corruption: Raekha Prasad Meets the Gulabi Gang', *The Guardian*, 15th February: 5.

Purvis, J. (1995) 'The Prison Experiences of the Suffragettes in Edwardian Britain', *Women's History Review*, 4(1): 103–133.

Rege, S. (1998) 'Dalit Women Talk Differently: A Critique of Difference and Towards a Dalit Feminist Standpoint Position', *Economic and Political Weekly*, WS39–WS46.

Rowena, J. (2012) 'The "Dirt" in the Dirty Picture: Caste, Gender and Silk Smitha, Part 2'. *Round Table India*. [Online] 8th October 2012 [Accessed on 9th October 2012]. Available from: http://roundtableindia.co.in/index.php?option=com_content&view=article&id=5822:the-dirt-in-the-dirty-picture-caste-gender-and-silk-smitha-part-2&catid=119:feature&Itemid=132.

Roy, A. (1994a) 'The Great Indian Rape-Trick I'. *South Asian Women's NETwork*. [Online] 22nd August 1994 [Accessed on 28th August 2014]. Available from: www.sawnet.org/books/writing/roy_bq1.html

Roy, A. (1994b) 'The Great Indian Rape-Trick II'. *South Asian Women's NETwork*. [Online] 3rd September 1994 [Accessed on 28th August 2014]. Available from: www.sawnet.org/books/writing/roy_bq2.html.

Roy, A. (2014) 'The Doctor and the Saint. Ambedkar, Gandhi and the Battle against Caste'. *The Caravan*. [Online] 1st March 2014 [Accessed on 13th September 2014]. Available from: www.caravanmagazine.in/reportage/doctor-and-saint.

Saari, A. and Chatterjee, P. (2009) *Hindi Cinema: An Insider's View*. New Delhi: Oxford University Press.

Sharma, A. (2012) 'North-east Racial Slur Could Get You Jailed for Five Years'. *India Today*. [Online] 3rd June 2012 [Accessed on 13th February 2013]. Available from: http://indiatoday.intoday.in/story/north-east-racial-slur-home-ministry-sc—st-act-jail-term/1/198828.html/.

Soundararajan, T. (2014) 'Strange Fruit: India's Caste Culture is a Rape Culture'. 24th June 2014. Available from: http://otherworldsarepossible.org/strange-fruit-indias-caste-culture-rape-culture. Cross-posted from *The Daily Beast & Women in the World*.

Srinivas, M. N. (1956) 'A Note on Sanskritization and Westernization', *The Far Eastern Quarterly*, 15(4): 481–496.

Stephen, C. (2011) 'A NAME OF OUR OWN', *Journal of Dharma*, 36(4): 419–434.

Stephen, C. (2013) 'Popular Mythologies and Their Implications for Violence against Women'. *Round Table India*. [Online] [Accessed on 25th October 2013]. Available from: http://roundtableindia.co.in/index.php? Option=com_content&view=article&id=

7000:popular-mythologies-and-their-implications-for-violence-against-women&catid=120:gender&Itemid=133.

Taneti, J. (2013) *Caste, Gender, and Christianity in Colonial India: Telugu Women in Mission*. New York: Palgrave Macmillan.

Thounaojam, S. (2012) 'A Preface to Racial Discourse in India North-east and Mainland', *Economic and Political Weekly*, XLVII(32).

TrustLaw (2011) 'FACTSHEET: The World's Most Dangerous Countries for Women'. [Online] [Accessed on 3rd August 2012]. Available from: www.trust.org/trustlaw/news/factsheet-the-worlds-most-dangerous-countries-for-women.

White, A. and Rastogi, S. (2009) 'Justice by Any Means Necessary: Vigilantism among Indian Women', *Feminism & Psychology*, 19(3): 313–327.

Yuval-Davis, N. (2006) 'Intersectionality and Feminist Politics', *European Journal of Women's Studies*, 13(3): 193–209.

12 Fault lines

Black feminist intersectional practice working to end violence against women and girls (VAWG)

Camille Kumar

The ending Violence Against Women and Girls (VAWG[1]) movement is a critical site for intersectional practice (Kelly, 2013). Prominent intersectionality theorists, activists and artists and have focused on the experiences of Black[2] women and violence (Crenshaw, 1991; Jordan, 1980). In spite of this extensive work, women who work to end VAWG are often excluded from discourses about intersectional feminism as we are seen to be engaged in caring work, viewed as neither academia nor activism.

If caring work is recognised as inherently revolutionary (Zetkin, 1896), then the VAWG movement is simultaneously a practice (doing with intention), activist (seeking to create change) and academic (seeking to deepen understanding and foster learning) and therefore a critical place for intersectional practice and analysis.

It is a precarious time for the ending VAWG movement in the UK. Neoliberalism, patriarchy and white supremacy threaten the sustainability of specialist women-led BME[3] VAWG services. These conditions bring into question our identity as a movement, highlighting the limitations of existing structures; and pin-pointing key ideological differences.

'You can find my kind living right on the fault line' (Dessa, 2011)

Fault lines are cracks in the Earth's surface found in areas vulnerable to earthquakes. Fault lines symbolise areas of weakness. Some argue that fault lines threaten a movement's survival and, in response, impose a dominant voice. However, Lorde's work testifies to the power of recognising difference as a resource (Lorde, 1984). Intersectionality constitutes fault lines as spaces of dissent and subversion. This reflective chapter investigates current fault lines in the ending VAWG movement using an intersectional framework.

Intersectional practice requires relinquishing positions of power, and the cultivation of humility in recognising our failures. Intersectional practice insists on multiple truths (Hill-Collins, 2000), refusing single objective certainty. Intersectional practice enables us to organise around the identity category of 'woman', whilst working to reject oppressive gender binaries. Intersectionality requires accountability from individuals for the violence they perpetrate, simultaneously holding multiple truths of broader socio-cultural causes of VAWG.

Intersectional practice requires decolonising work. In shifting marginalised people to the centre of the frame, perspective changes. In remembering and celebrating Black women whose work is marginalised/ erased in His-story, insight deepens. Intersectional practice invites a continuous building on the organising, familial, intellectual and community traditions of Black women, to strengthen a practice rooted in empathy, justice, dialogue and connection.

'Who in the hell set things up like this?' (Jordan, 2005)

The Global North's feminist movement of the 1970s has wrongfully claimed itself as the origins of feminism (Lorde, 1979). The complex forms of resistance undertaken by women across the Global South are continually erased. We have flashes of this rich Her-story (Wilson, 1978; Robinson, 2010; Hiralal, 2003; Byam, 2008) in the stories of Indian female abortionists (Gordon, 1974), African female slave emancipators (Bush, 1984), Sojourner Truth's *Ain't I a Woman* speech (Truth, 1851), and the secret women's business of the domestic sphere, where subversive worlds are created and handed down through oral traditions. The UK ending VAWG movement exists because of the revolutionary work of our sisters and ancestresses in the Global South. The origins of the UK ending VAWG movement are also situated in the context of the British cultural tradition of white, middle-class, abled benevolence (Incite, 2006).

The UK ending VAWG movement emerged over 40 years ago, with Women's Aid in Chiswick, London, recognised as the first European domestic violence refuge (UN Women, Undated). Across the UK, women rebelled: squatting in buildings for safe refuge, organising marches against VAWG, holding consciousness-raising groups to un-learn the teachings of patriarchal heteronormativity and exploring sexual desire in the sanctum of women-only spaces. Meetings were held in kitchens, in the back rooms of temples, at bus stops, in lesbian and trans-bars, anywhere free from the surveillant male gaze.

This was not utopia. The projects were as imperfect as the society from which they were born. Where white women developed campaigns, white women's experiences were centred, where middle-class women established services, middle-class needs were centred. In response, a diversity of services and campaigns were born: African and Caribbean, Asian, Chinese, Latin American, disabled, lesbians, trans, refugee and migrant women organised. The existence of specialist services, centred around intersecting identities, became critical to the development of intersectional practice in the UK (Larasi, 2013). As projects grew, women began to access projects in large numbers, requiring more women-power than volunteering enabled. In the 1980s, local government authorities began to fund (some) VAWG services through grants.

'Don't be tempted by the shiny apple' (Chapman, 1989)

Funding brings a complex host of problems (Incite!, 2007). Forced competition and an imposed culture of scarcity attack the bonds required for collaborative work and intensify inequalities (Rojas Durazo, 2007). The biggest threat currently facing BME VAWG services is white women's[4] VAWG services (Imkaan, 2015).

Funding becomes the ground for fragmentation within the VAWG movement on multiple intersecting dimensions with devastating results. First, fragmentation is counter to the spirit of intersectionality and second, there is a depletion of resources or fear of the depletion of resources. These destructive aspects of funding leach the energy and rigorous concentration demanded by an intersectional VAWG movement. Funding entrenches a culture of dependence, tying the future of organisations to funding structures. In the 2008 banking 'crisis' and imposed 'Austerity' regime, VAWG services face significant cuts. In one year alone, public spending on VAWG services was reduced by 30% nationally with disproportionate impacts on BME and young people's services (Towers et al., 2012).

Funding structures transfer organisational resource from feminist movement building towards service provision, shifting the focus of the work from collective structural change to individualised personal development. An attack on collective working is an attack on intersectional practice. As one women's organisation representative put it: 'Voluntary sector services are supposed to be something different to statutory services . . . [yet] voluntary organisations are increasingly under pressure to compete using the same language in the same way . . . what's the point then?' (Women's Resource Centre, 2012).

Funding displaces control of resource allocation from survivors[5] to the white male elite, generating damaging compromises. For example, government control of refuge funding forces refuges to exclude women who are ineligible for housing benefits, including migrant and asylum-seeking women, women in employment and private renters, perpetuating inequality and entrenching vulnerabilities.

In the early 2000s, local authorities shifted from grant funding to competitive tendering. G4S and SERCO, both transnational securities firms operating prisons and immigration removal centres across the world, respectively responsible for the murder of asylum seekers (Allison and Hattenstone, 2014), and the systematic sexual abuse of asylum seekers in the UK (Mason, 2015), are currently contracted to deliver sexual violence services (G4S, Undated; SERCO, 2013). Ending VAWG organisations now 'compete' with these corporations to provide the same services they had developed over decades of campaigning and radical action. In a climate of survival of the fittest measured by anti-feminist competitive processes, it is a challenge to hold onto the idea that feminist principles of intersectionality are actually the key to survival and liberation.

Reflecting on the Her-story of the movement provides insight into how funding-induced compromises have contributed to the current situation. The Herstory also raises questions about whether the ending VAWG movement is still a movement – a group of people working together to advance their shared political ideas –

or whether it has become a 'sector' – organisations providing services for the government. The question of sector or movement is critical as the answer guides our decisions around goals, political identity and organisational activities. As a sector, there are no grounds to argue against SERCO and G4S delivering sexual violence services to women. As a movement, actively resisting the take-over of VAWG services by organisations that themselves perpetuate VAWG becomes critical and urgent. The urgency for the survival of the VAWG movement is the urgency of intersectionality. Intersectionality was born out of struggle, degradation, depletion and threatened annihilation in order to survive it.

'All the ones who had a hard day / I prepared a place on my dance floor . . . / Welcome to my Queendom' (Latifah, 1989)

Intersectionality troubles the singular categorisation of people (Brah, 1996). Intersectional practices are based on an understanding of collective organising as life-affirming and revolutionary. BME led by and for[6] VAWG services are examples of Hill-Collins' concept of 'safe spaces' (2000), acknowledging the power of BME women being together without interference from men of colour or white people. The safety of any 'safe space' is not absolute; each individual is positioned in a personal social web of intersectionality (Parker, 1978; The Combahee River Collective, 1977). However, 89% of BME women interviewed in a national research project felt safe because they were supported by a BME VAWG service (Imkaan, 2012).

Previously marginalised and ignored by the government, the experiences of BME women have been in the spotlight over the last decade. In the 2016 VAWG strategy there are nine references to BME women (HM Government, 2016), compared to only one in the previous strategy (HM Government, 2010). The government's public focus on forms of VAWG disproportionately affecting BME women, including 'harmful practices',[7] and sexual violence in conflict is increasing.

Over the same period, BME VAWG services have suffered financial cuts of between 20% and 100% (Imkaan, 2015). The government is electing to fund mainstream services over BME services (Khandekar, 2016), while some local authorities are actively seeking to shut down BME VAWG services (Southall Black Sisters, 2008). Compounding this structural racism, some white women's organisations competitively market their own alleged capacity to deliver BME specialist provision. The dramatic loss of BME VAWG services reveals deep fault lines, radiating within the intersections of racism, imperialism and patriarchy. Exploration of this fault line might start with interrogating the arguments used in articulating the need for BME VAWG services.

The UK Government is most responsive to arguments framed around cultural, faith and linguistically derived needs. Many BME VAWG organisations have relied on this construction uncritically. Intersectional analysis provides insight into the impacts of this collusion.

First, the 'culture, faith, language' construction takes responsibility for violence away from the perpetrator and the matrix of domination (Hill-Collins, 2000) that forms the context for each survivor, problematising instead aspects of a survivor's faith, ethnic origin, culture and/or language. This conveniently and wrongly locates VAWG solely within BME communities. More insidiously, what does it do to a woman of colour if she is made to feel her experiences of violence are because of an aspect of her identity? How does this connect to the broader projects of Imperialism and White Supremacy?

Second, sexist racist stereotyping colludes with culture, faith and language constructions to reinforce biological 'race' myths creating false racialised hierarchies of need. An intersectional lens, focused on different groups of marginalised women, reveals the impact of these constructions. For example, 'strong' Black women represented as not requiring specialist services (Mama, 1989) results in the significantly disproportionate loss of Black women's services (Imkaan, 2015). 'Submissive' Asian women represented as needing services to protect them from their own 'backwards' cultures results in the infantilisation of Asian women and an associated assumption that white women's services are better equipped to respond to Asian women survivors, evidenced by the 2015 Save Apna Haq Open campaign – a BME women's service in Rotherham. The dehumanising exoticisation of Chinese women and Latin American women results in their services being invisibilised and undervalued. Further, racist constructions of 'foreign' identities obscure the needs of mixed heritage and intergenerational British-born BME women. These racist constructions rely on the fragmentation of identity in order to deny the intersectional experiences of BME survivors.

Third, sexist racist constructions disavow the primary motivating factor for women accessing BME VAWG services: a shared lived intersectional experience of violence, racism and exclusion and the transformative possibilities inherent in BME women-only 'safe space' (Imkaan, 2012). This disavowal furthers the white supremacist myth that BME communities are inherently problematic. It also enables (some) white women's services to assert that their services meet the needs of 'all women' through the recruitment of culturally and linguistically diverse staff members, disregarding the transformative potential of BME services.

Fourth, anti-intersectional, racist constructions of BME women's experiences enables the UK Government to evoke the protection of BME women as justification for harmful policies. For example, by interlinking forced marriage and 'foreign' communities, the government uses the 'protection' of women as justification for stricter immigration legislation, putting migrant women at further risk (Wilson, 1978). By interlinking female genital mutilation (FGM) and religion, the government uses the 'protection' of women as justification for the racialised profiling and invasive questioning of BME women at airports.[8]

Intersectional practice requires a rejection of 'culture, language and faith needs' framing of VAWG. Intersectional practice challenges BME VAWG services to consider: *How do we articulate the specificity of BME women's experiences of VAWG in the context of global racist, capitalist, abled, homo-transphobic patriarchy?* Intersectional practice demands white women's services consider: *How does your understanding and actions impact on BME women's services and anti-racist movements?*

'Last night I heard the screaming' (Chapman, 1988)

Neo-liberal, capitalist, state apparatus actively destroy community structures. For Global South located and diasporic communities this destruction is an extension of violent colonising practices of imperialism. Neo-liberalism and imposed 'Austerity' work together with this History to erode local community bonds, creating transient urban and deprived rural populations, perpetuating a culture of individual responsibility and 'other'-blaming. Application of an intersectional lens reveals the extent to which neo-liberal state structures produce social conditions of isolation and fragmentation with devastating psychological impacts. In the absence of community-based structures, the ending VAWG movement is forced to rely on state structures: policing and legislative systems for responding to VAWG; and parliamentary systems as signifiers of cultural rejection of VAWG. This inherently contradictory, contested relationship requires relentless compromise and numerous contradictions – a fault line.

Hard-won changes to policing guidelines and criminal legislation continue to impact on the lives of thousands of women. Police receive 115 domestic violence call outs per hour (HMIC, 2014), forming a critical component of the current response to VAWG crises. Simultaneously, the flawed/broken pursuit of 'justice' through a system that is designed to exploit and profit from the marginalisation of Black (Lammy, 2017), Muslim, Asian (Dodd, 2011), LGBTQI (Bent Bars, Undated), migrant (Hibiscus, Undated), disabled (Loucks, 2007) and young people (Gibbs and Hickson, 2009) is rigorously critiqued by Black and Indigenous activists, academics and practitioners around the world (Incite!, 2006; Sisters Inside, Undated; Davis, 2000; Lammy, 2017; Smee, 2013).

The vast majority of women who experience VAWG will never pursue a criminal justice process. An estimated 75% of rape survivors and 95% of BME survivors will never report to the police (RCEW, Undated; Imkaan, 2016). There are a multitude of intersecting reasons for this, some of which may be answered by reform including survivor-centred evidence tests and increased capacity for fast-tracked cases. Reform will not provide an answer to other reasons, for example, survivors not perceiving their experiences as abuse, not wanting to put family members through the CJS, and, most profoundly, love. The vast majority of women are abused by people they love, and the CJS is neither nuanced enough, nor empathetic enough to handle this complexity. CJS framings of VAWG allow the UK Government to affect an ideological stance against VAWG, while engaging in practices and policies that provide scaffolding for, and/or actively collude with ongoing violence.

The failure to address VAWG as intersectional and through interventions that are intersectional is a violence. Despite evidence of the significant number of survivors who are criminalised (Corston, 2007), in the last 15 years, the female foreign national prison population has doubled (Women in Prison, Undated). Despite the UK Government's public focus on 'sexual violence in conflict', asylum-seeking women's experiences of violence are routinely dismissed (Singer, 2013), prolonging incarceration and abuse in 'immigration removal centres'.

While publicly grandstanding a commitment to 'getting tough' on VAWG, the government's imposition of 'Austerity' is reducing women's access to employment, benefits, housing and health care, thereby increasing vulnerabilities of all women to VAWG. Despite recognising the significantly high numbers of children subject to child protection proceedings because of domestic violence (Edelson, 1999), the UK Government is funding a new program that sterilises women who have had successive children removed from their care (Pause, Undated).

Intersectional practice requires us to be critical of the criminal justice systems framing of VAWG, to ask: *What could intersectional justice look like? How do we shift beyond CJS reform towards creating nuanced intersectional systems of accountability that keep women safe and enable collective liberation?*

'Your silence will not protect you' (Lorde, 1984)

The tension for VAWG services between honouring women's autonomy and upholding 'safeguarding' duties is a fault line requiring intersectional attention. Multi-Agency Risk Assessment Conferences (MARAC) and broader participation in surveillance activities are a starting point for exploration.

MARAC is an adaptation of the 'Coordinated Community Response' model developed by the Duluth Centre (Domestic Abuse Intervention Programs, Undated). The model was introduced into the UK in 2003 ostensibly to reduce devastatingly high 'domestic homicide' figures, i.e. Two women a week killed by a partner or former partner (Home Office, 2016).[9]

MARAC requires completion of a common risk assessment form, and 'high risk' survivors are prioritised for MARAC. MARAC is a regular meeting between professionals from voluntary and statutory services. Relevancy of information shared is determined by the MARAC Chair and may include information about a survivor's employment, education, faith, housing, sexual and romantic relationships, friendships, family, immigration status, income and travel history. At first glance, the MARAC is a comprehensive system ensuring the safety of people most 'at risk'. However, utilising an intersectional framework, other consequences are exposed.

First, the 'risk framing' shifts the focus from supporting survivors to 'reducing risk', something that is neither quantifiable nor in her control. In this way, the survivor's individual resources, protective factors and needs are obscured by the professionals' assessment of risk. Furthermore, 'risk framing' creates false hierarchies of VAWG types, minimising intersecting forms of abuse including emotional abuse, coercive control and sexual abuse.

Second, actual risk assessing is an ongoing practice, not a static form-filling exercise. The perceived immediacy of danger at the time of completing a risk assessment form, practitioner's skills in identifying indicators, the amount of information survivors hold about their rights, extent and manifestation of trauma, levels of knowledge about a perpetrator's past actions and levels of trust all impact on a risk assessment. Furthermore, a risk assessment form completed by a random practitioner fails to account for the constant fluctuations in risk survivor's experience.

Intersectional practice requires us to be mindful of power. For MARAC referral, survivor consent is considered good practice but is not required. Survivors are never invited to attend meetings and there is no requirement for minutes to be provided to them. Making decisions 'in the best interests' of another's safety without requiring her consent, let alone her direct input, is a paternalistic, imperialistic configuration of power, undermining the autonomy of each survivor.

Centring different groups of women reveals further complications of MARAC. For example, for an undocumented woman, the potentially fatal impacts of her information being shared with immigration authorities are evident. A woman in poverty may experience further harm if information is shared with a welfare agency that sanctions her payments. A trans-woman may feel intensely humiliated in being outed to a roomful of strangers without her consent. A Black woman whose brothers are regularly harassed by police in Stop and Search[10] may have her family exposed to further harassment if information is shared with police. Utilising the standpoint of these intersecting positions, the MARAC system stands implicated in perpetuating violence.

The success of MARAC is also questionable. MARAC has enabled local authorities to collect copious amounts of data on intimate aspects of women's lives. Despite MARAC extensively operating across the UK for over 10 years, domestic homicide rates are not decreasing (Bentham, 2016; Banks, 2015). While attention is sometimes paid to State surveillance practices disproportionately impacting males including Stop and Search and Prevent,[11] the subtle and complex systems of surveillance operating in women's lives is less frequently explored.

Women are surveilled in our access to health care (Greene, 2017), welfare systems (Henman, 2008), migration (Wilson, 1978), public spaces (YouGov, 2012) and at home (Monckton-Smith, 2017). For different groups of women, intersecting surveillance structures are employed. For migrant women, surveillance structures may involve immigration controls requiring weekly attendance and finger printing at a police station. For visibly Muslim women, this may involve being followed by security in retail stores. For working-class women, surveillance may include the extensive intrusions of social care into their homes. For women involved in the sex industry, CCTV in hotels and frequent brothel raids are utilised. For disabled and trans-women, medical institutions form part of this panopticon of daily life.

Part of the work of the ending VAWG movement has been raising awareness of and seeking to disrupt surveillance in interpersonal relationships, however on the question of state surveillance practices the movement is largely silent. The movement itself utilises surveillance practices in its own work, for example through the use of CCTV in refuges, online information recording systems and participation in multi-agency meetings including MARAC, Safeguarding Hubs and Sexual Exploitation Panels.

Intersectional practice requires us to shift our question from: *How can we safeguard victims of violence?* To: *What intersecting risks are ignored when we utilise government safeguarding frameworks? Are we safeguarding survivors or ourselves?*

'Work does not liberate women' (hooks, 1981)

The issue of sex-work has polarised the movement and is a fault line in urgent need of attention. Some in the movement understand sex-work to be inherently exploitative and a form of VAWG. Others believe sex-work to be legitimate employment.

What would happen if the movement were to make space for hearing unique experiences from a range of people? From working-class sex-workers, migrant sex-workers, sex-workers who survived child abuse, sex working mothers and many others. To hear also from those affected by the sex industry, including survivors of trafficking, women who are raped by male partners enacting porn-derived fantasies, children of sex-workers and others. By making space for this diversity of experience, what could we learn? How would our thinking and feeling about the issues change?

Intersectional practice requires us to move away from individual 'knowing' towards collective learning. Looking to Herstory for lessons, seeking insights from other social justice movements and intersecting individual experiences to create collective truths. For example, we look to labour rights movements, and the exploitative nature of all labour is brought into focus, complicating the argument that sex-work must be stopped because it is 'exploitative'. We look to the experiences of survivors of sexual exploitation and the distinction between consensual and coerced sex-work is troubled as women describe the complex push and pull factors that often lead to experiences of trafficking. We look to the experiences of sex-workers asserting that the stigma attached to sex-work is the hardest aspect of the job. We look to queer critiques of heteronormativity and the connections between prostitution – the exchange of sexual labour for money – and marriage – the exchange of sexual and domestic labour for financial security (Extravaganza, 2005). We look to Marxist feminist analysis of feminised labour – caring work, domestic work, nursing, teaching, cleaning, cooking – and intersections in the regulation of female sex and of female labour become clearer.

Further, intersectional practice requires us to look at who our arguments align us with. Some anti-sex-work arguments around morality align with Christian right groups who are not seeking the same justice we are seeking. Some pro-sex-work arguments around the rights of migrant sex-workers align with practices of slavery, ensuring the supply of Black female bodies from the Global South for white men in the Global North (hooks, 1981); also not the liberation we are seeking.

Intersectionality reminds us that there are no single issues, that all social justice issues are interconnected. Through this we start to see that the sex-work 'issue' is not something we can work out later (after the revolution). The nuanced questions and complex emotions emerging from this issue are central to our struggle. We move from questions about the justifications and ethics of sex-work, to asking questions: *What false assumptions create this binary of 'liberated' and 'oppressed work'?* (hooks, 1981) *How do the structures of capitalism, imperialism, patriarchy, racism, ableism and homo-transphobia intersect to create situations where all women's labour is exploited? How do we honour women's choices while working to disrupt oppressive structures?*

Conclusions

> If you have come here to help me you are wasting your time. But if you have come because your liberation is bound up with mine, then let us work together.
> (Watson, Undated)

The fault lines in the VAWG movement are deep and wide-ranging. In a world where mistakes are interpreted as failures and failures as weakness, it is painful to be honest about the unexpected consequences of our campaigning and struggles. However, our activities, practices and rhythms must be consistent with the liberated future we are imagining into existence.

Intersectionality offers a framework to understand why oppressive societal rules cannot be re-written by isolated movements for social change. No matter how well-intentioned, unless all oppressive structures are collectively addressed, until all the parts of us can come along, we are in a project of eternal reform not revolution (Parker, 1978).

This exploration of fault lines is exhausting work. In a patriarchal neo-liberal world where 'objectivity' and 'fake truths' are revered, giving up the entitled position of knowing feels precarious. Engaging in intersectional practice that offers more questions than answers and blurs lines is a brave and challenging act.

Intersectional practice offers an alternative configuration of power that celebrates 'power with', rather than 'power over'. Intersectional practice encourages us to move away from polarised places to ask: *How can we push the boundaries of our understanding to allow for multiple truths to co-exist?*

In Angela Davis' recent trip to London, she said 'we live in the imaginations of the women who came before us' (Davis, 2017). The ending VAWG movement continues to nurture and raise me; giving me insight into some of the world's most terrifying 'everyday' realities, as well as inspiring transformation. I have witnessed women recover from violence and live extraordinary everyday lives. It supports me in my own journey of healing. The offering here is a reflective intersectional critique of the ending VAWG movement for the purpose of survival and creation of new intersectional possibilities, not a criticism for the relegation of this movement, which has always and continues to struggle for survival.

Notes

1 Violence Against Women and Girls is an umbrella term used in the UK to describe forms of violence used against women because they are women, including sexual violence, domestic violence, forced marriage, female genital mutilation, exploitation and trafficking.

2 In this piece, Black refers to women whose herstories originate from Africa and the Caribbean.

3 Black and Minority Ethnic (BME) is the term used in the UK to position communities originating from Africa, Asia, the Caribbean and Latin America, including the Indigenous Peoples of Australasia, the Americas, the islands of the Atlantic, Indian and Pacific Oceans. See Dabiri et al., 2015 for some contestations of the term.

4 I use the term 'white women's services' to position services governed and managed by white women, where a significant number of staff and survivors using the service are women of colour.

5 I use the term survivors to refer to women who experience any form of VAWG. This includes those who live and those who are killed, either at the hands of their perpetrators, the state and/or as a result of suicide. All women experiencing violence have survived something, even when it results in death.

6 'Led by and for' means services that are governed, managed and staffed by the same community they are providing services for.

7 UN term adopted by the UK Government: 'All practices done deliberately by men on the body or the psyche of other human beings for no therapeutic purpose, but rather for cultural or social-conventional motives and which have harmful consequences on the health and rights of the victims' (Kouyate, 2009). The term is contested; arguably all forms of VAWG are harmful practices borne out of patriarchal culture.

8 In 2017, 'Operation Limelight' gave UK Border Force, local police and airport staff powers to separate and question family members returning from countries identified as 'FGM practising communities'. The UK Government describes it as 'a proactive airside operation looking at inbound and outbound flights to 'countries of prevalence' for FGM' (HM Government, 2014).

9 This figure only includes deaths through recognised homicide and ignores suicides, forced suicides and 'accidents' in the context of domestic abuse.

10 Stop and Search refers to police powers to stop and search individuals if they have 'reasonable grounds' to suspect a crime/carrying items that may be used in a crime. Black people are eight times more likely to be stop and searched by police in the UK (Dodd, 2017).

11 Prevent is the UK 'counter-terrorist programme to stop terrorist-related activity. Prevent is a key element of CONTEST, the UK Government's counter- terrorism strategy' (H.M. Government, 2011). See, Cobain, 2016.

References

Allison, E. and Hattenstone, S. (2014) G4S, the company with no convictions – but does it have blood on its hands? *The Guardian*, 22 December 2014.

Anzaldúa, G. (1987) *Borderlands/La Frontera: The New Mestiza*. San Francisco, CA: Aunt Lute Books.

Banks, C., McLaughlin, H., Bellamy, C., Robbins, R. and Thackray, D. (2015) Domestic violence, adult social care and MARACs: Implications for practice. Manchester, UK: Manchester Metropolitan University.

Bent Bars Project (undated). Available from: www.bentbarsproject.org/.

Bentham, D. (2016) Revealed: Shocking rise in domestic abuse of women in London. *Evening Standard*, 5 September 2016.

Border Force (2014) FGM: Border Force targets 'high risk' flights at Heathrow to stop female genital mutilation. *Home Office: Gov. UK*. Available from: www.gov.uk/government/news/fgm-border-force-targets-high-risk-flights-at-heathrow-to-stop-female-genital-mutilation (Accessed: 11/05/2018).

Brah, A. (1996) *Cartographies of Diaspora: Contesting Identities*. Oxford, UK: Routledge.

Bush, B. (1984) Towards emancipation: Slave women and resistance to coercive labour regimes in the British West Indian colonies, 1790–1838. In Richardson, D. (ed.) (1985) *Abolition and its Aftermath: The Historical Context, 1790–1916*. London: Frank Cass and Company.

Byam, M. (2008) The modernization of resistance: Latin American women since 1500. *Undergraduate Review*, 4: 145–150.

Chapman, T. (1988) Lyric from 'Behind the wall'. New York: Elektra Records.

Chapman, T. (1989) Lyric from 'All that you have is your soul'. New York: Elektra Records.

Cobain, I. (2016) UK's 'Prevent counter-radicalisation' policy 'badly flawed'. *The Guardian*, 19 October 2016.

The Combahee River Collective (1977) A Black feminist statement, in James, J. and Sharpley-Whiting, T. D. (eds) (2000) *The Black Feminist Reader*. Oxford, UK: Blackwell Publishers.

Corston, J. (2007) The Corston Report: The need for a distinct, radically difference, visibly-led, strategic, proportionate holistic, woman-centred, integrated approach. Home Office, Ministry of Justice, GOV.UK. Available from: http://webarchive.nationalarchives.gov.uk/20130206102659/http://www.justice.gov.uk/publications/docs/corston-report-march-2007.pdf (Accessed: 11/05/2018).

Crenshaw, K. (1991) Mapping the margins: Intersectionality, identity politics, and violence against women of color. *Stanford Law Review*, 43(6): 1241–1299.

Dabiri, E., Okolosie, L., Harker, J. and Green, L. (2015) Is it time to ditch the term 'black, Asian and minority ethnic' (BAME)? *The Guardian*, 22 May 2015.

Davis, A. (2000) The color of violence against women: Keynote address at the Color of Violence conference. *Colorlines*, 3(3).

Davis, A. (2017) Angela Davis in conversation. Recording of a conversation with Jude Kelly at Women of the World Festival, 11 March.

Dessa (2011) Lyric from 'Kites'. Album: *Castor the Twin*. Minneapolis, MN: Doomtree Records.

Dodd, V. (2011) Asian people 42 times more likely to be held under terror law. *The Guardian*, 23 May 2017.

Dodd, V. (2017) Stop and search eight times more likely to target black people. *The Guardian*, 26 October 2017.

Domestic Abuse Intervention Programs (undated). Coordinated community response.

Edelson, J. (1999) The overlap between child maltreatment and woman battering. *Violence against Women*, 5(2): 134–154.

Extravaganza, V. (2005) Extract from the film *Paris is Burning*. Burbank, CA: Miramax Home Entertainment.

G4S Online (undated) Available from: www.g4s.uk.com/en/What-we-do/Health-Services/Sexual-Assault-Referral-Centres (Accessed: 29/09/ 2017).

Gibbs, P. and Hickson, S. (2009) *Children: Innocent Until Proven Guilty*. London: Prison Reform Trust.

Gordon, L. (1974) *Woman's Body, Woman's Right, Birth Control in America*. New York: Penguin Books.

Greene, S., Ion, A., Kwaramba, G., Lazarus, L., Loufty, M. and HIV Mothering Sunday Team (2017) Surviving surveillance: How pregnant women and mothers living with HIV respond to medical and social surveillance. *Qualitative Health Research*, 27(14): 2088–2099.

Henman, P. and Marston, G. (2008) The social division of welfare surveillance. *Journal of Social Policy*, 37(2): 187–205

Hibiscus (undated). Available from: http://hibiscusinitiatives.org.uk/index.php/evidence/.

Hill-Collins, P. (2000) *Black Feminist Thought: Knowledge, Consciousness, and the Politics of Empowerment*. 2nd ed. London: Routledge.

Hiralal, K. (2003) 'We shall resist': The role of Indian women in the Passive Resistance Campaign 1946–1948. Workshop on South Africa in the 1940's Kingston: South African Research Centre. HM Government 2010. *A Call to End Violence Against Women and Girls*. London: HM Government.

HM Government (2011) *Prevent Strategy*. London: HM Government.

HM Government (2016) *Violence Against Women and Girls Strategy 2016–2020*. London: HM Government.

HMIC (2014) Increasingly everyone's business: A progress report on the police response to domestic abuse. HM Inspectorate of Constabulary: Gov. UK. Available from: www.justiceinspectorates.gov.uk/hmicfrs/wp-content/uploads/2014/04/improving-the-police-response-to-domestic-abuse.pdf (Accessed: 11/05/2018).

Home office 2016. Domestic homicide reviews: Key findings from analysis of domestic homicide reviews. Home Office, Ministry of Justice, GOV.UK. Available from: https://assets.publishing.service.gov.uk/government/uploads/system/uploads/attachment_data/file/575232/HO-Domestic-Homicide-Review-Analysis-161206.pdf (Accessed:11/05/2018).

hooks, b. (1981) *Ain't I a Woman?: Black Women and Feminism*. Boston, MA: South End Press.

Imkaan (2012) *Vital Statistics 2: Key Findings Report on BMER Women's and Children's Experiences of Gender-based Violence*. London: Imkaan.

Imkaan (2015) *State of the Sector: Contextualising the Current Experiences of BME Ending Violence Against Women and Girls Organisations*. London: Imkaan.

Imkaan (2016) Minutes from meeting of national network of BME VAWG service providers. London: Imkaan.

Incite! (2006) *Color of Violence: The INCITE! Anthology*. Cambridge, MA: South End Press.

Incite! (2007) *The Revolution Will Not Be Funded: Beyond the Non-profit Industrial Complex*. Cambridge, MA: South End Press.

Jordan, J. (1980) *Passion: New Poems 1977–1980*. Boston, MA: Beacon Press.

Jordan, J. (2005) 'Poem about my rights', in *Directed by Desire: The Collected Poems of June Jordan Port*. Townsend, WA: Copper Canyon Press.

Kelly, L. (2013) Introduction, in Rehman, H., Kelly, L. and Siddiqui, H. (eds) (2013) *Moving in the Shadows: Violence in the Lives of Minority Women and Children*. London: Ashgate.

Khandekar, O. (2016) Rooms of their own: Support groups for minority women struggle to stay afloat. *The Caravan: A Journal of Politics and Culture*, 1 March 2016. Available from: www.caravanmagazine.in/lede/rooms-of-their-own-uk-anti-abuse-minority-group-struggle (Accessed: 11/05/2018).

Kouyate, M. (2009) Harmful traditional practices against women and legislation. Paper prepared for Expert Group meeting on good practices in Legislation to address harmful practices against women.

Lammy, D. (2017) Lammy Review: An independent review into the treatment of, and outcomes for, Black, Asian and Minority Ethnic individuals in the Criminal Justice System. London: HM Government.

Larasi, M. (2013) A fuss about nothing? Delivering services to Black and minority ethnic survivors of violence: The role of the specialist BME women's sector, in Rehman, H.,

Kelly, L. and Siddiqui, H. (eds) (2013) *Moving in the Shadows: Violence in the Lives of Minority Women and Children*. London: Ashgate.
Latifah, Q. (1989) Lyric from 'Come into my house'. Album: *All Hail the Queen*. New York: Tommy Boy Records.
Lorde, A. (1979) An open letter to Mary Daly, in Lorde, A. (1984) *Sister Outsider: Essays and Speeches*. Trumansburg, NY: The Crossing Press.
Lorde, A. (1984) *Sister Outsider: Essays and Speeches*. Trumansburg, NY: The Crossing Press.
Loucks, N. (2007) *No One Knows: Offenders with Learning Difficulties and Learning Disabilities*. London: Prison Reform Trust.
Mama, A. (1989) *The Hidden Struggle: Statutory and Voluntary Sector Responses to Violence against Black Women in the Home*. London: London Race Research and Housing Unit.
Mason, R. (2015) Theresa May 'allowed state-sanctioned abuse on women' at Yarls Wood. *The Guardian*, 3 March 2015.
Monckton-Smith, J., Syzmanska, K. and Haile, S. (2017) Exploring the relationship between stalking and homicide. London: Suzy Lamplugh Trust. Available from: http://eprints.glos.ac.uk/4553/ (Accessed 29/09/2017).
Parker, P. (1978) *Movement in Black*. New York: Firebrand Books.
Pause (undated). Available from: www.pause.org.uk/.
Rape Crisis England & Wales (undated). Statistics. Available from: https://rapecrisis.org.uk/statistics.php (Accessed: 29/09/2017).
Robinson, R. (2010) *Black Women and Suffrage: A US Herstory Untold*. Dusseldorf: VDM Verlag Dr Muller.
Rojas Durazo, A. C. (2007) 'We were never meant to survive': Fighting violence against women and the Fourth World War, in Incite (2007) *The Revolution Will Not Be Funded*. Cambridge, MA: South End Press.
SERCO (2013) Contract news update 16. *SERCO* website. Published 15 May 2013. Available from: www.serco.com/news/media-releases/2013/contract-news-update-16 (Accessed: 14/09/2017).
Singer, D. (2013) Women seeking asylum: Failed twice over, in Rehman, H., Kelly, L. and Siddiqui, H. (eds) (2013) *Moving in the Shadows: Violence in the Lives of Minority Women and Children*. London: Ashgate.
Sisters Inside Australia. Available from: www.sistersinside.com.au.
Smee, S. (2013) At the intersection: Black and minority ethnic women and the criminal justice system', in Rehman, H., Kelly, L. and Siddiqui, H. (eds) (2013) *Moving in the Shadows: Violence in the Lives of Minority Women and Children*. London: Ashgate.
Southall Black Sisters Campaign (2008) Available from: www.southallblacksisters.org.uk/campaigns/save-sbs-campaign-2008 (Accessed: 28/09/2017).
Towers, J. and Walby, S. (2012) *Measuring the Impact of Cuts in Public Expenditure on the Provision of Services to Prevent VAWG*. London: Trust for London and Northern Rock Foundation.
Truth, S. (1851) Ain't I a Woman?, in Collins, O. (ed.) (1998) *Speeches That Changed the World*. Louisville, KY: Westminster John Knox Press.
UN Women (undated) The history and origin of Women's Sheltering Virtual Knowledge Centre to End Violence Against Women and Girls. Available from: www.endvawnow.org/en/articles/1368-the-history-and-origin-of-womens-sheltering.html?next=1369 (Accessed: 29/09/2017).
Watson, A. (date unknown) Original source unknown; attributed to Lila Watson, Gangulu woman and activist.

Wilson, A. (1978) *Finding a Voice: Asian Women in Britain*. London: Virago.

Women in Prison (undated) Key facts. *Women in Prison* website. Available from: www.womeninprison.org.uk/research/key-facts.php (Accessed: 20/09/2017).

Women's Resource Centre (2012) *Surviving the Crisis: The Impact of Public Spending Cuts on Women's Voluntary and Community Organisations*. London: Women's Resource Centre.

YouGov and End Violence Against Women Coalition (2012) Sexual violence in the capital. Available from: https://yougov.co.uk/news/2012/05/25/sexual-harassment-capital/ (Accessed: 20/09 2017).

Zetkin, C. (1896) Only in conjunction with the proletarian woman will socialism be victorious. Speech at the Party Congress of the Social Democratic Party of Germany, 16 October 1896. Published in Foner, P. and Schoenhals, K. (1984) *Clara Zetkin Selected Writings*. New York: International Publishers.

13 The impossibility of adulthood with a learning disability and the possibilities of digital activism

Rachel Robbins

Introduction

Intersectionality is a concept borne out of the trauma and violence of single axis approaches to oppression (Nayak, 2015). The unique circumstances of the lives of people with learning disabilities means they are more likely to be exposed to traumatic life events (Hatton and Emerson, 2004). These circumstances include an increased likelihood of institutionalisation, reliance on care-giving, constructions of vulnerability and capacity, increased likelihood of poverty and prejudicial attitudes. Furthermore, disabled people (including people with learning disabilities) are currently facing a much harsher welfare regime. For example, CAB provided debt advice to more than 72,000 disabled people (cited by DRUK, 2014). The Papworth Trust (2013) noted nine out of ten disabled people were forced to cut back on food or paying household bills, in relation to the bedroom tax.[1]

When it comes to the matter of life or death, the health care provided to this group of adults is widely acknowledged and evidenced as dangerous. In March 2007, MENCAP published 'Death by Indifference' highlighting six case studies of the deaths of adults with learning disabilities which they argued could have been avoided and were possibly a direct result of discrimination and health care inequalities. A progress report followed five years later detailing a further 74 deaths (MENCAP, 2012). The avoidable death by drowning of 18-year-old Connor Sparrowhawk in an NHS unit for people with learning disabilities demonstrated a sustained disregard of his life and family relationships. It also led to an investigation that showed that Southern Health (the organisation charged with his care) had failed to investigate more than 1,000 unexpected deaths of patients with learning disabilities and/or mental health issues over four years (Mazars, 2015). This failing is not just a problem of poor individual practice, but also a systemic issue in which people with learning disabilities already marginalised have become commodities within a privatised healthcare economy which separates adults with learning disabilities from their families based on cost-effectiveness (Brown et al., 2017).

This chapter has three main arguments: first the label 'adult with a learning disability' is produced through an intersectional process resulting in oppression; second, working socially using intersectionality with adults with a learning disability within current systems is becoming an impossibility; and third, that scholars of intersectionality and social movements need to consider the relevance of the digital space and the context of social media activism. These arguments can be evidenced using the life of Connor Sparrowhawk as told by his mother: ‘One of the main things that struck us when Connor approached 18 was the lack of aspiration attached to his future, particularly by social services’ (Ryan, 2018: 59).

The intersection of adulthood and learning disability

As this book is aimed at an international audience, it is worth clarifying terminology, starting with the category of adult with a learning disability. Learning disability is an historic and socially constructed category and has replaced previous attempts at categorisation such as ‘mental handicap’ or the more insulting, ‘feeble-minded’ or ‘idiot’. According to a UK Government policy briefing (Parkin, 2016: 4): ‘A learning disability affects the way that someone communicates and understands information. This means that someone may have difficulties:

- understanding new or complex information;
- learning new skills; and
- coping independently.’

Whilst the language is polite, the category remains problematic. This attempted definition is primarily a means of identifying people as welfare recipients or service users by accentuating difference and deficit. Learning disabilities is a label that serves to support medical and welfare services administration, rather than the person who is labelled. The label is devised by and for providers of services. It does not acknowledge the role of power and historical policies of eugenics and segregation which have underpinned the categorisation.

The government policy briefing goes on to highlight how learning disability can affect both children and adults. The impact of intersecting learning disability with a developmental model of age has a profound impact on understandings of those subject to the label. Acquiring the label ‘adult with a learning disability’ is an intersectional process, which is historically contingent on understandings of adulthood and disability. The concept of intersectionality was devised to draw attention to the experiences of Black women and how those experiences can be ‘theoretically erased’ (Crenshaw, 1989: 139). Intersectionality considers how multiple social identities and forms of discrimination intersect in ways that cannot be understood in isolation from one another. Racism defines the sexist experiences and vice versa. ‘Power relations of racism and sexism gain meaning in relation to one another’ (Hill-Collins and Bilge, 2016: 10–11). The claim that ‘adult with a learning disability’ is the outcome of an intersectional process is designed to show how disabilism impacts upon the adult experiences, as well as how expectations of adulthood inform the experience of disability and that this is subject to power relations.

As Hancock argues, the concept of intersectionality is characterised by its relationship to activism: 'one key intellectual project of intersectionality: Making the women of color in general, but the intersectionally disadvantaged in particular, a visible and legible part of public discourse with an eye towards getting their policy needs met' (2016: 10–11).

Activism is intrinsically strategic and acknowledges that identities are not static, but the result of social conditions and historic processes. To unpack the identity of 'adult with a learning disability', it is important to interrogate those categories ('adult' and 'learning disability') and experiences (disabilism within adulthood and expectations of adulthood with a disability) as historically located and produced through power relations.

If seen in opposition to childhood, adulthood is rarely acknowledged as a period of oppression and might appear misplaced in a discussion of disadvantage. However, the construction of adulthood and the designation of adult within the power relations of welfare provision is historically contingent and is subject to ideological and economic structural forces. Parton (2006) discussed the changing nature of the child within social work to show the two contradictory strands in policy discourse in relation to children. In the first, it is acknowledged through discourses of children's rights that children are people in their own right and should be a focus of policy and practice. However, childhood is also identified 'as a key site for overcoming current and future problems' (Parton, 2006: 83). Therefore, children are often defined as a future rather than as a present. The child is imbued with rights but little agency. But what of adulthood?

Neiman suggests that rather than a definition of adulthood, society uses markers: 'Leaving your parents' home, paying your own bills, having successful intimate relations are all signs of being an adult and anyone who fails to show such signs by a certain age will be suspected of one pathology or another' (2014: 123). These markers of adulthood are being delayed, disordered or revised for many either through personal choice, economic constraints or structural inequalities, leading to the suggestion that adulthood is in crisis. Neiman argues that this is, in part, related to the structural: 'Our inability to grow up is not, or not only, our fault. The social structures within which we live are constructed as to keep us childish' (2014: 17).

The structural is related to the dominant ideology and context of neo-liberalism, which views the market as the central organising principle of social relations (Penn and O'Brien, 2009). Neo-liberalism has its roots in the classical liberalism of the 17th century based on an ideal individual who is essentially rational and self-interested. The neo-liberal subject is self-reliant and free from state interference (or from another perspective, support and provision). Whilst it is suggested that as a society we will all benefit from any entrepreneurial economic growth, the risk of economic collapse is individualised. While the classical liberal subject is an entrepreneur and producer, the neo-liberal subject and their relation to the state is primarily as consumer (Bauman, 2012). As Silva (2013) demonstrates, this economic and social structure has disrupted the previous standard life course, causing some to see younger generations as entitled and immature for failing to meet markers of adulthood. As with childhood, there are contradictory messages about becoming adult. Adulthood is a time to set out long-term markers of stability, such as independent living, work and families, but there is no societal responsibility to provide for this. In the reverse of childhood, adults are granted agency but fewer rights and less security. To thrive, they are expected to make the right consumer choices. This has a devastating impact on disadvantaged sectors of society, including those labelled with a learning disability.

In mobilising intersectionality, to work socially with adults with a learning disability we should not see 'adulthood' and 'learning disability' as 'mutually exclusive categories of experience and analysis' (Crenshaw, 1989: 139) any more than we would see 'race' and gender in this way. Here, I am not suggesting that an adult with a learning disability is analogous with a Black woman, because, of course, these two categories are also not mutually exclusive. Instead, it is to highlight the dangers of a single axis of analysis when working within oppressive systems, such as the UK welfare system.

There have been several notable shifts in the UK operation and discourses of welfare in recent times: the move from public to private provision, from collective to individual risk, from the notion that welfare is a safety net for all to the discourse of us/them or tax-payer/scrounger. Recent UK governments of all shades have leant on a discourse of dependency in relation to welfare. Emboldened through the political use of the global crash to restrict welfare spending and roll back state provision, the evocation of cultures of worklessness are prominent in UK politics (McDonald et al., 2013). This tactic places an emphasis on the importance of a person's ability and choice to work, whilst circumnavigating the structural shifts in employment in a post-industrial country. The discourse of dependency suggests that there is a group of people, who do not want to work, with different values from the general population. Dependency has always been a feature of welfare provision: 'The social construction of normal life course through social policy associates dependency only with certain stages of life-course, specifically with childhood and old age' (Priestley, 2000: 427–428).

The disabilism of welfare provision denies dependency as a feature of adulthood. Dependency is linked to the denial of choice and self-determination. For people with learning disabilities this erosion of personhood is achieved the through the threat and fact of segregation into residential care.

An intersectional analysis of the position of the adult with a learning disability shows that their existence is caught between a rock and a hard place. Concerns have been raised by the incidences of learning disability within benefit sanctions (DRUK, 2014). Only 6% of adults with learning disabilities are in employment in the UK (Public Health England, 2011), yet individuals are held to account for this structural inequality. This occurs when the identity as adult within welfare is foregrounded and the learning disability (the ability to keep appointments, deal with complex arrangements, lower levels of literacy) disappears. On the other hand, when the learning disability is foregrounded, we find large numbers of adults with a learning disability being consigned to the euphemistic regime of

Assessment and Treatment Units (ATUs). ATUs are a form of medicalised residential segregation. Learning disability becomes a medical area of expertise. The provision of assessment and treatment are used to contain behaviours associated with the challenge of navigating services. It is no accident that the move to an ATU often occurs at the bureaucratic start of adulthood, during the transition from children to adult services (Lenehan, 2017).

An intersectional analysis considers what the intersection of adulthood and learning disability tells us about power and inequality in the construction of both adulthood and disability. Adults dependent on welfare are currently being 'responsibilised' rather than the limiting economic climate or the job market being addressed. This is bought into sharper relief when viewed through the lens of learning disability. Learning disability becomes something to be contained rather than supported when viewed through the lens of the treatment of adults. A single axis of analysis distorts these experiences (Crenshaw, 1989). Intersectional analysis demonstrates how adults with learning disabilities 'are caught between ideological and political currents that combine first to create and then to bury' them (Crenshaw, 1989: 160). The value of multidimensionality is further exposed in the experience of the migrant disabled woman:

> The immigrant racialized woman is constructed as an outsider; add disability to this construct and she is rendered socially invisible. If she is identified, she is designated by the term 'problem' and she lives, beneath the shadow of that problem which envelops and obscures her. It must be noted that racialized women who have disabilities – deemed to be neither waged workers nor homemakers (unpaid workers) – are constructed as a social burden. They are constructed as recipients, rather than givers of care.
>
> (Dossa, 2009: 24)

Adulthood is supposed to be economically productive (for women re-productive). The current obsession with welfare dependency and the impact of exclusionary categories relegates the adult with a learning disability as failed because they need care, rather than existing within any mutual relationships of care. Learning disabled adulthood becomes an impossibility.

The impossibility of intersectionality-informed social work with adults with a learning disability

There is a tendency to see social workers and service users as two distinct groups, in binary opposition. Not only can these identities intersect, both are operating in the same climate and context. That neo-liberalism has achieved a hegemonic position in the lives of people with learning disabilities reliant on welfare, so it has within social work (Gwilym, 2017). Despite the complex beginnings of social work within the charity sector (Alcock, 2003) and radical politics (Hugman, 2009) the majority of UK social workers are currently employed by the state and fulfil their role as set out and regulated by the state (Garrett, 2010). Whilst many enter the profession attracted by potential political activity or justice-seeking (Humphrey, 2011), neo-liberalism militates against this (Gwilym, 2017).

In the UK, social work retains a generic qualification across services for adults and children, but practices are divergent. Recent legislative and policy changes have meant that social care for adults has emerged as a separate and distinct area of service provision, after the separation from children's services in 2006 (DH, 2006). The statutory duties of qualified social workers within children's assessment, protection and family support are clear. Qualified adult social work, on the other hand, is rarely acknowledged within policy agendas, even when those agendas address traditional social work areas (such as dementia care or personalisation). Consequently, the role of the adult social worker has become hazy and indistinct in the wider field of adult social care. The statutory role for adult social workers is now perhaps most associated with risk assessment and safeguarding (Lymbery, 2014). If it is understood that UK social work is 'state mediated' and therefore a politically dominated profession (Lymbery, 2014) it is peculiarly lacking in resilience against political agendas, despite its radical roots. 'Intersectionality is a way of understanding and analysing the complexity in the world, in people and in human experiences' (Hill-Collins and Bilge, 2016: 2). Intersectional practice requires a practitioner who can think outside of state mandated categories.

Ideally, to work socially with adults labelled as learning disabled requires the adoption of a social model of disability (Oliver, 2009), which seeks to establish disability and its associated disadvantages as a product of unequal power relations, rather than deficits situated in the individual. Yet, any desire to adopt a social model is undercut by the legislation underpinning the support that the state offers. Eligibility criteria requires that for a person's needs to qualify for services they must relate to an impairment or illness, so that the person cannot achieve at least two outcomes in their day-to-day life, impacting significantly on their well-being (Care and Support (Eligibility Criteria) Regulations, 2015). This is a deficit, individualised model of disability.

Ideal practice would also entail working alongside disability rights movements and collectives. However, current practice is dominated by an individual case-based approach, which has become a managerially defined form of practice. 'Community based approaches and groupwork remain secondary to the casework principle, now rebranded as care-management' (Horner, 2009: 23). Creativity and solidarity are further eroded by austerity, which has led to a tightening of eligibility criteria as local councils are forced to respond to smaller budgets. Continuing budget cuts are expected to impact significantly on adult social care (LGA, 2017). Financial imperatives have overtaken the stated social justice aims of the profession. This can be difficult to trace as policy-driven cost-cutting often hides behind the language of disability rights, using the language of independence, autonomy and choice as justification for reduced resources and support. Many adults who received support as children find themselves outside the remit of adult social care.

Social workers have seen their role restricted, a tightening of eligibility criteria and the rise of managerialism to keep in check ambitions of working with adults with a learning disability in an intersectional, holistic framework. The marketisation of care has also produced competition for the support work of adults with learning disabilities from two different fields – the charity/independent sector and the medical profession. This has reproduced the rise of institutional and residential care. The latter half of the 20th century saw a decrease in the use of segregation, demanded by disability rights organisations and overseen by social work practitioners. However, institutions have since seen a significant and growing role to play in the current provision of services.

Morris points out: 'Powerlessness characterises the experiences of residential care and the nature of institutionalisation affects even those of us who are not in residential care. The possibility of institutionalisation hangs over many disabled people' (1991: 127). This fear is justified and demonstrable through scandals such as Winterbourne View. A BBC Panorama documentary of the levels of abuse led to the convictions of 11 members of staff and drew attention to the out of town, out of sight care of adults with learning disabilities. (Winterbourne View was a privately owned, publicly funded hospital located on an industrial estate on the edge of Gloucestershire.) This scandal has not led to the closure of hospitals, or a reduction in out of area placements. Brown et al. explain this lack of movement in monetary terms:

> In 2015–16 we estimate that the value of the Inpatient Healthcare Market to the 'independent' sector is in the region of £284 million. Most of that provision operates on a for profit basis and our sons and daughters are its currency.
>
> (2017: 8)

Whilst local authority provision is being starved of resources to work with adults with learning disabilities, and eligibility criteria are tightened so that only those with significant needs can be provided for, the independent sector is being paid from the public purse to provide residential care. There are also perverse financial incentives for local authorities to move vulnerable adults into long-stay residential care away from their own jurisdiction (Brown et al., 2017).

This is first and foremost a dilemma for people with learning disabilities and their families. However, it highlights the growing impossibility of the social work task with adults with learning disabilities. Social workers should have a key role in advocating for families so that they access the right support. However, advocacy work while in line with the stated aims of their employers and their legislative duties under the Care Act brings social workers into conflict with the financial constraints and modes of operation imposed on their employers. Mladenov argues: 'neoliberalism confronts the disabled people's movement with two difficult tasks; to defend self-determination while criticising market-based individualism, and to defend the welfare state while criticising expert-based paternalism' (2015: 445).

Similarly, social workers must seek to avoid the co-option of disability rights language to support coercive practice. The difficulty lies in providing support and advocacy that acknowledges the expertise of service users and their families but that can also hold onto the tension of individual rights, family perspectives and collective identities.

Changing the context: Digital activism

Connor Sparrowhawk was a young man with a label of learning disability and a diagnosis of autism. Connor was 18 years old when he entered an ATU, funded by the NHS and run by Southern Health: 107 days later he was dead. He died an entirely preventable death, drowning in an unsupervised bath despite his mother raising concerns about his epilepsy. If Connor had not been labelled as having learning disabilities, the death of a physically healthy young man whilst under NHS care, would have generated outrage. If Connor had not entered that ATU, he would not be dead.

An intersectional analysis can support the understanding that Connor had become an impossibility on reaching adulthood. Just after entering the ATU, the following occurred:

> In the early hours of that morning, Connor was restrained after he lunged at a support worker. He was pinned face down to the floor by four staff, and sectioned under the Mental Health Act. That was the day he stopped being a sixth-former.
>
> (Ryan, 2018: 66)

Intersectionality requires an understanding and 'development of a historical critique' (Crenshaw, 1989: 157) which recognises how categories of difference emerge and are treated. Segregation is a means of controlling the lives of people with learning disabilities. This is justified through a construction of adulthood as productive and responsible but disability as unproductive and burdensome and the growth of an expert class to deal with 'the problem'.

Intersectionality also requires a consideration of context, or what Yuval-Davies (2011) has named 'situated intersectionality'. 'Situated gaze, situated knowledge and situated imagination construct how we see the world in different ways' (Yuval-Davies, 2011: 4). This is a challenge to scientific objectivity. Combined with intersectionality it becomes a challenge to chart the impact of that 'situatedness' on the varying positions within different social, economic and political projects. Intersectionality should be applied to understand privilege *and* marginalisation. LB's death was not simply a result of his marginalisation but also the privilege of others to feel able to act with the arrogance of position. Through examining how the layers and intersections of power work, we can tie intersectional analysis to Foucault's (1978) assertion that power is not just about oppressing and constraining but that oppressive institutions can also be productive. 'Where there is power, there is resistance' (Foucault, 1978: 95). The constraints of the ATU and medical model provision opened up a new site for action.

The story of LB is bleak. However, in the spaces carved out through solidarity, friendship and collectivity there have been chinks of hope offered to his family and other families experiencing living (and dying) with the label of learning disability. Intersectionality emerged as critique of social movements and their tendency to exclude minority interests, while privileging the interests of the most advantaged (The Combahee River Collective, 1982; Crenshaw, 1991). Intersectionality can also be mobilised as strategy to ensure inclusion of wider and inter-related interests within groups (Laperrière and Lépinard, 2016). Following Connor's death, however, there was no strategic, concerted effort to bring together a social justice movement: 'We had no idea that Connor's death would generate a groundbreaking social movement and lead to the uncovering of systematic failure to investigate the deaths of certain patients in the UK' (Ryan, 2018: 97).

Yet, there emerged a strong, imaginative and lively campaign around justice for his loss and the fight for the lives (and deaths) of people with learning disabilities to be understood and valued. Key to the movement, which became known as #JusticeforLB, was the use of digital technology and social media. A full account of the campaign can be found in Sara Ryan's (2018) biography of her son and the campaign. Some key details are: a blog which intended to document the lighter side of life with Connor, which morphed into recording the experiences of dealing with the ATU staff; a twitter network of friends, allies, professionals, lawyers and academics who demonstrated solidarity with the hashtag #JusticeforLB and the handle @JusticeforLB (managed by George Julian – a knowledge-transfer ally); a private member's bill; and the crowd-funded live-tweeting of Connor's inquest.

Digital activism is ripe for intersectional analysis. Social media both promotes new forms of misogyny, racism and oppression as well as new forms of activism and resistance (Locke et al., 2016). Whilst providing some democratising features it can also be exclusionary on the grounds of digital literacy and disability (Turley and Fisher, 2016). These contradictions were experienced by Sara Ryan. Whilst the digital experience provided a platform and network, it also led to increased surveillance, set out in a staff briefing which followed Connor's death:

> We were made aware that a blog, containing details of our staff on the unit by [redacted] in March. It was agreed that [redacted] would monitor the blog and raise any potential issues as previously the entries had mentioned staff by name and had been potentially defamatory towards staff.
>
> (cited by Ryan, 2018: 98)

The surveillance of the blog was designed around the protection of institutional reputation and not the life/death of Connor. It also has a gendered dimension. Mother-blaming and autism have a long history. Kanner (1943) attributed autism to a lack of maternal affection and this view was popularised and mainstreamed by Betteleheim (1967). Whilst this is now a recognised fallacy, mother-blame and high expectations of motherhood remain for those with an autistic child (Courcy and des Riveres, 2017). The impact of mother-blame is demonstrated in Sara's reflection:

> Through a combination of working full-time, writing a blog about our experiences of health and social care, failing to tell staff in a specialist unit to observe a young patient with epilepsy in the bath and calling a consultant 'Dr Crapshite', I killed Connor.
>
> (Ryan, 2018: 196)

The live crowd-funded tweeting into Connor's death (by George Julian) was one opportunity to redress the power imbalance. Whilst the NHS trust could provide a team of lawyers, Connor's family relied on the work of a charitable organisation for their preparation and representation. The broadcast of tweets allowed others to see the process unfold and provided much needed transparency and accountability.

Intersectional analysis becomes most useful when considering the moves between the digital space and the mainstream, providing real-world impacts. The campaigning led to mainstream media coverage of the death of a young man who could easily have been dehumanised by talk of processes, social care jargon and medical conditions. Intersectional theorists and researchers have drawn attention to the neo-liberal project of boundary control through securitisation, detention and surveillance (Yuval-Davies, 2011; Hill-Collins and Bilge, 2016). The borders around the category of adults with learning disabilities are framed within national borders, with each state using specific tools and methods to contain. The attempt is to individualise, remove from networks and if necessary to de-humanise to reduce institutional blame or reputation. This leaves families in a liminal space with no recourse to being heard, or being heard in harmful ways (as toxic, obstructive, uncaring, overbearing). Social media in this case has pushed at that boundary. This can be seen in other digital activist campaigns (Turley and Fisher, 2018; Brown et al., 2017) which have pushed feminist concerns into mainstream coverage.

Conclusion

Neo-liberalism and austerity are means of supressing imaginative ways of active engagement against oppression. Intersectionality provides a response to this as it challenges processes of identity formation and disrupts the taken-for-granted, 'the discourse of inevitability' (Davies, 2008) of neo-liberalism. It asks us to look outside the comfort of disciplinary and other borders.

Digital activism will play a major role in future 'waves' of feminism. Some caution is required in its use. New technologies do not replace old strategies and collectives. Historical knowledge is still power. Ryan acknowledges:

> while access to social media gives sidelined families a platform, I can't help thinking that some of the skills derived from my training as an academic have helped during the campaign – research skills including analysis, reflection and critical engagement contribute to effective campaigning.
>
> (2018: 139)

The Justice for LB campaign demonstrates social media use requires continued vigilance on the uses of power, as well as providing an imaginative, collective resource. The instigators and followers of #JusticeforLB demonstrate an understanding of both the potential of social media campaigning, but also the multiple jeopardies that require tenacity and sassiness[2] to overcome. However, the use of digital spaces helps amplify their concerns. It moves people with learning disabilities and their families from a borderland to a connected centre.

Notes

1 Under the Welfare Reform Act of 2012, the government removed what it called the Spare Room Subsidy. Under the changes, tenants in social housing, had their benefits reduced if they had a spare bedroom. This has had a disproportionate impact on foster carers, divided families and disabled people.

2 The deliberate choice of 'sassiness' follows Maya Angelou's poem – 'And Still I Rise' – as comment on the labels attached to those who inhabit the liminal and treacherous spaces provided by intersectional erasure.

References

Alcock, P. (2003) *Social Policy in Britain [2nd Edition]*. Hampshire, UK: Palgrave.

Bauman, Z. (2012) *Liquid Modernity [2nd Edition]*. Cambridge, UK: Polity Press.

Betteleheim, B. (1967) *The Empty Fortress: Infantile Autism and the Birth of the Self*. New York: Free Press.

Brown, M., James, E. and Hatton, C. (2017) *A Trade in People: The Inpatient Healthcare Economy for People with Learning Disabilities and/or Autism Spectrum Disorder*. Lancaster, UK: Centre for Disability Research.

Brown, M., Ray, R., Summers, E. and Fraistat, N (2017) '#SayHerName: A case study of intersectional social media activism', *Ethnic and Racial Studies*, 40(11): 1831–1846.

The Combahee River Collective (1982). 'A Black Feminist Statement', in Hull, G. T., Scott, P. B. and Smith, B. (eds.) *But Some of Us Are Brave*. Westbury, NY: Feminist Press.

Courcy, I. and des Rivières, C. (2017) '"From cause to cure": A qualitative study on contemporary forms of mother blaming experienced by mothers of young children with autism spectrum disorder', *Journal of Family Social Work*, 20(3): 233–250.

Crenshaw, K. (1989) 'Demarginalizing the intersection of race and sex: A Black feminist critique of anti-discrimination doctrine, feminist theory, and anti-racist politics', *The University of Chicago Law Forum*, 140: 139–167.

Crenshaw, K. (1991) 'Mapping the margins: Intersectionality, identity politics and violence against women of color', *Stanford Law Review*, 43(6): 124–1299.

Davies, B. (2008) 'Practicing Collective Biography', in Hyle, A. E., Ewing, M. S., Montgomery, D. and Kaufman, J. S. (eds.) *Dissecting the Mundane: International Perspectives on Memory Work*. Lanham, MD: University Press of America.

DH (2006) *Our Health, Our Care, Our Say: A New Direction for Community Services*. London: HMSO.

Dossa, P. (2009) *Racialized Bodies, Disabling Worlds: Storied Lives of Immigrant Muslim Women*. Toronto: University of Toronto Press.

DRUK (2014) 'Disability Rights UK submission to the Work and Pensions Select Committee Inquiry into benefits sanctions policy'. At: www.disabilityrightsuk.org/disability-rights-uk-submission-work-and-pensions-select-committee-inquiry-benefits-sanctions-policy (accessed December 2016).

Foucault, M. (1978) *History of Sexuality Volume 1: An Introduction*. New York: Vintage Books.

Garrett, P. M. (2010) 'Recognizing the limitations of the political theory of recognition: Axel Honneth, Nancy Fraser and social work', *British Journal of Social Work*, 40(5): 1517–1533.

Gwilym, H. (2017) 'The political identity of social workers in neoliberal times', *Critical and Radical Social Work*, 5(1): 59–74.

Hancock, A.-M. (2016) *Intersectionality: An Intellectual History*. New York and Oxford, UK: Oxford University Press.

Hatton, C. and Emerson, E. (2004) 'The relationship between life events and psychopathology amongst children with intellectual disabilities', *Journal of Applied Research in Intellectual Disability*, 17(2): 109–117.

Hill-Collins, P. and Bilge, S. (2016) *Intersectionality*. Cambridge, UK: Polity Press.

Horner, N. (2009) *What is Social Work: Context and Perspectives [3rd Edition]*. Exeter, UK: Learning Matters.

Hugman, R. (2009) 'But is it social work? Some reflections on mistaken identities', *British Journal of Social Work*, 39(6): 1138–1153.

Humphrey, C. (2011) *Becoming a Social Worker: A Guide for Students*. London: Sage.

Kanner, L (1943) 'Autistic disturbances of affective contact', *Nervous Child*, 2: 217–250.

Laperrière, M. and Lépinard, E. (2016) 'Intersectionality as a tool for social movements: Strategies of inclusion and representation in the Québécois women's movement', *Politics*, 36(4): 374–382.

Lenehan, C. (2017) *These Are Our Children: A Review by Christine Lenehan, Director, Council for Disabled Children*. London: Department of Health.

LGA (2017) 'Adult social care funding state of the nation 2017'. At: www.local.gov.uk/sites/default/files/documents/1.69%20Adult%20social%20care%20funding-%202017%20state%20of%20the%20nation_07_WEB.pdf (accessed December 2017).

Locke, A., Lawthom, R. and Lyons, A. (2016) 'Feminisms and social media', *Feminism & Psychology*, 28(1): 128–129.

Lymbery, M. (2014) 'Social work and personalisation: Fracturing the bureau–professional compact?' *British Journal of Social Work*, 44(4): 795–811.

Macdonald, R., Shildrick, T. and Furlong, A. (2013) 'In search of "intergenerational cultures of worklessness": Hunting the yeti and shooting zombies', *Critical Social Policy*, 26, September.

Mazars (2015) 'Independent review of deaths of people with a learning disability or mental health problem in contact with Southern Health NHS Foundation Trust April 2011 to March 2015'. At: www.england.nhs.uk/south/wp-content/uploads/sites/6/2015/12/mazars-rep.pdf (accessed December 2016).

MENCAP (2007) 'Death by indifference'. At: www.mencap.org.uk/sites/default/files/2016-06/DBIreport.pdf (accessed December 2016).

MENCAP (2012) 'Death by indifference: 74 deaths and counting'. At: www.mencap.org.uk/sites/default/files/2016–08/Death%20by%20Indifference%20-%2074%20deaths%20and%20counting.pdf (accessed December 2016).

Mladenov, T. (2015) 'Neo-liberalism, postsocialism, disability', *Disability and Society*, 30(3): 445–449.

Morris, J. (1991) *Pride against Prejudice: Transforming Attitudes to Disability*. London: The Women's Press.

Nayak, S. (2015) *Race, Gender and The Activism of Black Feminist Theory: Working with Audre Lorde*. Hove, UK: Routledge.

Neiman, S. (2014) *Why Grow Up? Subversive Thoughts for an Infantile Age*. London: Penguin.

Oliver, M. (2009) *Understanding Disability: From Theory to Practice*. Hampshire, UK: Palgrave.

Papworth Trust (2013) 'Nowhere to go, no way to pay: Applying the bedroom tax with discretion'. At: www.papworthtrust.org.uk/sites/default/files/Bedroom_tax_report_FINAL_In_house_copy%20-%20smaller%20version.pdf (accessed December 2016).

Parkin, E. (2016) 'Learning disability – Overview of policy and services'. House of Commons library briefing paper number 07058.

Parton, N. (2006) *Safeguarding Childhood: Early Intervention and Surveillance in a Late Modern Society*. Hampshire, UK: Palgrave Macmillan.

Penna, S. and O'Brien, M. (2009) 'Neoliberalism', in Gray, M. and Webb, S. A. (eds.) *Social Work: Theories and Methods*. London: Sage.

Priestley, M. (2000) 'Adults only: Disability, social policy and the life course', *Journal of Social Policy*, 29 (3): 421–439.

Public Health England (2011) *People with Learning Disabilities in England 2011*. London: HMSO.

Ryan, S. (2018) *Justice for Laughing Boy: Connor Sparrowhawk – A Death by Indifference*. London: Jessica Kingsley Publishers.

Silva, J. M. (2013) *Coming Up Short: Working-class Adulthood in an Age of Uncertainty*. Oxford, UK: Oxford University Press.

Turley, E. and Fisher, J. (2016) 'Tweeting back while shouting back: Social media and feminist activism', *Feminism & Psychology*, 28(1): 128–132.

Yuval-Davies, N. (2011) *The Politics of Belonging: Intersectional Contestations*. London: Sage.

14 The activism of intersectionality

A tool for feminist political articulations, possibilities, tensions and challenges[1]

Itziar Gandarias Goikoetxea

Introduction

The 'activism of intersectionality' refuses tendencies towards problematic discreet categorisations of 'activism' and 'intersectionality'. The application of intersectionality in political activism highlights the tensions and difficulties that arise when different women meet to generate joint political activities. The focus is on the experience of articulation of the Platform of the World March of Women of the Basque Country[2] (WMW, www.emakumeenmundumartxa.eus/), where autochthnous and migrant women gather. For that, intersectionality is put to work in activism in order to recover its radical and transformative character originating in Black feminisms. The 'activism of intersectionality' is a tool with a political potential to be reclaimed and yet to be discovered.

In the last two decades, intersectionality has been welcomed by feminist and gender studies worldwide. Nevertheless, various authors are sceptical about its use as the magical remedy to overcome limited theoretical frameworks that respond exclusively to gender (Falcón and Nash, 2015). Ahmed (2012) and Nash (2010) speak of a current fetishisation of intersectionality, with the danger of reducing it to an acritical and rigid proposal, to the detriment of its dynamic, political and transformative character. Other authors consider it an old-fashioned concept (Taylor et al., 2010) or a 'buzzword' (Davis, 2008). All of these critiques point mostly towards the difficulties and conflicts that come up at the practical stage. These tensions surface in the context of tangible social realities of power inequalities when carrying out joint activism between migrant and local women in the Basque Country. In the articulation of the World March of Women we have realised that the matrix of different social dominations configures different experiences of life and concrete inequalities that put us in very different positions to do activism. The precarious and poor employment conditions that migrant women have to occupy to survive, mainly as domestic and care workers, generate difficulties in being able to take part in assemblies and activities, even during the weekend. Lorde (1984: 139) states that 'survival is not a theory'; for migrant women activism is the constant daily struggle to survive.

The relevance of intersectionality to feminist activism is not new. As acknowledged by Crenshaw herself (1989: 153), Sojourner Truth (1851), over a century ago, with her emblematic question, 'Ain't I a woman?' exposed how her experience as a Black woman and a slave was different to that of white women of the time, involved in the struggle to vote. Later, during the seventies and eighties, the Black feminist Combahee River Collective, used 'simultaneous oppressions' in their 1977 feminist statement to articulate their intersectional struggles as Black women. The Combahee River Collective statement was/is pioneering in challenging the struggles based on identities deeply rooted in Black and feminist activist movements. These demands from the end of the seventies were picked up by Black feminist activists like Angela Davis (1983), Audre Lorde (1984), Patricia Hill-Collins (1993) and Chicana and feminist lesbians (Moraga, 1983; Anzaldúa, 1987) who, during the entire decade of eighties, denounced the exclusions of Black women within the political activist movements in which they were participating. Feminist, Black liberation movements, as well as leftist movements of the time were articulating themselves around a homogeneous and selective subject, in which Black women, some of whom identified as lesbians and working class, were positioned as 'outsiders insiders': 'I chose the term "outsider insider" because it seemed to be an apt description of individuals like myself who found ourselves caught between groups of unequal power' (Hill-Collins, 1999: 85).

Based on the lived experiences of Black women, Crenshaw (1991) distinguishes two types of intersectionality, both with direct implications for feminist activism. On the one hand, Crenshaw develops the notion of 'structural intersection' out of her analysis of Los Angeles Afrodescendant women who suffered from gender violence, racism and patriarchy. Structural intersection is the overlapping of systems of discrimination (gender, race and social class) which has specific impacts on the lives of people and social groups.

On the other hand, Crenshaw identifies 'political intersectionality' out of her analysis of relations between antiracist and feminist movements, where women of colour live an 'intersectional disempowerment' (Crenshaw, 1991: 1243) at the crossroads between at least two subordinate groups, the feminist movement and the antiracist movement. Crenshaw (1991) reveals the division of political energy that this implies for women of colour, as in the majority of cases both groups have separate and discriminatory agendas. Paying attention to the discourses of both movements, Crenshaw (1991) emphasises how the constructions of racism and sexism are based exclusively on the experiences of both groups' dominant conceptions, obviating the lived experience of the intersectionality of racism and patriarchy. Crenshaw (1991) observes how these mutual exclusions entail the danger of reproducing the same mechanisms of domination and subordination against which the movements themselves hope to fight against.

Intersectionality is problematised when put to work in activism. The imperative is to understand how the 'activism of intersectionality' can reconfigure centre and margin positions. Intersectional activism makes visible the relations of power within the political articulations between different feminist subjects. Intersectionality is more than a theory and academic concept; it is essential to anti-racist feminist activism and enables the liberation of individuals, communities and societies situated at the margins.

Reflections on putting intersectionality to work in the political activism of Women World March

The World March of Women is an international movement of feminist actions that unites women and organisations to eliminate the causes of poverty and violence against women. Since the year 2000, The World March of Women's movement has mobilised hundreds of women from over 70 countries worldwide, around the struggle against all forms of discrimination and inequality, through regional, national and international actions. In the case of the Basque Country, the WMW unites different feminist and women organisations and trade unions and although it was organised from 2000, it achieved a big mobilisation in 2005, with the 2nd International Action. Since 2013, and as regards the 4th International Action, we have started a process of reorganisation with the entering of new feminist and migrant women groups. In that process, intersectionality was the lens to understand how the interrelation of diverse oppressions creates the basic conditions for joint political activism. The following is a brief description of each group:

Women of the World Babel is a Basque and migrant women's organisation that promotes empowerment meetings of women with different personal, social and cultural history.

Garaipen is a feminist women's group constituted by Basque and migrant women gathered for social and multicultural leadership.

Medeak is a radical feminist group born in 2000, placing the 'body' at the centre of political action. Medeak identify themselves as radical, transsexuals and transgender with the objective of reclaiming the margins.

Women Assembly of Bizkaia is a feminist women's organisation based in Bilbao and with a history of struggle for the rights of women over the last 35 years.

Bilgune Feminista is a nationwide Basque feminist organisation born in 2002 that fights for one sovereign and feminist Basque Country.

Through assemblies every three months, during a period of two years, we have reorganised the running of the articulation and redefined four new fields of action that fit the largest diversity of the groups: (i) transsystemic violence, (ii) bodies and sexualities, (iii) sustainability of life and (iv) network work and diversity management. Each one of the four fields of action was defined by a different group. This construction of the areas of action is a practice of political intersectionality (Crenshaw, 1989) as the axes of action are presented as open, so that each group can then use them to its specific reality. Therefore, intersectionality is about the ability to go over my own demands, in order to see the ones belonging to the rest of the people, and build an opening political agenda that we all see as our own. The process of implementing the activism of intersectionality for the articulation of political struggles in and through these groups within the World March of Women's movement has not been free from difficulties. The following three tensions have been identified: (i) the crystallisation of 'lacking' and 'emptied' intersectional subjects (ii) the 'coat rack' subject or the danger of classification and univocality, and (iii) the utopia of the 'etcetera'.

Crystallisation of lacking and emptied intersectional subjects

Applications of intersectionality can fall into a discursive trap that exposes inherent tensions in political activism with regards to identity politics; between on the one hand, claiming a position of oppression in order to resist, whilst on the other hand, re-inscribing the very position of oppression that is resisted.

Puar warns us of this danger in the case of women of colour:

> What the method of intersectionality is most predominantly used to qualify is the *specific difference* of 'women of color,' a category that has now become, I would argue, simultaneously emptied of specific meaning in its ubiquitous application and yet overdetermined in its deployment. In this usage, intersectionality always produces an Other, and that Other is always a Woman of Color.
> (2011: 52)

In other words, intersectionality can become a mechanism for the production of a new essentialised intersectional subject or in terms of Puar (2011: 52), 'emptied of specific meaning'.

In its origins intersectionality challenged essentialism and reductionism. However, in practice, the economy of intersectionality could potentially reinscribe the political exclusion of racialised women as a feature of their embodied identities. This locates the failure of political representation in the 'complex' identities of 'intersectional' subjects, who are constructed as unrepresentable in terms of 'race' or 'gender' alone (Carasthatis, 2013). On this issue, Brown asks: 'What kind of political recognition can identity-based claims seek that will not resubordinate the subject itself historically subjugated through identity categories such as "race" or "sex," especially when these categories operate within discourses of liberal essentialism and disciplinary normalization?' (1993: 391).

There is the risk of crystallising marked subjects, with the danger of generating bodies in which oppression would seem to be emerging from their very existence. Thus, presenting women of colour as 'lacking' subjects or victims of their own characteristics, who are in need of specific interventions, aimed at reducing their lacks and deficits. In the case of the WMW, there is a condescending glance and suspicious scrutinising tendency that positions and represents migrant women as not feminist enough, as 'lacking' women needing to be enlightened by Basque feminists:

> I recognize that there is a tendency to look at them meticulously, putting in question their work and activities, because when they are autochthnous women some knowledge of activisms is presupposed but with migrant women we keep thinking think they still have to learn it.
> (Women Assembly of Bizkaia)

This reflects an assumed supremacy of the autochthonous position in relation to the migrant woman, fixing and crystallising the migrant position; in Mohanty's (2003) terms, as the 'Third World Women' that need to be saved by and to learn from Western feminists. This aspect of the economy of intersectionality can only function through the subject being 'emptied of specific meaning' (Puar, 2012). In this economy of intersectionality these 'Third World Women' are supposed to be empty of knowledge and experience of activism and are therefore in need of enlightenment by local Basque feminists.

The 'crystallisation' and 'emptiness' constructions of the migrant as lacking in knowledge disavows the power dynamics within intersecting systems of power, privilege and oppression that shape and configure the intersectional experiences of oppressions of migrant women. Instead of fostering agency, this crystallising emptiness essentialises migrant women as deprived victim subjects with respect to normative and privileged subjects who, in convenient contrast, are hardly questioned. Harris (1990) warns that if we do not break with essentialism, we are always going to be forced to choose which pieces of our identity represents us and, therefore, the women situated at the margins will hardly stop being something more than a crossing of axes of domination.

The coat rack subject or the danger of univocality

There exists the danger of considering social categories as pre-existing elements and external to the subject; categories that we incorporate and dress onto the subject, as if they were a coat rack (Nicholson, 2000). Nicholson uses the image of the coat rack to illustrate how the body becomes a coat rack, onto which different types of devices related to personality and behaviour are hung. The risk is of constructing gender as representative of what women share, and that race, class, age and other identity positions become indicatives of what we don't share.

This 'additive' model (Spelman, 1988) holds the danger of classification and univocality. The danger of classification consists of thinking of intersectionality in terms of a race competition (Platero, 2012), about what is the most relevant category or axis of oppression; not conducive to the articulation of difference in feminist activist struggles. As Moraga and Castillo point out (1984: 22), struggling to combat only our discrimination 'will only isolate us within our own oppression, it will separate us rather than radicalise us'.

We have been aware that 'oppression is full of contradictions' (Hill-Collins, 1993: 36). On one hand, our awareness as Basque women, of our positions of privilege in terms of race, as white European women, does not involve setting aside or precluding our intersectional experiences of oppressions as women, as Basque and as working class. For example, Basque feminists from the Bilgune collective articulate their intersectionality of class oppression, national-cultural oppression[3] and sex-gender oppression. In that sense, the face-to-face meetings of WMW Platform have widened the homogenous visions that migrant women had, in relation to the reality of Basque women. For instance, migrant women during the assemblies are now aware of the subordination of the Basque language, seeing the difficulty of some Basque women expressing themselves in Spanish. One of the first political decisions was, we collectively agreed, to prioritise Basque as a language in the assemblies, with volunteer translators to Spanish, even though Spanish is well known.

On the other hand, we have also been aware that the 'woman' category itself is limited. In terms of accounting for the diversity of meanings that the 'woman' notion adopts for each one of us, our question was: Is the experience and the meaning of woman the same, for an African woman who has just migrated and works as a domestic worker; for a Basque adult woman who is trying to reconcile her work and family life; or, for a young mum whose mother-tongue is Basque and with a situation of work precariousness; or for a lesbian who wants to have a masculine aspect and to whom being interpellated as a woman causes discomfort?

The tensions arising from the 'activism of intersectionality' became apparent in 2015, during the preparation of the actions for the passing of the feminist caravan through Bilbao. To work on the axes of network action and diversity management, we created a specific group formed by migrant women from different countries and autochthnous women. We decided to do a street action: for this, we constructed a 'panties market stall' where we represented reflections of individual and collective resistances on panties, thongs and nappies. It became apparent that use of the term 'panties' had different significances for all of us. For example, for young Basque women the panties were a sexual liberation symbol, but for women with functional diversity, nappies represented problematic constructions of dependency, vulnerability and need.

The tensions in these differences towards our activist street actions demonstrated that the activism of intersectionality in relation to difference is emotionally hard, painful and generates conflict. Often, to avoid conflict we look the other way and don't confront our differences. But, as Lorde (1984) states, we need not to be afraid of differences, because those differences can be a creative force for change. The following example, concerning differences in relation to the 'panties market stall', demonstrates the inherent and complex contradictions that have to be grappled with within feminist activist alliances. Furthermore, it demonstrates the necessity of intersectionality to feminist activism. Some African women outlined their disagreement with the realisation of the 'panties market stall'. They understood this action as a violation, as for them, the symbol of the panties reinforced racist sexualised stereotypes of African women as Jezebels, including connotations of African women as prostitutes. It became clear that the street action of the 'panties market stall' could have the effect of excluding rather that uniting the African women who would refuse to participate because of what the 'panties market stall' symbolised. What happened next was that there was not much time for prolonged or in-depth discussions because the activity was scheduled to take place within a few days. In the end without a thorough discussion the activity was not suspended, the African women gave in and the panty stall was organised.

This forced concession of the African women, who were uncomfortable with the 'panty' action showed at least two things about power dynamics. First, that within feminist articulations there are shifting power asymmetries and not all women have the same authority and legitimacy when making decisions or proposing activities. Here, the challenge of intersectionality within feminist activism reminds us of the complexity of Spivak's question (1988), '*Can the Subaltern Speak?*' Second, that inviting women to participate in an activity is not enough and does not guarantee political intersectionality; the issue of inclusion is fraught with unequal power dynamics. As a political tool, intersectionality treats power, privilege and oppression as concurrent and relational (Collins and Bilge, 2016). This involves bringing conflicts around differences to the core of our activism debates. Putting political intersectionality to work in activism requires working through conflicts and disagreements generated by those differences in power. Political intersectionality, involving critical reflection of power constituted in and through difference, is emotional and hard work to do collectively.

The utopia of the etcetera

The concept of intersectionality, unlike that of double or triple discrimination, avoids carrying out an analysis limited to an aggregation or arithmetic sum of oppressions recognising the fluid multidimensionality of social relations (Harris, 1990). Reductionist additive logics, such as double or triple discrimination, hold the danger of assimilating diversity as mere manifestation of differences, omitting inequalities produced at the convergence and simultaneousness of the axes of differentiation. In the practice of intersectionality, this risk has moved onto the intersections. In other words, it would seem that studying a bigger number of intersections produces more sophisticated analyses, as if intersectionality could apprehend all of the subject's positions (Falcón and Nash, 2015).

Efforts to resolve this tension are through the use of the '*etcetera*' that somehow lightens the load and operates as a strain relief. However, putting the etcetera to practice exposes significant issues. On the one hand, the order given to the categories is neither accidental nor coincidental. Which categories do we automatically name and which ones do we not? Why does gender, class or origin appear automatically to us in this long list, whereas others, like language or functional diversity, are harder to name? What does it depend on? Are some categories more universal than others?

On the other hand, the etcetera appears as a feminist theoretical utopia, 'a promised land' (Nash, 2010: 3) to encompass all identities. The question becomes: what are the implications for activism, research and scholarship regarding the possibility or not of including all intersections? The etcetera entails a sign of the complexity, the variety and the heterogeneity of identities that we are eager to capture but can never reach. Butler frames the use of the etcetera, as a desperate, defensive, anxious remedy to the complexity of identity:

> The theories of feminist identity that elaborate predicates of color, sexuality, ethnicity, class and ablebodiedness invariably close with and embarrassed 'etc' at the end the list. Through this horizontal trajectory of adjectives, these

> positions strive to encompass a situated subject, but invariably fail to be complete. This failure, however, is instructive: what political impetus is to be derived from the exasperated 'etc' that so often occurs at the end of such lines? . . . This illimitable etcetera, however, offers itself a new departure for feminist political theorizing.
>
> (Butler, 1990: 143)

Butler's proposal is the illimitable etcetera as a site of feminist praxis. In this sense, critical analysis of the etcetera (Platero, 2012) offers possibilities and reveals a political subject that is not evident or irreducible, but continuously constructs him/herself through action.

Regarding the WMW Platform, we have learned that putting intersectionality to work in activism does not involve the groups having to speak of all the oppressions, or feeling satisfied by using the word intersectional or the etcetera postscript to magically resolve the complexity of the positions we occupy. As put forward by the Bilgune feminist group, intersectionality requires us to speak from the specific oppressions that determine our experience. Our different partial situations are the starting point because:

> Intersectional does not mean that now all of us need to speak of all the oppressions constantly. I, for example, read reality from my situation as a woman, Basque, precarious, that speaks Basque and from there I am going to make politics. I don't have to speak about all oppressions all the time. Intersectionality means that I speak of what affects me, you speak of what affects you and we can build something in common.
>
> (Bilgune Feminist group)

The challenge resides in developing, collectively, a political intersectional articulation of struggles, that, on the one hand, is sufficiently wide for the different demands to be placed within it, and, on the other hand, is in tune with diverse women's particular realities. A situated political articulation that pays attention to the multiplicity of struggles that is open and unfinished. The task is placing 'human difference as a springboard for creative change' (Lorde, 1984: 115) as a condition of the activism of intersectionality.

The challenges and horizons of intersectionality

Based on Crenshaw's original proposal (1989, 1991) of intersectionality as a provisional and revisable notion, it is necessary to think about intersectionality as an open tool, to rethink the inherent dilemmas of difference within feminist activism. Regarding the argument presented in this chapter that intersectionality is essential to activism demonstrated through the experience of articulation of the World March of Women in Basque Country, three challenges that must be addressed have been identified. The first is related to dealing with the interrelation between subjectivity and intersectionality. The second refers to the urgency of repoliticising intersectionality; giving it back its initial transformative and radical character. The third is about addressing intersectionality from the outlook of the contingent situations where it emerges.

Dealing with the subjective aspects of intersectionality

The turn towards examining the emotional component of intersectionality (Staunaes, 2003; Kwan, 1999; Nayak, 2015) emphasises the urgency of understanding how the structures of domination produce processes of subjectification. Is it possible to distinguish, through emotions, the axes of intersection, using the metaphor of the crossroads? What are the implications of being simultaneously located in the spaces of 'periphery' and 'centre'?

In regards to the focus on the emotional component of intersectional, Jordan-Zazhery outlines the consequences of measuring intersectional experiences and separating the elements that make up identity:

> When you look at me, what do you see: a woman who is black or a black woman?' In my eyes, this is a moot question since my blackness cannot be separated from my womaness. In fact, I am not sure if I want them to be separated. What I want is for individuals not to use my social location to justify punishing me or omitting me from the structures and practices of society. Sometimes my identity is like a 'marble' cake, in that my blackness is mixed intricately with my womaness and therefore cannot be separated or unlocked.
>
> (2007: 260–261)

The metaphor of the cake illustrates the impossibility of disaggregating the elements that make up identity; it is impossible to separate the sugar, the flour or the yeast once the cake is baked. The goal of intersectionality is not to find the different ingredients that make up identity; this is an additive and fragmented model of oppressions that ends up rebuilding and essentialising all forms of identity (Yuval-Davis, 2006).

Insistence that 'the intersectional experience can be emotionally overwhelming' (Nayak, 2015: 92) and cannot be ignored is not a recent plea. Back in the seventies, the Combahee River Collective noted that, 'the psychological toll of being a Black woman and the difficulties this presents in reaching political consciousness and doing political work can never be underestimated' (1977: 215). The emotional component of the activism of intersectionality cannot be ignored because understanding how and why the experience feminist activism is emotionally overwhelming is key to the survival of feminist activism. Nayak cautions us against configuring intersectionality into a 'unifying mechanism' (Nayak, 2015: 93). The challenge is to stay with and inhabit the inevitable tensions that intersectionality exposes within feminist activism. In other words, not resorting to the excuses that there isn't enough time to debate, explore or listen thoroughly because a task or street action needs to be done.

Repoliticising and radicalising intersectionality

One of the tensions, exemplified by the street action of the 'panties market stall' explored earlier in this chapter was the extent to which the act of appealing to diversity and enumerating the differences is a way of concealing and not facing the inequalities that generate differences. The problem is not difference but unequal power relations: 'Difference is less a problem for me than racism, class exploitation, and gender oppression. Conceptualizing these systems of oppression as difference obfuscates the power relations and material inequalities that constitute oppression' (Hill-Collins, 1993: 494).

With respect to the World March of Women, this continues to be a challenge, but we have taken some steps forward. The participation of migrant women in the Platform has been very relevant, to show not only the differences in relation to origin, class and legal status between Basque and migrant women, but also to lay on the table the material and access inequalities to rights and resources that exist amongst us. This was reflected in the joint definition that was constructed around the axes of diversity and network:

> We are women that come from diverse geographies with different experiences, journeys, knowledges, abilities, identities, ways of struggling and demands that we want to defend value and recognise without establishing hierarchies. We recognise ourselves as diverse whilst unequal in rights conditions.
>
> (Communications Dossier, World March of Women)

Ahmed (2012) and Bouteldja (2016) ask whether referring to intersectionality in discourse and analyses does not work as a strategy to avoid talking about racism or classism. Puar has examined how intersectionality is associated with a calling for inclusion, converting itself into a tool for 'managing diversity' (2012: 53) within existing conventional categories. Ward (2007) and Bilge (2013) argue that intersectionality has been emptied of its initial capacities to produce counter-hegemonic knowledge in order to be absorbed within neo-liberal culture and ideology. Bilge (2013) uses the term 'Whitening intersectionality' (2013: 412) in regards to the academically European colonisation of intersectionality. The whitening of intersectionality is not limited solely to the bodily issue, in other words, it is not exclusive to white women, it incorporates white hegemonic thinking, and internalised colonialism (Moraga and Castillo, 1984). It is an uninterrupted and racialised process of socialisation that determines and generates perceptions, emotions and racial white ways of thinking about racism, even within racialised people themselves. Ahmed (2012) underlines how, in situations in which it is difficult or uncomfortable for us to listen to the racism we reproduce, intersectionality can be used as a defence against listening or feeling questioned. These are warnings that feminist activists must be vigilant of, given time and resources, including emotional energy, in socio-political and economic contexts of increasing demand and pressure and decreasing material resources.

The convergence of intersectionality and diversity has led to a depoliticisation and de-radicalisation of the theoretical and political contributions to intersectionality. This has subordinated the demands of intersectionality that we question the categories used and (re)consider how these categories and our analysis will differ, if our starting points are the material realities of the people situated at the margins (Falcon and Nash, 2015). The examples in this chapter, and in particular the 'panty' street action, provide a clear message that placing the issues of race and racism inside intersectionality is crucial, in terms of counteracting the practices of hegemonic post-racial and neo-liberal thinking that avoid talking about racism in virtue of intersectionality.

Towards a situated intersectionality

As an alternative proposal to manage the tension between particularisms and universalism, some authors have proposed the concept of 'contextualised' intersectionality (Falcón, 2012). This refers to continuously building a politics of localisation (Boyce-Davies, 1994; Kaplan, 1994), and examining how intersectionality is being interpreted and what meanings it adopts in each context.

In that same direction, Romero Bachiller and Montenegro (2013) propose moving from intersectionality as a junction of axes, to intersectionality as 'situation'. Here, forms of oppression are materialised in semiotic contexts and specific materials where forms of oppression appear. From this vantage, the focus is on those manifestations and identities that are presented in a determined and localised manner. Intersectionality as 'situation' proposes that there are particular contexts where certain differences emerge as relevant compared to others. The emergency of certain positions is not a product of chance but responds to systems of oppression in which they have been socio-historically placed (Romero Bachiller and Montenegro, 2013). Therefore, not all the bodies appear as potentially vulnerable in the same way.

The distribution of the vulnerabilities, starting from the processes of differentiation, with the inequality that is attached to them, is a product of the 'systematicity of contingencies' (Brah, 1996: 117): a reiterated repetition of differentiations that causes certain bodies to be historically configured and rebuilt as marked bodies. However, it is relevant to note, when referring to the 'systematicity of contingencies', that an essential ontological character, through which certain characteristics or differences emerge, is not determined. These characteristics or differences are incarnated and materialised in social practices, on a daily basis (Brah, 1996). A situated intersectionality would go from thinking in terms of marked bodies, to the ways in which bodies emerge in specific power relations frameworks. The objects of analysis are the practices of differentiation that produce bodies, rather than the bodies produced by axes of domination. As shown by Brown (1997), we are not only oppressed but also produced, by discourses of power and historically complex and contingent practices of domination that complicate the metaphor of the intersection of different social categories.

Conclusions

Starting from the initial transforming and critical character of the concept of the activism of intersectionality, its potentialities and the tensions have been explored in putting intersectionality to work in anti-racist feminist activism. Making use of Weil's recommendation (1952) about mistrusting and suspecting the words adorned with capital letters, the aim is to question and place, under critical suspicion, the current academic success of intersectionality.

There is an urgency for critical examination of the complexities of intersectionality within activism. Intersectionality is a tool, requiring continuously rethinking that is subject to context and place. The activism of intersectionality grapples with contingent, unsettled and contextual positionality. The activism of intersectionality offers a way of mediating 'between the tension of restating a multiple identity and the necessity of developing political identities' (Platero, 2012: 115). It is precisely this continuous tension that allows us to continue to rethink and discuss the utility and challenges of the activism of intersectionality. The strength of intersectionality resides in its resistance to firmness and immobility.

Intersectionality has been mainly applied in the analysis of the intersection of oppressions in subjects situated at the margins (Nash, 2008), however, it has barely accounted for the ways in which privilege and oppression can be mutually constitutive in individual and collective experiences. Intersectionality is a device that shows how privilege is articulated and how the positions of privilege and oppression, occupied by us, can co-exist simultaneously. The challenge resides in moving from the interconnection of categories imposed by the logic of domination, to the logic of fusion and inseparability (Lugones, 2005).

Three current challenges found in the activism of intersectionality, as a tool for the practice of feminist politics are: first, attending to the emotional experiences of lived intersectionality; any intersectional structural analysis is limited to the point of redundancy without it.

Second, intersectionality is not an inclusive strategy of differences. Simply talking about differences does not bring any transformation (Razack, 1998). The activism of intersectionality can generate political articulations amongst different feminist identities. The activism of intersectionality is an intrinsic element of 'the activism of Black feminist theory' (Nayak, 2015) for active building of common places that express shared situations, without denying the differences and without abandoning the existing complexity, singularity and multiplicity.

Rather than creating new readings of intersectionality that will surpass the previous ones, the activism of intersectionality returns to the roots of sustaining anti-racist feminist activism on Black feminist theoretical foundations. Crenshaw's concept of intersectionality (1991) is rooted not in the pages of a law review journal, but in the political labour of Black women activists. Exploring the possibilities and the challenges in the activism of intersectionality there is the insistence that we question and deconstruct the glasses through which we read power in order to re-read power in activism.

Notes

1 This text is based on the author's thesis: 'Until all women are free: Encounters, limits and challenges for articulations between migrant women and local feminists in Basque Country', assigned to the Social Psychology Department in Universitat Autònoma of Barcelona. The author would like to thank the women who participated and recognise their daily fight for a fairer world for women; and expressly to Sheida Besozzi for her help with the translation and Suryia Nayak and Rachel Robbins for their comments to this text.

2 For more information visit the website: http://emakumeenmundumartxa.eus

3 Basque Country is a non-recognised nation, without political legal area and with its own language. Basque culture is a dominated and oppressed culture. Taking into account the nation/culture component in constructing feminist subjects, means that patriarchy and the sex/gender system it imposes are embodied in a particular socio-economic and political model (the class component). The Spanish and French states condition the situation of the women of Euskal Herria as citizens, refusing the national sovereignty as Basque people. As Basque women we locate our struggle for a new social relationships model for Euskal Herria, where sex/gender will not create domination (Bilgune Feminista, 2010).

References

Ahmed, S. (2012) *On Being Included.* Durham, NC: Duke University Press.

Anzaldúa, G. (1987) *Borderlands: La Frontera* (Vol. 3). San Francisco, CA: Aunt Lute.

Bilge, S. (2013) Intersectionality undone: Saving intersectionality from feminist intersectionality studies. *Du Bois Review: Social Science Research on Race*, *10*(2), 405–424.

Bilgune Feminista (2010) Creating feminist identities to change Euskal Herria. Recovered from: http://bilgunefeminista.eus/eu/ENG.

Bouteldja, H. (2016) Raza, Clase y Género: ¿Nueva divinidad de tres cabezas? *Clivajes. Revista de Ciencias Sociales* (6), 1.

Boyce-Davies, C. (1994) *Black Women, Writing and Identity: Migrations of the Subject.* London: Routledge.

Brah, A. (1996) *Cartographies of Diaspora, Contesting Identities.* London & New York: Routledge.

Brown, W. (1993) Wounded attachments. *Political Theory*, *21*(3), 390–410.

Brown, W. (1997) The impossibility of Women's Studies. *Differences: A Journal of Feminist Cultural Studies*, *9*(3), 79–101.

Butler, J. (1990) *Gender Trouble: Feminism and the Subversion of Identity.* New York: Routledge.

Carasthatis, A. (2013) Identity categories as potential coalitions. *Signs: Journal of Women in Culture and Society*, *38*(4), 941–965.

Collins, P. H. (1993) Toward a new vision: Race, class, and gender as categories of analysis and connection. *Race, Sex & Class*, 25–45.

Collins, P. H. (1999) Reflections on the outsider within. *Journal of Career Development*, *26*(1), 85–88.

Collins, P. H. and Bilge, S. (2016) *Intersectionality.* Hoboken, NJ: John Wiley & Sons.

Combahee River Collective (1977) 'A Black feminist statement'. Reprinted in L. Nicolson (ed.), *The Second Wave: A Reader in Feminist Theory*, New York: Routledge.

Crenshaw, K. (1989) Demarginalizing the intersection of race and sex: A Black feminist critique of antidiscrimination doctrine, feminist theory and antiracist politics, *The University of Chicago Legal Forum*, 139–167.

Crenshaw, K. (1991) Mapping the margins: Intersectionality, identity politics, and violence against women of color. *Stanford Law Review*, *43*(6), 1241–1299.

Davis, A. Y. (1983) *Women, Race and Class*. New York: Vintage Books.

Davis, K. (2008) 'Interseccionality as a buzzword': A sociology of science perspective on what makes a feminist theory succesful. *Feminist Theory*, *9*, 67–85.

Falcón, S. M. (2012) Transnational feminism and contextualized intersectionality at the 2001 World Conference Against Racism. *Journal of Women's History*, *24*(4), 99–120.

Falcón, S. M. and Nash, J. C. (2015) Shifting analytics and linking theories: A conversation about the 'meaning-making' of intersectionality and transnational feminism. *Women's Studies International Forum*, *50*, 1–10.

Harris, A. P. (1990) Race and essentialism in feminist legal theory. *Stanford Law Review*, 581–616.

Jordan-Zachery, J. (2007) Am I a Black woman or a woman who is black? A few thoughts on the meaning of intersectionality. *Politics and Gender*, *3*(2), 261–262.

Kaplan, C. (1994) The politics of location as transnational feminist practice. In I. Grewal and C. Kaplan (eds.), *Scattered Hegemonies: Postmodernity and Transnational Feminist Practices*. Minneapolis, MN: University of Minnesota Press.

Kwan, P. (1999) Complicity and complexity: Cosynthesis and praxis. *Depaul Law Review*, 45–56.

Lorde, A. (1984) *Sister Outsider*. Trumansburg, NY: The Crossing Press.

Lugones, M. (2005) Radical multiculturalism and women of color feminisms. *Revista Internacional de Filosofía Política*, (25), 61–76.

Méndez, R. L. P. (ed.) (2012) *Intersecciones. Cuerpos y sexualidades en la encrucijada*. Barcelona: Bellaterra.

Moraga, C. (1983) *Loving in the War Years: Lo que nunca pasó por sus labios*. Boston, MA: South End Press.

Moraga, C. and Castillo, A. (1984) *This Bridge Called My Back: Radical Writings by Women of Color*. San Francisco, CA: Ism Press.

Nash, J. (2008) Re-thinking intersectionality. *Feminist Review*, *89*, 1–15.

Nash, J. (2010) On difficulty: Intersectionality as feminist labor. *The Scholar and Feminist Online*, *8*(3), 1–10.

Nayak, S. (2014) *Race, Gender and the Activism of Black Feminist Theory: Working with Audre Lorde*. London and New York: Routledge.

Nicholson, L. (2000) Interpretando o gênero. *Estudos Feministas*, *8*(2), Florianópolis, Univ. Federal de Santa Catarina.

Puar, J. K. (2012) 'I would rather be a cyborg than a goddess': Becoming intersectional in assemblage theory. *PhiloSOPHIA*, *2*(1), 49–66.

Razack, S. (1998) *Looking White People in the Eye: Gender, Race and Culture in Courtrooms and Classrooms*. Toronto: University of Toronto Press.

Romero Bachiller, C. and Montenegro, M. (2013) The Intersectionality as a situation. In *International Congress of Critical Social Psychology*. Barcelona, February 2013.

Spelman, E. V. (1988) *Inessential Woman: Problems of Exclusion in Feminist Thought*. London: The Women's Press.

Spivak, G. C. (1988) Can the subaltern speak? In C. Nelson and L. Grossberg (eds.), *Marxism and the Interpretation of Culture*. Basingstoke, UK: Macmillan.

Staunaes, D. (2003) Where have all the subjects gone? Bringing together the concepts of intersectionality and subjectification. *NORA: Nordic Journal of Women's Studies*, *11*(2), 101–110. http://dx.doi.org/1080/08038740310002950.

Taylor, Y., Hines, S. and Casey, M. E. (eds.) (2010) *Theorizing Intersectionality and Sexuality*. Hampshire, UK: Palgrave Macmillan.

Truth, S. (1851) Ain't I a Woman? In O. Collins (ed.) (1988), *Speeches that Changed the World*. Louisville, KY: Westminster John Kmox Press.

Ward, J. (2007) *Respectably Queer: Diversity Culture in LGBT Activist Organizations*. Nashville, TN: Vanderbilt University Press.

Weil, S. (1952) *The Need for Roots*. London: Routledge.

Yuval-Davis, N. (2006) Intersectionality and feminist politics. *European Journal of Women's Studies*, *13*(3), 193–209. http://dx.doi.org/10.1177/1350506806065752.

15 Breaking the silence

Women, intersectionality, community radio and empowerment

Annette Rimmer

Introduction

The term 'intersectionality' is rarely seen in UK media literature, though there has long been outrage about the dismal statistics and invisibility/reductive representation of Black, Asian, LGBTQ, disabled, working class, refugee people – and women as homogenised, excluded groups (WFTV and BFI, 2016). Mediadiversified, a website conceived to draw attention to diversity issues in media, cites Crenshaw's original (1989) definition of intersectionality: 'women experience oppression in varying configurations and in varying degrees of intensity. Cultural patterns of oppression are not only inter-related, but are bound together and influenced by the intersectional systems of society'. Mediadiversified explains: 'In other words, certain groups of women have multi-layered facets in life that they have to deal with. There is no one-size-fits-all type of feminism' (Mediadiversified, 2016).

Their definition may be viewed as reductive, but is designed to open debate to a broad range of people and also to move the theory of intersectionality from its domain as an analytic tool used by feminist and anti-racist scholars (Nash, 2008), to its deployment as an active device for understanding and fortifying minority voices in media: '. . . it gives people better access to the complexities of the world and of themselves, it's what it does rather than what it is that lies at the heart of intersectionality' (Hill-Collins and Bilge, 2016: 5).

The chapter emerged from the pilot study for my thesis, 'Breaking the Silence: community radio, women and empowerment'. Through it I considered the potential of community radio as a vehicle of women's empowerment for those of us working to facilitate welfare, whether in social, community or youth work. My background in all three fields, and latterly as a radio producer, motivated me to unearth the stories of my female colleagues. Their narratives expose multi-faceted, intricate lives where, although much common ground is evident, especially regarding violence and oppression, homogeny is not.

As a radio volunteer, I am careful to situate myself within the research domain, aware of the 'insider-outsider' dilemma (Thomson and Gunter, 2011). I acknowledge the potential for exploitation and colonisation when narratives are interpreted by a white, middle-class researcher (despite the suspicious, critical approach arising from my working-class background and years of social work practice). For this reason, I have refrained from attaching my own interpretation to each individual quotation and tried to expose the women's sentiments as they emerged. But in truth, the study is, in its entirety, my own construction and the participants are witnesses selected to help build my case. As with most academic studies, the author's voice is the loudest. My approach combines the narratives of two community radio volunteers, Vee and Collette, with discourse on media, empowerment and on intersectionality 'as a major paradigm of research in women's studies and elsewhere' (McCall, 2005: 1771). McCall completely rejects 'the separability of analytical and identity categories' and laments that such important phenomena as intersectionality lacks discussion on how it should be studied. Whilst the study uses a feminist ethnographic and narrative approach, it acknowledges the dangers of colonisation pre-eminent in Tuhiwai Smith (2012), and Spivak's scepticism in 'Can the Subaltern Speak?' (1988). It is pre-occupied with exposing what Shetty and Bellamy (2000: 25) call 'lost voices' and recounted with the insight that: 'the existing system of dominant social relations "creates a culture of silence" where oppressed people are silenced, alienated and "a mere object of the director society"' (Freire, 1972: 16).

In order to support and encourage the womens' narratives, 'The River of Life' was used as a community development tool where a group of individuals plot their lives as journeys down a river, explaining each stage of the journey to the group (Thompson, 2008).

In addition to community radio women's voices, and by way of interpretation, the chapter integrates literature from diverse disciplines in order to 'understand and apply intersectionality more deeply in the real world' (Hancock, 2016: 21). It views 'social work' as a broad church of activity which facilitates welfare, empowers and strengthens communities through working and learning together.

> We view the term 'social work' in its widest sense and use it to describe anyone working to facilitate the welfare of disadvantaged people. We do not believe social workers are 'case managers', but are activists and campaigners working collectively together with us in the community.
>
> (Citizens as Trainers Group et al., 2004: 311)

It is crucial from the outset to understand 'empowerment' as a *process*, rather than an end result. Just as intersectionality is characterised through the 'dailiness' of life, empowerment likewise, most often takes place during the process of working and learning together. Rather than a grandiose trumpeted finalé, it is the everyday, nuanced and almost invisible process of change which may (or may not) ultimately, influence organisations or societies: 'Empowerment is about opening spaces for meaning-making within communities, so that local voices and stories are heard amongst the maelstrom of global cultures' (Burkett, 2013: 3).

The chapter emanates from my position as a white woman activist, who, after 30 years in community development, youth work, various fields of social work and teaching, was drawn into the media world in the midst of a jobless depression.

My subsequent introduction to community radio restored my confidence and reignited my belief in collective creativity and empowerment; the pursuit of learning and having fun together; combatting loneliness, depression and oppression.

At once, the seemingly 'worlds apart', distinct disciplines of social work and media collided, stepped back to consider each other, and then embraced. I discovered a growing body of literature, particularly from the majority world, discussing 'media, culture and social justice' and using 'community media' as an active tool of informal education and empowerment: 'Community media, through its diverse forms and processes, have the power to move community members from being dependent and passive to becoming actively involved in the creation of a more meaningful society' (Paranjape, 2007: 468).

There is no claim of originality in bringing the worlds of intersectionality, community radio and empowerment practice together; hooks (1994 and 2003) considered the invisibilising and silencing of Black history and cultural identity a convenient 'social amnesia' and the restoration of both became her life's work. Nasa Begum exposed the voice of Black Disabled, LGBTQ women and their exclusion from any of the traditional gender roles or community spaces occupied by these (so-called) 'distinct' groups. In addition:

> Specialists trained to treat one or other of our body parts have contributed to our dismembered body image (*and identity?*). Value judgements are assigned to our 'good parts' or 'bad parts'. Health is seen as a virtue, disease as evil and ugly.
>
> (Begum, 1992: 76)

She called for a 'breaking of the silences' surrounding the experiences of Disabled women. hooks, Begum and others build upon reire's (1972) theory that change can only happen when the 'dependent society' breaks out of the culture of silence and wins its right to speak.

Methodology

The study 'Breaking the Silence: community radio, women and empowerment' is cognisant of the tensions involved in understanding and researching intersectionality and empowerment, as exemplified by Van der Hoogt and Kingma in their discussions with Indigenous women:

> The conflict is between collective and individual rights, and the need to link and address social and economic exclusion with cultural discrimination. Holistic solutions are needed. Changing power relations is a long-term process, which also needs to deal with fighting gender-based violence.
>
> (2004: 47)

Here lie some obvious tensions in intersectional and empowerment practices where statutory and NGO funding tends to be short term, tends to target singular homogenised societal groups and tends to demand constant evaluation and measurable results:

> our last community radio funding was to engage 'older people'; there was no requirement to target specific kinds of older people. The group that jumps forward is white middle class older men – there are loads of those in radio already. We needed much more time, money and a definite remit to engage with – reach out to – give voice to – maybe older people who'd always been excluded – who may not even dream that they could be radio presenters (for example older women from poor communities, older trans, older women who'd grown up in care or experienced abuse, with dementia etc. etc.). We did manage this, but it was down to utter dedication and the commitment of staff who went the extra mile on a voluntary basis. What can you do in 18 months?
>
> (Community Radio staff member, 2016)

It is clear from this example that presumed homogeneity can make intersectional inclusive practice difficult and exacerbates the problems of marginalised groups.

Intersectional practice and feminist research, as used here, endeavour to restore and highlight nuances and complexities concealed by social amnesia and traditional methodologies. McCall is sceptical:

> Are these assumptions about the capacity of different methodologies to handle complexity warranted? Scholars have not left a clear record on which to base a reply to this question. Feminists have written widely on methodology but have either tended to focus on a particular methodology (e.g., ethnography, deconstruction, genealogy, ethnomethodology) or have failed to pinpoint the particular issue of complexity.
>
> (2005: 1772)

There is a level of agreement that intersectionality is a vaguely defined concept which lacks a defined methodology and even introduces new methodological problems in research (McCall, 2005; Nash, 2008). This study is a modest attempt to deploy intersectional practice and research in an (as yet) untested arena. Whilst scholars continue to wrangle with these important issues and explore the nature and methods of intersectionality, Geertz points out the crucial importance of establishing some kind of research framework designed by the *researched* as well as the researcher: 'Rather than attempting to place the experience of others within the framework of . . . a conception . . . understanding them demands setting that conception aside and seeing their experiences within the framework of their own idea of what selfhood is' (cited in Hood et al., 1999: 27).

There are other tensions involved in aspirations of community and individual empowerment. One of those tensions is brought about by the romanticism attached to 'community'. Burman draws out the risks of romanticising cultures or religions, reifying them and thereby possibly concealing gendered abuse:

> Included in this are the seemingly 'positive' ways of representing minority cultures – by romanticizing or exoticising them. Either way, culture is treated as static, is equated with religion and is treated as somehow a more primary axis of difference or identification than gender.
>
> (2004: 302)

However, in Freire's (1972) terms, empowerment arises from dialogue where safe spaces are created for conflict to be worked through and difference comes to be problematised and understood.

Community radio in context

> I've always loved radio. Well I'm Black, uneducated and I always thought I was a really quiet person and I never ever in a million years thought I could do my own radio show – no more than I could have been a beauty queen but somewhere I saw this ad and thought I'd come along for the laugh. See what all these knobs did. (Referring to the knobs on the radio desk, I think!) I always thought it was educated white middle class people on radio – ok now you've got Chris Evans but by and large especially women its plummy speaking women (impersonates posh talker) but it's not for the likes of us, it's not people like us who are normally on radio, so I never thought for one minute it would lead to what it has.
>
> (Collette, 2014)

Literature on community radio is scarce in the UK, therefore this study uses works from the Majority World (Paranjape, 2007; Wairimu et al., 2010; Fuller, 2007; Curry et al., 2013), where community radio goes back much further, possibly starting in Bolivia in 1947 (Fogg et al., 2009). It is also informed by work of Radioactive 101 (2014) who combine the disciplines of psychology, education, social work, drama and media and have been integral to the dissemination of evidence of community media as a tool of intersectionality and empowerment throughout Europe.

The Community Radio 'movement' (Stewart, 2006: 5) began in UK in the 1980s with voluntary, non-profit stations run by and for community members, not financial gain. 'Community' was (importantly) defined as 'of geography, of identity or of interest' (F.C.D.L. 2009). This is pertinent to intersectional practice, though open to criticism of homogenisation – for example one of the first 'identity' stations to be created was 'Gaydio' for the gay community in Manchester. 'Legacy' and 'Unity' serve older and younger Caribbean people (respectively) in Manchester. With regard to geographic community stations, 'Sunny Govan' radio serves part of Glasgow. Ofcom, the UK state regulating body, mandates that within each community station there is a representation of diverse voices within its area, so many stations broadcast in a variety of languages and reflect diverse cultures; a show in Polish may be followed by a show in Urdu or a Disability Rights or LGBTQ show. Whilst *no one show* will attend to all of the intersections in the identities of people and communities, Community radio is compelled (by the regulator) into attending to diversity:

> Community radio stations provide a new voice for hundreds of local communities across the UK. Fuelled by the hard work and enthusiasm of volunteers, they reflect a diverse mix of cultures and interests and provide a rich mix of mostly locally-produced content.
>
> (Ofcom, 2015)

There is insufficient space to critique community radio, but there are arguments, particularly from some Black commentators, that community radio, regulated by government, was intentionally designed to replace uncontrolled pirate stations. Kenlock laments the loss of radio controlled by and for the Black community:

> If you walked down any South London street in the early 1990's 'London's soul power' could be heard booming with pride from passing car stereos, at local youth centres and in businesses. This sense of community empowerment and embracing our Black British identity was the vision we had as the founders of Choice FM.
>
> (Kenlock, 2013)

That community licenses were given out to crush the power of oppressed voices is a moot point, but is certainly the case that the UK Government, through Ofcom, compels 'community radio to demonstrate measurable social gain and be accountable to the target community' (Ofcom, 2011). What is relevant to this chapter is the notion that the community radio movement comprehends and addresses intersectionality by providing sites of daily dialogue, problematising and action where Freire's 'culture of silence' (1972) and hooks' 'historical amnesia' (2003) are being tackled.

Community radio voices

I aimed to uncover the forgotten voices of intersectionality through the women's narratives: 'This "social amnesia" amounts to silencing people's stories. The lived experience of those groups is so rarely heard, that it is forgotten, ignored and even consciously rendered invisible by dominant groups in societies' (hooks, 1994: 31).

Volunteers are engaged through learning together, discussion, building friendships and supporting each other to produce radio broadcasts. In this space, individual issues are discussed, problematised and transformed into structural concerns. In Freire's terms it is an ongoing dialogic experience, without which, 'learning is utterly superficial. Learning engages the learners in the constant problematising of their existential situations' (1985: 56).

hooks (1994 and 2003) considers intersectionality as central to the ideal of collective learning and empowerment. Here a community radio volunteer explains the radio training group, for whom the common bond is an interest in radio:

> You are dealing with a group of people of very wide social backgrounds, the one common thing is radio so they might be unwaged, disabled, an ex-offender, have mental health . . . that's a whole different individual group of people's stories, their baggage they bring – I hate that word baggage. I shouldn't have used that. But its people's stories the good things, the bad sides and things like that.
>
> It was an incredibly diverse group. And I thought what was very, very good about the training (and yeah some of it will be about the nature of the group) But the training encouraged people who were completely differing backgrounds, who probably, NO *certainly* would never in ordinary life normally interact. Oh yeah, you're talking about people women who couldn't read or write, to people who are pretty adept, who communicate well and it was a situation that people would be very unlikely in their normal social groupings, to have interacted. So I learned loads, and not just about radio, but about completely different lives. Oh yeah it was very much a 2 way process and yeah there were times when one person 'd rub somebody up the wrong way . . . but as a group it worked very well.
>
> (CR volunteer, 2014)

There are daily examples of the stories and problematising which takes place in the space of community radio. Vee's narrative, whilst making her way down the river of life, reveals some painful educational experiences as a Disabled child:

> Teachers . . . once they found out I wasn't very well co-ordinated . . . the needlework teacher Mrs . . . we had to make an apron and I couldn't do that so she made the apron for me and she just gave me a running stitch to do 'cos I couldn't hold the needle properly. So instead of being patient she did it for me. On the other hand Ms . . . the housecraft teacher, she was like the spitting image puppet of Mrs Thatcher – she was a witch. She was giving instructions to the girls and all of a sudden she would stop and say – 'Hold on we'll have to wait for Vee 'cos she's not as quick as the rest of you.' She really humiliated me.

Continuing her journey down the river of life, Vee relates how she developed her identity and confidence with the help of music:

> I was very naïve and believed that I could get pregnant by someone holding my hand. And I was well developed. At the age of 12 I was 36D (bra size) so you can imagine what that was like – So by the time I went to youth clubs it was scary you know – cos all these boys with raging hormones and me with big boobs. Because of the way I looked I started to develop my personality really because I didn't have much else going for me really apart from my boobs, so that was when I started developing my sense of humour and other skills – also because I was always like the 'tag along'. All the other girls

> would get the boys and I'd tag along and so I developed other things like I started getting into music and I used to do all the discos at the youth club and that was how it all started really. I found out that when I was playing records I could be anyone I wanted to be really'.

Her early experience of radio at college:

> we set up our own little radio station – in the W centre and all it was a tape deck and we called it Arundel Radio Station and our tag line was 'WE are ARS and if you don't like it you can kiss it' (uproarious laughter) *I love it!*

And the impact of community radio on her life:

> To be honest It's got me through a lot of bad times in my life I think. It's given me opportunities. It's the first time I've really done something that I can honestly say that without any contradiction that I'm good at it. I'm really good at this, I am really good at what I do. And I can say that with a lot of confidence, the only time really I've been able to say that with a lot of confidence. I just love it. I just love my show and the great thing is it's all been off my own bat, nobody's told me what to do or what to put in it, its all come from my ideas it's been great to be able to channel my ideas into something that's actually tangible, it's audible.

A significant body of Media and Culture commentators have begun to echo Freire's theory that for marginalised people, community media is crucial to visibility:

> whilst one society remains silent, the other society is conceptualised as 'Goliath', dominant and in control of that very loud voice – characterised as globalised media. Community media, through its diverse forms and processes, have the power to move community members from being dependent and passive to becoming actively involved in the creation of a more meaningful society.
>
> (Paranjape, 2007: 468)

Later in her community radio development, Vee decided to start a Disability show, which she uses to raise awareness about Disability issues through discussion with other Disabled people or guests from local organisations:

> So really the show is about giving a voice to others. They are the experts and they have a voice and they give others information. We've had people talking about head injuries, epidermalitus. We've had people from carers organisations. About cancer during pregnancy (and that was 2 fellas). Mummy's star – this guy set it up 'cos his partner had cancer and she gave birth to a boy and she died 3 weeks later so he set up this organisation and called it

> 'mummy's star' 'cos that's how he talked about her death to his little boy. Nelly Globe – prostate cancer fella called . . . He wanted to raise awareness and help people get through it and raise money. Nelly was his missus and Globe 'cos she's his world . . . So radio is to educate, to inform and to entertain – that's it in a nutshell . . . Not a patronising teaching thing – mixed with music – informal.
>
> So not only has the radio empowered me I'm using it to empower others – but the great thing about community radio is that it lets you act from your own initiative, in fact it depends on your own initiative. Your show is your time that is your time to do what you like – as long as you stick to the rules and aren't rude, crude or obscene . . . or party political you can do pretty much what you like.
>
> (Vee)

Interestingly, the women in the study exposed new dimensions on the hotly debated definitions of 'empowerment' hitherto unseen by conventional literature-led discourse. They talked of empowerment as *being able to empower others*, of empowerment as *creativity*, of *having fun* as well as having a voice.

Collette began her journey down the river of life by choosing her name:

> You can't use my nick name of the 'jolly wog' so just use Collette.
>
> I'll start my journey just with my love of music really. My earliest memory is hearing 'Can't Buy Me Love' when I was 3 – I remember being in the hallway at our house and hearing that song coming out of another room and another memory I had was of 'A Hard Day's Night' which was 1965 or 66 playing in the street. So my earliest memories are tied up in music, I wasn't interested in dolls or anything like that but my main interests were music and football.
>
> I was born in King Side in the old terraced houses near the brewery and as far as I know my parents lived in one room and they weren't married so in those days it was shocking . . . and not only weren't they married but they were in an inter-racial relationship – my dad was Black Nigerian and my mum was white English so it was a terrible shocking thing.

Collette recounts being expelled at the age of 12 or 13 and has many observations about her education, the most poignant one being that it was wasted on her:

> Because I was hyperactive I was in and out of child guidance and I remember sitting at school looking out of the window. I used to love being outdoors I had so much energy inside of me and to make me sit down was hell.
>
> So I think of Community Radio training and Community Radio as being a sort of education – I do understand why you have to go to school but for me they should have saved the money (laughter) And the daft thing was I was quite bright. But to marry brightness up to sitting still and discipline . . .

> I used to love being outdoors I had so much energy inside of me and to make me sit down was hell and it was a rough inner city school in a rough area and I grew up amongst domestic violence, drugs dealing, prostitution it was rough. King Side in the 60's and 70's wasn't a place for the faint hearted!
>
> There were lots of jobs in those days, the hyperactivity hadn't been diagnosed but it was hard, not just 'cos I'm black with no 'O' levels, but there were limits on what I could do 'cos I'm blind in one eye. One job I lost because I was so football mad I got the sack from there 'cos we had a midweek game and I told them I was at the doctors and I took half a day off and went to the match and the woman who worked there as a secretary, her husband spotted me at the game so . . . 'you're supposed to be sick but you were singing at Queens Park Rangers'.

Such narratives have become significant published works (hooks, 1994; Lorde,1984) and are poignant portraits of lives described by Collette as 'not of the ma'nstream'. They demonstrate the power of voicing the miniscule and grand detail of one's life and that breaking the silence and finding one's voice is in itself a kind of *empowerment*: 'There is a rich, developing literature on voice. In narrative inquiry there is a relationship between researchers and participants and issues of voice arise for both' (Clandinin and Connelly, 2000: 146).

So an important first step to understanding intersectionality and empowerment is for people to express themselves, exchange stories and raise their voices about the things that matter to them, a process which, according to Burkett (2013) can also mean having fun. Burkett reveals the voices of young participants in the World Comics Network:

> Community members are not just audiences, they are creators. It's not only about drawing comics, it's about helping each other to tell and understand their stories, giving their opinion. At the end they agree on something – 'this kind of violence is wrong' or 'what solutions can we look at?' So it's about an opportunity for dialogue and peer learning.
>
> (ibid.: 11)

> I ended up being expelled from school at the age of 12 or 13 and I was off school for 2 years because no school in my town would have me, but my salvation again was music and I remember when I was 13 or 14 and the local uni used to have rock concerts and Leo Sayer was on and you were supposed to be 18 to get in. I was 13 I looked about 11 but the hippy type students (who must have known my age) just waved me in.
>
> (Collette, 2014).

> Well I got interested in politics and making serious radio shows, I think 'cos of the injustice to my parents and being mixed race. I mean look at my Father he was a violent alcoholic and illegal immigrant he never did a day's work

> and if you judge him as that that's fair enough to say he's a bad person – but just to judge him as a black man is wrong and that's why he was judged bad.
>
> (ibid).

In Burman's terms (2004), the practice here is 'attending to another's difference', but does it go far enough to challenge the large-scale homogenisation of difference, especially in the contexts of policy and practice, 'where the language of *homogenised difference or diversity* prevail and are often employed as a code for *inequalities*'? Intersectionality is seen as going beyond the recognition of difference, not only attending to another's difference but 'breaking out of the mire of 'stultifying uniformity' versus 'deviancy' implied by much of the discourse on difference:

> We need to go beyond enabling difference, since this paradigm only brings us more of the same (so to speak); that is, if we follow Foucault on this, it is the same old story of the regulation of the normal as part and parcel of the pathologisation of difference, and vice versa.
>
> (Burman, 2004: 294)

The crux of intersectionality as difference amongst groups, and the deviancy perspective on difference is a feature touched upon by Collette:

> In the past I used to be embarrassed about having a very white side to my culture – If I gave certain black people a lift in my car I would hide my CDs by white artists as they would have a dig at me for being a Coconut. These days however, I just say as I am half white and was raised virtually single handed by my white mother why'shouldn't I have a white side?

As Sweetman articulates, for those working to support others: 'If we are aware of intersecting inequalities we will be less discouraged if women disagree on race and class grounds, and see differences between them as more important than commonalities' (Sweetman, 2015).

Collette's comments also verify the importance of the minutiae of everyday life. It is in the 'particular', the minutiae, and not the generalised features of difference, where intersectionality exposes the misunderstandings of 'anti-oppressive' practice: 'I do believe that attending to differences is enabling: not by talking of differences in general, but by talking of particular, but situationally constructed, specificities' (Burman, 2004: 297).

> One of my colleagues at the radio is an 84-year-old very posh, highly educated. We get on brilliantly – she is lovely. We talk about really middle class things like religion, classical music and travel. I am more intimidated by class than colour. I am extremely aware and embarrassed by my lack of education and social graces so tend to stick within my own class, regardless

> of colour but sometimes the white educated person enjoys talking to someone like me and both sides can learn.
>
> (Collette, 2016)

It is dialogue with different others which enables learning, growing and self-awareness to take place and this is a collective and relational enterprise occurring in the community space. Empowerment and intersectionality, as Cornwall and Edwards relate: 'are not individual resources but depend absolutely on relational dimensions' (2014: 9).

McCall notes the importance of class, as confirmed by Collette. She calls for more examination of 'the structural inequalities among women, especially among different classes of women, since much less attention is devoted toclass than to race in the new literature on intersectionality' (2005: 1788).

'Different' voices have long been excluded from mainstream media, which struggles to fulfil its remit to represent the communities it serves. Smith (2015) suggests that this is not only to do with the 'deviancy perspective' discussed by Burman (2004), but is an intentional strategy designed to silence oppressed people:

> 'voice' isn't just a matter of speech – it also has to do with how people are seen and heard. Excluded groups tend to become a powerful motif in the minds of the dominators. They are viewed both as a threat to order – politically, socially and sexually; and as existing for the benefit of the powerful.
>
> (Smith, 2015)

The concept of 'empowerment' in terms of 'giving voice', continues to be disputed, contested, deliberated in the literature of all kinds of social work. However, in community media literature, it is held that gaining a voice is a prerequisite for liberation and social justice (Fuller, 2007).

> I have always had a great gift of the gab and sense of humour despite essentially being a shy private person and hiding behind a radio means I can utilise all that. Sometimes I do very serious heavy political topics which can be more hard work than fun but I find it rewarding as one of my big regrets in life is being expelled from school at the age of 13 thus having little formal education so I am always keen to educate myself I see my radio work as being part fun and part my chance to help the world.
>
> (Collette, 2016)

Those working in and amongst specificities, those borderlands or 'blurred zones' must, according to Smith (2015), steel themselves to hear the misery, as well as the glee in intersectional voices. An intersectional interpretation would extend this restricted, binary observation but the argument exposes the notion of voice as multiple, not singular.

> My identity depends on where I am and who I'm with. For example I was at a totally black funeral on Friday and was totally black in what I talked about and who I talked with, all my, what I ate (goat, rice and peas) and the music danced to (reggae) I didn't feel I was putting on an act, I automatically will talk about black things with black people.
>
> (Collette, 2016)

Community radio may be seen as an intersectional enabler – a simple 'voice-giver' and a space where social action can take place, it can have deep significance.

> I do feel I am 2 people in one and I can do shows that appeal seperately to black and white audiences without selling out either side. I am very happy that in the last few years mixed race/multi-racial has been recognised as being a separate identity to black. It was an insult to everyone. As I am now at a predominantly white station I do feel an extra responsibilty to educate the white audience about racial matters. I never felt that at ZZFM (another community radio station) as the shows and audience were far more integrated and knowledgable. By the way, when I said being classed only as black was an insult I of course meant it as the one drop rule thing. Like all black people are the same.
>
> (Collette, 2016).

Collette and Vee represent a critical perspective on mainstream media which has all but silenced intersectional voices, partly due to its deviancy perspective on those voices, but also because 'it sees itself as expert opinion formers and ordinary citizens as "ignorant meddlesome outsiders"' (Chomsky, 1991).

Conclusion

> Elements, essence and conceptual framework of the term 'intersectionality' have evolved through, and are evident in Black feminist writing and testimony.
>
> (Nayak, 2015: 153)

There is no claim here that community media represents the panacea for understanding intersectionality or empowering practice. However, it has been the aim of this chapter to contribute to the widening of the debate and to demonstrate how the 'elements, essence and conceptual framework' of intersectionality might be realised and activated through women's community radio voices.

This is not to say that community radio is not open to parallel criticisms levelled at all sites of intersectional practice which are seemingly embraced but regulated by statutory bodies and N.G.O.'s and might be a most useful tool of oppression (Kenlock, 2013). Experiences from India, Bangladesh and Black radio in the U.S. demonstrate a waryness of community radio as a potential source of opposition and dissent (Pavarala, 2015); this waryness is a constant presence for UK radio.

The processes through which individuals and groups identify themselves – and are identified and defined by institutions – is a major cause of inequality. Lamont et al., (2014) consider the role of institutions and cultural repertoires in fostering social resilience as providing buffers and scaffolds against the effect of inequality. Perhaps community radio is a 'buffer and scaffold' against oppression, but it represents a safe space for dialogue and social action, where women meet, talk and elevate their problems from individual pathology to structural levels. Here lies an important intersection of informal education (the underpinning theory of social work) with community media that 'sees the need to break down the mystification of life and understand our experiences in a critical way' (Beck and Purcell, 2010: 12).

The paternalistic notions of 'giving voice' and breaking the silence are highly symbolic concepts in radio, and should be held to account (Burman, 2004), but addressing 'voice poverty' (Pavarala, 2015: 14) is an essential precursor to, and tool of intersectional practice and empowerment: 'Denial of voice comes from systematic efforts to restrict access to modes of self-expression. The policy environment needs to be changed drastically to enable access and, thereby recognise people's voices' (ibid., 2015: 15).

That 'empowerment' is a much-debated concept is acknowledged here, but there is crucial agreement that it is not an 'end result' but a lengthy *process*, a journey on smooth or rocky terrain, made both bumpy and inspirational by the idiosyncrasies of intersectionality: 'empowerment is not a destination, nor something that can be "delivered" but a journey that is neither predictable nor linear in outcome' (Cornwall and Edwards, 2014: 119).

Freire's depiction of oppression as a hegemony of silence is augmented by hooks' vivid description of her own life and how Black culture and identities have been rendered invisible (1992). That community radio might extend a microphone and spotlight into these domains is highly symbolic and reframed by media scholars as an antidote to 'media darkness' and 'voice poverty': 'it can help communities re-constitute symbolic universes that have been disrupted by violence' (Rodriguez cited in Pavarala, 2015: 16).

Finally, to restate my position: the narratives here have been interpreted by a white, middle-class researcher, fully aware of potential exploitation and colonialisation. As Spivak points out: you cannot simply make the subaltern visible or lend her a voice, neither can you appropriate her voice. 'You don't give the subaltern voice. You work for the bloody subaltern, you work against subalternity' (1992: 46).

So my assertion is that community radio represents a significant force working against subalternity by challenging the orthodoxy of silence and providing a space for women to join together, learn skills and gain pride through vocalising their nuanced lived experiences of oppression and empowerment. Community radio is a significant vehicle of intersectionality and a plausible movement engaged in combatting oppression.

> What Community Radio is about is giving 'lesser' people (I don't know how you are going to phrase this) but people like myself who aren't of the

> mainstream — giving lesser people a chance. 'Cos you know yourself that (I'm not going to name any names) but there are people at the radio who will never get a chance in the mainstream and I include myself in that 'cos I just got turned down for a job but if I can go there (to community radio) and be something and have people say 'well done Collette' – have my friends and family being proud. I got a really nice text the other week from someone who'd listened to my show and they thought it was really good. That makes you feel 10 feet tall! I go out there and I'm struggling to get a job because I'm disabled. I go in there (community radio) and I'm something.
>
> (Collette, 2014)

> It's tangible, it's audible . . . the very reason I believe in community radio is because it does give you a sense of empowerment.
>
> (Vee)

References

Beck, D. and Purcell, R. (2010) *Popular Education Practice for Youth and Community Development Work*. Exeter, UK: Learning Matters.

Begum, N. (1992). Disabled Women and the Feminist Agenda. *Feminist Review*, (40), 70–84.

BFI (2016) British Film Industry. At: www.bfi.org.uk.

Burkett, I. (2013) Visual Voices: World Comics Network. *Practice Insights, The Community Development Magazine for the Busy Practitioner, Researcher, Policy Adviser, Student and Trainer*, (2), Spring 2013.

Burman, E. (2004) From Difference to Intersectionality: Challenges and Resources. *European Journal of Psychotherapy, Counselling & Health*, 6(4), 293–308.

Chomsky, N. (1991) Force and Opinion. At: www.CHOMSKY.INFO [accessed 14 August 2016].

Citizens as Trainers Group, Young Independent People Presenting Educational Entertainment, Rimmer, A. and Harwood, K. (2004) Citizen Participation in the Education and Training of Social Workers. *Social Work Education*, 23(2), 309–323.

Clandinin, D.J. and Connelly, F.M. (2000) *Narrative Inquiry: Experience and Story in Qualitative Research*. San Francisco, CA: Jossey-Bass.

Cornwall, A. and Edwards, J. (Eds) (2014) *Feminisms, Empowerment and Development: Changi'g Women's Lives*. London: Zed Books.

Crenshaw, K. (1989) Demarginalizing the Intersection of Race and Sex: A Black Feminist Critique of Antidiscrimination Doctrine, Feminist Theory, and Antiracist Politics. *The University of Chicago Legal Forum. Feminism in the Law: Theory, Practice and Criticism*, 1989, 139–167.

Curry, S.J., Pooley, J. and Taub-Pervizpour, L. (2011) *Media and Social Justice*, Basingstoke, UK: Palgrave Macmillan.

F.C.D.L. (Federation for Community Development Learning). At: www.fcdl.org.uk.

Fogg, A. Korbel, P. and Brooks, C. (2009) *Community Radio Toolkit*. Manchester, UK: Radio Regen.

Freire, P. (1972) *Pedagogy of the Oppressed*. London: Penguin.

Freire, P. (1985) *The Politics of Education: Culture, Power and Liberation*, Westport, CT: Bergin & Garvey.

Fuller, L.K. (Ed) (2007) *The Power of Global Community Media*. Basingstoke, UK: Palgrave Macmillan.

Hancock, A.M. (2016) *Intersectionality: An Intellectual History*. Oxford, UK: Oxford University Press.

Hill-Collins, P. and Bilge, S. (2016) *Intersectionality (Key Concepts)*, Cambridge, UK: Polity Press.

Hood, S., Mayall, B. and Oliver, S. (Eds) (1999) *Critical Issues in Social Research: Power and Prejudice*, Buckingham, UK: Open University Press.

hooks, b. (1992) *Black Looks: Race and Representation*, Cambridge, MA: South End Press.

hooks, b. (1994) *Teaching to Transgress: Education as the Practice of Freedom*, London: Routledge.

hooks, b. (2003) *Teaching Community: A Pedagogy of Hope*, London: Routledge.

Kenlock, N. (2013) After the Demise of Choice FM, Is It back to Pirate Radio for Black Britons? At: www.theguardian.com/commentisfree/2013/nov/14/demise-choice-fm-pirate-radio-black-britons-capital-xtra [accessed 18 May 2014].

Lamont, M., Beljean, S. and Clair, M. (2014) What is Missing? Cultural Processes and Causal Pathways to Inequality. *Socio-Economic Review*, 12, 573–608.

Lorde, A. (2007) *Sister Outsider*. New York: Random House.

McCall, L. (2005) The Complexity of Intersectionality. *Journal of Women in Culture in Society*, 30(3), 1771–1800.

Mediadiversified. At: https://mediadiversified.org [accessed 20 October 2016].

Nash, J.C. (2008) Rethinking Intersectionality. *Feminist Review*, 89, 1–15.

Nayak, S. (2015) *Race, Gender and the Activism of Black Feminist Theory: Working with Audre Lorde* (Concepts for Critical Psychology). London: Routledge.

Ofcom (2011) *Notes of Guidance*. At: http://licensing.ofcom.org.uk/radio-broadcast-licensing/community-radio/apply-for-licence/ [accessed 18 May 2014].

Ofcom (2015) *Community Radio*. At: http://licensing.ofcom.org.uk/radio-broadcast-licensing/community-radio/ [accessed 18 February 2015].

Paranjape, N. (2007) Community Media: Local is Focal. *Community Development Journal*, 42, 459–469.

Pavarala, V. (2015) Community Radio 'Under Progress' Resuming a Paused Revolution. *Economic & Political Weekly, EPW*, 1(51).

Radioactive 101 (2015). At: http://radioactive101.eu/ [accessed 3 September 2015].

Shetty, S. and Bellamy E.J. (2000) Postcolonialism's Archive Fever. *Diacritics*, 30(1), 25–48 .

Smith, M.K. (2015) 'Race' and Difference: Developing Practice in Lifelong Learning. At: www.infed.org [accessed 24 August 2015].

Spivak, G.C. (1988*) Can the Subaltern Speak? Marxism and the Interpretation of Culture*. Chicago, IL: University of Illinois, 271–313.

Spivak, G.C. (1992) Interview with Gayatri Chakravorty Spivak: New Nation Writers Conference in South Africa (Interviewer Leon de Kock). *Ariel: A Review of International English Literature*, 23(3), 29–47.

Stewart, P. (2006) *Essential Radio Skills*. London: A&C Black Publishers.

Sweetman, C. (2015) (Ed.) Gender and Development and Intersecting Inequalities: The Gap between Theory and Practice. *Gender and Development Journal, Virtual Special Issue on intersectionality*. Routledge, Oxfam Special.

Thompson, D. (2008) *How to Set Up a Refugee Organisation*. Sheffield, UK: Federation for Community Development Learning.

Thomson, P. and Gunter, H.M. (2011) Inside, Outside, Upside Down: The Fluidity of Academic Researcher 'Identity' in Working with/in School. *International Journal of Research and Method in Education*, 34(1), 17–30 [accessed 12 January 2015].

Tuhiwai Smith, L. (2012) *Decolonizing Methodologies: Research and Indigenous Peoples*. London: Zed Books.

Van der Hoogte, L. and Kingma, K. (2004) Promoting Cultural Diversity and the Rights of Women: The Dilemmas of 'Intersectionality' for Development Organisations. *Gender & Development*, 12(1), 47–55.

Wairimu Gatua, M. Owens Patton, T. and Brown, M.R. (2010) Giving Voice to Invisible Women: 'FIRE' as Model of a Successful Women's Community Radio in Africa. *Howard Journal of Communications*, 21(2), 164–181.

WFTV (2016) (Women in Film and TV). At: www.wftv.org.uk.

Conclusion: Contextual intersectionality

A conversation

Suryia Nayak, Marisela Montenegro and Joan Pujol

This conversation on contextual intersectionality, between Suryia Nayak, Marisela Montenegro and Joan Pujol, is a fitting conclusion to this edited collection of international perspectives on the activism of intersectionality. The conversation took place whilst walking together through Chorlton Water Park, Manchester, UK on a Sunday afternoon in June 2017. In the same way as the conversation took place, the chapter is structured by a series of questions that could be used as a social work framework for critical intersectional reflexivity. As the conversation developed, it became apparent that applying a contextual intersectional lens to issues of social justice in the Spanish context foregrounds issues that resonate with the challenges, tensions and opportunities highlighted throughout this book with relevance to an international audience of social work. It is apparent that the challenge of contextual intersectionality is of attending to 'the micopolitics of context' (Mohanty, 2003: 223) within contemporary 'political shifts to the right, accompanied by global capitalist hegemony, privatization, and increased religious, ethic, and racial hatreds' (Mohanty, 2003: 229).

Suryia: It is noteworthy that Crenshaw ends her seminal paper 'Mapping *the Margins: Intersectionality, Identity Politics, and Violence Against Women of Color'* (1991) by addressing the fetishisation of personal identity traits as the focus of intersectionality. In the penultimate sentence of the paper, Crenshaw states, '[r]ecognizing that identity politics takes place at the site where categories intersect thus seems more fruitful than challenging the possibility of talking about categories at all' (1991: 1299). In her concluding remarks, Crenshaw warns against a binary split between identity and context, stating:

> If as this analysis asserts, history and context, determine the utility of identity politics . . . Does this mean we cannot talk about identity? Or instead, that any discourse about identity has to acknowledge how our identities are constructed through the intersection of multiple identities?
>
> (Crenshaw, 1991: 1299)

The emphasis on context in Crenshaw's 1991 paper should be apparent by the fact that she is locating intersectionality in the context of 'violence against women of colour' and 'identity politics'. As a Black feminist activist, with over 30 years working to end violence against Black women, I appreciate the significance of the particularity of the critique of practices that fail Black women survivors of rape; however, to remain at the level of that particularity is to fall foul of the critique Crenshaw is asserting. This seems to reflect the obsession with personal traits as the determination of discrimination and to ignore Crenshaw's admonition that 'intersectionality is not being offered here as some new, totalizing theory of identity' (Crenshaw, 1991: 1244). Crenshaw's choice of the word 'mapping' (1991) in the title of her paper on intersectionality is a word implicated in context. Mapping intersectionality brings to mind Huggan's 'cartographic connections' (1989: 128), Boyce-Davies' 'compasses of racialization' (2013: 173–201) and the numerous other uses of the metaphors of location/context used in Black feminist, decolonial scholarship that I refer to as 'location as method' (Nayak, 2017: 203). The constitutive imperative of context in relation to axes of differentiation is that 'if you can't locate the other, how are you going to locate yourself?' (Minh-ha, 1991: 73). Here, context can be thought of as a method, a verb and an event (Nayak, 2017b: 206); context is the agent of intersectionality. There is no intersectionality without context. Picking up on the Black feminist concepts developed by Hill-Collins (2000) of 'situated knowledge' (2000: 270; Haraway, 1988), 'situated knowers' (Hill-Collins, 2000: 19) and situated standpoints (2000: 25), we could speak of a 'situated intersectionality'.

The lesson for social work is that intersectionality is not a theory 'in the abstract, an exhaustive list of intersectional social categories . . . to add them up to determine – once and for all – the different intersectional configurations those categories can form' (Carbado, 2013: 5). Discursive practices of social work epistemology and practices rest too easy at the foothills of intersectional configurations of axes of difference, rather than the excruciating, mountainous terrain of context, situation and positionality; a convenient place of 'conviviality', 'connivance' and 'compromise' (Mbembe, 2001: 66). Perhaps an international movement of 'social workers without borders' (www.socialworkerswithoutborders.org) would be '[n]ot so much intersectionality of identities, but intersectionality of struggles' (Davies, 2016: 144).

The lesson for Black feminist activists working socially is not to fall into the 'shadow boxing' trap described by James. Black women's embracing of intersectional identity positions, or '[e]ver present, often ignored, but completely inescapable . . . plurality' (James, 2000: 255) often translates into:

> black women paint[ing] varied portraits of the shadow boxer as radical; as lone warrior; successful corporate fund-raiser for, and beneficiary of, progressive issues; individual survivalist; and community worker, disciplined to the leadership of non-elites in opposing state corporate dominance . . . this, after all, is the shadow boxer's dilemma: to fight the authoritative body casting one off, while simultaneously struggling with internal conflict and contradictions'.
>
> (James, 2000: 255)

Suryia: Marisela and Joan, how does contextual intersectionality enable you to understand power and the production of subject positions in social work practice in the Spanish context?

Marisela and Joan: The Spanish State organises social work through general and specific services. General services focus on economic and health needs, while specific services follow a categorical logic, such as services for women or for older people. The conceptualisation of specific services corresponds to a construction of public policing that categorises and homogenises social groups (Subirats et al., 2008). Specific services approaches place people in a series of discrimination axes such as, gender, race, class, age and sexuality that translate complex life processes into stable regulatory frameworks. This control device defines which forms of life are possible and desirable (Motta, 2016) associated with identity formations and personal rights and establish asymmetric trajectories of inclusion/exclusion. The social work device constitutes a 'one-dimensional' subject (McCall, 2005).

Job placement services for migrant women in Barcelona highlight intersectional issues for public social policies and the practice of social work. Job placements in domestic service and caregiving workplaces offered to migrant women are socially and culturally unders'ood a' 'dirty' jobs; economically devalued and attributed, within patriarchy, to women (Anthias, 2001; Bettio et al., 2006; Gil, 2011; Mohanty, 2003: 245–246; Sassen, 2003). Contextual intersectionality enables (a) critical examination of how gender and culture interact in the definition of 'adequate' workplaces for migrant women and (b) complicities within the practice of social work:

> Consequently we argue that social services condense semiotic–material elements that help to shape subjects and dynamics in the host societies, generating processes of social stratification for some collectives of immigrant women, precisely intending to combat poverty and exclusion. Hence, social services and resources targeted at immigrant women thus become accomplices in reproducing the Spanish patriarchal system that has not yet been abolished, while also creating processes of hierarchization and social stratification.
>
> (Montenegro and Montenegro, 2013: 338)

Suryia: In the UK context, the configuration of social work into specialist children and family, mental health, disability and older people services performs the dividing practices (Foucault, 1965) that 'system of differentiations' (Foucault, 1982 : 792) require for the rationalisation of unequal power relations (Madigan, 1992). This imposed fragmentation fails the woman situated in the contextual intersectionality of disability, mental distress, caring for children and classified as older; she becomes divided between, upwards of four, different service configurations. The anti-intersectional stratifications of UK social work are not fit for 21st-century, rapidly changing and fluid configurations of socio-economic living conditions. The imperative for intersectional social work practice is to attend 'to specificity of the experience of difference whilst attending to the indeterminacy of difference' (Nayak, 2017a: 1). The point is that difference is constituted in and through context. So, in the example of the woman living in the intersectionality of disability, mental distress, caring for children and classified as older, a contextual intersectional lens would focus on the contexts that (re)produce these identity categories, for example a capitalist patriarchy.

Suryia: Using examples from the specificity of your geopolitical contexts, how can the practitioner/user divide be understood through the lens of contextual intersectionality?

Marisela and Joan: In the Spanish context, intersectionality highlights how power relations configure subordinate positions in localised situations or chronotropes. Significant axes of differentiation depend on specific relational contexts (Agha, 2007; Yuval-Davis, 2014; Zebracki and Milani, 2017). Thus: 'forms of social distinction and inequality are produced in complex combinatories of social location in its broadest sense, forged through multiple sites. Hierarchical relations linked to social divisions are emergent and subject to historical contingencies, variable, irreducible and changeable' (Anthias, 2011: 214).

Social service interventions problematically construct an asymmetry, between the service provider and a legitimately needy service recipient. This binary is characterised as two internally homogeneous categories, in dichotomies of active/passive, rational/emotional, provider/needy (Montenegro, 2003). This division functions as a social organiser, defining social work relationships and legitimates paternalistic or 'good intentions' interventions (Hagelund, 2005). The professional-user divide stratifies both positions and locates one of them in a position of inferiority with respect to the other. A contextual intersectional perspective draws attention to how this axis of differentiation interacts with other social markers, in particular intervention processes, and how subject positions are built through the entanglement of multiple categorisation devices.

For migrant women in Barcelona, social categories such as gender, class, legal situation, ethnicity and user status are intertwined in the practice of 'labour insertion'. The training and counselling of migrant women tend to suggest their labour insertion in the field of domestic work and personal care based on the following arguments. First, because migrant women are represented as a 'difficult to insert' collective, their insertion must be urgently facilitated. Second, gendered and racialised representations of migrant women as 'affectionate and family oriented', equates to suitability for domestic and caring activities. Finally, migrant women are constructed as 'women in high risk' and in need of urgent intervention. This argumentation legitimates 'insertion practices' that position migrant women in the vicissitudes and precarious conditions inherent to this labour market. In practice this argumentation reproduces oppressive hierarchical practitioner/client dichotomies.

Suryia: The contradiction you expose in the term 'insertion', which in a UK context might be translated as 'integration', is that the mechanisms of 'labour insertion' for migrant women actually functions as the opposite of insertion or integration. Insertion practices position and represent migrant women as an 'excess and lack' to be placed in supplementary jobs, for example as domestic auxiliaries. I am reminded of Derrida's logic of supplementarity: '[t]he supplement comes in place of a lapse, a nonsignified, a nonrepresented, a nonpresence' (Derrida, 1997: 303). This brings me to the relationship between Derrida's logic of supplementarity and the logic of intersectionality because both of these lines of logic deconstruct the logic of binaries.

The Black feminist concept of intersectionality and Derrida's concept of the supplement demonstrate that all experience/phenomenon is constituted of multiple, interdependent contextual meanings. In the logic of intersectionality and the logic of supplementarity there is no distinction between inside and outside or absent and present. Positioning migrant women as the supplement, surplus, substitute, is to position migrant women as the 'dangerous' undecidable, as inside/outside/absent/present. It is no surprise, then, that the logic of binaries functions to regulate and control subject positions, for example in 'migrant as lacking' and 'practitioner as expert'. Social work based on contextual intersectionality would reconfigure referrals, caseloads and record files to replace service user names, diagnoses and offenses, such as, 'patient Mrs A, service user Mr B, Offender juvenile C' with 'the names of the oppressive situations they inhabit such as racism, patriarchy, homophobia and capitalism' (Nayak, 2017b: 207).

Marisela and Joan: Service user, practitioner binaries represent the service users as subjects 'marked' by intersecting gender and cultural traits and professionals as 'neutral' liberated, secular and non-traditional subjects. The differentiation between the subject and object of intervention constitutes an axe of differentiation that interacts with other axes that becomes intelligible from a contextual conception of intersectionality.

Suryia: In your particular socio-geopolitical context(s) which axes of differentiation emerge as tools of legitimisation, such as processes concerning racial ethnic, gender identity categories in the form of legal papers?

Marisela and Joan: Specific social service provisions, in the Spanish state, are based on traditional axes of structural differentiation (age, gender and disability). To these structural axes, other axes of differentiation, with less governmental attention, have been added such as national origin and sexual orientation. The categories of gender and age are defined by the national identity card. Levels of disability are defined by the Assessment and Guidance Teams (EVO) (that belongs to the General Direction of Social Protection of the Department of Labor), and assign certain levels of disability; levels that may vary depending on state regulations. In the case of sexual orientation or gender identity, services are offered based on self-definition, and the type of resources received are allocated as a group (such as 'information campaigns') rather than at a personal level: 'personalised economic resources'. In cases of individualised attention, as in the case of HIV, these resources are part of the general health provision instead of assignment to a particular axis of differentiation. A focus on the differentiation procedures illustrates an intersectional perspective that considers the connection between the social context and the relevant axes of differentiation.

Training processes for migrants highlight the implications of incorporating the concept of intersectionality in the analysis of public policies. For example, some of these services are offered to migrants who have a residence card that is mandatory to obtain the certificate of the course. However, people without a work permit can take these courses, but they will not have official certification. A contextual intersectional perspective allows us to appreciate how legal status emerges as an important axis of differentiation. The intersectional analysis must identify the contextual forms of differentiation (the legal status in this example) and understand how these differentiations intersect with other axes of differentiation (for example, gender, race, age, sexuality). In this case, physical records (such as certificates, titles or residence cards) are artefacts that condense axes of differentiation (sex, gender, age, filiation) and facilitate the exercise and reiteration of power relations.

Intersectional contextual analysis incorporates socio-historical elements that define the axes of differentiation activated in a given context. In Spain, the differentiation procedures in the access and type of health care received must be understood in the context of the legal transformations of the Spanish National Health System (NHS) from a universal health provision to a stratified one according to nationality and employment. The Spanish Law 16/2003 of May 28,[1] of cohesion and quality of the NHS, considered in article 2 that the general principles that inform the law were: (a) the provision of services to users of the NHS in conditions of effective equality and quality; (b) the universal and public insurance by the state; and (c) public funding of the National Health System, according to the current financing system. The Individual Health Card (IHC) was given to anybody who registered in the city town. This situation changed with the Royal Decree-Law 16/2012, of April 20,[2] on urgent measures to ensure the sustainability of the National Health System and improve the quality and safety of its health provision, which argued that the health system was economically unsustainable and pernicious to the viability of the health business sector (p. 31278). Article 3, on the condition of insurance, stated that (a) public healthcare provision will be given to those holding the insured status, and (b) those who do not have insured status may obtain health care delivery by the payment of a special health agreement. The legal situation was further transformed by the Royal Decree 1192/2012, of August 3,[3] on the condition of the insured and the beneficiary for healthcare in Spain, with public funds, through the National Health System and the Royal Decree 576/2013 of 26 July,[4] establishing the basic requirements of the special agreement for health provision to people without the status of insurance or beneficiaries of the National Health System, amending the Royal Decree-Law 16/2012. The legislation was encoded into the Individual Health Card, transforming the IHC into an intersectional differentiation device that encodes gender, age, disability, nationality and employment. It has to be noted that the additional provision to the state budget (BOE, 16th December 2013, section I, p. 104817) establishes that the beneficiaries of the public health system must have their residence in Spain, and the health benefits are lost after spending more than 90 days out of the country. This is an example of capillary intersectional differentiation justified with economic arguments that exclude certain intersectional subject positions from public health provision.

Suryia: In the UK context, Anzaldúa's warning that '[r]rigidity means death' (2007: 101) underscores the necropolitics of Section 15 of the Immigration and Asylum Act 1999, which states 'that a person will have 'no recourse to public funds' if they are subject to immigration control; public funds include welfare benefits and public housing'. If rigidity equates to the borders that constitute 'migrant' bodies and territorial (geographic, legal and conceptual) boundaries of immigration, then the question is what is social work doing to refuse these as an agent of collective resistance for liberation?

Marisela and Joan: In the Spanish context, '[r]rigidity means death' (Anzaldúa, 2007: 101), in the situation where the law functions as a mechanism of exclusion for migrants without legal status and Spaniards that are out of the country for more than 90 days. This legal imperative is based on an anti-intersectional necro-political justification where apparent lack of resources justifies the exclusion of certain groups of people from health provision. Article 2 of the Royal Decree 1192/2012, of August 3, on the condition of the insured and the beneficiary for healthcare in Spain states that the following conditions need to be fulfilled to have the condition of insured:

1. To be an employee or self-employed worker, affiliated with the Social Security and in a situation of membership or similar to membership.
2. To hold the status of pensioner of the Social Security system.
3. Being a beneficiary of any other periodic Social Security benefit, such as unemployment benefit or other similar benefits.
4. To have exhausted the benefit or the subsidy for unemployment or other benefits of similar nature and to be unemployed, not proving the condition of insured by any other title.

After excluding many migrants and some Spaniards from the NHS, the Royal Decree 1192/2012 of 3rd of August, explicitly gives Spanish nationals that reside in the territory the condition of insured:

1. To have Spanish nationality and reside in Spanish territory.
2. To be nationals of a Member State of the European Union, of the European Economic Area or of Switzerland and to be registered in the Central Registry of Foreigners.
3. To be nationals of a country other than those mentioned in the previous sections, or stateless persons, and holders of an authorisation to reside in Spanish

territory, as long as it remains in force under the terms established in its specific regulations.

The establishment of a typology of 'insured citizens' allows the intersectional stratification of the population in different categories; stratification that is codified in the Individual Health Card. The IHC is the document that identifies and authorises access to public health system services, recognises the status of an accredited person and informs on health coverage. Therefore, the contexts of legal changes transform the right to public health for all into a stratified privilege for some, where the people of each level can receive – or not – a specific health benefit.

In addition, the difficulty of the administrative procedure for obtaining the card depends on a personal intersectional layering. The front of the card shows the details of the accredited person: (a) personal identification code; (b) name and surnames of the owner; (c) level of health benefits. The card incorporates a magnetic stripe with encoded information of personal and administrative details in order to guarantee the confidentiality of the personal data stored. When receiving health care, the card functions as the axis of differentiation that allows or denies the possibility of receiving certain health provisions. The health card constitutes a material condensation of intersectional codification of different personal categories that facilitate or deny access to certain medical treatments; a codification that can be historically traced.

Suryia: How do different axes of differentiation articulate, and thereby give representation, voice and position, to particular vectors of identity?

Marisela and Joan: Intersectionality questions essentialist identity models in recognising the conflict inherent in the configuration of subject positions (Brah, 1996; Hall, 1996). We must attend to the ways in which categories are constructed through symbolic and material assemblages. As different forms of social organisation mutually constitute in specific geopolitical spaces and socio-historical moments (Anthias, 2002; Yuval-Davis, 2014), differentiation is the result of positionality, and relational context. Contextual intersectionality understands that certain differences in particular contexts produce particular relationships of discrimination and subalternisation.

In social work, practice is considered a matter of social welfare and public interest, defined through complex processes, within power relations, dominant discourses, laws, policies, theoretical and methodological approaches, in which certain constructions arise while others remain inactive or disappear. These frameworks function as organisational principles that assimilate pieces of information and turn them into problems and definitions in which the solutions are included implicitly or explicitly (Verloo, 2006). It is crucial to observe who is involved in the definition of a particular political policy, as well as why some issues become relevant and others not. In short, the very process of constructing a problematic field where social work must be carried out is the result of discourses and practices that constitute something like an object of thought (political, moral, scientific) as a possible object of knowledge and governmental action (Foucault, 1976).

An example of these dynamics, in the Spanish context, are recent processes of recognition of rights related to gender, sexuality, kinship and family; as well as the appearance of services and specific social programs for LGBT people (Cruells and Coll-Planas, 2013). Sadurní and Pujol (2016) warn that these operations of inclusion of homonormative corporeality entail the exclusion of other bodies from recognition policies, and function, in the geopolitical arena, as yardsticks to distinguish between civilisation and barbarism. In the legislative context, Platero (2011) analyses the controversies surrounding the law 3/2007[5] that includes the right to change the legal name and the mention of sex in the documentation of adult Spanish citizens, under the requirement (in most of the cases) of a diagnosis of gender dysphoria and of having received medical treatment for two years: legislation that had an unequal reception in the collective of trans-people. The obligation of complying with the diagnosis of 'gender dysphoria', as a perquisite to exercising the right to change name and sex, places in biomedical expertise the authority of certification of the pathological character of the patient; this contributes to the differentiation and asymmetry of trans-identity with respect to cisgender identity, its constitutive exterior. On the other hand, by explicitly excluding the application of the law based on the status of citizenship, the rule of exclusion of non-citizens is reiterated. The space of public policy as an object of analysis, from an intersectional perspective, allows us to understand how different organisational structures work in a specific context to create hierarchies of medical/patient, trans/cisgender person, autochthonous/migrant, civilised nations/barbarians.

In the Spanish state, intervention spaces are generally organised on an axis of 'problematised' differentiation; the very existence of the service or project starts from the premise of a phenomenon understood as a social problem. Specialised services, for example, in gender violence assume the category 'woman' as central and unquestioned. Hankivsky and Cormier provide the following critique:

> Policy interventions have sought to extend to all women without taking into account that violence does not have a single cause and that women who experience it are differently situated. Violence against women cannot be read through the lens of gender without accounting for the intersecting factors that shape the lived realities of affected women and determine their needs and help-seeking patterns.
>
> (2011: 218)

In the investigation 'From victims to agents: imaginary and practices on gender violence in the couple against immigrant women in the Spanish State' (Cea, 2015), narrative productions were carried out with professionals working with gender violence. The analysis allowed axes of differentiation to be identified, exposing, on the one hand, that the legal status of migrant women determines their access to types of care in cases of partner violence. Without legal status, which in the Spanish state means possession of a Foreigner Identification Number (NIE), women are not eligible for certain economic aid or protection measures, such as access to foster homes. Thus, the institutional framework emerges as a limitation to how social services can be accessed by the very people who need them (Cea and Montenegro, 2014). On the other hand, the imaginaries about the places of origin of some immigrant women affect the ways in which they are served in the services. One of the service professionals says:

> I have seen many times in the public administration – which is my scope of action – that a Moroccan woman is not treated the same as one from here. This is a very strong situation for me. These stereotypes and prejudices are everywhere. There are professionals who do not review themselves and this marks their intervention. They are acts of racism, which are invisible, but are acts of racism as such. Therefore, if your point of departure in attention to citizenship is from prejudice, distrust, or 'to see what you want', the possibility of migrant women to get out of violence is small because they are faced with other barriers that hinder, for example, reporting, asking for guidance, etc. There is a continuous secondary victimization to women in these cases.
>
> (Cea, 2015: 124)

An intersectional perspective allows us to analyse culturalist discourses in terms of reiterative practices of differentiation and categorisation. Suárez (2008) defines this type of practice as 'discursive colonialism': a structural position of power where certain constructions of gender equity are established as valid against others.

The constitution of 'identity vectors' requires 'representation technologies' and procedures to, 'give voice' to such 'identities'. Taking an intersectional essentialist perspective leads to a reification of 'intersectional identities' and assumes that these positions have a representative character. The position of 'gay migrant', for example, constitutes a 'legal' position (in Foucault's perspective) that could have meaning within the practice of social service that assumes a 'voice' and a 'position of the subject' that sustains this voice. Contextual intersectionality blurs this position of the subject and exposes the contextual elements, including those within the social services, involved in the production of that position.

Suryia: Drawing on examples from your own contexts, activism and experience, how does intersectionality problematise knowledge production?

Marisela and Joan: Contextual intersectionality problematises knowledge/power relations that constitute social work practitioner/service servicer relationships. Contextual intersectional perspectives expose the mechanisms of disavowal that normalise and naturalise hegemonic power relations in the context of social work in particular and in governmental contexts in general.

Contextual intersectionality questions the effects that emerge from the dynamics of subalternisation. These dynamics are based on socio-historical power/knowledge mechanisms through which information is produced, categorised and interpreted. The concept of intersectionality is linked to a broad tradition of feminist works that question the scientific rationale that hegemonises production of knowledge (Harding, 1986, Haraway, 1988). Public policies and social work practices are nourished by the truths constructed by scientific production devices; devices that defines certain social situations and subject positions as problematic. These operations delimit the contours of the categories constituted as an object of intervention and homogenise the people who are part of the same axis of discrimination. In the Spanish context, this process can be exemplified in the interventions that define its object of intervention as 'immigrant women and their problems' (Agrela, 2004).

The definition of 'social problems' through the production of knowledge and forms of social intervention is a political issue (Cubillos, 2017). First, it occurs in a controversial field of theories, perspectives, methodologies and relationships where certain meanings are set against others. Second, it is framed in power matrices that contribute to defining what is 'good'/'bad', what is 'normal'/ 'abnormal', what is 'correct'/'incorrect': what is susceptible to change and what should be kept as is. Third, it has consequences that reinforce certain dynamics of subordination. Finally:

> many of the cherished categories of the intersectional mantra – originally starting with race, class, gender, now including sexuality, nation, religion, age, and disability – are the products of modernist colonial agendas and regimes of epistemic violence, operative through a Western/Euro-American epistemological formation through which the notion of discrete identity has emerged.
>
> (Puar, 2012: 54)

The epistemic violence of social service provision is in the claim to objective detachment through an invisible, omniscient observer (Haraway, 1997); academic and professional 'expertise' functions as an axis of differentiation and asymmetry. The lack of intersectional analysis of the position of the practitioner renders this position as not susceptible to scrutiny as 'subjects to be studied' (Agrela, 2004: 39). In teaching courses on intersectionality to public and private social service practitioners in Barcelona, we invited participants to examine their daily practice from an intersectional perspective. We structured an observation script to examine intersectionality in professional practice in three sections:

Accessibility: descriptions of the people who arrive at the service/activity.
How do people reach the service (word of mouth, referral, dissemination of the service . . .)?
In what language (s) is the service/activity disseminated?
Facilities/limitations to assist (public transport, schedules, physical barriers, child care space . . .).
Who 'does not' come to the service? Why?

Interactions: description of the people who participate in the different interaction spaces (meetings, attention sessions, virtual spaces).
How is participation in different spaces?
Who speaks, who listens?
Technical elements present in the interactions (templates, didactic material . . .).
Configuration of the physical space. Description: tables, desks, chairs, sofas, desks.
Body language in the interactions between participants.

Perceptions and feelings: impressions of the session and the participants.
What comes to your mind when you interact with different people in the context of your work?
Give an example of three people who participate in the service (users, professionals . . .) and explain the impressions and images that have been suggested to you.
What impression and images may have this people about you?
How do you feel in different work spaces? Why?
How do you think your cultural background affect your work?
How do you think different axes of oppression affect the attention/activities that are organised in your work space?

The observations produced intense debate regarding the intersectionality of positionality. The writing of one of the professionals propitiated the first debate:

> The spaces have white artificial light, air conditioning, monochromatic walls, rigid furniture and plastic; there are no infrastructures to regulate personal energy (food, drinks, space to rest . . .). The space follows Western norms and, therefore, adjusts to what we expect from a space.

The participant's analysis concluded that the organisation of the space, considered as innocuous and neutral, reproduce localised social and cultural practices. In this case, the space and what it contains (as well as what it does not contain) corresponds to what is normatively understood as a 'neutral' space for attention and provision of services.

The practitioner continued:

> The characteristics of the space simply do not help in some of the basic objectives of the project, those that have to do with proposing other ways of relating . . . And, in this sense, we must question the norm, the habit, and provide a different alternative that, even if only a little, breaks with the established norms. Space does not do it, it is not a good ally.

Here, the practitioner asks about the impact in context on the feelings of the service users, especially in the case of the two Moroccan service users. The analysis highlights the normative nature of service provision contexts and how they constitute how people inhabit them; the organisation of the space contributes to the intervened/intervened differentiation. This process of differentiation is interwoven, in the narrative of the professional, with that of the national and cultural origin of some of the users. Hence, the practitioner proposed that in the next meeting of the group, he will suggest that everyone sits on a rug on the floor and take tea during the session (practices associated with Moroccan customs). With this suggestion, he intends to intervene in the normativity of the physical space to generate changes in group dynamics. It had never occurred to the practitioner, even though he had worked with this group of service users for some time, that the configuration of the space is constitutive.

The next story spoke about the imaginaries that affect the practitioner's task. In this case, the rapporteur is also the object of inquiry. In his analysis, the axes of differentiation relate to social class and educational attainment. The practitioner observes these axes through an action that triggers different reactions towards different users:

> a user with university education arrives late to the session and I approach him with a reminder of punctuality. On the other hand, my tone is closer to admonishing to another user who does not have this level of education because I associate unpunctuality with disorganization.

Although the description does not recognise it, the asymmetric professional/user relationship reproduces the axes identified in the writing. The story performs a critical scrutiny of one's professional practice without questioning the role of authority with respect to one's professional position.

In the third story, a practitioner reflected on the relationship between her position and that of some service users regarding certain axes of differentiation:

> These days I have realized that it is easier for me to put my hand on the back (as a symbol of encouragement) of the women who share with me the characterization of being immigrant women, especially if they are from South America. By listening to their stories . . . I understand them without needing many words. They do not know that it is a characteristic that we share but I think and I feel that we tune in a particular way.

In this fragment, the practitioner identifies with the category 'immigrant woman'. Due to this identification, she empathises with the users who share this position despite the fact that the practitioner's membership in the category 'migrant woman' is unknown to the migrant service users. In this case, attributes such as skin colour, the fluent use of the Catalan language or her position as a practitioner are decisive in the ways in which she is 'read' in this context: as an autochthonous woman. The narrative shows a gap between her experience and the users' attributions. This suggests that the processes of differentiation that emerge from social stratification processes happen in different ways. In this case, the status of 'migrant' has different implications and recognitions for different people. Therefore, the dynamics of categorial stratification involve contingent elements that depend on the specific context of the interaction; elements and relationships that can only be analysed when they materialise in specific configurations. The practitioner's reflection continues:

> But, on the other hand, not sharing the category 'migrant woman' with the user can lead to self-deception. When understanding and accompanying a woman with a profile of high social class and 'autochthonous' . . . let's say that I have to fight against my prejudices of 'you have had everything'.

This extract introduces an interesting movement. On the one hand, in the two cases she addresses, she refers to the effects that emerge from the tangled functioning of different axes of differentiation. In addition, she reflects on how her position influences her professional practice. On the other hand, in this fragment, the effect of differentiation favours subordination dynamics that affect the position that could be considered 'privileged' in terms of economic status and national belonging. Stratification mechanisms are not deployed in the same way in all cases, but, also that the variation is involved in the hierarchal configurations, which result from specific relational contexts. Therefore, the effects of differentiation processes are diverse and should not be reduced to the constant iteration of dominant dynamics of subalternisation. A further angle concerning axes of differentiation and context arises when the practitioner reflects on the impression she believes the service users have of her:

> Most, except for those who are younger, judge me by my age. They think I'm too young for this job. Some, out of curiosity, ask me directly. Others confess to me, after a few sessions, that at first they distrusted me for this reason.

Here, the practitioner is reporting on the effects of differentiation that affect her position in the context of being a professional; in this case, the matter of age, and what is expected or not about age. Given that her recognition as a practitioner (differentiation) is linked to her knowledge and skills for proper professional practice (context), her expertise is called into question when she is asked about her age.

Contextual intersersectionality accounts for the effects of subalternisation that arise from axes of differentiation. Critical observation of how assumptions about service users constitute the professional attention they receive opens the possibility of analysing the procedures that contribute to the reproduction of these assumptions in specific spaces of intervention. It is important to ask about the configuration of the practitioner position and how these positions are legitimated, since intersectional studies on this position are scarce.

Suryia: Intersectionality is a theory that deconstructs borders, but it seems that contemporary debates and applications about intersectionality are contingent on one border or another, which runs counter to the spirit of intersectionality (Nayak, 2015).

Marisela and Joan: Although affirmative identity politics have enabled recognition of multiple subject positions, the fragmentation of these positions has led to a political paralysis. In the current international contexts of social and economic precariousness, Fraser asks:

> Why is there no broad coalition of new-New Dealers: trade unionists, unemployed and precarious workers; feminists, ecologists and anti-imperialists; social democrats and democratic socialists? Why no Popular Front insisting that the costs of fictitious commodification should be paid, not by 'society' as such, nor by nature reduced to a sink, but by those whose relentless drive to accumulate capital precipitated the crisis?
>
> (Fraser, 2013: 127)

Certain formulations of intersectionality have not enabled collective working. First of all, the intersectional perspective has accentuated, in some cases, identity policies by asking which of the axes of differentiation is the most relevant. For example, in the Barcelona context, the city council, adopting an intersectional perspective, has an office of 'gender mainstreaming', in which 'gender' is considered to be the main axis that intersects with the other axes. This prevalence of the gender category is reflected in the grant forms, where all areas must define gender indicators. Thus, it is assumed that a primordial axis (gender in this case) crosses any subject position in any situation, while other axes may or may not be present; an approach that tends to invisibilise other possible axes.

Second, the intersectional perspective has suffered the debates of identity authenticity; the question becomes if a certain person 'can' be included in a certain category. This debate has been virulent in the case of the inclusion of transgender women in women's groups, being analysed in terms of transphobia or male privilege. When an additive perspective of intersectionality is adopted, the debates of authenticity identify the positions of maximum intersectional oppression. If 'woman' is a position that suffers from oppression, 'Black woman' is a position that suffers a double oppression, and so on. Reading in terms of identity politics has led to the desirability of oppressed political positions (but not of the conditions of oppression), leading to what Hancock (2007) calls 'Olympiad of oppression'. Understanding oppression in terms of identity rather than contexts of oppression has led to the confrontation between different positions within social activism. Therefore, we consider necessary the development of an intersectional perspective that pays attention to how contextual arrangements define the axes of discrimination (i.e., having a legal status) instead of considering these axes (i.e., being a migrant) as attributes of the person. Subject positions are contingent and associated with specific production contexts. The contingency of position acknowledges that certain contexts generate 'blind spots' that make certain contexts of oppression invisible to certain people; these processes of invisibility must be denounced and transformed.

Finally, instead of focusing on a set of 'subjugated intersectional categories', we understand intersectionality as an analytical and practice toolbox to deal with experiences of people and groups within historical and contextual classificatory frameworks. To limit the intersectional toolbox to a set of subaltern positions obscures the relational character of power relations and produces an understanding of oppression dynamics in terms of personal traits. For example,'an analysis of the position of 'white gay man' in terms of homonationalism exposes how certain geopolitical contexts activate and appropriate the position of 'gay white man' to be included in 'the nation', contributing to the exclusion of other 'gay identities' (Puar, 2007).

Suryia: How can intersectionality enable us to think about the predicament at the heart of liberation movements articulated by Avtar Brah in the following way: 'At what point, and in what ways, for example, does the specificity of a particular social experience become an expression of essentialism?' (Brah, 1996: 95).

Marisela and Joan: Brah (1996) questions the existence of a definitive essence that transcends history and culture. At the same time, she recognises that dominated groups appeal to shared experiences that reaffirm a seemingly essential difference with dominant groups in what, following Spivak (1987)'and Fuss (1989), can be called 'strategic essentialism'. Strategic essentialism can, however, become pure essentialism; an essentialism where the struggle against one form of oppression leads to reinforcing another. Intersectionality allows for the articulation of diverse struggles by recognising that, for example, the struggle against the processes of racialisation and genderisation share common strategies and that we embody multiple axes of differentiation. However, the situation is not so simple.

Certain understandings of intersectionality consider the axes of differentiation as intrinsic characteristics of the subject; a socially assigned, constituting badge. From this perspective, a white heterosexual woman and a white lesbian woman have two distinct badges, with relatively different personal experiences and needs. We could argue that the category 'lesbian' is an example of 'strategic essentialism' that can be used politically to make visible the experiences and needs of women who feel identified with this category. But what about the intersection 'heterosexual white woman' or 'white lesbian woman'? It could be argued that they are categorical intersections that can be politically used to visualise privileged positions. However, the use of these intersectional categories tends to essentialise and homogenise the experience of certain groups of people. For example, in our study on social services for migrant women in Barcelona (Montenegro and Montenegro, 2013) we found that the use of the category 'Latin American woman' by practitioners assumed a particular experience of patriarchy in Latin American women; an experience that European women had liberated themselves from. This assumption established an 'intersectional hierarchy' where the 'European woman' was located in a 'better position' than the Latin American woman. This process of 'essentialisation' of women's experiences does not take into account the diversity of historical and social processes that mark the functioning of patriarchy in different countries, and in different social classes, in Latin America and Europe. In this sense, it is important to differentiate between the political use of identity to claim the recognition of certain experiences and identities, and the governmental appropriation of these identity categories as a form of population management.

Brah (1996) suggests the use of 'diaspora spaces' privileging 'routes' over 'roots'. In this sense, we are 'subjects in movement', where the axes of differentiation are temporary and in constant transformation. Under this understanding, 'the home' is a temporal territorialisation within a more general movement of diasporic nature. Following this metaphor, the social categories by which we are defined and define ourselves constitute 'home'; that space we feel is ours and in which we feel more or less comfortable. However, the social and personal categories constituting 'home' can be vertiginously transformed. This is exemplified in Brah's description (1996: 7–9) of her experience, at the end of the 1960s, when her body was 'read' as 'Indian' in the US and 'Pakistani' in Great Britain. The transformation of our position in the social system affects the categorical references that define us; a categorical vocabulary that mutates according to the social and historical context in which we find ourselves. The notion of 'diaspora spaces' suggests an intersectional space in transformation where psychosocial and geopolitical processes converge and where borders, axes of differentiation and locations are formed. The unequal distribution of vulnerabilities responds to systematic and repeated asymmetric differentiation practices that are updated in specific situations where certain differences become structurally significant.

Suryia: How can intersectionality be utilised to imagine/realise alternative social work relationships/models/interventions for liberation?

Marisela and Joan: Intersectionality constitutes a perspective that addresses the way in which subjectivation processes are traversed by unequal and hierarchical power relations. There are three figurations that we believe may be transformational in the realisation of intersectionsocial work interventions.

a) First, the concept of 'agency', referring to the ways in which people adapt to and transform the power structures in which they live. The action of social movements is an example of a collective agency. From the spaces of intervention, we need to generate procedures that take into account the personal and collective trajectories of the people we work with; those actions or initiatives community psychology define as 'invisible fights for dignity'. These are actions that deal with the conditions of oppression from the perspective of the participant. Recognising the agency of the participant questions the 'provider-lacking' dichotomy; a dichotomy often associated with the categories of people attended by the intervention services.
b) Second, we must continue to deepen participatory procedures that allow participants to make decisions regarding intervention processes. Contextual intersectionality is vigilant of the reproduction of subalternisation processes; thus, spaces for participation that question these power relations are needed.
c) Finally, the notion of articulation must be a basis for reflection and action. Strategic alliances can be established with non-governmental positions that

transform the context of the intervention. We could take into consideration the set of social agents that are producing discourses and practices for the critical transformation of power relations in terms, for example, of sexism, xenophobia, homophobia and transphobia, classism or capacitism.

Notes

1 Jefatura del Estado. Ley 16/2003, de 28 de mayo, de cohesión y calidad del Sistema Nacional de Salud, Pub. L. No. 10715, 128 Boletín Oficial del Estado 1 (2003).
BOE.es – Documento consolidado BOE-A-2003–10715
[Bloque 5: #a3] Artículo 3. De la condición de asegurado. 1. La asistencia sanitaria en España, con cargo a fondos públicos, a través del Sistema Nacional de . . .

2 Jefatura del Estado. Real Decreto-ley 16/2012, de 20 de abril, de medidas urgentes para garantizar la sostenibilidad del Sistema Nacional de Salud y mejorar la calidad y seguridad de sus prestaciones, Pub. L. No. 5403, 98 Boletín Oficial del Estado 1 (2012).
BOE.es – Documento consolidado BOE-A-2012–5403
Última actualización, publicada el 15/08/2016, en vigor a partir del 15/08/2016. Texto original, publicado el 24/04/2012, en vigor a partir del 24/04/2012.

3 Ministerio de Sanidad, Servicios Sociales e Igualdad. Real Decreto 1192/2012, de 3 de agosto, por el que se regula la condición de asegurado y de beneficiario a efectos de la asistencia sanitaria en España, con cargo a fondos públicos, a través del Sistema Nacional de Salud, Pub. L. No. 10477, I. Disposiciones generales, 186 Boletín Oficial del Estado 55775 (2012).
BOE.es – Documento BOE-A-2012–10477Todos los españoles, así como los ciudadanos extranjeros que tengan establecida su residencia en el territorio nacional, son titulares del derecho a la protección . . .

4 Ministerio de Sanidad, Servicios Sociales e Igualdad. Real Decreto 576/2013, de 26 de julio, por el que se establecen los requisitos básicos del convenio especial de prestación de asistencia sanitaria a personas que no tengan la condición de aseguradas ni de beneficiarias del Sistema Nacional de Salud y se modifica el Real Decreto 1192/2012, de 3 de agosto, por el que se regula la condición de asegurado y de beneficiario a efectos de la asistencia sanitaria en España, con cargo a fondos públicos, a través del Sistema Nacional de Salud., Pub. L. No. 8190, § I. Disposiciones generales, 179 Boletín Oficial del Estado 55058 (2013).
BOE.es – Documento BOE-A-2013–8190
Real Decreto 576/2013, de 26 de julio, por el que se establecen los requisitos básicos del convenio especial de prestación de asistencia sanitaria a personas que no . . .

5 Jefatura del Estado. Ley 3/2007, de 15 de marzo, reguladora de la rectificación registral de la mención relativa al sexo de las personas, Pub. L. No. 5585, § I. Disposiciones generales, 16 Boletín Oficial del Estado 11251 (2007).
BOE.es – Documento BOE-A-2007–5585
Documento BOE-A-2007–5585 . . . Ley 3/2007, de 15 de marzo, reguladora de la rectificación registral de la mención relativa al sexo de las personas.

References

Agha, A. (2007) Recombinant selves in mass mediated spacetime. *Language & Communication*, *27*(3): 320–335.

Agrela, B. A. (2004) La acción social y las mujeres inmigrantes: ¿hacia unos modelos de intervención? *Portularia: Revista de Trabajo Social*, (4): 31–42.

Anthias, F. (2001) The material and the symbolic in theorizing social stratification: Issues of gender, ethnicity and class. *The British Journal of Sociology*, *52*(3): 367–390.

Anthias, F. (2002) Beyond feminism and multiculturalism: Locating difference and the politics of location. *Women's Studies International Forum*, *25*(3): 275–286.

Anthias, F. (2011) Intersections and translocations: New paradigms for thinking about cultural diversity and social identities. *European Educational Research Journal*, *10*(2): 204–217.

Anzaldúa, G. (2007) *Borderlands/La Frontera: The New Mestiza*. 3rd ed. San Francisco, CA: Aunt Lute Books.

Bettio, F., Simonazzi, A., and Villa, P. (2006) Change in care regimes and female migration: The 'care drain' in the Mediterranean. *Journal of European Social Policy*, *16*(3): 271–285.

Boyce-Davies, C. (2013) *Caribbean Spaces: Escapes from Twilight Zones*. Chicago: University of Illinois Press.

Brah, A. (1996) *Cartographies of Diaspora: Contesting Identities*. London: Routledge.

Carbado, D. W. (2013) Colorblind intersectionality. *Signs*, *38*(4): 811–845.

Cea, P. (2015) De víctimas a Agentes: Imaginarios y prácticas sobre la violencia de género en la pareja contra mujeres inmigrantes en el Estado español (Ph.D. Thesis). Universitat Autònoma de Barcelona, Barcelona.

Cea, P. and Montenegro, M. (2014) Más allá de la visibilización: Problematizando discursos sobre violencia de género en la pareja contra mujeres inmigradas en España. *Quaderns de Psicologia*, *16*(1): 167–180.

Crenshaw, K. (1991) Mapping the margins: Intersectionality, identity politics, and violence against women of color. *Stanford Law Review*, *43*(6): 1241–1299.

Cruells, M. and Coll-Planas, G. (2013) Challenging equality policies: The emerging LGBT perspective. *European Journal of Women's Studies*, *20*(2): 122–137.

Cubillos, J. C. (2017) Reflexiones sobre el concepto de inclusión social. Una propuesta para el análisis de políticas públicas desde la teoría feminista. *Política y Sociedad*, *54*(2): 341–363.

Davies, A. (2016) *Freedom is a Constant Struggle: Ferguson, Palestine, and the Foundations of a Movement*. Chicago, IL: Haymarket Books.

Derrida, J. (1997) *Of Grammatology*. trans. G. C. Spivak. Corrected Edition. Baltimore, MD: The Johns Hopkins University Press.

Foucault, M. (1965) *Madness and Civilization: A History of Insanity in the Age of Reason*. New York: Random House.

Foucault, M. (1976) *Historia de la sexualidad. vol. I: La voluntad de saber*. Madrid: Siglo XXI.

Foucault, M. (1982) The subject and power. *Critical Inquiry*, *8*(4): 777–795

Fraser, N. (2013) ¿Triple Movimiento? *New Left Review*, (81), 125–139.

Fuss, D. (1989) *Essentially Speaking: Feminism, Nature and Difference*. London: Routledge.

Gil, S. (2011) *Nuevos Feminismos. Sentidos Comunes en la dispersion. Traficantes de Sueños*. Madrid: Traficantes de Sueños.

Hagelund, A. (2005) Why it is bad to be kind. Educating refugees to life in the Welfare State: A case study from Norway. *Social Policy & Administration*, *39*(6), 669–683.

Hall, S. (1996) Introduction: Who needs 'identity'? In S. Hall and P. du Gay (Eds.), *Questions of Cultural Identity* (pp. 1–17). London: SAGE Publications.

Hancock, A. (2007) When multiplication doesn't equal quick addition: Examining intersectionality as a research paradigm. *Perspectives on Politics*, *5*(1):63–79.

Hankivsky, O. and Cormier, R. (2011) Intersectionality and public policy: Some lessons from existing models. *Political Research Quarterly*, *64*(1): 217–229.

Haraway, D. (1988) Situated knowledges: The science question in feminism and the privilege of the partial perspective. *Feminist Studies*, *14*(3): 575–599.

Haraway, D. (1997) *Modest-witness Second-millennium: Feminism and Technoscience: FemaleMan-Meets-OncoMouse*. New York: Routledge.

Harding, S. G. (1986) *The Science Question in Feminism*. Ithaca, NY and London: Cornell University Press.

Hill-Collins, P. (2000) *Black Feminist Thought: Knowledge, Consciousness, and the Politics of Empowerment*. 2nd ed. London: Routledge.

Huggan, G. (1989) Decolonizing the map. *Ariel*, *20*(4). 115–131.

James, J. (2000) Radicalizing feminism. In J. James and T. D. Sharpley-Whiting (Eds.) (2000) *The Black Feminist Reader*. Oxford, UK: Blackwell Publishers.

Madigan, S. P. (1992) The application of Michel Foucault's philosophy in the problem externalizing discourse of Michael White. *Journal of Family Therapy 14*: 265–279

Mbembe, A. (2001) The intimacy of tyranny. In Ashcroft, B., Griffiths, G., and Tiffin, H. (Eds.) (2006) *The Post-Colonial Studies Reader*. 2nd ed. Oxford, UK: Routledge.

McCall, L. (2005) The complexity of intersectionality. *Signs*, *30*(3), 1771–1800.

Minh-ha, T. T. (1991) *When the Moon Waxes Red: Representation, Gender and Cultural Politics*. New York: Routledge.

Ministerio de Sanidad, Servicios Sociales e Igualdad. (2014) Los perfiles de la discriminación en España: Análisis de la Encuesta CIS-3.000. Percepción de la discriminación en España. Madrid: Ministerio de Sanidad, Servicios Sociales e Igualdad.

Mohanty, C. T. (2003) *Feminism without Borders: Decolonizing Theory, Practicing Solidarity*. Durham, NC: Duke University Press.

Montenegro, K. and Montenegro, M. (2013) Governmentality in service provision for migrated women in Spain. *Social and Personality Psychology Compass*, *7*(6): 331–342.

Montenegro, M. (2003) Identities, subjectification and subject positions: Reflections on transformation in the sphere of social intervention. *International Journal of Critical Psychology*, *9*: 92–106.

Motta, J. I. J. (2016) Sexualidades e políticas públicas: Uma abordagem queer para tempos de crise democrática. *Saúde Debate*, *40*(spe), 73–85.

Nayak, S. (2015) *Race, Gender and the Activism of Black Feminist Theory: Working with Audre Lorde*. London: Routledge.

Nayak, S. (2017a) Declaring the activism of black feminist theory. *Annual Review of Critical Psychology*, *13*: 1–12.

Nayak, S. (2017b) Location as method. *Qualitative Research Journal special issue: Bordering, exclusions and necropolitics*, *17*(3): 202–216.

Platero Méndez, L. (Raquel) (2012) Son las políticas de igualdad de género permeables a los debates sobre la interseccionalidad? Una reflexión a partir del caso español. *Revista del CLAD Reforma y Democracia* (52).

Platero, R. (2011) The narratives of transgender rights mobilization in Spain. *Sexualities*, *14*(5), 597–614.

Puar, J. (2007) *Terrorist Assemblages: Homonationalism in Queer Times*. Durham, NC and London: Duke University Press.

Puar, J. (2012) 'I would rather be a cyborg than a goddess': Becoming intersectional in assemblage theory. *Philosophia: A Journal of Feminist Continental Philosophy*, *2*(1): 49–66.

Sadurní, N. and Pujol, J. (2016) Homonacionalismo en Cataluña: Una visión desde el activismo LGTBI. *Universitas Psychologica, 14*(5): 1809–1820.

Sassen, S. (2003) *Contrageografías de la globalización*. Madrid: Traficantes de Sueños.

Spivak, G. C. (1987) *In Other Worlds: Essays in Cultural Politics*. New York: Methuen.

Suárez, L. (2008) Colonialismo, gobernabilidad y feminismos poscoloniales. In L. Suárez and R. Hernández (Eds.) *Descolonizando el feminismo: Teorías y prácticas desde los márgenes*. Madrid: Cátedra Ediciones.

Subirats, J., Knoepfel, P., Larrue, C., and Varonne, F. (2008) *Análisis y gestión de políticas públicas*. Barcelona: Editorial Ariel.

Verloo, M. (2006) Multiple inequalities, intersectionality and the European Union. *European Journal of Women's Studies, 13*(3): 211–228.

Yuval-Davis, N. (2014) Intersectionality, inequality and bordering processes. Presented at the Conference: XVIII ISA World Congress of Sociology, Yokohama, Japan.

Zebracki, M. and Milani, T. M. (2017) Critical geographical queer semiotics. *ACME: An International Journal for Critical Geographies, 16*(3): 427–439.

Index

Note: This index uses UK spelling. Page numbers in *italic* refer to tables; those in **bold** refer to boxes